Web Development
with the Mac®

Web Development with the Mac®

Aaron Vegh

Wiley Publishing, Inc.

Web Development with the Mac®

Published by
Wiley Publishing, Inc.
10475 Crosspoint Boulevard
Indianapolis, IN 46256
www.wiley.com

Copyright © 2010 by Wiley Publishing, Inc., Indianapolis, Indiana

Published by Wiley Publishing, Inc., Indianapolis, Indiana

Published simultaneously in Canada

ISBN: 978-0-470-53399-4

Manufactured in the United States of America

10 9 8 7 6 5 4 3 2 1

For general information on our other products and services or to obtain technical support, please contact our Customer Care Department within the U.S. at (877) 762-2974, outside the U.S. at (317) 572-3993 or fax (317) 572-4002.

Library of Congress Control Number: 2010921249

*For Richard Moll, my high school teacher
who introduced me to the Mac.*

For my dad, who gave me my first Mac: the Classic.

For Chris Pierson, who made me an expert.

*And for those nameless armies of Apple engineers
that continue to prove that the Mac matters.*

About the Author

Aaron Vegh is the principal owner of Innoveghtive Inc., a web development agency based near Toronto, Canada. Although Innoveghtive has been around for only the past three years, Aaron has been exchanging websites for money since the late 1990s. During his earlier career, he worked for a variety of companies, including investment banks, magazine publishers, and multinational technology corporations.

An avowed autodidact, Aaron taught himself every skill in this book, turning away from his English degree from McMaster University and his master's of publishing degree from Simon Fraser University.

Today, Aaron is a regular presenter at his local Macintosh User Group and an ardent attendee at local Mac developer events. He blogs at `aaron.vegh.ca` and tweets prolifically at `twitter.com/aaronvegh`.

Credits

Acquisitions Editor
Aaron Black

Project Editor
Christopher Stolle

Technical Editor
Dennis Cohen

Copy Editor
Marylouise Wiack

Editorial Director
Robyn Siesky

Business Manager
Amy Knies

Senior Marketing Manager
Sandy Smith

Vice President and Executive Group Publisher
Richard Swadley

Vice President and Executive Publisher
Barry Pruett

Project Coordinator
Kristie Rees

Graphics and Production Specialist
Andrea Hornberger

Media Development Project Manager
Laura Moss

Media Development Assistant Project Manager
Jenny Swisher

Media Development Associate Producer
Josh Frank or Shawn Patrick

Proofreading
Laura Bowman

Indexing
BIM Indexing & Proofreading Services

Contents

Part III: Web Design 185

Chapter 7: Design Concepts 187

Acknowledgments

A s you can imagine, a book like this doesn't spring from the loins of a sea goddess; it comes from the persistent labors of colossal machinery, and I'm indebted to each human piece of it.

For graciously putting me in touch with the good folks at Wiley, I'm thankful to Andy Finnell (on Twitter as @macgeek02). Without that initial contact, none of this would be happening.

My acquisitions editor, Aaron Black, was a pleasure to deal with and a true asset to the Wiley editorial team. He was an encouraging figure during the tough moments, and I felt he had my back in selling the idea for this book.

My project editor, Christopher Stolle, was my day-to-day contact while the book was being written. One couldn't hope for a more professional or qualified midwife to see this book to reality.

At home, writing a book of this magnitude took many, many hours away from my family. It's a measure of our strength that they were fully supportive during those long periods of required solitude, and I'm very grateful for the chance. It's makeup time now.

Introduction

The great Carl Sagan once said, "If you wish to make an apple pie from scratch, you must first invent the universe." It feels like that on the web too; before you can build a website, you have to learn a whole galaxy of technologies.

Back when the web was new, it was enough to learn a smattering of HTML. Not anymore: HTML has evolved, and it's just a starting point. Nowadays, if you want to mount a credible website, it needs to be beautiful, functional, and useful.

To achieve this, you need an understanding of techniques that cross traditional disciplinary boundaries. For many companies, getting a professional website means hiring a high-priced agency that's staffed with project managers, programmers, and designers.

Or does it? Can one person running his or her own agency do it all? Can he or she be the one who understands the mechanics of web serving, the details of front-end web development, the touchy-feely world of design, and the logic of application development?

My friend, I'm here to give you a most emphatic "yes."

Who Is This Book For?

This book is useful to anyone who wants to learn about web development. If you work for someone else, you'll find something here to enhance your existing skills. If you run a small company and you're looking to build your own site, this will give you the start-to-finish techniques for getting your site online.

But this book will mostly benefit the independent developer: that lone wolf, that single-minded individual, that seeker of personal fortune. You want to develop your business, and you want to find meaningful clients with substantive websites. You want to be their alpha and omega.

To be sure, being the jack-of-all-trades is not a status gained overnight. You'll build your skills gradually, adding pieces over time. But with focus, dedication, and stubbornness, you'll wake up one morning with this realization: "Yeah, I'm the complete package."

Why the Mac?

I've been using the Mac OS since 1987. That's so long ago that Microsoft was actually making the best software for the platform in the form of Microsoft Word. So, you might imagine that I'm a little biased in favor of the platform. Of course, having spent a substantial amount of time in Windows and Linux, I like to think that my bias is justified.

The advent of Mac OS X back in 2001 paved the way for the Mac as the ultimate web development platform. With its foundations as a Unix operating system, the Mac provides the same technologies that power the Internet; setting up the same environment as the one that will run your production server is a huge benefit.

But the Mac is also a very successful commercial operating system, and it therefore offers a number of terrific applications that make developing websites more enjoyable.

This book is an almost-600-page love song to the Mac OS; there's only one platform that gives you everything you need to do what's in these pages — and that's a Mac.

Tools You Need

Before you get started with this book, you should have a few tools that will make your life easier. The following list offers the best applications as well as some free ones:

- **Text editors.** The Mac doesn't include a built-in text editor. The TextEdit application may sound like it would meet your needs, but by default, this program writes to Rich Text Format (RTF). You need a text editor to write your code, regardless of the language. There are three great options for the Mac:
  - **TextMate.** To my mind, TextMate is the finest text editor on any platform. It's incredibly fast, has great syntax highlighting, and offers a massive set of add-on features. It just feels right to me. TextMate is available from `http://macromates.com` for about $60.
  - **TextWrangler.** From the makers of BBEdit, the longest-living text editor on the Mac, comes the free TextWrangler. It has all but a few of the high-end features of its commercial big brother. Find it at `http://barebones.com`.
  - **Coda.** From Panic Software, Coda is a combination text editor and file transfer solution. It's intended for web developers who have to manage websites, and I find it indispensable for ongoing maintenance. It's available at `http://panic.com` for $99.
- **File transfer programs.** Anyone who works with the web needs a way to transfer files to remote servers. A file transfer application is the way to go, and there are a couple of good options:
  - **Transmit.** Also from Panic, Transmit is the gold standard of FTP applications, and it includes support for secure transfers, WebDAV, and even Amazon's S3 service. It's a $30 download from `http://panic.com`.
  - **Cyberduck.** This is an open-source application that attempts to replicate the features of Transmit, although the interface isn't as polished. Still, you can't beat the price. You can get it from `http://cyberduck.ch`.

How This Book Is Organized

This book has four major parts to describe the different areas that you, as a web developer, must become comfortable with:

- **Part I** describes what I like to think of as the infrastructure technologies that make the web work. You'll learn about DNS, domain names, and hosting. You'll then move into the Unix operating system, and you'll learn how to use Linux to set up a complete hosting environment.

- **Part II** is all about the front-end technologies; you'll learn about HTML, CSS, and JavaScript. These are the tools that will give you the expertise to build static websites.

- **Part III** is where you'll learn about web design — from the basic concepts to the techniques that will drive your website. I also include search engine optimization (SEO) here to help people find your site. You'll also learn how to use Photoshop to build professional-quality site designs.

- **Part IV** is the big payoff; you'll leverage your expertise in static web development and add the dynamic component. You'll learn about databases, PHP, Ruby, and the Rails framework to build large-scale web applications.

Finally, I have included an appendix that provides advice and tips if you're involved in the business end of this field, another appendix with further resources, and a glossary.

This book is a very practical, hands-on guide to web technology. Because it covers a lot of ground, it requires close attention; this is not light reading on your back porch! Instead, I heartily encourage you to sit down at your Mac with this book at your side. Work through the many examples herein, and make sure that you're able to replicate my results. And even more important, continually demonstrate your understanding of the material by playing with your new knowledge; go beyond the examples and try new things for yourself. Be patient and be persistent, and this book will reward you.

Throughout this book, you'll also find icons with more information about a given topic:

- **Caution.** This describes something you should avoid doing or the consequences you might suffer if you attempt to do something that's opposite of what's suggested you do.

- **Cross-Ref.** This tells you where you can find related information to the techniques being described. In some cases, these are reminders of topics that have already been discussed.

- **Note.** This offers additional — albeit parenthetical — information that I have to share on a particular topic. Notes may not be required reading but can contribute to your overall appreciation for the material.

- **Tip.** This presents another way to do something or a shortcut for doing a particular task.

Being a self-employed web developer is a challenge, but with the right advice — and the right attitude — it can be an exciting and lucrative career.

Internet Infrastructure

Bringing Your Business Online

Whether you want to build one site for yourself or five a month for your clients, you need to know how certain parts of the Internet fit together. In this chapter, I cover the Domain Name System, domain registrars, and hosting options for your website. By the time I'm done here, you should have a good understanding of how to get a website up and running; in fact, you'll do just that on your own Mac, which you'll configure as your primary development machine.

Domain Name System

Every Internet-connected device has an address, known as an *Internet Protocol address*, often just shortened to IP address. Like a telephone number, your computer's IP address has a fixed format: four groups of numbers in a range from 0 to 255, separated by periods.

Because every Internet-facing device must have a unique IP address, the limitations of this protocol become apparent: There are only 4.2 billion possible addresses. While that may sound like a lot, we're actually running out. Some estimates suggest that we'll use the last IP address in 2011. By then, we should have migrated to a new version of the protocol, known as IPv6.

You can use an IP address to connect to any other computer on the Internet. For example, you can open a web browser and type the address **http://74.125.67.100/**, which gives you the Google home page, shown in Figure 1.1.

However, Google — or any other company, for that matter — doesn't advertise itself by its IP address because you're unlikely to remember that string of numbers. That's why we have the Domain Name System (DNS). Like a massive virtual phone directory, the DNS infrastructure provides hostname lookup services: You provide a domain name (like `google.com`), and the system returns an IP address. This happens behind the scenes in most any Internet application, such as web browsers and email clients.

In This Chapter

Domain Name System

Registrars

Web hosting

Setting up your development environment

Creating your own website

Figure 1.1

You can access the Google home page by using its IP address.

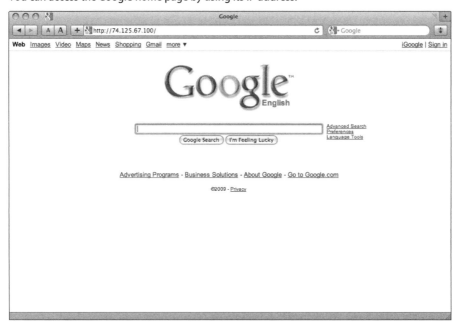

DNS is an amazingly powerful service and is one of the core technologies of the Internet. Like the Internet, DNS is highly *distributed* in nature. This means that there's not just one server that provides hostname lookup but many servers, with each one referring to another in a hierarchy. When a request is made for a website, for example, your computer queries your Internet Service Provider's (ISP's) DNS server for that name. If the DNS server has the record for that name, it provides the IP address for it. If no record is present, the server forwards the request to the ISP's DNS server and up the chain until an answer is found. A simplified diagram is shown in Figure 1.2.

You can find out the IP address of any domain name by using the Terminal application on your Mac. If you haven't used it before, you'll find it in `/Applications/Utilities/`.

NOTE

Terminal provides access to the command-line interface for the Mac operating system. If you're not familiar with the conventions of typing commands and working with text-based feedback, Terminal may seem like a foreign land to you. Hang in there: I'll introduce the command line gradually throughout this book. With enough practice, you'll find yourself appreciating the advantages of the command line and know when it provides the best solution for your needs. For remote administration, Terminal is a necessity, so I'll spend as much time as possible using it for working with online resources.

Figure 1.2

A typical DNS request

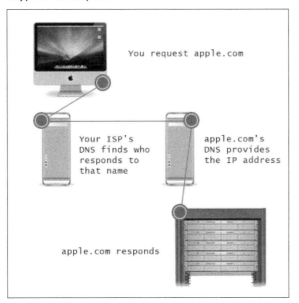

With Terminal open, you see a prompt where you can type in commands. Type **dig google.com** and then press Return. You see the following:

```
achilles:~ aaronvegh$ dig google.com
; <<>> DiG 9.4.3-P1 <<>> google.com
;; global options:  printcmd
;; Got answer:
;; ->>HEADER<<- opcode: QUERY, status: NOERROR, id: 21768
;; flags: qr rd ra; QUERY: 1, ANSWER: 3, AUTHORITY: 4,
   ADDITIONAL: 4
;; QUESTION SECTION:
;google.com.                    IN    A
;; ANSWER SECTION:
google.com.             159    IN    A     74.125.67.100
google.com.             159    IN    A     74.125.45.100
google.com.             159    IN    A     209.85.171.100
;; AUTHORITY SECTION:
google.com.             345565 IN    NS    ns4.google.com.
google.com.             345565 IN    NS    ns1.google.com.
google.com.             345565 IN    NS    ns2.google.com.
google.com.             345565 IN    NS    ns3.google.com.
;; ADDITIONAL SECTION:
ns4.google.com.         345565 IN    A     216.239.38.10
```

```
ns1.google.com.         345565 IN     A       216.239.32.10
ns2.google.com.         345565 IN     A       216.239.34.10
ns3.google.com.         345565 IN     A       216.239.36.10
;; Query time: 775 msec
;; SERVER: 10.0.1.1#53(10.0.1.1)
;; WHEN: Sun May 31 10:05:01 2009
;; MSG SIZE  rcvd: 212
```

The command `dig` takes a single argument by default: the name of the domain for which you want information. You see a number of sections: a QUESTION SECTION, which says that you're looking for A records for `google.com`; an ANSWER SECTION, which tells you there are three main IP addresses (known here as A records) that respond to the domain; and an AUTHORITY SECTION, which shows you the DNS servers for the domain.

A DNS server manages different kinds of records. The A record provides the address for a web server; an NS record provides additional name server addresses; and an MX record provides *mail exchangers*, which are servers that respond to email requests.

You can use `dig` to query specific DNS records. If you want to know the mail servers for a domain, you can use a less verbose form of `dig` that provides exactly what you're looking for:

```
achilles:~ aaronvegh$ dig apple.com mx +short
20 mail-in3.apple.com.
20 eg-mail-in2.apple.com.
10 mail-in11.apple.com.
10 mail-in12.apple.com.
10 mail-in13.apple.com.
20 mail-in1.apple.com.
20 mail-in2.apple.com.
20 mail-in6.apple.com.
100 mail-in3.apple.com.
10 mail-in14.apple.com.
```

The short syntax leaves out the verbose formatting of the initial example, providing just the addresses. MX records also include a priority; the lower the number, the higher the priority. Given the importance of email, having more servers increases the redundancy, ensuring that messages are delivered even when some machines go offline.

The `dig` command is very useful if you're dealing with a domain that isn't responding. One of the first troubleshooting steps I do is to check if the DNS server has the right IP address for the A record: Copy the IP address that `dig` provides and then paste it into a browser.

The next thing you want to know about a domain name is the address of its DNS server. You can acquire that by using a tool called `whois`. This is a way to query the DNS system directly, pulling domain registry information for your domain. What you get back from this command varies depending on the registry — records for .com domain names provide voluminous contact information and legal text. But here's a brief domain example:

```
achilles:~ aaronvegh$ whois vegh.ca
Domain name:              vegh.ca
Domain status:            EXIST
Approval date:            2000/11/16
Renewal date:             2009/12/01
Updated date:             2008/09/26
Registrar:
    Name:                 DomainsAtCost Corp.
    Number:               45
Name servers:
    ns1.mydyndns.org
    ns2.mydyndns.org
```

Domain records for `.ca` domains show certain important dates, the name of the registrar, and the information you're looking for: the active name servers. With this information, you can confirm that the domain name is pointed at the correct DNS server (that is, the server that knows the IP address of the domain in question), and if the site is having trouble responding in a browser, you can try another tool, `ping`, to see if that server is functional:

```
achilles:~ aaronvegh$ ping ns1.mydyndns.org
PING ns1.mydyndns.org (204.13.248.76): 56 data bytes
64 bytes from 204.13.248.76: icmp_seq=0 ttl=55 time=29.105 ms
64 bytes from 204.13.248.76: icmp_seq=1 ttl=55 time=33.558 ms
64 bytes from 204.13.248.76: icmp_seq=2 ttl=55 time=33.210 ms
```

The `ping` tool is wonderful. It sends a special, tiny packet to the server in question (here, it's `ns1.mydyndns.org`), and if that target server is online, you receive a one-line response that shows the amount of time that request took. And it does this once a second until you tell it to stop with the shell's interrupt command: Control+C.

It's also worth noting the dangers that `ping` introduces. While the amount of data that `ping` sends is tiny, it still provides work for the target server to accomplish. If millions of computers decided to ping it at the same time and for prolonged periods, that server could go offline under the load. This happens from time to time in coordinated attacks called *distributed denial of service attacks*. That's why `ping` won't work for some servers, such as `apple.com`, as Apple has disabled its servers' responses to pings. To that utility, it would appear that the Apple server is offline:

```
achilles:~ aaronvegh$ ping apple.com
PING apple.com (17.251.200.70): 56 data bytes
^C
--- apple.com ping statistics ---
13 packets transmitted, 0 packets received, 100% packet loss
```

Registrars

As you've already seen, domain names are the primary way to find stuff on the Internet. Without a good, memorable domain name, you'd be reduced to buying giant books with names in one column and IP addresses in another. Can you imagine the kind of difficulty that would cause? Oh, right — you do that with phone numbers today.

It's not an entirely fair criticism of the telephone; for its lack of mnemonics, there's a lot more that a phone number tells you than an IP address ever will. In North America, an area code and even the first three digits of the number give you geographical information about the target phone. And while IP addresses are also assigned geographically, you sure aren't going to be able to keep track of them.

Enter domain names. With their connection to the DNS system, Internet users have an easy way of reaching resources online. But where do these domain names get registered, and how do they work?

I'll answer the second question first. Domain names are composed of a number of parts, usually three. These parts represent a hierarchy that specifies the domain's ownership. Figure 1.3 demonstrates these parts with one of my favorite domains.

Figure 1.3

The parts of a domain

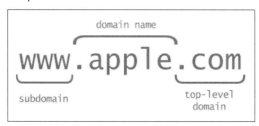

The top-level domain is always at the farthest right. The .com domain is the highest level and is the *root* of this domain name. Immediately to the left is the domain name itself and then to the far left is a subdomain. There can be any number of subdomains, but the most commonly seen one is www, for services available on the World Wide Web.

What top-level domains are available? The ones you have seen the most are in the four spheres originally introduced:

- .com for commercial domains
- .net for general use
- .org for nonprofit and institutional use
- .edu for use by educational institutions

There are also country-specific domains such as `.ca` and `.uk`. Only recently have other top-level domains proliferated; for example, `.mobi` is used for sites intended for handheld devices, and `.info`, `.biz`, and, `.name` round out the more popular choices. Still, it appears that `.com` remains the most favored choice for businesses; while the number of available English names is clearly running low, clever new brands are exploiting words without vowels as a new path to remaining with a `.com` domain. `Flickr.com` comes to mind.

So, if you want a domain name, where do you go? Each top-level domain authorizes companies to act on their behalf as *registrars*. These companies will sell you access to a name within their top-level domain for a period of a year or more. And as it turns out, there's a galaxy of choice in this industry because when most any company can become a registrar, most companies choose to do so.

If you run a business that requires you to purchase domain names fairly frequently, then choosing a domain registrar can be a pretty important decision. Imagine you owned 50 or more domain names, each for different clients. Each domain has its own *terms* (when it comes due) and *settings* (such as contact information and name servers). In my early days, I had domains registered with a number of different companies. Not only did I have to keep track of when to pay, but I also had to remember whom to pay! So, take this advice: Keep your domain name registrations centralized.

To avoid problems with domains in different places, choose a registrar sooner rather than later. When you're evaluating potential companies, consider these factors:

- **Price.** Compare the cost of a domain for one year among your potential registrars. You can see ranges for a `.com` domain from $12 to $35.

- **Availability.** Not all registrars offer a broad selection of top-level domains. Most give you `.com`, `.net`, and, `.org`, but not everyone can give you country-specific domains.

- **Auto-renew.** When your domain name comes due at the end of its term, you should be able to either receive a message or, ideally, have the domain automatically renewed. There's no greater faux pas in this business than having one of your client's domains turn into a parking site because you didn't renew your registration!

- **DNS features.** This isn't a definite requirement, but it's useful enough that it's worth noting. Some higher-priced registrars (notably Network Solutions) include complete DNS management as part of their service, giving you full power over how your domain is used. If you find yourself needing to manage domains at this level, you may want to have it as part of your domain registration.

When you buy a domain from a registrar, you're usually getting nothing more than the right to use that name. How you use it is up to you. Every registrar lets you control what DNS server the domain uses. It's the DNS server's job to indicate what servers will respond to each particular request type.

Let's look at an example. For my personal use, I registered the domain `vegh.ca`. The most important service this domain provides is email, but I also have a web server. Using the DNS system, I can point the web-hosting component (the `A` record) to my own web-hosting server while I point the mail components (the `MX` records) to Google Apps, which provides extremely high-quality (and free) email service.

If your registrar doesn't have DNS service (and most don't), you can make these kinds of settings by arranging them with your hosting company. By default, the same server handles A and MX records, but you can change that if you want.

Web Hosting

If you think there are a lot of domain registrars out there, you'll be dazzled by the number of web-hosting companies. Anyone can host a website; all you need is a fat pipe (a high-speed connection) to the Internet and some servers. You could even host your own website in your home or office, but I don't recommend it; while it makes for a great learning experience, it's a risky proposition for any website that needs maximum uptime. Consider some of the requirements beyond the basics I've already mentioned:

- **Synchronous network connection.** Home and office Internet connections, via cable or DSL, are *asynchronous*, which means you have a fast download speed and a much slower upload speed. These service providers are optimized for consumers of the Internet, not producers. There just isn't enough bandwidth to support web serving beyond a very basic site.

- **Redundant power supply.** The server sitting in your basement or office is subject to the same questionable hydro power as the rest of your facility. Professional hosting companies have diesel-powered backup generators that can ensure your server keeps going long after the power has gone out.

- **Security.** Both physical security and network security are important considerations. Professional companies keep their servers locked in cages inside secure facilities with 24-hour monitoring. They also have dedicated hardware firewalls that screen out various crackers and viruses.

- **Onsite service.** With your own server, if a hard drive dies (and, oh yes, it happens), you probably don't have a replacement on hand. You may not even have a backup! A hosting company can provide both, turning an unmitigated disaster into a hiccup.

The good news is that you can have all the benefits of professional web hosting without paying a ton of cash. But you need to be very careful about who you entrust with that cash; if you run a business doing web development, you're going to host your clients' sites yourself or you're going to recommend a company. Either way, your reputation is at far greater risk than your cash, so choose wisely.

The first decision you have to make is what kind of hosting you need. There are many options, but they usually fall along these lines:

- **Shared hosting.** This is the most common variety of hosting. A hosting company puts many customers on a single machine by using *name-based hosting*: There's one IP address for the machine, but it serves up different websites based on the domain name requested. The upside for the hosting company is that it can reduce its hardware investment and lower your price. The downside is that one active customer on the same server as you could slow your site down to a crawl. You also have a number of limitations, which typically include a limited number of databases and, most painful of all, no way to access the server via the command line. If you have a client who wants nothing more than cut-rate hosting for a single site, then shared hosting is the way to go; otherwise, take a look at the next level.

- **Virtual Private Server.** Also known by its acronym, VPS, this is a fairly recent hosting option as more powerful processors have become available as well as very good open-source virtualization software. In this case, a server runs a basic operating system, whose only task is to run instances of virtual machines. These virtual machines look and act like dedicated servers, giving you full remote access and the ability to install your own software if you want. But you still may suffer from performance issues, as your virtual server is using the same physical resources as others on the machine. However, given the cost advantages of this option, I consider it a terrific choice if you're just getting started.

- **Dedicated hosting.** Just as the name suggests, this is a computer at the hosting company that belongs entirely to you. You'll have your choice of the hardware that's used, so you can choose processor, memory, and hard drive capacity. You'll usually also have set bandwidth limits, although they're often generous enough that you won't have to worry about them. The hosting company will give you your choice of operating system: Windows, some commercial forms of Unix, and various flavors of Linux. The cost of this option can be much higher than other forms of hosting, but no other option gives you the same level of performance and support.

- **Collocation.** This final option is for the ultimate die-hard geek. You buy your own machine and then bring it to the hosting company; the only thing they provide is the bandwidth. You get the primary advantages of the hosting environment — namely, the Internet connection, power supply, and onsite security — but you give up nothing in terms of control. This can also be an expensive option, so for my money, I typically prefer the dedicated hosting option.

For my own business, I have a dedicated server that costs less than $200 per month. If that sounds like a lot, consider that I have a few dozen sites hosted there for various clients. The amount they pay varies according to the arrangements I made with them in the building of their sites as well as the amount of resources they consume. Overall, though, these clients more than pay for the cost of the server.

When it comes to choosing a hosting company for your own business, there are many factors to consider, such as their pricing, the features they offer, and, in some cases, where the company is located. But the chief concern, in my estimation, is customer service. Will your company respond to an emergency in hours rather than days? What will they do for you if the hardware fails? How hard is it to talk to a human? Don't just trust the company to tell you these things; go online and find out what others are saying. Every company has detractors online, but the best companies also have their promoters.

In Chapter 2, I discuss setting up a dedicated or virtual host with your operating system of choice. You do that by creating a virtualized Linux server right on your Mac to give you a sense of what you can accomplish with a remote server in the real world.

Setting Up Your Development Environment

The goal of this book is to turn you into a credible expert on all facets of web development. So far, I've covered the infrastructure of the web and provided some advice on what services to use. With that taken care of, it's time to turn to where most of the work is actually done: on your Mac.

Your Mac is a very powerful web development environment. It comes ready to use with the technologies that you need to build any website: the Apache web server, the PHP web scripting language, the Ruby on Rails web development framework, and more.

CROSS-REF

For more on Apache, see Chapter 3. For more on PHP, see Chapter 15. For more on Ruby on Rails, see Chapter 17.

Let's take a few moments to ensure your Mac is set up to serve web pages. During the course of your work, you'll create your sites on a Mac and then transfer them to your web host for production use.

NOTE

Technologists speak about using different environments in the course of software development. There are usually at least two environments: *development* is where the software is created. Once completed, the software is moved to *production*. In larger organizations, there's usually an intermediary environment, known as *testing* or *staging*. Ideally, the development and production machines would run the same operating systems — or operating systems that are similar enough that it doesn't matter. Thus, creating your sites on a Mac and then posting them to a Linux server rarely presents an issue.

As you would expect on a Mac, turning on the web server is as simple as clicking a button. Go to the System Preferences application and then open the Sharing pane, shown in Figure 1.4. Click the Web Sharing check box to turn on the web server.

With Web Sharing active, you see a note on the right side of the window that indicates the URL of your now-active server. In my case, I have a domain that I use specifically for my internal network: `amazingmac.ca`. You'll most likely see `.local` as your domain, giving you a URL of `http://<your computer name>.local`. If you click on that link (yes, it's a live link), your browser opens to that URL. If this is the first time you've ever used Web Sharing, you see an introductory page for the Apache web server. There's another shortcut you can also use: Typing **http://localhost** provides the same access to the web server.

There's also another link here: the same URL as the main server, with your username appended. This is a standard feature of the Apache web server, where every user on the system has his or her own dedicated web directory. On Mac OS X, that directory is the Sites folder, shown in Figure 1.5. Any folder put here could be accessed by the web server. Based on this screenshot, you'd be able to type **http://localhost/~aaronvegh/choicebelize** and get that website.

Figure 1.4

Activating the Web Sharing feature in the Sharing preference pane

Figure 1.5

The Sites folder in your home directory

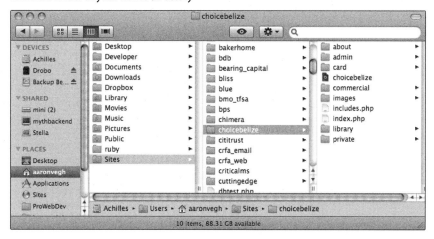

By default, the files accessed by simply typing **http://localhost** are located in /Library/ WebServer/Documents, at the root of your hard drive. In my opinion, this is an inconvenient place to have your development files. So, when I get my hands on a new Mac, I make a small change to the web server's configuration file, making the server's main directory my own Sites folder. This would turn http://localhost/~aaronvegh/choicebelize into http:// localhost/choicebelize, making life a lot easier. But be careful; if you share your Mac with other users, this procedure could cause problems. Only do this if you have a Mac to yourself.

In the Finder, press ⌘+Shift+G to bring up the Go to Folder pane. Type **/etc/apache2** and then click the Go button. You should see a file called httpd.conf. This is the configuration file for the Apache web server. Open that file in your favorite text editor.

NOTE

Although I've covered the topic of text editors in the introduction, it's worth repeating here: Don't use the TextEdit application included with Mac OS. Although it may look like a text editor, it is in fact a *rich text editor*, which includes all kinds of formatting in its default setting. Saving over a plain-text configuration file with TextEdit would do a great deal of harm to the operation of your web server. Before continuing, ensure that you're using one of the text-editing applications that I recommend in the introduction.

The Apache configuration file is long but fairly straightforward. Feel free to examine it; you'll find that the top section includes directives for the server in general (such items as where the server files are located, the modules it uses, and the user and group the server operates as), followed by directives for particular directories. It's the latter group that you're interested in right now; you want to change the directive called DocumentRoot, pointing it at your own Sites folder. Find this line in the file:

```
DocumentRoot "/Library/WebServer/Documents"
```

Change it to this (replacing, of course, my username with yours):

```
DocumentRoot "/Users/aaronvegh/Sites"
```

You have to make a change in one other location. Just a few lines down, find this line:

```
<Directory "/Library/WebServer/Documents">
```

Change that to your directory:

```
<Directory "/Users/aaronvegh/Sites">
```

You're done; save the file. You should be asked for your administrative password when you do this. With the new configuration file saved, you need to restart the Apache server for the settings to take effect. You could do this by going to the Sharing pane and deselecting the Web Sharing check box. But we're geeks. Open Terminal and then issue this command:

```
achilles:~ aaronvegh$ sudo apachectl restart
```

You're asked for your password and then the server restarts. Don't worry if this seems arcane; I cover this more in the next few chapters.

For now, you should test your configuration. Follow these steps to create a web page:

1. **In your favorite text editor, create a new file.**

2. **Type the following into your new file:**

```
<html>
    <head>
        <title>My First Web Page</title>
    </head>
    <body>
        <h1>Hello, World!</h1>
        <p>This is my first working web page.</p>
    </body>
</html>
```

3. **Save the file to your Sites directory and then name it** `index.html`**.** There may already be a file there by that name; feel free to overwrite it or rename the original, as this is just the default Apache welcome page.

4. **Open a browser and type** http://localhost **as the URL.**

You should see something similar to Figure 1.6 in your browser.

Congratulations! You now have a functioning web development environment.

Figure 1.6

Your first web page

Creating Your Own Website

I've spent this chapter talking about the things you need to start building websites, either for yourself or as a business. Once you have the technology out of the way, the first site you need to build is your own! Many companies — and I raise my hand guiltily here — neglect their own sites because they're too busy building them for others. Try not to fall into this trap.

Especially when you're new to building websites, take the time to create a site that does its best to advertise your services. All my clients came to me via word of mouth from my existing, happy clients. But the first thing prospective new clients do is visit my website. Once they see that it looks professional, with just that hint of edginess, they know they can trust me to do the job.

Be realistic about your site. Don't make a giant kingdom of web pages because they'll become outdated. Your clients only care about two things: the work you've done and how to get in touch. Focus on these, and you'll have accomplished the job.

"But wait," you may be crying. "How do you build a website?" I know. Bear with me while I get through the basics. In the next few chapters, I cover the technology that you'll use to build websites before I move on to the hard skills: HTML, CSS, and design.

But all the while, keep your thoughts on what your own site will look like and what kind of statement it will make. Applying what you learn here to what you want to accomplish will make learning easier — and more rewarding.

Summary

The technologies covered in this chapter represent the foundations of the Internet. Before you can move on to learn about websites — much less build them — you have to know how the Internet works. What I've covered here — from how the domain name system works, to troubleshooting, to picking domains and registrars, to selecting a hosting provider — will put you in good stead as we move forward.

Unix Is the Engine

N ow that you've had a chance to familiarize yourself with some of the services your business will depend on, it's time to get to know the engine that runs at the core of them all: Unix. Originally developed in 1969 at AT&T Bell Labs, this operating system formed the infrastructure atop which most of today's Internet was built.

The What and Why of Unix

A time traveler from the mid-1970s would probably not be out of place in front of a modern computer running one of the many variants of Unix now available. Unix came with a number of features that have made it the universal computing option, even to this day:

- It's a *multi-tasking*, *multi-user* operating system, which means the computer can run different processes at the same time and for different users. This made Unix a great option for time-sharing purposes, but today, that power makes the OS suitable for a variety of server tasks.

- It's a *highly portable* operating system, owing to its foundation in the C programming language on which it was built. The C language provided developers with a very low entry point for programming and produced lean, fast code that compiles on a variety of hardware platforms. This means that Unix can — and does — run on pretty much any computer you can find.

- It's an *open system*, with highly orthogonal components. *Orthogonality* represents the ability of a system to have independent processes, not dependent on other pieces for their operation. The foundation of this notion is the use of plain-text files for data storage as well as the proliferation of software tools that do one simple action rather than fewer single tools that perform many actions.

Owing to its features, portability, and openness, many large institutions embraced Unix, powering an industry for large-scale computing. While companies such as Sun, HP, and IBM each had their own brand of Unix (Solaris, HP-UX, and AIX, respectively), it was the Berkeley Software Distribution, or BSD, that drove Unix into the

mainstream. That's because while the commercial, high-priced Unix systems were busy running corporate payrolls and modeling financial data, BSD Unix was a liberally licensed academic package that you could acquire and run on your own computer.

Ultimately, it was this availability that led to the development of an entire generation of free, open-source software tools built on this foundation of knowledge: first, the GNU suite of tools and then the Linux kernel. Taken together, these tools are known as GNU/Linux, and they represent the pinnacle achievement of the open-source movement: a completely free (both monetary and in terms of license) operating system and software suite. Nowadays, you can choose from hundreds of available distributions, download them, and then run them on your computer. You can view and modify the operating system code and contribute changes back to the community or you can keep the changes for your own use.

Compare this freedom with the traditional commercial software world, perhaps best represented by the Microsoft Windows platform. A company wanting to deploy its applications on a Windows server has to both pay for a license and take for granted that the operating system meets its needs — the company has no access to the inner workings of that software and can't inspect the source code for security purposes. So, if a bug is discovered in the software, that company's only resort is to file a bug report with Microsoft and then hope for the best.

In the open-source world of Linux, that company could inspect the source code, fix the deficiency, and roll out a new version. It could also contribute that patch back to the community, thus improving that software for everyone. Over time, this network effect has led to Unix being recognized as an incredibly secure, stable operating system.

It was no surprise, then, when Apple turned to a variant of Unix for its next-generation version of the Mac OS. Essentially, the Mac is a beautiful and powerful graphical interface built on top of Unix's secure and tested foundations. When you open Terminal, included with Mac OS X, you're in a real, honest-to-goodness Unix environment. When you start up Web Sharing on the Mac, you're starting up the most powerful and pervasive web server software available: Apache. When you look at file information on your Mac, you're dealing with the same specifications you would on a Unix machine: owners, groups, and permissions.

Some variant of Unix is used to power more than 70% of all web servers on the Internet as well as the vast majority of email. FTP and SSH are foundational Unix technologies and are often used to move data across the Internet. Why would you use Windows in this environment when a new Mac out of the box comes with all this stuff built in? That's part of why you have a Mac — it's part of what makes the Mac a terrific development tool — and that's why you'll be dealing with Unix in your work.

In this chapter, I examine your options for a production server. This is the machine that you'll use to serve both yourself and your clients. In Chapter 1, I talked about the various hosting options that are available, and I recommended either a virtual private hosting service or a dedicated package. Once you make your choice, you'll be looking to select an operating system to install on it.

Choosing a Distribution

The terms of the Linux open-source license are very interesting: You're free to download and run the operating system, and you're free to view the source code and make changes to your heart's content. But if you want to redistribute those changes, it must be done with the same free licensing terms. In this way, the Linux license is viral: Alterations made to the software also become freely available, and a huge, virtuous cycle ensues.

One unintended side effect of this cycle is the intense proliferation of Linux *distributions*, which are variants of the Linux operating system custom-built for specific purposes. There are hundreds, perhaps thousands, of distributions available. With those numbers, a great deal of churn occurs as new distributions become available, while older, lesser-known ones die out. In the distribution race, as in most open-source software, the best ideas win.

So, while I might offer a quick look at some Linux distributions in the course of this book, there are clearly only three major contenders in the Linux space at this time. As a web developer, you're most likely to be exposed to at least one of these three, and when it comes time to choose a distribution for your own server, that OS is most likely to come from this list. I assume that if you're inclined to a different distribution, you have sufficient interest to make that decision worthwhile.

Ubuntu Linux

At least in terms of mindshare, Ubuntu Linux is the de facto king of Linux distributions. While Linux has fought for years the (mostly true) criticisms that it's difficult to install and use, the mission of Ubuntu has been to provide a beautiful, accessible, and useable Linux system that's suitable for personal desktop use. Ubuntu is based on Debian Linux, a venerable distribution whose main strength has been its software packaging system. I discuss package management later in this chapter.

One reason for the success of Ubuntu is undoubtedly its aggressive update timetable. Every six months, you see a new version of Ubuntu, featuring the latest improvements contributed by the community as well as enhancements developed by Canonical, the company that owns Ubuntu.

While desktop Linux is an interesting and worthwhile pursuit, your interest is really on the server side of things — after all, in Mac OS X, you already have the most enviable desktop environment! But Ubuntu also shines here: Combined with the Debian-derived package management system, Ubuntu offers stable, long-term support for its distributions; every two years, the company releases an LTS (long-term support) version of Ubuntu Server, which is maintained with critical updates and security fixes for five years. This is the kind of support that makes Ubuntu a smart choice on the server.

Popularity is also a powerful inducement to choose a distribution. In the case of Ubuntu, you're much more likely to find support for solving your problem than if you were running a lesser-known distribution. For example, try searching for "Ubuntu synaptics driver" and "Slackware synaptics driver" on your favorite search engine. At the time of this writing, I get ten times the number of results and that much more certainty that someone else has tried getting Ubuntu to work on his or her MacBook.

Red Hat Linux

Red Hat was one of the first entrants in the commercial Linux space — a tough market to break into, given that the operating system is free! But Red Hat proved that you could make money in the open-source game by giving away the software and then selling support. This strategy works well in the enterprise space, where large companies would rather let the experts handle their server infrastructure — and they have the cash to do it. As a result, Red Hat has become a very successful company that has plowed a lot of support back into the Linux community. Nowadays, Red Hat offers a few products that are worth knowing about:

- **Red Hat Enterprise Linux (RHEL).** This is the company's flagship commercial product. Unlike during its early days, the company sells RHEL to large companies, in the form of subscriptions, with their server variants starting at $350 per year. Of course, you may be wondering how Red Hat can sell an operating system and still be in conformance with the Linux free license. In truth, you can download the operating system if you know where to look. You can, of course, do this yourself if you want to run RHEL, but you won't find it as a free option if you're purchasing a dedicated server from a hosting company.

- **CentOS.** This is the most popular independent build of Red Hat Enterprise Linux. As of this writing, RHEL is at version 5, and there's a free version provided by CentOS, also at version 5. The goal of the CentOS project is to both provide a completely free version of the Red Hat OS and ensure complete binary compatibility with its parent. This means that a program or library file that runs on one platform can run on the other, as they're interchangeable. Essentially, CentOS is the same as the current version of RHEL but with any copyrighted Red Hat branding removed — all of which makes CentOS a very good choice for your server: great support from a long-term dedicated Linux developer, broad community support, and wide availability from web-hosting companies. This is, in fact, my current brand of Linux on my own server.

- **Fedora Core.** In many ways, this is the parent of both RHEL and CentOS. When the first Fedora distribution was launched in 2003, it was intended as a leading-edge Linux system that provided all the latest technologies in one package. The intention was to create a proving ground for new technologies, the best and most stable of which would then be introduced in RHEL. While some web-hosting companies offer Fedora as an option for your server, I can't recommend it. Your infrastructure requires stability more than fancy new features.

SUSE Linux

While I previously made light of the Slackware distribution, it does hold a place in the current Linux pantheon. Created in the early 2000s in Germany, SUSE Linux was a repackaging of Slackware for the European market, where it became very popular. Today, SUSE is owned by

Novell, which has adopted a strategy similar to that of Red Hat; they provide an enterprise edition of their software and maintain a leading-edge version that's tested by the community. SUSE Linux Enterprise is their stable, supported product; openSUSE is their test bed. On the desktop, the Novell distribution provides a terrific user experience, easy installation, and strong support.

Also, unlike with the enterprise offering from Red Hat, you can very readily go to the Novell website and download their SUSE Linux Enterprise Server. However, its downloads page places the very scary text "Evaluation Download" next to the link. Indeed, users who download this operating system are doing so under the auspices of an Activation Code, which lets you use the software. Have I scared you off yet? Strangely, I've been unable to find an analog to the Red Hat CentOS, which should be available if the SUSE operating system is an open-source project.

All companies that work in the Linux space have to walk a very fine line between commercial viability and community acceptance. In my opinion, the Novell strategy crosses that line. Its absence from many web-hosting companies' operating system offerings supports that viewpoint.

Mac OS X Server

In the midst of all these very capable Linux offerings, you might be wondering where the Apple server operating system fits. Mac OS X Server can be thought of in the same category as other commercial Unix systems, such as HP-UX and Solaris; it provides a rock-solid foundation on which to run your server applications. The advantages of Mac OS X Server are its management tools. For every task where you might use a command-line tool in Linux, Apple has provided a beautiful, user-friendly graphical application. To manage users and groups, web serving, email, file transfer, and more, Mac OS X Server provides terrific software.

However, you may find the cost of choosing Mac OS X difficult to justify. For example, relatively few hosting companies offer Apple hardware in their hosting environments, and those that do appear to charge significantly more for it. Also, because Mac OS X Server is used by relatively few people, getting help on the Internet is that much more difficult. Ultimately, my feeling is that the Mac makes an unbeatable desktop operating system, while Linux is the best choice for a server.

Installation and Setup

Most often, when you're dealing with a web-hosting company, you won't have to deal with the installation of Linux; you make your choice during the purchase process, and the company takes care of the rest. However, I strongly advocate running your own installation of Linux, both as a client and as a server, to give you a deeper understanding of its inner workings.

If you're like me, you learn best by trying things for yourself; it's the Geek Way. And Linux definitely qualifies as a geeky pursuit! So, if you're going to learn the ins and outs of this OS, you need to get your hands on a system that can run Linux. You probably have members of your family who have discarded computers or you know someone whose employer is offloading three-year-old PCs at the end of their lease cycle. For a pittance, you can acquire a fully viable Windows PC, onto which you can install the Linux distribution of your choice.

But perhaps you have a very tight budget or, more realistically, a spouse who will completely lose it if you bring yet another gadget into the house. Fortunately, if you own a Mac made since 2006 (that is, if your Mac has an Intel processor), you have a terrific solution: virtualization. Using a software product such as VMware Fusion or the free VirtualBox from Sun, you can run any operating system within a virtual machine on your Mac. The good news is that if you have a lot of RAM in your computer, performance can be quite excellent.

To demonstrate how to install and set up a basic Linux system, I'm going to use VirtualBox and install Ubuntu Desktop. Follow these steps:

1. **Type** www.virtualbox.org/wiki/Downloads **into your browser to open the VirtualBox downloads page, as shown in Figure 2.1.**

Figure 2.1

The Sun VirtualBox downloads page

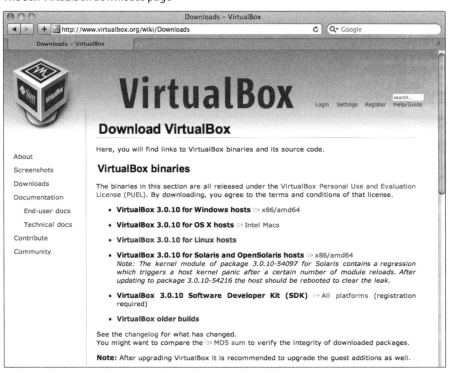

2. **Click the download link for OS X hosts and then save the file to your desktop.**

3. **Type** www.ubuntu.com/getubuntu/download **in your browser to open the Ubuntu download page, as shown in Figure 2.2.** As of this writing, the current version is 9.10.

4. **Choose your nearest download location from the pop-up menu and then click Begin Download.** Save the file to your desktop.

5. **While Ubuntu is downloading, mount the VirtualBox disk image by double-clicking the** .dmg **file you downloaded.** A VirtualBox volume appears on your desktop. When you open that volume, you find the installer application, as shown in Figure 2.3.

6. **Double-click the** VirtualBox.mpkg **icon and then follow all the steps, accepting all the default options.**

7. **Once the installation is complete, open the VirtualBox application, now located in your** /Applications **folder.**

8. **Click Next to create a new virtual machine to run your instance of Ubuntu Linux.**

Figure 2.2

The Ubuntu Linux download page

Figure 2.3

The VirtualBox mounted disk image

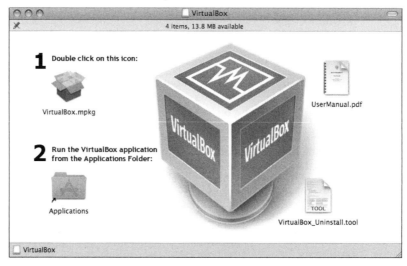

Figure 2.4

The VirtualBox application

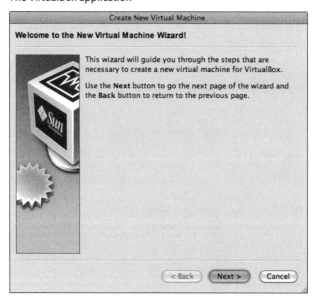

9. **Click Next, type a name for your virtual machine, choose the operating system, and then click Next.** For example, I typed **Ubuntu Linux** and then chose Ubuntu from the Version pop-up menu, as shown in Figure 2.5.

10. **In the next two screens, configure the memory and hard drive.** For memory, you may opt for the suggested minimum of 384MB, but more memory — if you have it — gives you better performance. For the hard drive, choose the Create a New Hard Disk option and then ensure that you choose the following settings: a dynamically sized drive image, with a maximum size of your choosing (the default is 8GB). When you're done, a Summary screen appears, as shown in Figure 2.6, to show you your settings.

11. **Click Finish to have VirtualBox create your new machine.**

Figure 2.5

The Create New Virtual Machine wizard

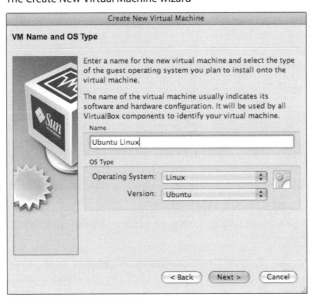

Figure 2.6

The Summary screen

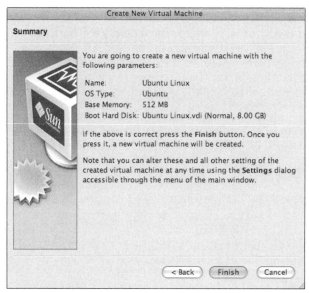

With your virtual machine created, you can now launch it for the first time. But with a blank hard disk image, what's going to happen? Not a whole lot, which is why you need to assign your newly downloaded Ubuntu installation image as the startup disk. Follow these steps:

1. **Open the Ubuntu virtual machine, and in the main window, click Settings in the toolbar to open the Settings window.**

2. **Click Storage in the toolbar of that window and then click the CD/DVD-ROM tab, shown in Figure 2.7.**

3. **Click the Mount CD/DVD Drive check box, which activates the options, click the ISO Image File radio button, and then click the file icon to choose a file.** The Virtual Media Manager window appears.

4. **To choose your downloaded Ubuntu Linux image, click the Add button in the Virtual Media Manager toolbar, and then choose the image from your hard drive.** The image is now listed in the Virtual Media Manager window, as shown in Figure 2.8.

5. **Click Select to use that image and then click OK to close the Settings window.**

Figure 2.7

The CD/DVD-ROM settings screen for your virtual machine

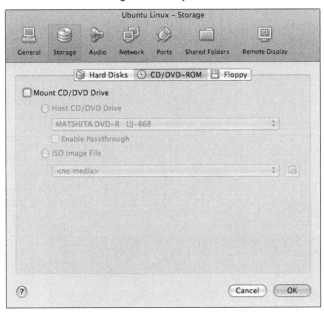

Figure 2.8

The Virtual Media Manager window

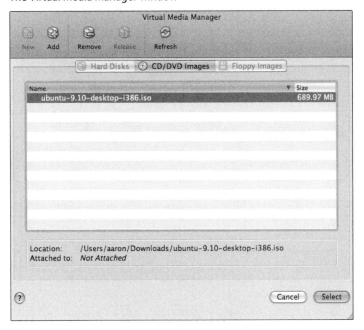

You're now ready to launch your virtual machine for the first time. Click the Start button to launch your virtual machine, and the first thing you see is a message from VirtualBox warning you about key locking. When your virtual machine is the active window, all keyboard and mouse actions are constrained within that window. By pressing the left ⌘ key on your keyboard, however, you can release that lock and use other Mac applications normally.

With that out of the way, Ubuntu launches. You should see the initial splash screen, shown in Figure 2.9. Press the arrow keys to move to Install Ubuntu and then press Return to choose it.

Congratulations! Having reached this point, you're now able to install any version of Linux that you like and play around with different settings to provide unique results. The greatest feature of using a virtual machine is that you can screw up completely and simply reset it with a fresh installation. In fact, the more mistakes you make, the better you'll learn.

Figure 2.9

The Ubuntu Linux splash screen

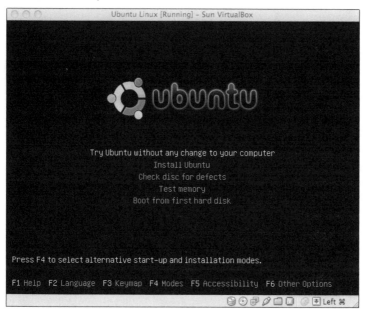

The Ubuntu installation process is, as promised, quite simple and easy to follow. Because you learn best by doing, I only briefly talk about the major steps involved as you follow the procedure.

If this is your first time, you should accept every default suggestion that the installer presents to you. In my case, the installer automatically detected my time zone and keyboard layout. During the hard disk partitioning step, the installer recommended — and I accepted — the option to use the entire disk. It's a virtual disk anyway, so that's fine.

CAUTION

If you're running Ubuntu (or any other Linux) on a machine that's also running another operating system, then you should pay close attention to this step! While the Use entire disk option is fine for machines (virtual or real) running only Linux, this is the step where you would partition the disk to preserve the other operating system. Ubuntu also helps with this step, but it's worth warning you: If you're not careful, you could lose important data here.

Some distributions offer either a complete directory of software packages to install at this time or more simplified groups of software (with names such as Office Tools or Web Serving). Ubuntu takes the responsibility out of your hands on this one: If you're installing the Desktop version of the OS, you're getting a default installation that includes the most commonly used applications for a wide variety of uses.

Once the installation is complete, the system reboots. At this point, you want to detach the virtual disk that you connected before installing; the easiest way is to click the tiny CD icon at the bottom of the virtual machine window and then choose your physical optical drive as the source.

At last, you have your own Linux system, running as a virtual machine on your Mac, as shown in Figure 2.10! Take some time to explore the operating system a bit. Run the software updates that are offered to you, open some applications, and play some Mahjongg. You might also want to install the VirtualBox Linux Additions, a suite of drivers that make working with your virtual machine easier; you can mouse freely in and out of the Linux environment, you'll have better mouse control, and, best of all, you'll have decent screen resolution. Check the VirtualBox website for documentation on how to install the additions.

After you've had a chance to explore your new Linux OS, you're going to set it aside to learn about some of the basics of working with any Unix-based file system, whether that be Linux or Mac OS X.

Figure 2.10

The default Ubuntu desktop

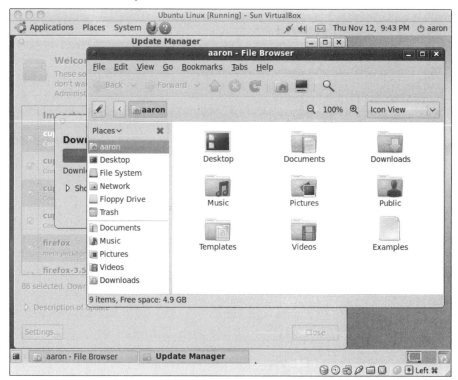

Users, Groups, and Permissions

I began this chapter by describing Unix as a multi-user operating system. Back in the days of time-sharing, this was a critical feature: the ability to have users share their own environments, complete with their unique settings that would become available no matter what terminal they used to log on to the central server. Multi-user capability isn't just a convenience; it's a matter of security on an operating system: As the administrator of a machine, you need to control who can do what.

Consider the layout of the file system on your own Mac. If you open a new Finder window (either click the Finder icon in the Dock or, while in the Finder, press ⌘+N), you see that the top-level folder is your user home folder, as shown in Figure 2.11.

However, your home folder isn't the root of your hard drive; you can get to it in the Finder by choosing your hard drive (named Achilles in Figure 2.11) and then navigating to the Users directory. Inside, you find not only your home directory but also that of any other user on your system.

Figure 2.11

Your user home folder

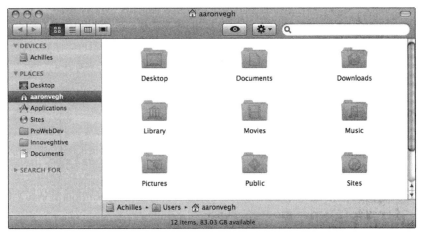

On the Mac or any Linux system, you find that you only have permission to write files into your home directory; everywhere else requires additional privileges. For example, navigate to the /System directory and then try to create a new folder (⌘+Shift+N). You're denied permission with a dialog box that says, "The operation could not be completed because you do not have enough access privileges."

As long as you keep your documents within your home folder, you should never experience a permissions issue on the Mac; in fact, most new users never realize that there's a complicated permissions model at work on their computers. However, when you become the administrator of a machine, permissions are an unavoidable topic. So, let's turn to your Linux system to investigate users, groups, and permissions.

If you chose to run Ubuntu Linux on your virtual machine, Terminal exists in the Accessories menu under Applications. Start Ubuntu, and you get a new window with a flashing cursor prompt; for example, aaron@ubuntu-test:~$.

In Ubuntu, the default Terminal prompt consists of your username (aaron), the hostname of the machine (ubuntu-test), and the current directory (~, which is Unix shorthand for the home directory). The dollar sign indicates that Terminal is ready for user input. Let's begin by asking for a listing of the files in the current directory. I'll use the ls command and then show you the result:

```
aaron@ubuntu-test:~$ ls
Desktop    examples.desktop  Pictures  Templates Documents  Music
    Public    Videos
```

The `ls` command returns a list of all the files and folders in the current directory. It's hard to tell in this listing, but the Ubuntu Terminal applies the color blue to directory names, while simple files are in white. However, that's still not a very useful display. Let's ask Terminal for more details on the files in this directory:

```
aaron@ubuntu-test:~$ ls -l
total 32
drwxr-xr-x 2 aaron aaron 4096 2009-05-18 20:12 Desktop
drwxr-xr-x 2 aaron aaron 4096 2009-05-18 20:12 Documents
-rw-r--r-- 1 aaron aaron  357 2009-05-18 20:05 examples.desktop
drwxr-xr-x 2 aaron aaron 4096 2009-05-18 20:12 Music
drwxr-xr-x 2 aaron aaron 4096 2009-05-18 20:12 Pictures
drwxr-xr-x 2 aaron aaron 4096 2009-05-18 20:12 Public
drwxr-xr-x 2 aaron aaron 4096 2009-05-18 20:12 Templates
drwxr-xr-x 2 aaron aaron 4096 2009-05-18 20:12 Videos
```

There's quite a bit of useful information here. Let's define what these columns are:

- **File permissions are in the first column.** The first character is a `d` to represent a directory, a `-` to indicate a regular file, or an `s` to indicate a *symbolic link*, the Linux equivalent to the alias file type in the Mac OS. The next nine characters are a representation of that file's permissions, arranged in three groups of three. Each set of three characters shows the presence of read, write, and execute permissions for the owner, group, and world (that is, everyone else), respectively. If the letter is present, then that bit is active for the file. For example, the Desktop folder has read, write, and execute permissions for the owner, but the group and the world can't write to it.

- **The file count is in the next column.** Where the line refers to a file rather than a directory, this number is always 1. For directories, the number indicates how many items are inside.

- **The owner and group of the file are next.** When you create a file, the owner is automatically set to be your username and group. On Ubuntu, a group is created with the same name as the owner, and each is assigned to every file you create. On the Mac, your user is assigned to a group called staff. Groups help system administrators assign permissions to multiple individuals. I discuss these assignments later in this chapter.

- **The file size is shown next.** It would be cool if directories showed the size of their file contents; instead, they always indicate the space the directory itself takes up in bytes: 4096. If you're dealing with large file sizes, you may find bytes difficult to parse, especially as they aren't grouped with commas or spaces! But if you use the command `ls -lh`, you can display those file sizes in sensible units, such as kilobytes or megabytes.

- **The next column shows the file's modified date.** If you update a file, its modified date as well as that of its parent folder changes to the new time.

- **And lastly, of course, is the name of the file.**

Let's keep our attention on the permission bits — that cluster of nine characters representing the file's access rights. I start by creating a new file by using the Linux `touch` command:

```
aaron@ubuntu-test:~$ touch myfile.txt
aaron@ubuntu-test:~$ ls -l
total 32
drwxr-xr-x 2 aaron aaron 4096 2009-05-23 16:21 Desktop
drwxr-xr-x 2 aaron aaron 4096 2009-05-18 20:12 Documents
-rw-r--r-- 1 aaron aaron  357 2009-05-23 16:20 examples.desktop
drwxr-xr-x 2 aaron aaron 4096 2009-05-18 20:12 Music
-rw-r--r-- 1 aaron aaron    0 2009-05-23 16:45 myfile.txt
drwxr-xr-x 2 aaron aaron 4096 2009-05-18 20:12 Pictures
drwxr-xr-x 2 aaron aaron 4096 2009-05-18 20:12 Public
drwxr-xr-x 2 aaron aaron 4096 2009-05-18 20:12 Templates
drwxr-xr-x 2 aaron aaron 4096 2009-05-18 20:12 Videos
```

You can see that the new file myfile.txt has been created, and that it's empty, at 0 bytes. Note also the permission bits, which indicate that aaron (the owner) can read and write to the file, while everyone else can just read it. There's no execution bit because this is simply a data file and can't be (nor should it be) launched like a program or directory.

What if I want to change the permissions for this file? I can make it so that anyone can write to this file:

```
aaron@ubuntu-test:~$ chmod 666 myfile.txt
aaron@ubuntu-test:~$ ls -l myfile.txt
-rw-rw-rw- 1 aaron aaron 0 2009-05-23 16:45 myfile.txt
```

The Unix chmod command — change mode — allows you to change the permission bits on a file. The arguments passed include an octal representation of the permissions as well as the file name in question. The first argument requires some explanation.

Each of the three permission groups — the owner, group, and world permissions — can be represented by a single number. When you put those numbers together, you get the octal representation that you pass to chmod. The values in Table 2-1 will help you learn an easy mnemonic.

Table 2-1 Octal Permission Values

Octal Value	Permission
4	Read
2	Write
1	Execute

To determine a permission bit for a given group, just add up the values for each permission type. For example, to note a read and write permission, add the 4 and the 2 to get 6. For read and execute permission, add the 4 and 1 to get 5. Once you do this for each of the three groups, you have your complete octal value to use as an argument for chmod. You should always have a larger number for owner permissions than the others; you don't want to give yourself the least control over your own file!

There's one more trick you can do with chmod: Using the recursive flag, you can change permissions for many files at once. As a web server administrator, you may find yourself altering permissions for an entire folder of files. It's fairly easy to execute:

```
aaron@ubuntu-test:~$ chmod -R  666 mydirectory/
```

This gives read and write permission to all files inside the mydirectory folder. And do note the uppercase R; it matters.

On the Mac side, you can do the same trick by using Terminal (it's located at /Applications/ Utilities). Everything I previously described also works on a Mac. But the Mac also provides a graphical interface for file permissions with the Get Info window, as shown in Figure 2.12.

In Mac OS X 10.6 Snow Leopard, you need to click the small lock icon and then type your password to change file permissions. Don't let this scare you off. You can set separate read or read and write permissions for the file's owner, group, and everyone. Note the lack of an execute permission; this is the Mac's way of suggesting to you that the system should know the difference between data files and applications. This only becomes an annoyance in the case of shell scripting, where your data files are, in fact, executable.

Now that you can change permissions on files, let's take a closer look at owners and groups. As you've already seen, the owner and group mechanism provides a way to give finer control over who can do what to a file. While it's normally assumed that the creator of the file can read and write to it, you may want to also give that authority to others; the group is the means to accomplish that.

To create a new user on a Linux system, you use the adduser command. This command takes a lot of potential arguments, but a simple form is what you'll use most often:

```
aaron@ubuntu-test:~$ sudo adduser theNewGuy
```

What's with the sudo? It's a command that stands for *super user do*, which allows regular users (such as you, the default user) to execute commands that only the administrator — known on Linux as *root* — could accomplish. Not every user has sudo capability by default; you have to be included in the group known as wheel (on Ubuntu and Red Hat systems). In the meantime, when you use the sudo command, you're asked for your password and then allowed to execute as if you were the root user. You have this power for approximately ten minutes; after that, you're asked for your password again the next time you run sudo.

Returning to `adduser`, in the previous example, you're passing the minimum required argument for the command: the name of the new user. That means you end up with a lot of defaults set for this user, which is usually fine. A number of events occur: A new folder is created in the `/home` directory of the system, with the same name as the new user; a new entry is created in the file `/etc/passwd` (which tracks the names and passwords of all users); and a new group is created with the same name as the user. This information is tracked in `/etc/group`.

While the new user has been created, you've not yet assigned a password. To do this, execute this command:

```
aaron@ubuntu-test:~$ sudo passwd theNewGuy
```

You're prompted for a new password, and you're asked to repeat it to be sure you typed it correctly; for security reasons, Terminal doesn't echo the password as you type, so be careful!

Once the user is created, you can test it by using the `su` (switch user) command:

```
aaron@ubuntu-test:~$ su theNewGuy
theNewGuy@ubuntu-test:~$
```

You're asked for `theNewGuy`'s password and then you can see that the prompt has changed, showing that the new user is logged in. At any time, if you want to log out from the new user, just type **exit**.

Before you move on, let's take a look at some of the tools that are available to manage users and groups. I've already mentioned the `/etc/passwd` file; this is where the user information is stored. If you want to look at it, issue the command `cat /etc/passwd`:

```
aaron@ubuntu-test:~$ cat /etc/passwd
alex:x:0:0::/home/alex:/bin/bash
mark:x:1005:1008::/home/mark:/bin/bash
weg:x:1006:1009::/home/weg:/bin/bash
jason:x:1007:1010::/home/jason:/bin/bash
stephanie:x:1008:1011::/home/stephanie:/bin/bash
```

This is the end of my server's `/etc/passwd` file here. You'll see the username, followed by an x, which represents the encrypted password for the user. This is followed by the ID numbers of the user and primary group, respectively. After that, you'll find the home directory; recall that this is created automatically by the `adduser` command. Finally, the file shows the default shell for that user. In the case of most regular users, the shell is Bash (Bourne-again shell). This is the program that users run when they log on with a Terminal application.

Figure 2.12

The Mac's Get Info window, with file permissions at the bottom

If you want to learn about the groups that users belong to, you have to look at another file, /etc/group:

```
aaron@ubuntu-test:~$ cat /etc/group
polkituser:x:118:
avahi:x:119:
haldaemon:x:120:
admin:x:121:aaron
aaron:x:1000:
sambashare:x:122:aaron
```

The group file shows the complete list of groups on the system (I'm only showing the most recent entries on my own machine). For each list item, you see the ID number of that group — compare this to the ID number in the `passwd` file. Finally, you see a comma-delimited list of the users that belong to the group. If you want to be a crack hacker, you can edit this file to append usernames to a group name. All it takes is a save and you're done.

Let's give this a try. While logged in to your Linux system as the primary user, create a new file:

```
aaron@ubuntu-test:~$ nano sharethisfile.txt
```

The `nano` command puts you into a Terminal-based text-editing environment. I like `nano` because of its simplicity; if you're not a `vi` or `emacs` aficionado already, then you'll be most comfortable here. The commands are along the bottom of the screen: Control+O to save, Control+X to quit, and Control+W to search. If you want to flip through your file a page at a time, use Control+V to go down and Control+Y to go up. Finally, if you want to delete a line of text, put your cursor on the line and then press Control+K. That's it. You're now a `nano` expert!

When you open `nano` on the command line, you'll provide a file name. If it exists, you'll edit that file; otherwise, you'll create it. In this case, you've now got a blank screen. Go ahead and type some text and then save and close the file (Control+O and Control+X, respectively).

As you saw earlier, when you create a file, the default setting is to allow write permission for the creator and read-only permission for the group and world. Now let's assume that you want another user on your system, such as `kate`, to read your file. The best way to do this is to create a group that both you and Kate belong to; let's call that group `developers`:

```
aaron@ubuntu-test:~$  sudo addgroup developers
Adding group 'developers' (GID 1001) ...
Done.
```

This creates the entry in the `/etc/group` file and assigns it with an ID. Now, let's open it to add your users:

```
aaron@ubuntu-test:~$ sudo nano /etc/group
```

Use Control+V to page down to the end of this file, and at the end of the `developers` line, add your username and Kate. The line should look similar to this:

```
developers:x:1001:aaron,kate
```

Save and close the file. Now assign the new group to your file and grant write permission to it:

```
aaron@ubuntu-test:~$ chgrp developers sharethisfile.txt
aaron@ubuntu-test:~$ chmod 664 sharethisfile.txt
aaron@ubuntu-test:~$ ls -l share*
-rw-rw-r-- 1 aaron developers 0 2009-05-23 16:45 sharethisfile.
   txt
```

You're done. Feel free to test the results: Switch the user to Kate, type her password, and try using `nano` to write and save a change to that file.

Package Management

Among operating systems, Linux enjoys an enviable advantage when it comes to the availability of software. The open-source community provides a multitude of *packages*: software titles that run on Linux. But this strength has also proven to be its weakness. Unlike commercial operating systems, such as Windows and Mac OS, there are no official releases of Linux, so there have often been problems targeting a particular brand of Linux with a software title. To run properly, software needs to know what version of the Linux kernel (the central system control module) is running, what window manager you have, and what software libraries are installed. In the bad old days, Linux hackers would find themselves in dependency hell, searching for different solutions in an hours-long attempt to install the software that their target package needed to run.

The advent of package management systems has changed all that. This was an innovation by Debian (the parent distribution of Ubuntu), which introduced the world to `apt`, the Advanced Packaging Tool. The principle behind package managers is that they can examine the available packages already installed on the system and automatically install all the software you need to run the package you request. For example, if you want to install Lynx, the text-based web browser, you could use the following command:

```
aaron@ubuntu-test:~$ sudo apt-get install lynx
Reading package lists... Done
Building dependency tree
Reading state information... Done
The following extra packages will be installed:
   lynx-cur
Suggested packages:
   lynx-cur-wrapper
The following NEW packages will be installed:
   lynx lynx-cur
0 upgraded, 2 newly installed, 0 to remove and 0 not upgraded.
Need to get 1214kB of archives.
After this operation, 4911kB of additional disk space will be
   used. Do you want to continue [Y/n]?
Get:1 http://us.archive.ubuntu.com jaunty/main lynx-cur
   2.8.7dev11-2 [1199kB]
```

```
Get:2 http://us.archive.ubuntu.com jaunty/main lynx 2.8.7dev11-2
    [14.3kB]
Fetched 1214kB in 3s (364kB/s)
Preconfiguring packages ...
Selecting previously deselected package lynx-cur. (Reading
    database ...
102156 files and directories currently installed.)
Unpacking lynx-cur (from .../lynx-cur_2.8.7dev11-2_i386.deb) ...
Selecting previously deselected package lynx. Unpacking lynx
    (from .../lynx_2.8.7dev11-2_all.deb) ...
Processing triggers for man-db ...
Processing triggers for doc-base ...
Processing 1 added doc-base file(s)...
Registering documents with scrollkeeper...
Setting up lynx-cur (2.8.7dev11-2) ...
Setting up lynx (2.8.7dev11-2) ...
```

This command causes a lot of text to appear in Terminal. The command first does a dependency check, examining which packages should be installed to support Lynx. You're offered a list of those packages, and assuming you accept them, those packages are downloaded and installed without any further intervention. It's a thing of beauty.

In this section, I'm going to run through package management for Ubuntu and Red Hat by using their respective package managers of choice. When you're done here, you should be able to install any software you need on your server.

Apt

You've already seen apt at work earlier in this section. It's actually a suite of tools that help you install, query, and remove packages from your system. Originally written as a front end for the Debian dpkg to operate on its .deb package file format, apt now also works with the more popular Red Hat .rpm format. These are both popular container formats for software applications that come with the application's binary files and configuration directives that tell the system where the files go.

I'm going to discuss two programs that make up the core of apt: apt-get and apt-cache. You'll use the former to install and remove packages, and you'll use the latter to query packages and the repositories they come from.

But what are *repositories*? These are the online locations where the software packages are kept. In the case of Ubuntu, there are repositories for every major version of Ubuntu (the current version as of this writing is 9.10, code-named Karmic Koala), and within those version repositories, there are categories of use, such as the standard main repositories, which are officially supported packages that include bug fixes and security patches.

But there are also other repositories available: the restricted repository includes items not available with a completely free open-source license; universe contains software not officially supported by Ubuntu; and multiverse contains software that's not at all freely licensed (such as many third-party display drivers). All these repositories are available to you and specified in the file /etc/apt/sources.list. Feel free to nano that file and have a look. And if you feel daring, you might decide to add other repositories from third parties: Ubuntu includes one in this file in an *inactive state*: the lines are there, but they're commented out with a preceding hash mark.

```
## Uncomment the following two lines to add software from
   Canonical's 'partner' repository.
## This software is not part of Ubuntu, but is offered by
   Canonical and the respective vendors as a service to Ubuntu
   users.
# deb http://archive.canonical.com/ubuntu jaunty partner
# deb-src http://archive.canonical.com/ubuntu jaunty partner
```

If you remove the hash character from those last two lines, the software in those repositories becomes available. Remember, if you want to edit these files, you need to issue the command sudo nano /etc/apt/sources.list; the sudo command is required to give you administrative privileges.

You've already seen the most common use of apt-get in action: the install command. Let's flip it around: If you want to remove a package from your system, you can issue this command:

```
aaron@ubuntu-test:~$ sudo apt-get remove lynx
[sudo] password for aaron:
Reading package lists... Done
Building dependency tree
Reading state information... Done
The following packages will be REMOVED:
   lynx
0 upgraded, 0 newly installed, 1 to remove and 0 not upgraded.
After this operation, 45.1kB disk space will be freed. Do you
   want to continue [Y/n]?
(Reading database ... 102229 files and directories currently
   installed.)
Removing lynx ...
```

There are a few more tricks that you'll perform with apt-get. The first is update, which looks at every package on your system and collects every updated version available:

```
aaron@ubuntu-test:~$ sudo apt-get update
```

When you issue this command, Terminal reports back with every repository in its list and then returns the command prompt. Are there any packages to be updated? Issue the upgrade command to find out:

```
aaron@ubuntu-test:~$ sudo apt-get upgrade
Reading package lists... Done
Building dependency tree
Reading state information... Done
```

```
The following packages will be upgraded:
    ntpdate
1 upgraded, 0 newly installed, 0 to remove and 0 not upgraded.
Need to get 62.6kB of archives.
After this operation, 0B of additional disk space will be used.
    Do you want to continue [Y/n]?
```

Just press Return at this point to select the default option of Y. The ntpdate update package is downloaded and installed, and you're done.

Don't worry if you've never heard of ntpdate (although in this case, it's a client to the Network Time Protocol daemon, which keeps your system's clock up to date); the point with this update mechanism is that it keeps the software on your computer current, most often with bug fixes and security improvements. It's a good idea to run the update and upgrade cycle regularly to ensure your system runs optimally.

There's one more trick you may find yourself doing with apt-get: dist-upgrade. This is a big one: With one command, you can upgrade to the most recent major version of Ubuntu. If you're running, say, Ubuntu 8.04 now and want to move up to 9.10, issue that command, and the system takes care of the rest. Suffice to say you won't use dist-upgrade very often, but it's a great way to stay current with Ubuntu, especially when you're running a dedicated server from your remote office.

So far, I've talked about how to install and manage packages. But how do you know what you've got installed already, and how do you find what packages are available? That's what apt-cache is for. This little tool lets you query both the repository and your own system's package database to give you the complete package information.

One of my most-used commands is the search command. Let's say you're looking for a text-based web browser:

```
aaron@ubuntu-test:~$ sudo apt-cache search text browser
elinks - advanced text-mode WWW browser
elinks-data - advanced text-mode WWW browser - data files
elinks-doc - advanced text-mode WWW browser - documentation
html2text - advanced HTML to text converter
lynx - Text-mode WWW Browser (transitional package)
```

The list is much longer than this, but the intelligent search capability provides the most relevant results at the top, turning up two good options: elinks and the classic Lynx. You can then use the names of the packages given here in your command to apt-get install.

There are also tools for providing information about packages in more detail. You can try the show command to get in-depth information on any package. Let's try it with a package you'll get to know much better later in this book:

```
aaron@ubuntu-test:~$ sudo apt-cache show php5
Package: php5
Priority: optional
```

```
Section: web
Installed-Size: 20
Maintainer: Ubuntu Core Developers <ubuntu-devel-discuss@lists.
   ubuntu.com>
Original-Maintainer: Debian PHP Maintainers <pkg-php-maint@lists.
   alioth.debian.org>
Architecture: all
Version: 5.2.6.dfsg.1-3ubuntu4.1
Depends: libapache2-mod-php5 (>= 5.2.6.dfsg.1-3ubuntu4.1) |
   libapache2-mod-php5filter (>= 5.2.6.dfsg.1-3ubuntu4.1) | php5-
   cgi (>= 5.2.6.dfsg.1-3ubuntu4.1), php5-common (>=
   5.2.6.dfsg.1-3ubuntu4.1)
Filename: pool/main/p/php5/php5_5.2.6.dfsg.1-3ubuntu4.1_all.deb
   Size: 1122
MD5sum: a7bc1c04d5f59af5d335c9008eeb3547
SHA1: 2c1500cf11422861d43044a99c1f0079cbf6c113
SHA256: 76cb4cf346b8e519364eb540a11bf3c6c5cb89fa3fa10dbcae7f34fe
   3029a1f2
Description: server-side, HTML-embedded scripting language
   (metapackage)  This package is a metapackage that, when
   installed, guarantees that you  have at least one of the three
   server-side versions of the PHP5 interpreter  installed.
   Removing this package won't remove PHP5 from your system,
   however it may remove other packages that depend on this one.
PHP5 is an HTML-embedded scripting language. Much of its syntax
   is borrowed from C, Java and Perl with a couple of unique PHP-
   specific features thrown in. The goal of the language is to
   allow web developers to write dynamically generated pages
   quickly. This version of PHP5 was built with the Suhosin
   patch.
Homepage: http://www.php.net/
Bugs: https://bugs.launchpad.net/ubuntu/+filebug
Origin: Ubuntu
```

There are two other commands that can show you all the currently installed packages: pkg-names and dump. The former can give you a quick list of every package name installed on the system; the latter is more for debugging purposes, as it provides more information on every package and can take a minute or more to scroll through Terminal. In fact, when using the latter command, you may want to channel the output into a text file:

```
aaron@ubuntu-test:~$ sudo apt-cache dump > cache.txt
```

The > is the redirect operator, moving the result of the first expression into the file indicated by the second. In this case, the file cache.txt is created, and the contents of the cache are dumped inside. If you want to append data to the end of an existing file, you can use the >> operator, known as the *concatenation operator*. Give it a try and then view the results with nano. If you're looking for a particular package, remember to use Control+W to search.

Yum

If you're running a Red Hat distribution such as CentOS, then you'll most likely want to use yum, which is also the default package management system for Red Hat Enterprise Linux, Fedora Core, and its namesake distribution, Yellow Dog Linux.

NOTE

Long-time Mac fanatics may recognize Yellow Dog Linux. This distribution was, for quite some time, the only Linux version available for PowerPC processors. As many as ten years ago, if you owned a Mac and wanted to run Linux on it, you were using Yellow Dog. Its pedigree comes from Red Hat, which is why this family of distributions also shares this package manager. Yum stands for Yellow Dog Updater, Modified.

The principle behind yum is identical to apt: The system uses a number of online repositories to draw from packages. The tool figures out the dependencies required to install the requested software package and then takes care of the details automatically. I won't go through as much detail on yum, owing to its similarity to apt; instead, I'll run through the basic commands.

To install a software package, issue the install command:

```
[aaron@cl-t030-220cl ~]$ sudo yum install lynx
```

Note the different command prompt from earlier examples; I'm running these on my own dedi-cated host, which is a CentOS system. As with the Ubuntu version, this command checks the installed repositories (located at /etc/yum.repos.d/) and pulls down the latest version of Lynx that's compatible with your system version.

To remove software, use the remove command:

```
[aaron@cl-t030-220cl ~]$ sudo yum remove lynx
```

You get a neatly formatted listing of the proposed actions:

```
Dependencies Resolved
================================================================
   Package        Arch        Version            Repository      Size
================================================================
Removing:
 lynx           i386        2.8.5-28.1.el5_2.1   installed
   4.4 M
Transaction Summary
================================================================
Install      0 Package(s)
Update       0 Package(s)
Remove       1 Package(s)
Is this ok [y/N]:
```

The default answer is N. If you want to remove the software, type **Y** at the prompt and then press Return.

yum provides a friendly interface for querying packages, in ways similar to apt-cache. For example, to get information on a single package:

```
[aaron@cl-t030-220cl ~]$ sudo yum info php
Installed Packages
Name    : php
Arch    : i386
Version: 5.1.6
Release: 20.el5_2.1
Size    : 2.9 M
Repo    : installed
Summary: The PHP HTML-embedded scripting language. (PHP:
    Hypertext Preprocessor)
Description:
PHP is an HTML-embedded scripting language. PHP attempts to make it
easy for developers to write dynamically generated webpages. PHP also
offers built-in database integration for several commercial and
non-commercial database management systems, so writing a
database-enabled webpage with PHP is fairly simple. The most common
use of PHP coding is probably as a replacement for CGI scripts.
The php package contains the module which adds support for the PHP
language to Apache HTTP Server.
```

And if you want to find a package, the search command works here too:

```
[aaron@cl-t030-220cl ~]$ sudo yum search text browser
zvbi.i386 : Raw VBI, Teletext and Closed Caption decoding library
viewvc.noarch : Web-interface for CVS and Subversion version
    control repositories
zvbi.i386 : Raw VBI, Teletext and Closed Caption decoding library
lynx.i386 : A text-based Web browser.
```

Ah, there's Lynx. Now, when it comes time to upgrading, yum also has you covered. As with apt, you can make it a two-step process: checking for and then pushing the upgrade process. Or you can live on the edge and run the second command by itself:

```
[aaron@cl-t030-220cl ~]$ sudo yum check-update
NetworkManager.i386                     1:0.7.0-4.el5_3
   update
ORBit2.i386                             2.14.3-5.el5
   base
SysVinit.i386                           2.86-15.el5
   base
acpid.i386                              1.0.4-7.el5_3.1
   update
alpine.i386                             2.00-2.el5.rf
   dag
alsa-lib.i386                           1.0.17-1.el5
   base
```

This command simply tells you what's available for the currently installed packages. The list here contains just the first few entries. To proceed, issue the `upgrade` command:

```
[aaron@cl-t030-220cl ~]$ sudo yum update
```

The output from this command is too voluminous to repeat here. Every package that requires an update is listed, and you're asked to approve the upgrade.

Package managers make for a terrific advantage in favor of Linux. The open culture that makes the operating system something of a Wild West is corralled quite nicely with tools such as `apt` and `yum`, while at the same time providing unfettered access to a galaxy of software, much of which I discuss in later chapters.

Summary

With VirtualBox running Ubuntu, you now have a second operating system running on your Mac, providing an unbeatable playground for the Linux skills that you'll need to manage your own web server.

In this chapter, I covered some of the basics of Linux administration, including how to create and work with users and groups as well as the always-tricky business of dealing with file permissions. Once you have these essentials figured out, you'll find yourself well-positioned when dealing with day-to-day server administration tasks.

With these basics out of the way, it's time to get into some practical Linux applications — the ones you'll use to apply the knowledge gained in this chapter. In other words, this is where the fun really begins.

Unix Applications

Now that you have a working Linux system at your disposal, it's time to make it work for you. In this chapter, I'm going to cover some of the tools that are at the very core of the web developer's arsenal: the OpenSSH remote access and file transfer protocol, the Apache web server, and running your email through Google Apps. Finally, I talk a bit about some steps you can take to ensure your server remains secure out in the bad, bad World Wide Web.

If you're new to server administration, some of these technologies may seem alien and scary. You may have also noticed providers out there who offer to take care of the hosting for you. I can't stress enough how important it is for you to take on these tasks yourself. If you end up with a shared hosting service or you hire someone to manage your server for you, you're taking a huge risk that a part of your critical infrastructure is out of your control.

It's amazing how often services give out after business hours. If your database server goes down and your client is screaming to have his or her site brought back online, would you rather fix the problem yourself right now or put in a call to someone who doesn't care as much about your client? Give me Option A anytime; that's how you stay in business.

In other words, you need to be the master of your own domain.

Using Secure Shell

In the old days, if you wanted to remotely control a Unix system, you used a program called Telnet, which provided a simple means for a remote user to have access to the target computer's command line; it's exactly like being at the computer.

Also, if you wanted to move a file from one computer to another, you used an archaic technology called FTP — File Transfer Protocol. Unfortunately, FTP is still very much in vogue.

What do these two technologies have in common? They're both woefully insecure: All communication between the remote client and the server is unencrypted. Anyone who intercepts your traffic would be able to pick up your communications, including the credentials you use to log on to the server as well as the files you pass back and forth. Use either of these technologies long enough, and you're pretty much guaranteed to hand away control of your server to some bored 14-year-old in his basement or, worse, a criminal ring of networking crackers, bent on using your server to launch their armies of spam bots.

Fortunately, there's an alternative to both technologies, and it comes in one package: SSH. This stands for Secure Shell, and it provides a means to encrypt communications between a client and a remote server. Anyone intercepting your communication receives only encrypted gibberish. You, on the other hand, can transfer data in both comfort and style.

As a Mac user, you already have everything you need to use SSH; you can both connect to remote servers by using an SSH client and receive requests as an SSH server. The client is available on the command line, but you have to push a button to activate the server. Let's go push that button. Follow these steps:

1. **Open System Preferences and then choose the Sharing pane, shown in Figure 3.1.**

2. **Click the Remote Login check box to activate the SSH server.**

Figure 3.1

The Sharing pane, with the Remote Login option selected

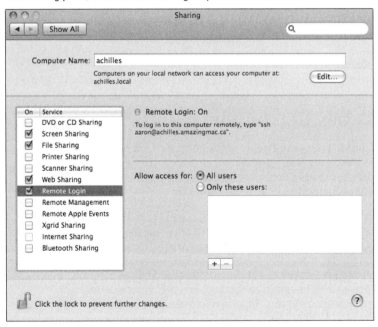

There you are — instant SSH activation. You can even test it right now, although this test is somewhat ludicrous: You're going to use SSH to remotely access your own Mac.

In Terminal, **type ssh *username@localhost*** and then press Return.

Of course, substitute your own username for username@localhost. You're asked for your password; this is your regular Mac password. Here's what you should see:

```
Last login: Tue Jun  2 20:29:56 2009
achilles:~ aaronvegh$
```

Congratulations! You've just used a remote protocol to get command-line access to your own Mac. Okay, that's not very interesting.

Working with OpenSSH

If you followed my instructions in Chapter 2, you should have a brand-new installation of Ubuntu Linux in a virtual machine. Because it's a desktop-style installation, you have all the normal stuff (such as a graphical interface, office software, Internet applications, and games) but none of the server stuff, such as an SSH server.

Using the skills you picked up in the last chapter, installing the server is easy. Open Terminal in your Ubuntu virtual machine. At the command prompt (here, it's shown as aaron@ubuntu-test:~$), type the following:

```
aaron@ubuntu-test:~$ sudo apt-get install ssh
```

The ssh package offered by Ubuntu is a *meta-package*: It provides both the client application and the server application in one. The apt-get utility not only installs the software but also starts the server. You're now ready to remotely log on to your Ubuntu machine from your Mac. All you need is the address of the remote server. For most real-world use, you simply use the domain name of the server. But your virtual machine likely doesn't have a domain name. Instead, you use the machine's IP address. Here's how to get it: In Terminal on the Ubuntu machine, type the following:

```
aaron@ubuntu-test:~$ ifconfig
eth0  Link encap:Ethernet  HWaddr 08:00:27:63:16:f6
      inet addr:10.0.1.106  Bcast:10.0.1.255  Mask:255.255.255.0
      inet6 addr: fe80::a00:27ff:fe63:16f6/64 Scope:Link
      UP BROADCAST RUNNING MULTICAST  MTU:1500  Metric:1
      RX packets:1362 errors:0 dropped:0 overruns:0 frame:0
      TX packets:904 errors:0 dropped:0 overruns:0 carrier:0
      collisions:0 txqueuelen:1000
           RX bytes:1889984 (1.8 MB)  TX bytes:71405 (71.4 KB)
      Interrupt:11 Base address:0xc020
```

The command `ifconfig` (which stands for interface configuration) provides detailed information about your network interfaces. I'm only showing the relevant interface returned by the command, traditionally known as `eth0`. There's another device that's always shown, called `lo`, for the loopback interface, which essentially represents the computer's connection with itself.

The relevant detail in the previous listing is the entry next to `inet addr`. The IP address is `10.0.1.106` (this is different depending on your own local area network settings). This is the value that you use to connect to your remote virtual machine from your Mac.

Take a careful look at the IP address. If it's not on the same subnet as your Mac, then you're not going to be able to connect. That's because VirtualBox defaults its network settings to Network Address Translation (NAT) mode. It creates a network just for the virtual machine, rendering it directly inaccessible to your Mac. The easiest solution to this problem is to switch to Bridged Networking mode, but as of this writing, it only works if you have an AirPort card in your Mac. If you do have an AirPort card, follow these steps:

1. **If your virtual machine is running, shut it down.**

2. **With the Ubuntu virtual machine selected in VirtualBox's main window, click the Settings button and then choose the Network pane.**

3. **Under the settings for Adapter 1, change the Attached to setting from NAT to Bridged Adapter and then change the Name setting to en1: AirPort.**

4. **Click OK and then restart your machine.**

If you don't have an AirPort card, all is not lost. Refer to the VirtualBox manual for other options.

Let's try logging on to the machine now. On your Mac, return to Terminal and then type this on the command line (substituting your own username and IP address, of course):

```
achilles:Desktop aaronvegh$ ssh aaron@10.0.1.106
The authenticity of host '10.0.1.106 (10.0.1.106)' can't be
    established.
RSA key fingerprint is 39:9d:90:de:cf:c2:00:f0:47:4d:ea:72:b0:2d
    :9c:63.
Are you sure you want to continue connecting (yes/no)? yes
Warning: Permanently added '10.0.1.106' (RSA) to the list of
    known hosts.
aaron@10.0.1.106's password:
0 packages can be updated.
0 updates are security updates.
Last login: Wed Jun  3 23:01:29 2009 from muppet.amazingmac.ca
aaron@ubuntu-test:~$
```

As this is the first time you're using SSH to log on to the remote machine, you see a little more information than you will later. Whenever SSH connects to a new machine for the first time, you're asked if you're sure that you want to do this. Now, you could be all hyper-paranoid and laboriously match the RSA key fingerprint given to the one on the remote machine, but given that you just set it up, you can be confident that your connection hasn't been hijacked. So, type **yes** to continue connecting. This causes an entry to be added to a file hidden in your home folder at `.ssh/known_hosts` that shows the IP address and its public key.

NOTE

The SSH suite uses a form of cryptography that has proven incredibly resilient to attack. It's called *public-key cryptography*, and it works by generating two keys: one is private and kept on the server, and the other is public and handed to anyone you want to work with (the SSH client, for example). In this system, only the private key can unlock communications sent with public-key encryption, which guarantees the security of your transmission.

You're now logged on to the remote machine! You've taken the first step to being able to reach out to any machine and work your administrative magic. But let's get one convenience out of the way right now. Typing your password at the SSH command is both potentially insecure and tiresome. So, you're going to take advantage of a special feature of SSH called SSH client keys. Given that you've seen how your local machine stores the server's public key, you might be able to guess how this works. You're going to generate a set of keys for your own Mac and then place your public key on the remote server. Thus, when your Mac connects to the remote server, your key will check out, and you'll be admitted without a password.

To generate your key pair, open Terminal and then type **ssh-keygen -t rsa**. You're asked for a place to save the private key, located in a hidden folder inside your home directory (`.ssh/id_rsa`). Just press Return to accept that location. You're then asked to type a passphrase and confirm it. Just hit Return twice to set an empty passphrase. Yes, this is a potential security risk, but it's outweighed (in my mind) by the time saved over dozens of daily SSH logons.

The key is generated, and you should see something like this:

```
Your public key has been saved in /Users/aaronvegh/.ssh/id_rsa.
    pub.
The key fingerprint is:
93:e9:fd:b5:1a:0f:6c:2b:43:dd:fd:3d:51:5c:e6:1b aaronvegh@
    achilles.amazingmac.ca
The key's randomart image is:
+--[ RSA 2048]----+
|                 |
|               o |
|              +. |
|         o   E+  |
|        S . . .+ |
|       . o... .o.|
|        ... = . +|
|         oo * oo |
|          o+.o . |
+-----------------+
```

There's a lot of interesting stuff here, and I'll describe the most important first. Your public key is saved in a file alongside the private key: `id_rsa.pub` and `id_rsa`, respectively. The next part of the response provides a couple of fingerprints for your key: a long hexadecimal string with your username and a `randomart` image; the latter is intended to provide a unique visual representation of your key. If you wanted to confirm whether your key is valid, you could look at its `randomart` representation and then compare it with your memory.

The next step is to move your public key to the server. This requires two steps: creating a place for your key on the server and then actually moving the file:

```
achilles:~ aaronvegh$ ssh aaron@10.0.1.106 "mkdir .ssh; chmod 700
   .ssh"
achilles:~ aaronvegh$ scp .ssh/id_rsa.pub aaron@10.0.1.106:.ssh/
   authorized_keys2
```

After each command, you're asked for your password. Note that the first line takes advantage of a powerful feature of SSH: the ability to pass a command directly to the remote machine from the local command line. Here, I'm creating a directory on the user's home folder and then setting permissions on it.

The second command uses the other utility in the SSH suite: SCP, or secure copy. This utility lets you move files from local to remote. I'll talk more about that shortly. In this case, you're moving your public key into a file called `authorized_keys2`; that's the place SSH looks when authenticating logon attempts.

With these steps completed, you should now be able to log on to the remote machine automatically:

```
achilles:~ aaronvegh$ ssh aaron@10.0.1.106
Last login: Wed Jun  3 23:03:30 2009 from achilles.amazingmac.ca
aaron@ubuntu-test:~$
```

Using SCP

Invoking long-distance commands is only half the fun with SSH; when it comes time to move files from your machine to a remote server, SCP is the way to do it. For most uses, SCP has replaced FTP as the predominant file transfer option of choice; where it hasn't, you have a real security issue. Wherever possible, you should insist on using SCP for moving your files.

On the Mac, you have a broad selection of clients for using SCP. My personal favorite is Transmit from Panic Software, shown in Figure 3.2, which offers a broad selection of file transfer protocols, SCP among them. There's also an open-source client called Cyberduck, which has many of the same features. Note that the majority of users refer to SCP as secure FTP, or SFTP.

However, while you can work with SCP in a fancy graphical client — and you will, don't worry — there are plenty of situations where having command-line mastery benefits you. So, let's take a look at how SCP works.

Figure 3.2

Transmit from Panic Software, with an SSH
connection setting

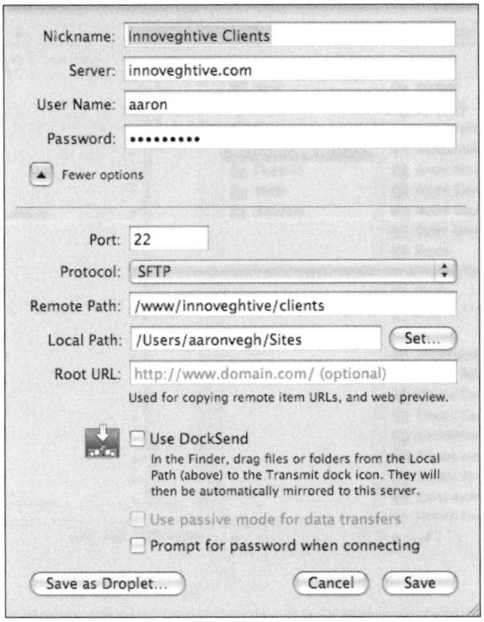

Perhaps the best way to explain SCP's operation is to compare it with its standard counterpart:
the Unix command `cp`. This is the command you use in Terminal to copy a file. It has a very simple structure:

```
$ cp <file> <destination>
```

So, to copy a file from one place to another, you simply supply two file paths:

```
achilles:~ aaronvegh$ cp Desktop/Sarah\ Soccer\ Schedule.pdf
    schedule.pdf
```

I've copied a PDF document from my desktop into my home folder. At the same time, because I
can specify the complete file path, I'm providing a new file name for that PDF. I now have two
copies of my daughter's soccer schedule — one with a much shorter name.

SCP works exactly the same way, except that instead of just providing a destination path, you
also have to supply a destination server. The command's structure looks like this:

```
$ scp <file> <user@server>:<destination>
```

So, to copy the schedule up to the server, I'd use this command:

```
achilles:~ aaronvegh$ scp schedule.pdf aaron@10.0.1.106:schedule.
    pdf
schedule.pdf                          100%  861KB 860.6KB/s   00:00
```

Because I set up the server key earlier, I wasn't asked for my password before the file was sent.

This represents most of what you need to know about SSH. Give it a try with your own files. Your next step is to take advantage of the power of SSH by learning the language of the command line.

Using the shell

You've already taken a brief look at life on the command line back in Chapter 2. You looked at the `ls` command, `touch`, `nano`, and some permission utilities. In this section, you'll go into greater depth to use the shell to:

- Navigate the file system
- Work on multiple files
- Create symbolic links
- Perform searches
- Pipe the output of one command into the input of another
- Automate tasks by using shell scripts
- Learn some useful shortcuts

At the end of this section, you may not be a Shell Master, but you'll have enough skill to get around and then move to the next level when you're ready.

You'll start with file system navigation by using the `cd` command. This one stands for change directory and allows you to move from folder to folder. You should know your current location by this command prompt:

```
achilles:~ aaronvegh$
```

This is the prompt you see when you open your Mac's Terminal window. The tilde character (~) is Unix shorthand for your home directory. Its *absolute* file path (the location relative to the root level of the hard drive) is /Users/aaronvegh. Let's use the `cd` command to move to another directory:

```
achilles:~ aaronvegh$ cd Desktop/
achilles:Desktop aaronvegh$
```

The prompt has changed to show the new location. However, it doesn't show the complete file path. For that, you can use a quick little command called `pwd`, or print working directory:

```
achilles:Desktop aaronvegh$ pwd
/Users/aaronvegh/Desktop
```

You don't have to just give absolute path names to get where you want to go. You can also use *relative paths*, which are denoted between the current folder and another. I've already shown you an example when I switched to the Desktop folder. In that case, I showed a relative path from the home directory. By using the two-dot shorthand, you can move to the parent directory. For example, to move from the Desktop folder back to the parent home folder, use the following command:

```
achilles:Desktop aaronvegh$ cd ..
achilles:~ aaronvegh$
```

To get to any other directory, you can give an absolute path. This is any path that begins with the / character, which denotes the root of the boot volume. For example, to get to the directory where the PHP scripting language keeps its configuration file, use this command:

```
achilles:~ aaronvegh$ cd /private/etc/
achilles:etc aaronvegh$
```

And wherever you're in the file system, you can always get back to your home directory simply by typing **cd**:

```
achilles:etc aaronvegh$ cd
achilles:~ aaronvegh$
```

Navigating on the command line requires a fair amount of hunt-and-peck. By using a combination of cd and ls, you can get to where you need to go.

Now let's move some files. A common file system issue is simple housecleaning. You've got a mess of files that you want to either organize or put in the trash. Let's look at both situations. First, you create a new directory by using the command mkdir:

```
achilles:~ aaronvegh$ mkdir APlaceToPutIt
achilles:~ aaronvegh$ ls
APlaceToPutIt   Documents      Library       Pictures
Desktop                Downloads     Movies       Public
Developer              Dropbox       Music        Sites
```

You could give any path as the location and name of your new directory; here, I'm providing the directory name in the current location. Now use the mv command to move all the files on the desktop to the new folder.

```
achilles:~ aaronvegh$ mv Desktop/* APlaceToPutIt/
achilles:~ aaronvegh$ ls Desktop
achilles:~ aaronvegh$
```

The mv command is very similar to the cp and scp commands that you've already examined. As the first argument, it takes the target file, and as the second argument, it takes the destination. Here, you're using a wildcard, the asterisk, to denote that you mean all files in the Desktop directory. And to prove that it worked, I'll do a listing on the Desktop directory; the prompt returns to indicate there's nothing there. Honestly, I had a pile of files there before.

That asterisk can be pretty powerful. On the server, you may find yourself with a lot of similar files. In my case, I usually end up with all kinds of files with the `.sql` extension on the end:

```
achilles:Desktop aaronvegh$ ls
CIP ENews prototypes
Complete WebCopy.pdf
Insurance Calculator Flash.html
Insurance Calculator.html
Insurance Calculator.swf
JLR Images.zip
Planning.numbers
Sarah Soccer Schedule.pdf
azure.sql
jrl.sql
kodiak.sql
```

These SQL files are exports from my local database; I perform an export and then upload them to the server. After that, I have no need of them. Using the * character, I can easily pick them out from the command line:

```
achilles:Desktop aaronvegh$ rm *.sql
```

The `rm` command removes files indicated in the argument. Here, I use the wildcard to stand in for any file name, followed by the `.sql` extension. This has the desired effect of deleting my three database export files.

You need to be very careful of the `rm` command; if you're not paying attention, you could delete critical files. This becomes especially important advice when you add the powerful recursive switch to `rm`. With the simple addition of `-R` to `rm`, the utility descends into any folder below the target and then deletes everything. Let's try this on copies of some files. Follow these steps:

1. **Create a new directory in your home folder by typing** mkdir DeleteTest **in Terminal.**

2. **Copy some files to the new directory with a command like** cp -R ~/Desktop/* DeleteTest/. **The** -R **switch is also a recursive here, allowing the copy to bring the contents of directories along too.**

3. **Delete the whole lot by typing the command** rm -R DeleteTest.

The terrible power of the recursive switch is that it can take effect on files you never intended. This is not such a problem when you copy, perhaps, but deleted files are gone forever. Just imagine if you gave the wrong argument to `rm -R`: a mere slip on the keyboard, substituting a `/` for your intended target, would attempt to delete your root volume! That's why whenever I use `rm`, I always take a deep breath before hitting Return and read my command one more time.

Let's move on to symbolic links. If you're a longtime Mac user, you know about the concept of *aliases*, which are virtual pointers to original files. You can create an alias on a Mac by selecting an item in the Finder and either pressing ⌘+L or holding down the ⌘ and Option keys while dragging. In Figure 3.3, I've created an alias of a PDF on my desktop. If you double-click on either the alias or the original, the PDF opens.

Figure 3.3

An alias on the Mac: `Complete WebCopy.pdf`, along with its alias file

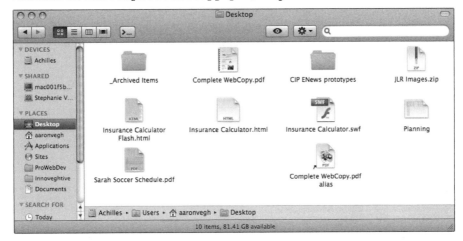

The Unix world has a similar construct called the symbolic link, also known as a *symlink*. To create one, use the `ln` command with the `-s` switch:

```
achilles:Desktop aaronvegh$ ln -s Complete\ Web\ Copy.pdf
    symlinked_pdf
```

The syntax follows the same convention as other file utilities: target, followed by destination. This gives you a new file that connects to the original:

```
achilles:Desktop aaronvegh$ ls -l sym*
lrwxr-xr-x  1 aaronvegh  staff  20  6 Jun 23:57 symlinked_pdf ->
    Complete\ Web\ Copy.pdf
```

The new file explicitly points to the original with the `->` characters. And this works equally well for directories, not just files. For example, on your Linux server, you may want to provide quick access to a web directory from a user's home folder. Assuming your home folder is at `/home/aaron` (as it might be on an Ubuntu system), you might create a symlink like this:

```
aaron@ubuntu-test:~$ ln -s /www web
aaron@ubuntu-test:~$ ls -l web
lrwxrwxrwx 1 aaron aaron 4 2009-06-07 00:04 web -> /www
```

Getting to the /www directory (where your web files are located) would now be a simple matter of changing into the web symlink:

```
aaron@ubuntu-test:~$ cd web
aaron@ubuntu-test:~/web$ ls
index.html
```

Although it looks like you're in the web directory from the command prompt, you're actually in the /www folder.

For my next trick in the shell, you'll learn how to perform file searches on the command line. This can be useful when you know a certain file name exists but you've lost track of where it might be. Users of late-model Macs know that Spotlight, the system-wide search technology, keeps a constantly updated index of all the files on the system, providing instant results when a search query is typed in the search field, as shown in Figure 3.4.

Figure 3.4

Mac OS X 10.6 Snow Leopard includes a feature called Spotlight, which provides instant file results on a given search query.

The Unix subsystem has a similar — albeit not as fancy — utility called locate. Instead of updating the file index instantly, the locate system runs daily to keep a listing of files on the system. You can then use a command to find the file you're after:

```
aaron@ubuntu-test:~/web$ locate myfile.txt
/home/aaron/myfile.txt
```

Linux runs a script every day called `updatedb` to keep the index up to date. You can run this yourself at any time if the file you want isn't yet in the index:

```
aaron@ubuntu-test:~$ sudo updatedb
```

Depending on the size of your file system, this could take a few minutes to complete.

Another tool for searching is called `grep`, which stands for global regular expressions print. The `grep` utility is used to search text, both within files and in the output of other commands. Regular expressions are a language for pattern-matching, allowing you to perform any kind of string-based search-and-replace operation. You'll only scratch the surface of what `grep` can offer here, which should suggest to you that `grep` is a powerful tool indeed.

NOTE

Regular expressions are an important part of using the command line, and they come in handy from time to time in your role as a web developer. However, teaching them here is beyond the scope of this book. When the time is right, I heartily encourage you to become more familiar with this useful, although difficult, language.

Because Unix machines deal primarily with text files, regular expressions were necessary to parse information out of vast collections of data. You might use a simple `grep` search to find information in a web server's log file. These files tend to grow into thousands of lines, making them impossible to scan manually if you're looking for particular information. A log file stores a number of pieces of information: the IP address of the requestor, the time of the request, and the resource being requested.

I have an ad system running on my server, and every hour, it has to run a maintenance script, which keeps things tidy. One way to be sure that this script is running is to query my log files. Knowing the name of the script I'm looking for, I can use `grep` to see if it's there:

```
[root@cl-t030-220cl httpd]# cat innoveghtive-access-log | grep
   maintenance.php
67.205.74.25 - - [06/Jun/2009:05:00:01 -0400] "GET /adserver/
   maintenance/maintenance.php HTTP/1.0" 200 -
67.205.74.25 - - [06/Jun/2009:06:00:01 -0400] "GET /adserver/
   maintenance/maintenance.php HTTP/1.0" 200 -
67.205.74.25 - - [06/Jun/2009:07:00:01 -0400] "GET /adserver/
   maintenance/maintenance.php HTTP/1.0" 200 -
```

You've already seen `cat` at work; that command outputs the contents of the given file. But I'm also using something else here: a powerful feature known as a pipe (|) character. The | character is a means to take the output from one command and make it the input for another. In short, I'm saying, "Here are the contents of my web log file; now search it for the text *maintenance. php*." So, instead of `cat` returning the entire contents of my log file, it returns only what gets filtered through `grep`. And happily for me, it shows that, indeed, my maintenance script is running on the hour.

Another way I like to use `grep` is in combination with the `ps` command. This one lets you view the active processes on the system; if you want to know whether your SSH server software is running, `ps` is one way to find out. All you have to do is invoke the command (with the appropriate switches: `aux` selects every process by every user on the system) and then channel the output through `grep`:

```
aaron@ubuntu-test:~$ ps aux | grep ssh
root      2142  0.0  0.2   5436  1068 ? Ss    Jun06   0:00 /usr/
    sbin/sshd
```

A given line in the results returned from `ps` tells you a lot: the user who invoked the command (`root`, in this case), the process ID, some information about the processor load, and the path of the application. In this case, SSH is running just fine.

In just this short time, you've covered a lot of ground on the shell. You can move around the file system, copy and move files, delete them (carefully!), create symlinks, search files, and pipe the output of one tool into another. Let's see if you can put those tricks together in an automated way by creating a shell script to reveal the full power of the command line.

A *shell script* is a set of commands placed in a file and then executed like a binary file. A common task on a web server is the backing up of files. A backup is a potentially complicated operation, involving several commands and several steps. So, you create a script that can handle it for you.

NOTE
The script you're going to create here is very simple. More complicated scripts can be written by using logic to determine different courses of action depending on conditions at runtime. You rarely need that kind of power, but if you do, there are many online resources to point you in the right direction.

The first step in writing a shell script is determining what you want to accomplish:

- First, delete any existing backups that have been archived by this script.
- Then, create a ZIP archive of the files you want to back up.
- Finally, move those files to the remote server by using SSH.

You could easily switch the first and last steps, but I prefer to know that my script starts with a clean slate. Before you write this script, create a set of files that you can test this with. On your Mac, create a directory and then add some files to it:

```
achilles:~ aaronvegh$ mkdir tobebacked
achilles:~ aaronvegh$ cd tobebacked
achilles:tobebacked aaronvegh$ touch file1.xml file2.xml file3.
    xml
```

Now, follow these steps:

1. **In Terminal, create the file that will house your script by using the** nano **editor to write it:**

```
achilles:~ aaronvegh$ nano backup
```

2. **In the** nano **editor, type this text:**

```
#!/bin/bash
ssh aaron@192.168.1.105 "rm ~/backups/*"
tar -czvf backup.tgz ~/tobebacked/
scp backup.tgz aaron@192.168.1.105:backups/
rm backup.tgz
```

3. **Press Control+O to save the file and then press Control+X to close the file and return to the command prompt.**

4. **To execute this file, you need to set the proper permissions, so run** chmod **and then note how the execute bit is set:**

```
achilles:~ aaronvegh$ chmod 744 backup
achilles:~ aaronvegh$ ls -l backup
-rwxr--r--   1 aaronvegh  staff   146   7 Jun 01:10 backup
```

5. **Run the shell script:**

```
achilles:~ aaronvegh$ ./backup
tar: Removing leading `/' from member names
/Users/aaronvegh/tobebacked/
/Users/aaronvegh/tobebacked/file1.xml
/Users/aaronvegh/tobebacked/file2.xml
/Users/aaronvegh/tobebacked/file3.xml
backup.tgz                        100%  187    0.2KB/s   00:00
```

You're done. Go ahead and shell into your Ubuntu machine to confirm that the file has been uploaded. Run the script again to see the backup replaced with a more recent version (look at the time stamp by running ls -l).

While most of the commands in the shell script are things you've already learned, there are a couple items that are new here. First, the shell script opens with the line #!/bin/sh. The #! is a notation known as the *shebang*, and it represents a signal to the operating system that the following content is shell script. The /bin/bash is the path of the program that does the interpreting — in this case, Bash. All current versions of Mac OS X include Bash, as do all versions of Linux; this is the predominant shell in use today.

The second new feature in this script is the use of the tar command. Using this tape archive command, you can collate a number of files into one and then zip the files into a compressed archive (the tar command includes the -z switch, which provides the ZIP file compression). This is common practice in the Linux world; putting files together and compressing them makes transmission over the network very easy. If, at the other end, you want to restore your files, simply pass this command on your Ubuntu machine:

```
aaron@ubuntu-test:~/backups$ tar -xvf backup.tgz  Users/
   aaronvegh/tobebacked/
    Users/aaronvegh/tobebacked/file1.xml
    Users/aaronvegh/tobebacked/file2.xml
    Users/aaronvegh/tobebacked/file3.xml
```

I'll close off this section about learning the shell with some tricks of the trade. Often, you'll find that some files are too long to type. Fortunately, the shell comes with a feature called tab auto-completion. To try it out, begin typing the first few characters of a file or directory and then hit the Tab key; if those first few letters match a unique item in the scope, the name auto-completes.

Another time-saving trick is the history file. Every command you type is stored in a log file. If you want to repeat a command, simply press ↑ and the most-recent command appears at the prompt, ready to execute. Often, you'll use this when you mistyped the previous command and want to make a single change. It's very useful when that last command is a long one!

Similarly, you can see all the commands in the log by typing **history** at the prompt; you'll see a listing sorted from least to most recent.

Now, with your newfound knowledge of how to run the shell, you're ready to move on to some specialized applications.

The Apache Web Server

What is a web server? At its most basic, it's software that receives requests by using the HTTP protocol and then responds with files. The *hypertext transfer protocol* is a client-server system for moving files between a local client (such as your web browser) and the server (such as the Apache web server). When the client requests a particular page from the server, it replies with a header, which contains a message — such as `HTTP/1.1 200 OK` — and the `body` of the response, which contains the page requested.

The best web servers perform this seemingly simple operation with aplomb under even the heaviest loads; Apache is known for its ability to handle many concurrent connections. But the server includes a number of other features that make it the software of choice for the majority of the Internet's web servers:

- **Support for most scripting languages.** Apache includes bindings for Perl, Python, PHP, and Ruby.
- **Support for various authentication schemes.** This includes `mod_auth_digest` and encryption using SSL (secure sockets layer) and its successor, TLS (transport layer security).

- **Support for URL rewriting.** This uses `mod_rewrite`, which provides the ability to seamlessly redirect traffic on a server.
- **Support for custom log files.** This uses `mod_log_config`.
- **Support for on-the-fly file compression.** This uses the `gzip` standard, helping to shrink the size of pages served up.
- **Support for virtual hosting.** This allows the same server to respond to requests for multiple domain names.

Apache is also free and available on every platform. What's not to like? Let's get to know it a little bit better.

How Apache works

The first step to learning Apache is to install it on your Ubuntu machine. As you've already seen, it's very straightforward when using that system's package manager:

```
aaron@ubuntu-test:~$ sudo apt-get install apache2
```

Notice that `apt-get` installs a number of other packages to support Apache; this is a normal part of the dependency-checking process that makes Linux package management such a pleasure to use. After running this command, you now have a complete web server installed.

When Apache is activated, it reads the contents of its configuration file, which you took a brief look at in Chapter 1. As Linux configuration files go, it's a pretty long one, but it's mostly comments to document the features that are available.

Open the configuration file on your Ubuntu virtual machine. In Terminal, type **sudo nano /etc/apache2/apache2.conf**. You then enter the `nano` editor, with the contents of your server's Apache configuration, as shown in Figure 3.5.

NOTE

Apache goes by different names on different versions of Unix. While on Ubuntu, the package goes by the name `apache2`; on many other platforms (including Mac OS X), the package is known by its more generic name `httpd` (for hypertext transfer protocol daemon — a *daemon* is an always-running process that responds to incoming requests). Consequently, the location and name of the configuration file vary. Look in your Linux version's `/etc/` folder if you're unsure.

This configuration file contains a few sections; let's page through it together (remember, press Control+V and Control+Y to page down and up, respectively).

Figure 3.5

The Apache configuration file in nano

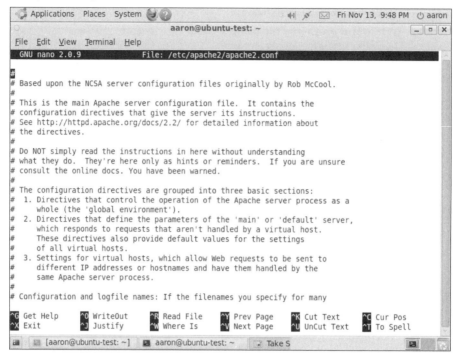

First up are the directives that control the behavior of the server in general. There are four important settings made in this section:

- **The execution environment of the web server.** The line is ServerRoot "/etc/apache2", indicating where the configuration files for the server are located.

- **The user and group under which the server operates.** The lines are:

```
User ${APACHE_RUN_USER}
Group ${APACHE_RUN_GROUP}
```

  The values for those variables are kept in the file envvars alongside the configuration file. On my Ubuntu machine, they're both www-data; this is the user that needs to be able to access the files in your web server's document repository.

- **The resource limits under which the server operates, including the self-descriptive** Timeout, MaxKeepAliveRequests, **and** KeepAliveTimeout. You generally won't need to change these settings.

● **The add-on module settings, included with these lines:**

```
# Include module configuration:
Include /etc/apache2/mods-enabled/*.load
Include /etc/apache2/mods-enabled/*.conf
```

This last setting requires some explanation. As you've seen in the description of Apache's features, many of its most powerful components come in the form of these add-on modules. Many of these come with Apache, while others can be downloaded and installed. If you look in the /etc/apache2/mods-enabled folder, you see all the modules that Apache includes by default. But there's another folder called /etc/apache2/mods-available, which has many more that you can use; all you have to do is copy the module's load and conf files from the -available to -enabled directories.

The next section of the Apache configuration file describes the operation of the main server. If you're using Apache to serve files for just one domain, this is where those files should be kept. Because the configuration of the main server is so similar to that of virtual servers, the Ubuntu Apache maintainers have decided to make the main server a virtual one; there's no main configuration in this configuration file. Instead, you find these lines at the very end of the configuration file:

```
# Include the virtual host configurations:
Include /etc/apache2/sites-enabled/
```

This works exactly like the modules section that you saw earlier. Any file placed in this directory is included in the server configuration. If you look in that folder, you see a file called 000-default, which contains the configuration directives for the main server. Open it in nano.

The top part of the configuration looks like this:

```
<VirtualHost *:80>
    ServerAdmin webmaster@localhost
    DocumentRoot /var/www
    <Directory />
        Options FollowSymLinks
        AllowOverride None
    </Directory>
```

The configuration opens with the VirtualHost directive, which specifies an IP address and port. In this case, the asterisk indicates a wildcard for the IP address, which means that this configuration responds to requests on any IP address that this machine supports. Port 80 is the default port for the HTTP protocol.

The DocumentRoot directive specifies where the files for this server are located. If you look at that directory on Ubuntu, you see just one file:

```
aaron@ubuntu-test:~$ ls /var/www
index.html
```

You'll look at that file shortly. Back in the configuration file, you see a set of directives for certain directories inside the `DocumentRoot`. I'm only showing the one for the root (/) of the hard drive; directives for other directories follow after. Apache provides for dozens of directives, and these two are very commonly used. The first, `FollowSymLinks`, allows the server to find files through symlinks. The `AllowOverride None` directive prevents the use of `.htaccess` files, which can provide directives to the server during runtime operation.

While not a complete list, here are some other important configuration directives that you'll come to know, along with an example of their uses:

- `ServerName`. In a virtual server setup, you use this directive to indicate the domain name being served: `ServerName www.amazingmac.ca`.

- `ServerAlias`. This command is used in tandem with `ServerName` to provide an alternate name that the server can respond to. I use this to let the server respond to just the domain name without the "www" prefix: `ServerAlias amazingmac.ca`.

- `DirectoryIndex`. By default, a page request to Apache that doesn't include a file name (such as the root request with just the domain name) responds with a file called `index.html`. With this directive, you can specify other file names, including different file types. You can include multiple files, but if each of these is in a directory, the first one in this directive takes precedence: `DirectoryIndex index.html index.php default.html`.

- `Options`. This directive controls the features available to the files in a particular directory. There are a number of options available:
  - `All`. The default setting
  - `ExecCGI`. Allows CGI scripts to run from this directory
  - `FollowSymLinks`. Follows symlinks set up in this directory
  - `Includes`. Executes server-side includes files
  - `Indexes`. Shows a text-based listing of the directory's files if no index file is present:

```
<Directory /www>
    Options Includes Indexes FollowSymLinks
</Directory>
```

For the time being, you don't need to make any changes to the configuration provided by the default Apache installation. If you did make a change (because exploring and testing are what make you a better developer!), you need to restart the server. Apache comes with a small utility to help you do just that:

```
aaron@ubuntu-test:~$ sudo apache2ctl restart
[sudo] password for aaron:
apache2: Could not reliably determine the server's fully
    qualified domain name, using 127.0.1.1 for ServerName
```

Again, like the Apache configuration files, the name of the utility differs depending on the distribution. On Mac OS X, for example, it's simply `apachectl`.

The warning from the server is there to remind you that you have no domain name attached to this virtual machine. You're okay to ignore that for now, as you're just using it for testing purposes.

You can test the server by opening a browser on the Mac and then typing the IP address of the virtual machine. Figure 3.6 shows what Ubuntu's Apache server produces by default.

To complete the circle, let's look at the file that Apache is serving up here. On your virtual machine, apply the `cd` command, go to the `/var/www/` directory, and then run the command **nano index.html**:

```
<html><body><h1>It works!</h1></body></html>
```

As HTML content goes, this is pretty sparse, although it gets the job done. I cover HTML in proper detail in Chapter 4.

For now, this completes your tour of Apache. Let's move on to another vital service to be provided by most servers: email.

Figure 3.6

The default page for the Ubuntu Apache server

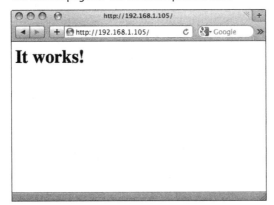

Using Google Apps for Email

While the protocols that govern the flow of web page traffic are pretty simple, email transmission is somewhat more complex. Moving an email from your computer to its destination requires the involvement of no less than three different servers, as shown in Figure 3.7.

At the beginning of the transaction, a mail transfer agent (MTA) receives the email from your client program (such as the Apple built-in Mail program). This MTA is identified in your mail program as the outgoing, or SMTP, server. Often, this server is running either Sendmail or Postfix, two of the most popular mail servers available for Linux.

The MTA looks up the receiving domain of the email you've sent and sends the message along to the receiving domain's mail server; this is another MTA that's most likely running Sendmail or Postfix. Depending on the configuration of that server, there could be one or more transitions to other MTAs, particularly in large organizations where the users in the domain might be distributed among many machines.

Finally, the message is delivered to a mail delivery agent (MDA), which is the server application that you would have entered as your incoming, POP, or IMAP server. Usually, this is a server application called Dovecot, or Cyrus, although there are many others.

Figure 3.7

How an email moves from start to finish

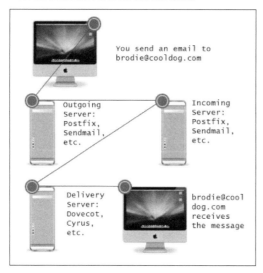

If this were five or six years ago, I would be proceeding with an in-depth explanation of how to install and configure your own mail server to sit alongside your Apache server. But the landscape has become terribly complicated lately; email has moved from a convenience to a necessity. Any downtime in email availability is a big deal.

Meanwhile, the commitment required to keep a mail server in good working order has grown significantly. Not only do you have to manage your users' accounts among multiple domains, but you have to control the amount of disk space that each can use, curtail the spread of viruses, eliminate spam, and walk each user through the seemingly byzantine steps of setting up their client programs.

No question about it: Email has become harder to manage over the years. That's why I was thrilled by the introduction of a new service by Google: Google Apps for Domains.

What Google provides

You know Gmail: It's Google's massively popular web-based email service. In an era where Microsoft and Yahoo! provided lackluster web-based email, Gmail was a revelation: massive storage space, a terrific user interface, and fantastic spam and virus protection. Over time, while the incumbent webmail services languished, Google continued to innovate, adding features like POP download, IMAP access, integrated instant messaging, and much, much more.

But the most important Gmail feature — for me, at least — is the ability to have your own personal Gmail at your own domain. Now, ordinary folks can have arguably one of the best email services available without having to put an "@gmail.com" at the end of their address.

Did I mention that you can get this for free?

Before Google made this service available, I had laboriously set up an email server myself and provided it to my hosting clients. No longer; when a client hosts his or her site with me and wants to also get email, I push it to Google. The features are better, the overall experience is better, I don't pay a cent, and it's completely trouble-free.

For the rest of this section, I'm going to take you through the process of setting up a domain with Google Apps. While Apps is a complete service that offers a calendar, office tools, and email, it's only the latter that I'll concern you with here. You can explore the rest on your own. Follow these steps:

1. **Go to** www.google.com/apps/intl/en/group/index.html **and then click the Get Started button.** This is the Google Apps home page. The service comes in a Premier Edition that costs $50 per user; you can avoid that one and use the Standard Edition. If you do need 25GB of storage per user, forced secure connections, and a 99.9% uptime SLA, then Premier is for you.

2. **Type the domain you want to use.** I'm assuming here that you already own the domain in question; otherwise, you can buy one during this process for a reasonable $10 per year. Ensure that you have clicked the option to indicate that you're the administrator of the domain (see Figure 3.8); this will give you the authority to change your DNS settings to point to Google.

3. **Type your user information.** You're presented with a form, where you need to type your name, email address, phone number, and country. There's also a check box that notes that you're aware that unless you modify your domain's DNS settings, email will not work. But you knew that. You can optionally also provide information about your company here before clicking the Continue button to reach the final step in the registration process.

Figure 3.8

Choosing your domain during Google Apps signup

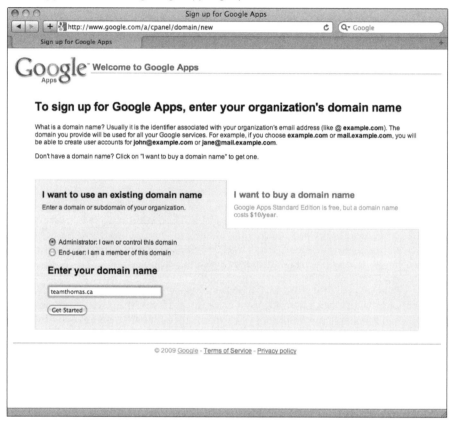

4. **Create an admin account.** You must create a new email address at the domain; this will be the account responsible for administering the whole domain. Once you provide that, along with a password, complete the *captcha* — the scrambled, difficult-to-read text — and agree to the terms of service, you can move on (see Figure 3.9). Don't feel bad if the captcha image is unreadable; you'll be able to try again if you get it wrong.

5. **Verify that you own the domain.** With your account registered, you now need to assure Google that you own the domain in question. You can do so in either of two ways: by uploading a special file to the domain's web server or by making a DNS change. The former is the easier method, so choose that one (see Figure 3.10).

Figure 3.9

Setting up the admin account on Google Apps. Beware the captcha.

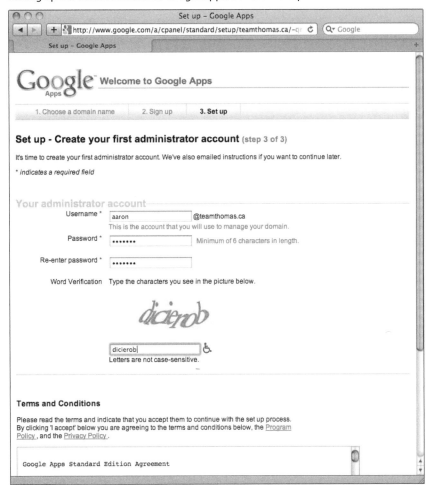

6. **Prepare a file and upload it to the server.** You're asked to create a file called `googlehostedservice.html`, and you're given an alphanumeric code to place inside. Then, upload that file to the root level of your website. Once done, click the button on this page that says you've completed the steps above. Without further ado, your file should check out, and you're taken to an introduction to the service.

You're now successfully registered with the Google Apps service. You can review the guide that is presented to you or click the Dashboard button to get home (see Figure 3.11).

Figure 3.10

Verifying the domain

As you can see, the Email service isn't quite ready to go; an Activate Email link is there below that entry. If you click that, you'll receive instructions on how to update your domain's DNS settings to point to Google. In Google's user-friendly fashion, it provides a pop-up menu of a number of popular hosting companies; if yours is among this list, you receive specific instructions on how to update the DNS records.

Essentially, you need to sign in to your hosting service (or domain registrar, perhaps, if it provides DNS services) and replace any current MX settings with those in Table 3-1.

Figure 3.11

The Google Apps Dashboard

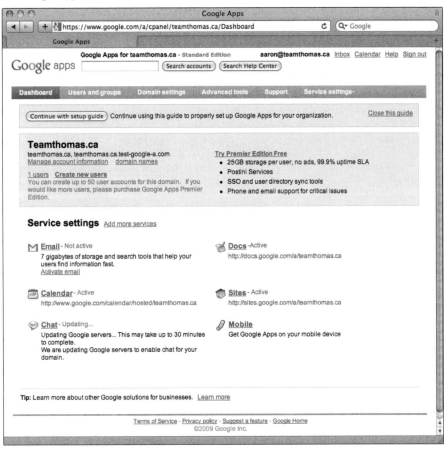

Table 3-1 Google MX Servers

Server	Priority
ALT1.ASPMX.L.GOOGLE.COM.	20
ALT2.ASPMX.L.GOOGLE.COM.	20
ASPMX.L.GOOGLE.COM.	10
ASPMX2.GOOGLEMAIL.COM.	30
ASPMX3.GOOGLEMAIL.COM.	30
ASPMX4.GOOGLEMAIL.COM.	30
ASPMX5.GOOGLEMAIL.COM.	30

If you're typing these yourself, be sure to include the trailing period after each domain name; it's a DNS thing.

The Priority setting indicates the order that each server is used. If the lowest-number server is unavailable, the DNS system will move to the next one up the chain. That Google provides seven servers should make you feel warm and cozy inside too; that's a lot of redundancy.

If your DNS provider doesn't let you type these numbers, at least ensure they're presented in this order.

DNS settings take time to propagate throughout the Internet, so give this process 24 to 48 hours to complete, although it can take as little as 4 hours.

Now, if you're migrating an existing domain with active email accounts, this is a good time to set up those accounts in Google Apps. In this case, make sure that you're using the same account names so nobody loses email. Let's go through the process of setting up a user for an email account. Follow these steps:

1. **In Google Apps, click the Users and groups tab.** You see a Create a new user link, as shown in Figure 3.12.

2. **Type an account name and password.** You can accept the temporary password or click the Set password link to provide one explicitly.

3. **Click the Create new user button to complete the action.**

Follow these steps for any other users that you want on your domain.

You can now receive email at these accounts. Your final step is to inform your users of how to set up their email clients. The easiest way to give your clients email is to simply point them to the included web-based email client. It's Gmail but at your own domain. The address is `http://mail.google.com/a/<yourdomain>`.

Figure 3.12

The Google Apps Users and groups page

You can also take advantage of Google's IMAP access to get your mail on a desktop email client, such as Mac OS X's Mail or the iPhone's Mail app. If you log on to the web-based email, you can find the instructions for setting up your email client to access your mail through IMAP. To do that, click the Settings link and then click the Forwarding and POP/IMAP tab, as shown in Figure 3.13.

Click the Enable IMAP radio button and then click the Configuration Instructions link to get detailed instructions for desktop mail clients and mobile mail clients.

At this point, you're probably waiting for your DNS changes to propagate. But from a settings perspective, you're done. Now you can sit back and enjoy the satisfaction of your users getting the best email service available.

Figure 3.13

Gmail forwarding and POP/IMAP settings

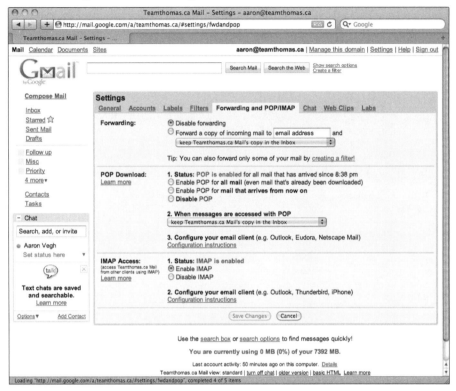

Securing Your System

You almost can't be too paranoid about security. When it comes to protecting your machine from the scoundrels of the Internet, the paranoiacs are right! Everyone has stories about servers being cracked, and I'm no different.

I once picked up a dedicated server for my client, and I made the mistake of setting up the firewall after activating my SSH server. Within a single day, the server had been compromised; it spewed spam all over the Internet and hosted more than one phishing site. I was forced to not only wipe that server and start over but also change IP addresses, as it appeared on many blacklists as a source of malware.

I'm not a security expert, but to get a reasonable degree of protection, you don't have to be. To ensure you aren't the victim of just any random attack on your machine, there are two precautions to take right away when the server comes online: install a firewall and install a port-knocking server.

Using iptables firewall

Every server that accepts traffic from the network on your computer does so through a *port*. This is a network connection in either the Transmission Control Protocol (TCP) or User Datagram Protocol (UDP). Ports are allocated to particular services: Web pages go through port 80; SMTP goes through ports 25 or 587; IMAP goes through port 143; and so on. Every open port to the network exposes that machine to the risk of intrusion by a bad guy. So, the first step to securing your system is to only run servers that you're actually using; there's no sense creating a risk for yourself over a server that has no purpose.

A firewall is your second step. For the servers that are running on your computer, you can prevent access based on the port coming in and even the requesting IP address. There are many choices for firewalls in Linux, but your best mainstream choice is a package called iptables. It works by passing every packet it receives through a set of rules. If it makes it through the rules, the packet is accepted by the destination service on the machine.

The iptables package is already installed on every late-model Ubuntu distribution. At any time, you can view the current rules by issuing this command:

```
root@ubuntu-test:/etc# iptables -L
```

You're shown three groups of rules: one for INPUT, one for OUTPUT, and one for FORWARD. Currently, all three groups should be empty of rules; iptables has a default set to allow all traffic in and out.

In your case, you'd like to accept traffic on the ports for Apache, Dovecot, and SSH. These are INPUT rules, which govern what traffic is allowed to come into the server. These are the critical rules for the security of your system; I'm not nearly as concerned about affecting the OUTPUT rules, which keep local services from accessing parts of the network, or the FORWARD rules, which can move packets to another machine on the network.

Because the rules are evaluated in a certain order, that order becomes important when you add rules to the chain. Let's see how adding rules works. To add SSH to the rules, use this command:

```
root@ubuntu-test:~# iptables -A INPUT -p tcp --dport ssh -j
   ACCEPT
```

The arguments are as follows:

- -A, **to append a rule to the chain.** This rule becomes the last rule on the INPUT chain, which governs inbound traffic.
- -p, **to specify the connection protocol.** You almost always use tcp as the value here.
- --dport, **to specify the destination port.** You can provide a port number or simply the name of the service, as I do here.
- -j, **to jump to the specified target.** This can be ACCEPT, REJECT (which notifies the sender that this happened), DROP (which doesn't let the sender know), or LOG (which simply logs the event and continues to process rules).

Now add a setting for Apache:

```
root@ubuntu-test:~# iptables -A INPUT -p tcp --dport www -j
    ACCEPT
```

So far, so good, but if all traffic is allowed by default anyway, why specify that these ports are open? Because your next rule drops any packet not already specified with these rules:

```
root@ubuntu-test:~# iptables -A INPUT -j DROP
```

There — no more unwanted traffic. But wait! You forgot to add a rule for Dovecot. Let's add it now and then look at the rules that you have:

```
root@ubuntu-test:~# iptables -A INPUT -p tcp --dport imap -j
    ACCEPT
root@ubuntu-test:~# iptables -L
Chain INPUT (policy ACCEPT)
target     prot opt source               destination
ACCEPT     tcp  --  anywhere             anywhere    tcp dpt:www
ACCEPT     tcp  --  anywhere             anywhere    tcp dpt:ssh
DROP       all  --  anywhere             anywhere
ACCEPT     tcp  --  anywhere             anywhere    tcp dpt:imap2
```

Wait a second here. If the firewall evaluates these rules in order, then it will reject a request on port 143 (IMAP's default port) before it gets to the right rule! You have to fix this. The first step is to drop the rule you just added. For this, you use the -D switch and then provide the number of the INPUT rule that you want dropped:

```
root@ubuntu-test:/etc# iptables -D INPUT 5
```

Check to confirm it's gone. Then, you put the rule in the right place. You won't append it now because you already have your last rule in place. Instead, you'll use the -I switch to insert the rule. You'll also specify what position among the rules to place it at — in this case, the fourth spot:

```
root@ubuntu-test:/etc# iptables -I INPUT 4 -A INPUT -p tcp
    --dport imap -J ACCEPT
```

That should do it. Now, when you restart your computer, these rules disappear. Ouch! Instead, you have to commit them and then set the system to restore the settings on reboot. Follow these steps:

1. **To save your settings to a file, execute the command** `sudo iptables-save > /etc/iptables.save`.

2. **To set the system to load this file on startup, create the file** /etc/network/
   if-pre-up.d/iptable_load **with** nano **and then type this text:**

   ```
   iface eth0 inet dhcp
     pre-up iptables-restore < /etc/iptables.rules
   ```

3. **Save and close the file.**

4. **Type** chmod 755 iptable_load **to change the permissions on this file so it can execute.** This file should now load the configuration at boot time.

Using a port-knocking utility

The configuration you created allows users to log on via the web server, mail delivery agent (Dovecot), and SSH. Of these services, the last is the one that poses the greatest threat; anyone who cracks shell access has immediate access to your machine. That's why I promote an even-greater level of protection for this service: a system called *port knocking*.

While there are security experts who will dispute the efficacy of port knocking, I've seen this technique prove successful in keeping my server safe from attack. It works by setting your firewall rules to deny access to SSH by default. Then, when a correct sequence of requests are made on (for example) three specific ports, the door is opened, adding a firewall rule that lets that IP address access the port.

It's not quite security through obscurity because although it's mathematically very difficult to guess which port number sequence might gain access, the attacker can't know that port knocking is even active on the server; there's no way to tell from the outside.

The port-knocking server isn't installed by default, so you have to remedy that first. From the command line, issue the following command:

```
aaron@ubuntu-test:~$ sudo apt-get install knockd
```

The installation finishes with the note that you must edit the configuration file to enable the server. Let's do that now. The configuration file is located at /etc/knockd.conf; when you open that file with nano, you should see the following:

```
[options]
    UseSyslog
    logfile     = /var/log/knockd.log
[openSSH]
    sequence    = 7000,8000,9000
    seq_timeout = 5
    command     = /sbin/iptables -A INPUT -s %IP% -p tcp --dport
  22 -j ACCEPT
    tcpflags    = syn
```

```
[closeSSH]
    sequence    = 9000,8000,7000
    seq_timeout = 5
    command     = /sbin/iptables -D INPUT -s %IP% -p tcp --dport
22 -j ACCEPT
    tcpflags    = syn
```

The software comes with a configuration ready-made for SSH. Amazing! Clearly, this is the protocol most people use knockd for. Given what you've learned about iptables in the previous section, this should be straightforward enough; when the server receives a sequence of port knocks at 7000, 8000, and 9000, it executes the command shown for iptables. This command adds an INPUT entry to the rule chain for the IP address that's knocking. You can have as many port numbers in the sequence as you like, although three is good. But be sure to change those numbers, as using the defaults is a security risk.

Before you test the configuration, make sure that you don't already have a rule in iptables for SSH (you will if you followed my previous instructions):

```
aaron@ubuntu-test:~$ sudo iptables -D INPUT -p tcp --dport ssh -j
    ACCEPT
```

This ensures that, by default, your firewall blocks all access to SSH.

To test this setup, you need a knock client package. Visit www.zeroflux.org/projects/knock to download the Mac client. It's a command-line application with a very simple syntax:

```
aaron@ubuntu-test:~$ knock ubuntu-test.local 7000 8000 9000
```

To confirm that it's working, run your Mac's SSH client and then log on to the Ubuntu server.

Summary

The tools you've investigated in this chapter are some of the most important you'll use; they form the backbone of the Internet and interact with the network in very direct ways. With your newfound knowledge of using the shell environment, you can access both your own Mac and remote machines for quick and easy configuration and maintenance. That will give you the power over various services that your web server will offer, including Apache.

But don't let that scare you off! With practice and by learning from mistakes, you'll come to understand how these pieces fit together.

Client-Side Development

xHTML

Hypertext Markup Language (HTML) is the tool you'll use to compose your web pages; think of it as the bottom layer in the great web development layer cake. HTML will help you write the content of the document — the text and media that make up a page. But it's a content-only language; you'll use a different technology — Cascading Style Sheets — to give your content its form.

If you've been exposed to HTML in the past, you may think that you can build a complete site using just this technology. But times have changed: I describe how to separate the content from its presentation. Before we get there, I explain the role of HTML in the web developer's portfolio. Later, I take you through the pantheon of HTML tags and then I get into greater detail with some techniques for writing great code.

Markup Languages

In simple terms, markup languages are used to describe content. Many kinds of markup exist, but by far the most popular is HTML. It's the language used for formatting pages in a web browser. In fact, web browsers can be thought of as little more than applications that parse HTML (among other languages).

The primary currency of markup languages is the *tag*. Tags provide instruction as to what the content represents. By surrounding a block of text in a p tag, for example, you're telling the browser that this text is a distinct paragraph.

The primary advantages of HTML are speed and ease of use. HTML's short learning curve is what has contributed to the explosive growth of the Internet; it's easy enough that anyone can pick it up.

HTML was created in 1990 to describe a way to link documents together in a network, hence the term *hypertext*. The standard was devised with the intention of connecting documents together with hyperlinks. The language became a standard adopted by the World Wide Web Consortium (the W3C), the international standards body for the Internet.

In This Chapter

Markup languages

Modern HTML: xHTML

Using tags

W3C standards

Using table-based layouts

The future of HTML

HTML was never intended to provide a rich graphical experience; early web pages are a testament to this, as shown in Figure 4.1.

Figure 4.1

The Apple website in 1997

However, as the Internet grew, developers found new ways to push the envelope of what HTML could do. From the very outset, designers were looking for ways to emulate the vivid richness of print layouts online. Over time, HTML was enhanced to offer greater stylistic control. Fonts, colors, and even content positioning became possible as innovative developers hacked around with the language.

In time, HTML started to show its age. As layouts became more elaborate, the problems of managing the code grew. As I saw at the time, there were two major problems with old-school HTML:

- The primary means of placing elements on the page became the `table` tag, which led to massive code bloat (I talk more about that later in this chapter).
- HTML was being increasingly used to describe content rather than just show it. Like the table problem, this led to pages that became very difficult to manage.

The problem got bad enough that the W3C came up with a brand-new solution. They built on the foundation of HTML and developed two technologies that would forever separate form and content. For the former purpose, they developed a technology called Cascading Style Sheets (CSS). For the latter, they reinvented HTML under a new moniker: xHTML.

Modern HTML: xHTML

The new xHTML language borrows heavily from the principles of another markup language called *eXtensible Markup Language*, or XML. XML is used as a means to transmit data in a standard, easily digested format. The tags that XML uses are specific to the type of data being transmitted. For example, this is what an XML document for an address book might look like:

```
<?xml version="1.0"?>
<!DOCTYPE Addresses PUBLIC "http://www.domain.com/ab.dtd">
<Addresses>
    <Address>
        <FirstName>Aaron</FirstName>
        <LastName>Vegh</LastName>
        <Phone>905-555-2900</Phone>
            </Address>
    </Addresses>
```

Every XML document has a Document Type Declaration (DTD). This is a document, sometimes located online, that specifies what tags the document can use. Although the DTD given here is fictitious, you might imagine that it specifies the fields shown. It also specifies the hierarchy of data: an `Addresses` object contains one or more `Address` objects, which in turn are composed of `FirstName`, `LastName`, and `Phone` fields.

One of the particular strengths of XML is its strictness; if a tag is out of place or typed incorrectly, the entire document is invalid and a proper XML parser fails to render the data. Compare this behavior with HTML: Where there are errors in the document, the browser fudges it, showing a layout that tries to approximate the intentions of the author. This behavior is the cause of much consternation on the part of web developers, who have to contend with the quirks of different web browsers; how they handle these issues with improper HTML is what leads to sometimes glaring differences in rendering.

With XML, such differences of opinion are dramatically reduced. Because the DTD provides a way to validate the document, there's little chance of misinterpretation, and you can count on your XML reaching your audience in the same condition you sent it.

Web developers were very jealous of this power. That's why the new version of HTML is actually an XML document! When done correctly, your xHTML document validates against a DTD defined by the W3C. Your browser receives exactly what it's expecting and renders your page with much greater reliability.

However, there was a problem on the way to paradise. Some web developers complained that xHTML was too strict. For many legacy sites, converting to xHTML would require massive amounts of work. For them, the W3C created a DTD that would provide the benefits of xHTML while providing some limited support for older tags. Hence, there are two DTDs for xHTML: a strict version, which is the preferred format, and a transitional version, which helps out the legacy coders.

N O T E

I lied: There's actually a third DTD, specifically intended for frameset documents. Because framesets are almost entirely passé, I prefer to pretend they don't exist, and I won't be talking about them here. If you're looking for a way to embed multiple pages into the same document, then follow through this and the next chapter first. If you still think you need to do that, then you can refer to www.w3schools.com/tags/tag_doctype.asp to learn more.

Because you're learning HTML for the first time, I'm going to try to impart some good coding habits and teach you only the strict flavor of xHTML. This version of HTML will produce rather plain-looking documents, but they'll be ready-made for your soon-to-be-developed skill in providing style with CSS.

Using Tags

To this point, I've spent far too much time talking about HTML and not enough time showing you how to use it. I'm going to remedy that now. To write your code, open your text editor of choice. You'll be creating various documents in the course of this chapter, so it would be useful to organize them in your `Sites` folder. I created a folder called `prowebdev` in my `Sites` folder, and I'll store my files there. With the files in the `Sites` folder, you can readily access them in your browser (assuming you set up your Mac's web server, as described in Chapter 1).

I'm going to start with a basic web page that introduces you to the elements of HTML. In your text editor, type this code:

```
<!DOCTYPE html PUBLIC "-//W3C//DTD XHTML 1.0 Strict//EN"
    "http://www.w3.org/TR/xhtml1/DTD/xhtml1-strict.dtd">
<html xmlns="http://www.w3.org/1999/xhtml" xml:lang="en"
    lang="en">
    <head>
        <title>Hello, World!</title>
        <meta http-equiv="Content-Type" content="text/
    html;charset=ISO-8859-1" />
    </head>
    <body>
        <h1>Hello, world!</h1>
        <p>This is my first HTML document. It's very strict.</p>
    </body>
</html>
```

Save the file as `helloworld.html`. Then, open a web browser and type the address (changing it depending on how you named your files): `http://localhost/prowebdev/helloworld.html`. You should see a page similar to Figure 4.2.

CROSS-REF

You can find the `helloworld.html` file on the website for this book: `www.wileydevreference.com`.

Figure 4.2

Your first web page

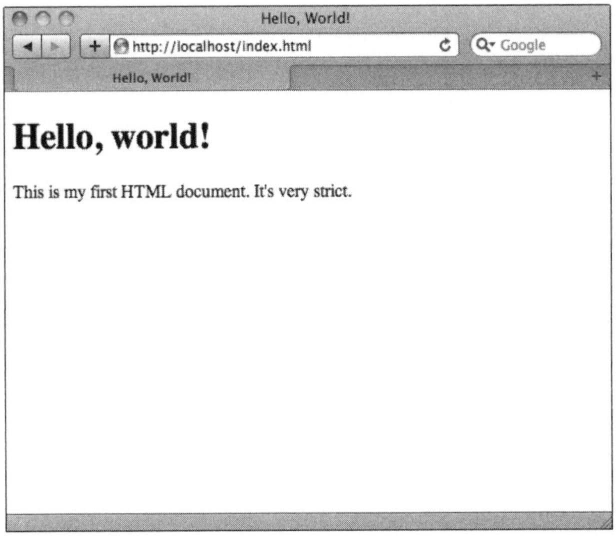

As you look at this code, you see some of the basic rules that make up the xHTML specifications:

- **Tags are composed of keywords inside angle brackets.**
- **There must always be both open and close tags.** The closing version of the tag is the opening tag with a slash before the keyword. There are some tags that are self-closing, such as the `meta` tag.
- **Some tags have *attributes*, which are essentially key-value pairs.** For example, look at the `html` tag in the example; the `xmlns`, `xml:lang`, and `lang` attributes are declared and defined there.
- **All tag names must be lowercase.**
- **Use indents to visually format the code in your text editor.** The indents imply the hierarchy of the tags: `head` and `body` are child elements of `html`; `title` is a child of `head`.

Almost all this code is pure housekeeping. The first line declares the doctype of this document; this is the code that you use to invoke the xHTML Strict doctype. Well-behaved web browsers that see this line will go into strict mode, providing consistent rendering for documents that meet the requirements of the doctype.

The next line declares the opening `html` tag. It contains three attributes that specify the language of the document and the `namespace`, which defines the tags that are available. These first two lines will be the same in all your documents; I keep them in a safe place and paste them into every HTML document that I create.

Every HTML document has two major sections: a `head` and a `body`. The `head` defines elements required for the whole page; the `title` tag is shown here, the contents of which appear in the browser's title bar. There's also a `meta` tag, which defines the text encoding of the document and is required for this doctype. In the `body` block are two text elements: a `header` tag (the `h1` is the top-level header) and a paragraph.

Let's fill out this basic document a bit more. First, you're going to tackle the elements that would normally appear in the `head` of a document. You've already seen the `title` tag, but there are several others. Here are some of the more common ones:

- `title`, which you've already seen, provides the title of the document.
- `meta` comes in many different flavors and provides *metadata* for the page. The metadata often describes the page for the benefit of search engines; content provided by these tags can appear in search engine results. These tags have two attributes: `name` and `content`. For each kind of `meta` tag, you provide the value.
- `link`, which provides a link to an external style sheet. I show you how this is used in Chapter 5.
- `script`, which provides a link to an external JavaScript document. I cover this in Chapter 6.

Let's add some `meta` tags to the `head` of your document. Just below the `title` tag, add these lines:

```
<meta name="description" content="A page to describe HTML
    basics." />
<meta name="keywords" content="hello world, html, basics" />
<meta name="author" content="Aaron Vegh" />
```

You can change the `author` name to your own name.

There are other `meta` tags, but these are the most common. You now have a complete `head` section for your document. Let's turn to the `body` of the page now.

There are nearly 80 tags in the HTML specification. If you use the language long enough, you learn most of them. That may seem overwhelming, but you'll find that the tags are very sensible and easy to pick up. The only trick is to gain the experience necessary to know which tag to use when. If there's one rule of thumb that I can share about HTML, it's this: Code for what the content is, not what the content looks like. Or to put it more academically, code semantically. Remember that xHTML is intended to describe content, not control how it looks.

Out of the tags that make up xHTML, I'm going to talk about a few dozen at most. And I'm going to group them into the categories that you'll find yourself using most often: for describing text and images, for putting data into tables, and for creating forms.

Text and images

Table 4-1 shows the tags you can use to describe text and images that appear in your HTML.

Table 4-1	HTML Tags for Text and Images
Tag	**Description**
a	Anchor tag; used to create hyperlinks
b	Bold tag
blockquote	Defines an excerpted segment of text of paragraph length or more
br /	Break tag; used to create a line break in text
em	Emphasis tag; used to differentiate important text
h1 to h6	Header tags; used to indicated header priority, where the h1 tag is the highest priority, while h6 is lowest
hr /	Horizontal rule tag; used to create a line to separate blocks of content
img /	Image tag; used to insert images in the page
li	List item tag; used to specify an item in an ordered or unordered list
map	Image map tag; used to specify coordinates and hyperlinks in an image
ol	Ordered list tag; used to create lists of numbered items
p	Paragraph tag; used to denote paragraphs of text
pre	Pre-formatted text tag; used to show literal text within an HTML document
strong	Strong tag; similar to the emphasis tag, this is used to highlight important text
sub	Subscript tag; used to create subscript characters
sup	Superscript tag; used to create superscript characters
ul	Unordered list tag; used to create bulleted lists of items

One of the most important tags in HTML is the anchor tag. In order to test it out, you're going to create a second page. Open your text editor and then create a new file. Type these contents:

```
<!DOCTYPE html PUBLIC "-//W3C//DTD XHTML 1.0 Strict//EN"
   "http://www.w3.org/TR/xhtml1/DTD/xhtml1-strict.dtd">
<html xmlns="http://www.w3.org/1999/xhtml" xml:lang="en"
   lang="en">
   <head>
      <title>Hello Back!</title>
```

```
    <meta name="description" content="A page to describe HTML
basics." />
    <meta name="keywords" content="hello world, html, basics,
coding, fun" />
    <meta name="author" content="Aaron Vegh" />
    <meta http-equiv="Content-Type" content="text/
html;charset=ISO-8859-1" />
</head>
<body>
    <h1>Hello Right Back!</h1>
    <p>You've arrived.</p>
</body>
</html>
```

Save this document as `helloback.html` alongside the `helloworld.html` file that you've already created. Everything about this file is the same as the first, except for the `body` content and the `title` tag.

CROSS-REF

You can find the `helloback.html` file on the website for this book: `www.wileydevreference.com`.

Let's go back to your original file to make some changes. Replace the content within the `body` tags with this:

```
<h1>Hello, world!</h1>
<p>In this document, you'll find a number of important HTML
    features:</p>
<ul>
    <li>The use of header tags</li>
    <li>Paragraphs</li>
    <li>Lists</li>
    <li>The occasional <b>bold tag</b></li>
</ul>

<hr />

<h2>Take note</h2>
<p>There's no point to using HTML unless you <a href="helloback.
    html">link to another page</a>!</p>
```

Save the file. If your browser is still tuned to your first attempt at this page, simply reload it to see the change, as shown in Figure 4.3.

Figure 4.3

Your page with more text elements

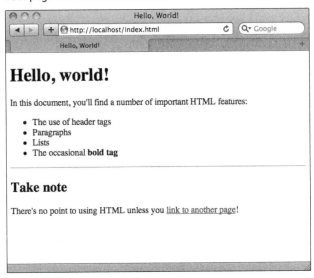

In just a brief block of code, you've managed to use many of the tags that you'll need for describing text. Go ahead and click that hyperlink at the end; it should take you to the `hello-back.html` page. If not, check the file name in your hyperlink and ensure the pages are together in the same directory.

I did forget to include one important tag: the image. Before you use the image tag, there are a few things to say about how images work on the web.

First, you have only three image formats to choose from. Each format has its limitations, so when you choose, balance the benefits against the weaknesses:

- **JPEG.** This is a lossy image format, with a range of compression depths. In other words, the more compressed the image, the smaller the file size, but the worse it looks. JPEG is best for images with a lot of color, such as photographs.

- **GIF.** This is a lossless image format. You can get smaller file sizes by reducing the number of colors used. GIF also offers a crude form of transparency, where individual pixels can be made fully transparent. GIF is good for simple images or illustrations with few colors.

- **PNG.** This is also a lossless format. Intended to replace GIF and JPEG, PNG offers a range of compression options and, most important, true alpha-based transparency. This results in larger file sizes. Also, Internet Explorer 6 doesn't natively support transparent PNG files.

You might find yourself using JPEG and GIF images most often in your sites, at least until your designs require image transparency (I discuss this in Chapter 12).

Second, I want to make a strong case for file organization. Consistency is key here, as larger sites tend to accumulate files to such an extent that you'll quickly be lost without a system. In this case, every website project I do has an `images` folder. Create one now alongside your two new HTML files. Into that folder, you'll place an image of your choice, as long as it's in one of the three formats.

If you're on a Mac (and, of course, you are!), the easiest way to get a PNG file is to grab a screenshot; the Mac natively supports PNG and produces screenshots in that format. So, choose an area of your screen, press ⌘+Shift+4, and then drag your mouse over the region you want to capture. On the release of your mouse, you hear a snapshot sound and then a file called `Screen shot <date>` appears on your desktop. Move that file to your new `images` folder and then rename it `sample.png`.

Now, let's go to `helloback.html`. Change the content within the `body` tags so it looks like this:

```
<h1>Hello Right Back!</h1>
<p>
    You deserve a picture:
    <img src="images/sample.png" alt="Desktop shot" />
</p>
```

Save this file and then visit it in your browser. You should see something similar to Figure 4.4.

It may not seem like much, but you've now learned a solid chunk of HTML.

Figure 4.4

Using the image tag

Tables

In the bad old days, web developers used tables to position elements on a page. Heck, even Apple did it! And yes, up until a couple of years ago, I did it too. In the practical web development business, if you wanted compelling layouts on the web, you had to use tables. It's an ugly hack, but it worked.

You're not going to do that now. Instead, I'm going to discuss how tables are meant to be used: to describe tabular data. Table 4-2 shows the available `table` tags.

Table 4-2 HTML Tags for Tables

Tag	Description
table	Table tag; the parent tag used to specify the table
tbody	Table body tag; used to indicate the table's main content
td	Table data tag; used to indicate a single cell in a table
tfoot	Table footer tag; used to indicate the table's closing content
th	Table header tag; used to indicate the headings of a table row or column
thead	Table head tag; used to indicate the table's header row
tr	Table row tag; used to indicate a row of cells

Create a new file in your text editor and then copy and paste the content from either of the two files used thus far; this gives you most of the document structure ready-made. Then, replace the content between the `body` tags with this content, which will construct a table of data:

```
<h1>Telling Lies with Statistics</h1>
    <p>You can use numbers to say anything:</p>

    <table>
        <thead>
            <tr>
                <th>Name</th>
                <th>Age</th>
                <th>Teeth</th>
            </tr>
        </thead>
<tfoot>
            <tr>
                <td colspan="2">Avg Teeth</td>
                <td>15</td>
            </tr>
        </tfoot>
        <tbody>
```

```
                    <tr>
                            <td>Cory</td>
                            <td>23</td>
                            <td>32</td>
                    </tr>
                    <tr>
                            <td>Max</td>
                            <td>7</td>
                            <td>12</td>
                    </tr>
                    <tr>
                            <td>Walt</td>
                            <td>85</td>
                            <td>2</td>
                    </tr>
            </tbody>
    </table>
```

Save the file as `hellotable.html`. Then, view the file by pointing your browser to `http://localhost/prowebdev/hellotable.html`. You should see a page similar to Figure 4.5.

CROSS-REF

You can find the `hellotable.html` file on the website for this book: `www.wileydevreference.com`.

Figure 4.5

A table in HTML

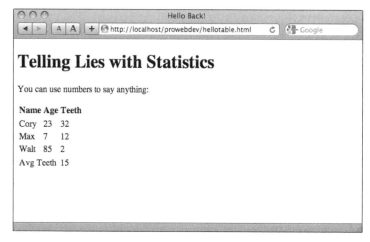

Telling Lies with Statistics

You can use numbers to say anything:

Name	Age	Teeth
Cory	23	32
Max	7	12
Walt	85	2
Avg Teeth	15	

Personally, I find the most distinguishing characteristic of tables in HTML to be their tediousness. It's quite possible that the number of characters of code surpasses the content. However, there's a great deal of sense to the use of `table` tags. A parent `table` element contains `thead`, `tbody`, and `tfoot` tags, each of which contains rows made up of cells. And, yes, the footer must go above the `body`, according to the W3C specification.

The governing principle of using tables in HTML is that while cells are the principal building blocks, they must be arranged in rows. The `tr` tag specifies the boundaries of a horizontal row inside a table, and the `td` tags within them must line up all the way down the line. Notice how my table has five rows of three columns.

Tables can get tricky where you want some cells to take up multiple rows or columns. In the bottom row of this table, I have a cell that spans two columns by using an attribute called `colspan`. There's also a `rowspan` attribute. When it comes to knowing where to place these multiple-spanning cells, imagine them growing down and to the right. If your cell spans columns, make your declaration in the left-most cell of the group to be spanned. Similarly, if your cell spans rows, make your declaration in the top-most cell of that group.

Feel free to experiment with this table to see if you can control cell spanning.

Forms

While the web was originally envisioned as a read-only medium of interconnected documents, it quickly became apparent that there would need to be a way for people to interact with these pages. The solution is a set of form tags, which allow you to create various elements that can be used to type data.

In this section, I cover how to create a form by using the available elements. At this point, however, you can't see what happens to the form data. Every form has an action attribute that specifies a script that handles the form data, and this is done on the server side. I cover this in more detail in Chapter 15. Table 4-3 shows the available tags for form creation.

Table 4-3	HTML Tags for Forms
Tag	**Description**
button	Button tag; used to provide a pushbutton control
fieldset	Field set tag; used to indicate a collection of related elements in a form
form	Form tag; the parent of the other tags
input	Input tag; used to provide a number of different inputs
label	Label tag; used to indicate a label for input tags
optgroup	Option group tag; used to indicate a collection of option tags
option	Option tag; used to indicate an option inside a select tag
select	Select tag; used to provide a choice of multiple options
textarea	Text area tag; used to provide multi-line text input

For this example, you're going to create the sort of contact form that you see on many websites. Open your text editor and then create a new file. You can use the same header information as you have in previous files; you're only changing the contents inside the body tag. Type the following into that area now:

```
<h1>Contact Us!</h1>
<p>Have a question? Need advice? Just fill out this form, and
   we'll get right back to you.</p>

   <form action="submit.php" method="post">
       <p>Your Name <input type="text" name="name" /></p>

       <p>Your Email Address <input type="text" name="email" /></
p>

       <p>Number of robot drones needed
       <input type="radio" name="drones" value="1-5" id="one2five"
/> <label for="one2five">1-5</label>
       <input type="radio" name="drones" value="6-10" id="six2ten"
/> <label for="six2ten">6-10</label>
       <input type="radio" name="drones" value="11+"
id="elevenPlus" /> <label for="elevenPlus">11+</label></p>

       <p>What features do you look for in a robot drone?<br/>
       <input type="checkbox" name="features[]" value="cackle"
id="cackle" /> <label for="cackle">Evil Cackle</label><br/>
       <input type="checkbox" name="features[]" value="lasers"
id="lasers" /> <label for="lasers">Frickin' Lasers</
label><br/>
       <input type="checkbox" name="features[]" value="hat"
id="hat" /> <label for="hat">Go-Go Gadget Hat</label><br/>
       <input type="checkbox" name="features[]" value="toaster"
id="toaster" /> <label for="toaster">Built-in Toaster</
label><br/>
       <input type="checkbox" name="features[]" value="laundry"
id="laundry" /> <label for="laundry"> Washing Clothes</
label></p>

<p>What do you need your drones for?
   <select name="purpose">
       <option>Choose one...</option>
       <optgroup label="Recreational">
           <option value="fishing">Fishing</option>
           <option value="frisbee">Frisbee</option>
       </optgroup>
       <optgroup label="Industrial">
           <option value="welding">Welding</option>
           <option value="bedmaking">Bed-making</option>
```

```
        </optgroup>
      </select></p>
      <p><input type="submit" value="Send Form" /></p>

  </form>
```

Save the file as `helloform.html` alongside the rest of your files from this chapter. Let's have a look at it in the browser; it should resemble Figure 4.6.

CROSS-REF

You can find the `helloform.html` file on the website for this book: `www.wileydevreference.com`.

Let's examine this code. The `form` tag has two important attributes. The first attribute, `action`, specifies the name of the file that will receive the data typed in this form. In the old days, this would certainly be a Common Gateway Interface (CGI) script written in Perl. Nowadays, there are a wide range of languages and techniques for handling form data on the server side; for this book, you're going to use PHP.

The other attribute here is the `method`. There are two choices here:

- GET places the form data into the string of the URL, making the data visible to anyone who looks at your location bar. If you switched the method here to GET, the URL would change to something like `submit.php?name=Aaron Vegh&email=aaron@vegh.ca`.
- POST places the form data into the HTTP headers, obscuring it from view. This is the preferred method for form data, as it's both more secure and cleaner.

NOTE

So, when might you use GET? Most often, when you create a hyperlink to another page. Sometimes, you may want to pass some information from one page to another. Using a GET method inside your `a` tag is an easy way to do this:

```
<a href="profile.php?color=Green">Go to your profile page</a>
```

When using GET, avoid passing information that's sensitive in nature, as anyone could see this URL and simply change the location string to achieve unexpected — and undesirable — results.

The form opens with the use of the versatile `input` tag. That tag's `type` attribute governs its appearance and comes with a number of rules for use depending on the type. In the first instance, you're simply using it as a text input box. The only other attribute used here is the `name` attribute; you use this attribute to put a name to every piece of data being collected in a form.

When it comes time to ask for the number of drones needed in this form, you start to see the `input` tag's versatility at work. This time, the `type` is a radio button, which is a control that allows only one of its options to be activated. Be sure to give each instance of the group of radio buttons the same name; only one of them is used when the form data is transmitted.

Figure 4.6

Your rendered form

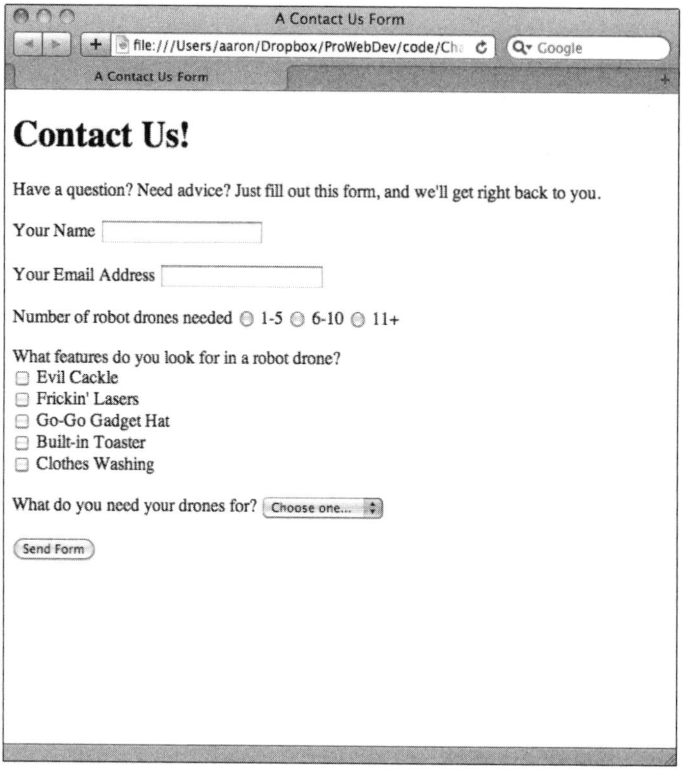

In the next question, you see yet another use of the `input` tag, this time in the form of the `checkbox`, which allows multiple options to be chosen. In this case, every option gets the same name along with a set of indexing square brackets ([ ]), which place the selected options into an array for transmission to the server.

The final question makes use of the `select` tag, which can provide either a pop-up menu (as it does here) or a *combo box*, a multi-line field with the values shown. If you want to have the user choose more than one value from this control, just add the attribute `multiple="multiple"` to the end of the opening `select` tag. To choose more than one value, hold down the ⌘ key while clicking on a value.

Finally, the `input` tag puts in a last appearance in a new form: the `submit` type. This creates a button that commits the form to the server, with the text that appears in the `value` attribute. Don't bother clicking that button; you don't have a file called `submit.php`!

There's one more item of interest in this form: the use of the `label` tag. Unfortunately, you rarely see this tag used in forms. But for the effort of including them, you get a great payback in the usability of your forms.

Labels are used to indicate the text that belongs to a form control, such as a radio button or check box. When added, you're able to click the text label to activate the control, making it that much easier (realistically, dramatically easier) for users to work with your form. Give it a try with this form in your browser and then compare the difference between clicking the tiny radio button and clicking its label. Convinced? Always be sure to use this tag in your forms.

That concludes my discussion of HTML tags. Now's your chance to practice; take some time to create your own sample web pages. Use as wide a variety of the tags as you can. Create paragraphs, links, lists, instructions, blockquotes, tables, and forms. Given the ease of use that is HTML's hallmark, you'll find yourself at home in no time.

W3C Standards

Standards are very important on the web. Without them, there would be total chaos, as different browsers rendered your web pages in different ways.

Wait. Actually, that's the case today. But I'm happy to report that the situation is improving; the W3C standards-setting body finally has the ear of all major browser developers in the market, especially the giant one based in Redmond, Washington — the one vendor whose browser so upset those standards as to make life very difficult for web developers everywhere. (Hint: Its name starts with "M" and ends in "icrosoft.")

Nowadays, if you code in strict xHTML, then you can code with the confidence of knowing that your page will appear the same in every major browser. But how do you know that your page is strictly complying with xHTML? You can use the services of the W3C Validator. This online tool examines the code you pass to it and then reports on whether it passes or fails. In the latter case, the Validator provides clues that can help you fix any issues.

To access the Validator, browse to `http://validator.w3.org`. You have three choices: to validate a file that exists on the Internet, to upload an HTML file, or to paste in code.

Let's choose the third option. Click the Validate by Direct Input tab, paste in the code from the form example that you just completed, as shown in Figure 4.7, and then click the Check button.

Figure 4.7

Submitting your HTML code to the W3C Validator

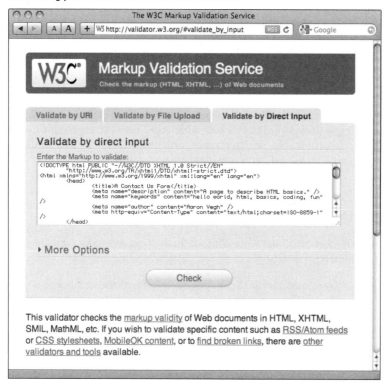

If you're using the same code I just did, you should see the result shown in Figure 4.8.

Phew! There's a warning there, but that has to do with the direct input method that you used; the Validator ignored your character-encoding tags. When you do get the gold star from the Validator, it offers the use of some graphical tags so you can show off to site visitors — and, more importantly, help spread the word about quality markup.

Figure 4.8

W3C Validator results: You pass!

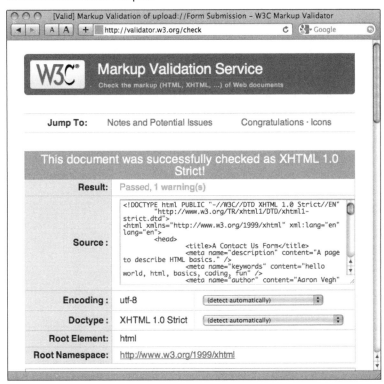

Sometimes, you don't get the gold star from the Validator. In those cases, you might see a screen similar to Figure 4.9.

There, there; no need for tears! Even the best web developers get this page. Yes, even me. In this case, I made only one error in the code: I left out a trailing slash on the end of an img tag. Yet, this triggered five errors in the Validator! The tool is nothing if not verbose. However, the first error shown often indicates the problem; fix and recheck, and you'll be fine.

In my time with the W3C Validator, I've run into a number of recurring problems. Follow these rules when you're coding, and you'll have clean documents in no time:

- **Make sure every tag is closed.** Where a tag is self-closing, ensure that you have the trailing slash included. The self-closing tags are few in number: `link`, `img`, `br`, `hr`, `area`, `input`, and `meta`. These are tags that don't describe content.

- **Always use lowercase.** Traditional HTML style specified (but didn't require) all-caps tagging; don't do it!

- **Don't miss required attributes.** Every `img` tag needs an `alt` tag, for example.

- **Check your element hierarchy.** All content must be within a block-level tag, such as a header, paragraph, or div (I cover this one in Chapter 5).

- **Don't make typos.** You will anyway, of course. It happens.

The good news is that if you forget the rules, the Validator reminds you. Once you spot your recurring errors, you'll be a human validator yourself — with a cape, a wacky sidekick, and a super-cool car.

Figure 4.9

W3C Validator results: You fail!

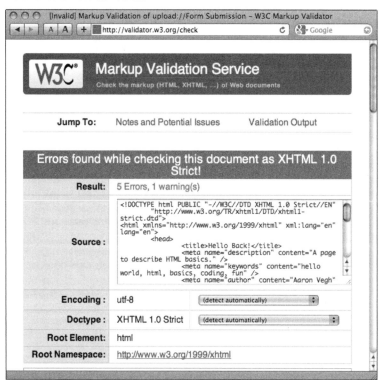

Using Table-Based Layouts

There are many schools of thought in the web development world, but nowhere is there more fervor than in the debate between those who espouse tables for layout and those who oppose them. Given the pitch to which this debate has risen, I think it's worth mentioning in greater detail.

I've already talked a bit about how tables are used to lay out documents. From your investigations into the `table` tags, you could probably guess how it's done: Imagine an HTML page that has a horizontal cell containing the site's logo, title, and navigation. Below that are a `body` containing a main column and a sidebar with subsidiary content.

With that picture in your mind, go ahead and code it. With the header template code you've been using in this chapter, put this code into the `body` of a new file:

```
<table width="100%" cellpadding="0" cellspacing="0" border="0">
    <tr>
            <td colspan="2">
                <h1>
                        <img src="images/sample.png" />
                        This is my table site! Fie on semantic
content!
                </h1>
                <p>
                        <a href="file1.html">Why Tables Rock</
a> | <a href="file2.html">Table-ictionary</a> |<a href="file3.
html">Table Styles</a>
                </p>
            </td>
    </tr>
    <tr>
            <td width="25%" valign="top">
            <!-- This is a comment; ignored by the browser -->
            <!-- This is our sidebar -->
                <h3>Other Sites that Use Tables</h3>
                <p>
                        <a href="#">Site 1</a><br/>
                        <a href="#">Site 2</a><br/>
                        <a href="#">Site 3</a>
                </p>
            </td>
            <td width="75%" valign="top">
                <!-- This is the main content area -->
                <h2>Table-opolis!</h2>
                <p>Tables are cool. I love tables; they make
layout fun.</p>
            </td>
    </tr>
</table>
```

This is a very simple table layout. Save it as `hellotablelayout.html` along with the rest of your files. Now view it in the browser, as shown in Figure 4.10.

CROSS-REF

You can find the `hellotablelayout.html` file on the website for this book: `www.wileydevreference.com`.

Hey, 1999 called: It wants its web page back! Now, I do tease a bit unnecessarily; you can use tables to construct highly visual sites, and you wouldn't know the difference (in fact, until you master the techniques in Chapter 5, you can't know the difference!). But consider the amount of code that it took to produce that page; it's about as simple as I could make it for this book. In more-engaging layouts, developers use cell-spanning techniques and another one called *nesting* — to put tables within cells — in order to achieve more-complex layouts.

Figure 4.10

A style-free, table-based layout

When that happens, you end up with a very long HTML file that is hard to maintain. I can't tell you about the hours I've wasted poring over code line by line to try to find the single missing `td` tag that was ruining my layout.

In fact, it was the overextension of the table layout craze that opened up a market for graphical HTML layout tools, such as Macromedia Dreamweaver (now owned by Adobe). With these WYSIWYG (What You See Is What You Get) tools, a developer could readily tell where the table cells were supposed to be, greatly minimizing time spent troubleshooting. Furthermore, a developer could nest and span with impunity, unconcerned with the massive amount of code being generated to support it.

The fact that most of these tools are either poorly maintained or gone altogether suggests that web technology has moved on. Coding semantically and pairing your well-formed code with CSS styling gets the job done faster — and with less code.

Stay tuned, and prepare to be amazed.

The Future of HTML

Before you finish this chapter, it's worth taking a look at the future of HTML. Everything you've learned about xHTML in this chapter will continue to be relevant for many years to come, but with the next version of HTML under development, you'll be able to implement some amazing technologies that were once the province of highly skilled Flash developers.

HTML5 — the successor to both HTML 4.1 and xHTML — is under development at the time of this writing. But web browser developers are keen to see the new language supported — Apple in particular. Safari 4, the browser currently shipping from Apple, provides native HTML5 support.

The new language incorporates both new tags (while deprecating others) and new APIs for enhanced functionality. Here are some highlights:

- A new canvas tag provides a way to draw simple images directly in your code as well as perform impressive animation effects.
- Media playback will be supported natively; currently, developers have to use embed and object tags to load external components for video and audio playback.
- An offline storage database will let web applications store documents on your computer, making web applications functional even when you're offline.
- More semantic tags will allow developers to build pages that are easier to read, both for themselves and for search engines.
- Form validations will let developers specify both required fields and formatting rules for text typed in forms. Currently, developers have to use a combination of JavaScript and server-side scripting to achieve solid form validation.
- A persistence mechanism will allow form data to pass from page to page without the intervention of a server-side script.

Any of these features and the many more that are currently included are still subject to change, pending the final release of the specification.

And when the specification is finally released, you'll have to wait for the major browsers to support it. That's bad news for those users who appreciate how long browsers hang around — I'm looking at you, Internet Explorer 6. Unless you know your audience is using an HTML5-capable browser, you'll have to continue supporting the existing technologies.

Summary

Through the course of this chapter, I covered the fundamentals of coding HTML, and I showed that proper HTML eschews form in favor of content. I covered the principles of how HTML documents are put together, with sections for `head` content and main `body` content. Within each section, I talked about the relevant tags: those that describe the page within the `head` tag as well as the content tags within the `body` tag. I talked about using HTML to produce headers, paragraphs, and lists and then I moved on to forms and tables. Remember the distinction between tables as used for tabular data and tables used for layout: the former is a good thing; the latter not so much.

Ultimately, the chief takeaway here is that HTML is for content only, not the appearance of it. When done right, HTML produces well-formed, albeit uninteresting, pages. But when you want to influence its appearance, you'll need CSS.

Cascading Style Sheets

A s Chapter 4 showed, well-written HTML is pretty boring. But with that boredom comes any number of benefits; chief among them is an excellent separation between *form* (how your page looks) and *content* (what your page is saying). By separating these functions, you make your job as a web developer dramatically simpler. Imagine a couple of scenarios:

- You've built a beautiful site based on HTML tables. Your client is thrilled — so thrilled, in fact, that she asks you to produce a version of the site that can be viewable on handheld devices, such as cell phones. You curse under your breath as you realize you have to re-author the entire site from scratch.

- In the course of developing a site for another client, you produce a large group of pages that use a daring header text style. When the client sees it, he hates it. You need to change that style to something easier on the eyes! But because you've put the style definition with every element that uses it, you need to laboriously clamber through your files to change them — and hope the client likes this one.

These are both very common scenarios. And in both cases, the use of Cascading Style Sheets, or CSS, would make the job a lot easier. In the first case, with properly formatted HTML, you can simply keep that file and then apply a new CSS style sheet to get yourself a mobile version. In the second case, every style is named and defined in just one place. Just switch up the style definition — and all styles are updated. Sweet.

For teams that work on websites, this separation of form and content makes collaboration a lot easier too: While one developer works on the HTML and the content that goes with it, a designer could tweak the styles to his or her heart's content.

Style sheets can be defined in one of three ways:

- **Inline.** Through the use of the HTML style attribute, you can define a style for a specific element within an HTML file. This is generally bad practice, but it can be necessary, for example, when formatting HTML email.

In This Chapter

Understanding CSS

Working with selectors

Page layout with CSS

Solving common problems

- **Embedded in the** head**.** Using the style tag in the head of an HTML document, you can define styles that apply only to that document. This works fine when you're only creating a single page.
- **In an external file.** Using the link tag in the head of an HTML document, you can specify an external CSS file to serve as the definition for all styles. This is the preferred method, as it provides all the advantages of the separation of form and content.

In this chapter, you'll use all three techniques for both demonstration and convenience. In practice, you should almost always use the external style sheet method, unless there's a compelling reason to do otherwise.

CSS technology is based on a simple metaphor of selectors and attributes. All your time with CSS is spent identifying elements to apply styles to. These identifiers are the *selectors*; the *attributes* are what set the style.

Your first step in learning CSS is to understand selectors — how to pinpoint elements in an HTML page. Next, you learn about the attributes: for text, images, tables, and forms. Then, you delve into positioning elements and laying out pages by using CSS. With enough practice, you should be able to create layouts very quickly and easily by using CSS — and leaving HTML table layout in the dustbin of history, where it belongs.

Understanding CSS

I've spent some time chiding those who use HTML to style content, and that may be unfair. For all its benefits, CSS has only recently become a practical technology. While the specification has existed since at least 2005, it has been poorly adopted by mainstream browsers until relatively recently. While browsers such as Mozilla Firefox and Apple Safari quickly picked up the latest CSS version 2 specification (which includes layout features), Microsoft Internet Explorer lagged for a long time. With the introduction of Internet Explorer 7 in 2006 (after a long five years under the previous version 6), CSS finally came to reside in all major browsers; however, Internet Explorer 6 remains a well-established browser, especially in corporate environments.

While web developers could have sat back and waited for the majority of web browsers to shift to the latest technology, they didn't; instead, the community has developed a number of hacks and workarounds that compensate for Internet Explorer 6's broken CSS implementation. I cover the specifics of those workarounds later in this chapter. But if you use the techniques described here, you can successfully target 99% of the browsers out there.

For the purposes of writing and testing your CSS code, I recommend using either Safari or Firefox and then making alterations to suit Internet Explorer. These two browsers have correctly adopted the CSS standard, so you can be sure that code found working there will stand the test of time.

Some developers who use Windows tend to code against Internet Explorer — after all, that's the browser that some 70% (and declining) of users use. But the detrimental effect is twofold: It not only goobers up the Internet for the law-abiding browsers, but it breaks their sites when

Microsoft updates their browser. Internet Explorer 8, released in March 2009, provides excellent CSS support. But it also provides a compatibility feature that breaks many pages coded for IE6 and IE7.

In other words, code correctly, and the future will reward you.

Working with Selectors

Selectors are the means by which you specify the elements you want to style. There are four different kinds of selectors:

- **Element selector.** Specify the name of the HTML element, and all elements of that type are thusly styled.
- **Class selector.** Using the HTML `class` tag, you can assign multiple elements the same style.
- **ID selector.** Using the HTML `id` tag, you can style a single page element. This is usually used for positioning elements.
- **Pseudo selector.** These are special selectors that apply in certain conditions. The `:hover` selector comes into effect when the mouse moves over an element. The `:first-line` selector styles the first line of a text element.

CSS provides a syntax for specifying the different kinds of selectors. The best way to explain that syntax is to just show it, so let's have a demonstration.

Open your text editor and then create a new document. If you followed through from Chapter 4, you'll have several documents that contain the same boilerplate HTML. Feel free to go back and copy that HTML into this new document. You start by creating the HTML that forms the content of your web page. Paste this text between the `body` tags:

```
<h1>Plasmo<span>Robotics</span></h1>
<p>You too can combine your <strong>love of plasma physics
   </strong> and <strong>robotics</strong> in this burgeoning new
   field!</p>
<ul>
   <li>Discover the power of plasma!</li>
   <li>Build sophisticated robotic components!</li>
   <li>Eliminate your enemies and get all the pie you can eat!</li>
</ul>
<p>But don't take our word for it! Listen to what others in the
   field have to say:</p>
<blockquote>
   <p>They said I should say this is a great field. I agree.<br/>
   <span class="attribution">Billy, Toronto</span></p>

   <p>All hail the mighty plasma robots! Now, where's my pie?<br/>
   <span class="attribution">Kevin, New York</span></p>
```

```
    <p>The convergence of plasma and robots is inevitable. The pie
    is just a bonus.
    <br/>
    <span class="attribution">Kelly, London</span></p>
</blockquote>
<p>Don't delay - <a href="#">order now!</a></p>
```

This is a fairly conventional HTML document that uses elements I covered in Chapter 4. The big difference you might notice is the use of the `class` attribute on the `span` tags. This allows you to target those elements independently of other spans. Save the document as `hellostyle.html` and then load it in your browser. You should see something similar to Figure 5.1.

Figure 5.1

Your basic HTML page

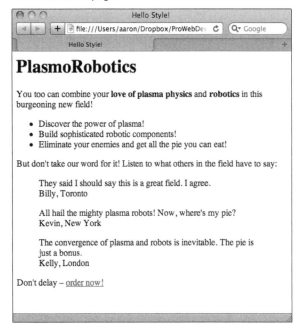

CROSS-REF

You can find the `hellostyle.html` file on the website for this book: `www.wileydevreference.com`.

The first way you apply style is with the embed method: You put a `style` tag in the `head` of the HTML document. Place this content anywhere between the `head` tags (I usually make it the last element in the `head`):

```
<style>

   body {
      background-color: #F6F6F6;
   }

</style>
```

Let's begin by investigating the anatomy of a style rule. A *rule* is a single cluster of declarations that target one or more selectors. The rule you just created begins by providing a selector called `body`. The braces enclose the individual declaration statements, which are composed of a property, a colon, and the value. Every declaration ends with a semicolon. Figure 5.2 shows the constituent parts of a style rule.

Figure 5.2

The anatomy of a style rule

declaration
declaration
strong { font-size: 16px; color: #A56E27; }
property
value
property
value
selector
declaration block

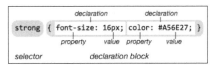

While you can write rules in any format, I recommend the style in the previous example: the selector and brace, followed by a carriage return and tab, with one line per declaration. It takes up more vertical space in your document, but you'll find your styles easier to read. Also, many text editors (such as Macromates TextMate and Coda from Panic Software) provide indexes of all the styles, so getting to the one you want is a snap, as shown in Figure 5.3.

Figure 5.3

TextMate's style index provides quick access to style rules.

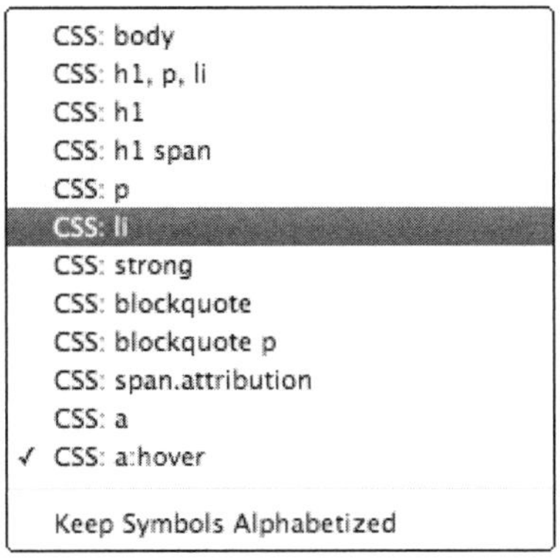

CSS: body
CSS: h1, p, li
CSS: h1
CSS: h1 span
CSS: p
CSS: li
CSS: strong
CSS: blockquote
CSS: blockquote p
CSS: span.attribution
CSS: a
✓ CSS: a:hover
Keep Symbols Alphabetized

Now let's see what you've accomplished. Save the document and then reload it in your browser; your document should now have a light-gray background.

You can style multiple elements at the same time. This is really useful when you want to set defaults for a number of elements. For example, type this after your last statement:

```
h1, p, li {
    font-family: "Lucida Sans", Helvetica, Arial, sans-serif;
    color: #336699;
}
```

Here, you're styling the h1, p, and li tags with the same properties. You're setting both the typeface and the color of those elements. When you have values that are more than one word, you must surround them with quotes.

But what's up with that value for color? In HTML, you can specify color values by using either one of the set keywords (such as *red*, *blue*, and *orange*) or a hexadecimal value. The latter method is preferred because of its accuracy; after all, why settle for any arbitrary blue? The hexadecimal value consists of three sets of two hexadecimal characters, each representing the red, green, and blue values. A *hexadecimal value* is a range of characters from 0 to 9, followed by A to F. When you put two of them together, you get a value for each color; the higher the value, the more there is of that color. Table 5-1 shows a range of color values to demonstrate how they work.

Table 5-1 HTML Color Values

Color	Hexadecimal Value	RGB Value
Black	#000000	rgb(0,0,0)
Blue	#0000FF	rgb(0,0,255)
Dark Gray	#C0C0C0	rgb(192,192,192)
Green	#00FF00	rgb(0,255,0)
Red	#FF0000	rgb(255,0,0)
Turquoise	#00FFFF	rgb(0,255,255)
Violet	#FF00FF	rgb(255,0,255)
White	#FFFFFF	rgb(255,255,255)
Yellow	#FFFF00	rgb(255,255,0)

As you can see, you can also supply the color as RGB values, specifying a number between 0 and 255 for each of the red, green, and blue colors.

Having set the default values for these three text elements, you can specify additional rules for them later. This is where you get the term *cascading* in Cascading Style Sheets; the system combs through all the style sources to build the complete rules for each element. Type this as your next rule:

```
h1 {
    text-transform: uppercase;
    border-bottom: 1px solid #336699;
}
```

These declarations make the `h1` tag uppercase and place a solid blue line underneath it. And because of the previous statement, the `h1` tag continues to be both blue and in Lucida Sans.

This cascade effect is both very powerful and a potential source of unexpected behavior. When your style sheets grow in size, you may find yourself inadvertently writing rules that encompass elements you hadn't planned on. Later in this chapter, I cover some techniques for dealing with these problems.

Let's see how to style the `span` tag. In your HTML, you use `span` to specify a string of text that is styled differently than the rest. In this case, you want to provide a different color. Type this as your next style rule:

```
h1 span {
    color: #333333;
}
```

When two selectors are placed beside each other, this expresses a hierarchical relationship; this selector styles the `span` that's inside the `h1` tag. Save the document and then refresh the page in your browser to see the effect. At this point, it should look like Figure 5.4.

Now, just as you enhanced the default styling of the `h1` element, you can do the same for the other text elements. Type these style rules next:

```
p {
    font-size: 14px;
}

li {
    font-size: 14px;
    color: #000000;
}

strong {
    font-size: 16px;
    color: #A56E27;
}
blockquote p {
    font-family: Courier, serif;
}
```

```
span.attribution {
    font-style: italic;
}

a {
    color: #336699;
}
```

Figure 5.4

Your page with some initial styling applied

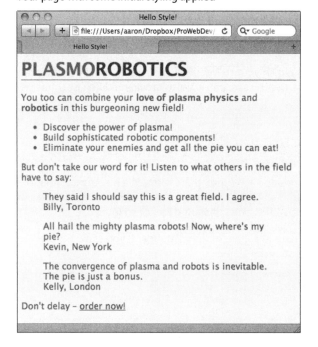

Lists in CSS also have a few styling possibilities. As you may recall from Chapter 4, there are two types of lists: *ordered* (which displays items numerically) and *unordered* (which displays items in bullet form). With CSS styles, you can control the number style to use on ordered lists (such as Arabic numerals, Roman numerals, and letters in upper- and lowercase), the kind of bullet the unordered list uses, and where the bullet is positioned relative to the item. In my own list, I've decided to change the style of the bullet from the default disc to the much-cooler square — after all, this is a site about robots! Type this rule in your style set:

```
ul {
    list-style-type: square;
}
```

When you save and reload the page, you should see a different bullet style.

So far, you've done little more than provide some text styles. This is traditional CSS and is already quite valuable for the web developer. Table 5-2 summarizes some of the useful text styles that you'll likely use.

Table 5-2 CSS Text Styles

Property	Description	Sample
`color`	Specifies a color for the text; units can be in keywords, hexadecimal, or rgb values.	`color: #000000;`
`font-family`	Sets the typeface and provides a list of fonts to specify the order in which they're used (depending on system availability)	`font-family: Helvetica, Arial, sans-serif;`
`font-size`	Sets the size of the font; units can be in pixels or ems.	`font-size: 14px;` `font-size: 1.2em;`
`font-style`	Styles the text with italic, oblique, or normal	`font-style: italic;`
`font-weight`	Styles the weight of text with bold, normal, bolder, or lighter	`font-weight: bold;`
`line-height`	Specifies the leading, which is the distance between lines in a paragraph; units can be a value, in pixels, or a percent.	`line-height: 160%;` `line-height: 14px;`
`list-style-image`	Provide your own bullet image for the `ul` tag.	`ul { list-style-image: url('lance.gif'); }`
`list-style-position`	Position the bullet or number either with a hanging indent (outside, which is the default) or within the text (inside).	`ul { list-style-position: inside; }`
`list-style-type`	Sets the style of the bullet (in a `ul` tag) or numeral (in an `ol` tag), as follows: **Bullets:** none, disc, square, circle **Numbers:** decimal, decimal-leading-zero, lower-roman, upper-roman, lower-alpha, upper-alpha, lower-greek, upper-greek	`ol { list-style-type: upper-greek; }`
`text-align`	Aligns text within an element; you can align left, center, right, or (full) justify.	`text-align: center;`
`text-decoration`	Provides ways to decorate the text with underline, line-through, overline, or (shudder) blink; you can set it to none to remove underlines from tags.	`text-decoration: underline;`
`text-transform`	Allows text to be capitalized, lowercase, or uppercase	`text-transform: capitalize;`

Now you're going to learn a little bit about the box model, which helps position elements.

The box model

There are two essential types of elements in HTML: inline elements and block elements. Think of *inline* as an element within a stream of text, such as the `span`, `strong`, and `b` tags. *Block* elements are free-standing elements. Think of the `p` and `blockquote` tags. For these block-level elements, CSS provides padding, borders, and margins. These three specifications make up the CSS box model, which treats every block level element as a box. Figure 5.5 shows how these specifications relate to the content.

Figure 5.5

The box model: padding, border, and margin around a block element

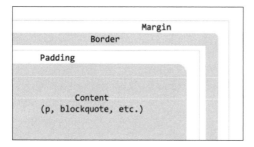

You can specify values for each of the padding, border, and margin elements of an item. You can also specify values for each side of each of these: `margin-top` or `padding-left`, for example. For this document, you'll specify the same value for all sides of each of these specs. Type the following rule next in your style definition:

```
blockquote {
    background-color: #EEEEEE;
    padding: 5px;
    margin: 2px;
    border: 1px solid #336699;
}
```

The values that you end up supplying to the padding, border, and margin are usually the result of trial and error to achieve the look you're after. In this case, I found that a padding of 5 pixels provides the correct-looking distance between my text and the border. A margin of 2 pixels provides a subtle bump for my `blockquote` box. Feel free to play with the numbers yourself to get a feel for how these values affect the look of your layout.

Table 5-3 summarizes the box model properties.

Table 5-3 CSS Box Model Styles

Property	Description	Sample
`border`	Sets all border sides in one rule; you can set border width, kind of stroke, and color; stroke choices include solid, dotted, dashed, double, groove, and none.	`border: 2px dashed #FF0000;`
`border-left` `border-right` `border-top` `border-bottom`	Set the specs for individual sides	`border-left: 1px solid #000000;`
`display`	Manually sets the element as a block or inline element; you can also set it to none to have the element invisible on the page.	`display: inline;`
`margin`	Sets the distance from the border to the box's surrounding elements; this sets all sides with one value or individual sides in the order of top-right-bottom-left.	`margin: 20px 5px 20px 10px;`
`margin-left` `margin-right` `margin-top` `margin-bottom`	Set the specs for individual sides	`margin-bottom: 10px;`
`padding`	The combined value for each side of the box; this can be set either one value for all or individually in the order of top-right-bottom-left.	`padding: 0px 5px 10px 5px;`
`padding-left` `padding-right` `padding-top` `padding-bot- tom`	Set the size of individual sides	`padding-left: 10px;`

To wrap up this `hellostyle.html` document, I thought it would be useful to demonstrate a pseudo-class selector. As I said earlier, pseudo classes are special cases for particular situations. Type this special case as your final rule for this document:

```
a:hover {
    color: #A56E27;
}
```

The `:hover` pseudo class takes effect when the user's mouse passes over the anchor tag. By setting the `color` property, you see the text color change when you move to the link. This is probably the most common case of the pseudo classes that you'll use, but there are others, as shown in Table 5-4.

Table 5-4 CSS Pseudo Classes

Property	Description	Sample
`:first-child`	Styles an element that is the first child of the parent element; think of the first p tag as having emphasis.	`p:first-child{ font-size:24px; }`
`:hover`	The style takes effect when the mouse is over the element.	`a:hover { color:#336699; }`
`:link`	Styles an unvisited link	`a:link{ font-weight:bold; }`
`:visited`	Styles a visited link	`a:visited{ font-weight:normal; }`

When you've finished styling the document, you should end up with something similar to Figure 5.6.

Figure 5.6

The final `hellostyle.html` file

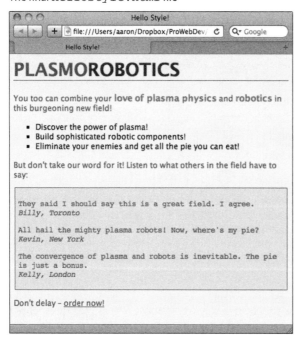

Formatting tables

When you're not using tables to lay out your pages anymore, you'll come to appreciate their actual purpose: to cleanly and beautifully render data. Product lists, sports scores, addresses, content-managed pages on a site, and much more can be rendered within tables. With the help of some CSS styling, you can turn dry facts into a crisp presentation.

You're going to create a new HTML file to build your sample table. Open your text editor and then using the same header content as with your previous files, type the following within the body tags:

```
<h1>Plasmo<span>Robotics</span></h1>
<p>Now you can order your own PlasmoRobotics kit! Make your
    choice below:</p>
<table>

    <thead>
        <tr>
                <th colspan="2">Product</th>
                <th>Price</th>
                <th>Description</td>
                <th class="last">Rating</th>
        </tr>
    </thead>

    <tbody>
        <tr>
                <td class="image"><img src="images/bot1.gif"
alt="The Chieftain" /></td>
                <td class="name">The Chieftain</td>
                <td>$399.99</td>
                <td>A solid performer with a taste for blueberry,
The Chieftain will be sure to entertain and enflame.</td>
                <td>&#9733;&#9733;&#9733;</td>
        </tr>

        <tr class="alt">
                <td class="image"><img src="images/bot2.gif"
alt="Alfa" /></td>
                <td class="name">Alfa</td>
                <td>$99.99</td>
                <td>The little PlasmoBot that could! Featuring
whistling show tunes and a penchant for dancing. A crowd
favorite!</td>
                <td>&#9733;&#9733;&#9733;&#9733;</td>
        </tr>

        <tr>
```

```
            <td class="image"><img src="images/bot3.gif"
alt="Groverdale" /></td>
            <td class="name">Groverdale</td>
            <td>$499.99</td>
            <td>It's super! This is our most popular bot. Has to
be seen to be believed!</td>
            <td>&#9733;&#9733;&#9733;&#9733;</td>
        </tr>

        <tr class="alt">
            <td class="image"><img src="images/bot4.gif"
alt="Parsley" /></td>
            <td class="name">Parsley</td>
            <td>$139.99</td>
            <td>Essential features dominate this workhorse. You
never have to think twice when Parsley's around — point and
scoot, that's what Parsley says.</td>
            <td>&#9733;&#9733;</td>
        </tr>

    </tbody>
</table>
```

Save your file as `hellotablestyle.html` and then open it in your browser. It should look similar to Figure 5.7.

CROSS-REF

You can find the `hellotablestyle.html` file and the images in this code on the website for this book: `www.wileydevreference.com`.

Before you proceed with styling this document, let me note a couple of points of interest in this HTML code. First, I created a table header that spans two columns, allowing a single header to represent both the product image and product name cells.

Secondly, the rating cell provides a good opportunity to make use of *HTML entities*. These are characters that can't normally be referenced on a standard keyboard. These entities come in many forms, from diacritical marks and accents, to various arrow symbols, to mathematical operators, to crazy stuff such as snowmen, sunshine, and pointing fingers. Each of these symbols is expressed with the ampersand, the pound sign followed by a number or name, and then a semicolon. There are hundreds of them; when I want something unique, I search for "html entities" on my favorite search engine. The W3C also provides a list of officially recognized ones at `www.w3.org/TR/html4/sgml/entities.html`. The star that I use in my example is not one of these, so if you're browsing in Opera for Windows, you won't see it.

Figure 5.7

The `hellotablestyle.html` file without styles

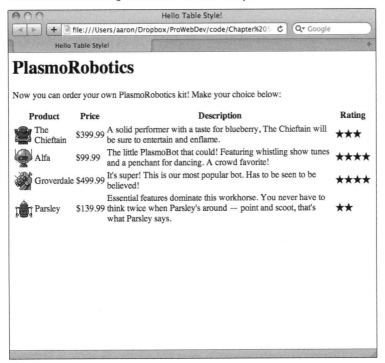

As I noted in Chapter 4, there are quite a few tags that make up an HTML table. While it makes tables laborious to code, each tag offers an opportunity to apply some CSS to it.

For this exercise, you're going to create a separate style sheet. I'm doing it here for two reasons. First, there are a larger number of styles, and having them in the HTML file becomes cumbersome. Second, you'll also use some styles that you set up for the last exercise, and there isn't enough time in the day to be repeating yourself.

Within the `head` tag of your HTML document, remove the `style` tag (if it's there) and then replace it with this `link` tag:

```
<link rel="stylesheet" href="hellostyle.css" type="text/css" />
```

The only attribute you need to change in this tag is the location of your CSS file. I named mine `hellostyle.css`, so make sure you match your file name to this.

CROSS-REF

You can find the `hellostyle.css` file on the website for this book: `www.wileydevreference.com`.

There's no fanfare to beginning a CSS file; you start by defining some of the same styles that you used in the previous example. You're going to set the style for the heading and the page background as well as set type defaults for all the elements you'll work with. Create a new text document and then type this code:

```
body {
    background-color: #F6F6F6;
}
h1, p, th, td, p {
    font-family: "Lucida Sans", Helvetica, Arial, sans-serif;
    color: #336699;
}
h1 {
    text-transform: uppercase;
    border-bottom: 1px solid #336699;
}
h1 span {
    color: #333333;
}
```

The only difference between this set of style rules and the previous example is the inclusion of the selectors for the `th` and `td` tags. Including these selectors sets the typeface and color for text that appears in your table cells.

The remaining style definitions are targeted against the elements that make up the table.

Recall from my explanation of the box model that the padding represents the distance from the edges of the block element to the border. This essential definition also holds true for table cells; new CSS users often confuse a table cell as the content, when in fact it's the stuff inside that counts. By default, there's a slight bit of padding, but as you can see when you look at the page now, there's not very much at all — the cells are closely grouped, both horizontally and vertically. So, you'll first increase the padding to give your table a little breathing room. Type this as your next style rule in your external style sheet:

```
th, td {
    padding: 10px;
}
```

By setting both the `th` and `td` selectors, you're taking care of both kinds of table cells. When you reload your page, the cells should have quite a bit more space between them. See Figure 5.8 for a comparison.

Figure 5.8

The table without padding (top) and with padding applied (bottom)

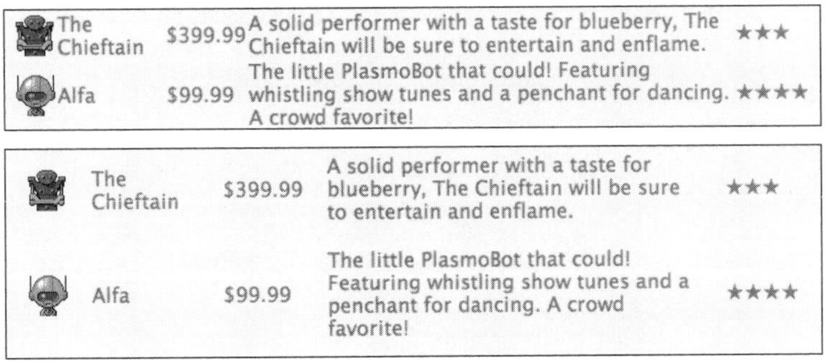

The extra space is helpful, but you need more. So, you're going to add a border to the table cells. For now, you're just going to do this for the `td` tags:

```
td {
    vertical-align: top;
    border: 1px solid #336699;
}
```

While I'm at it, I'm setting the `vertical-align` property for content within the cells; this binds the cell content to the top rather than floating it in the middle, which is the default setting. This is mostly a matter of taste, but I prefer my cell contents to line up across the top.

The `border` property works exactly as it does for other block-level elements: the line width, style, and color are in one declaration, and the border is positioned outside the padding. But there's a problem when you use a border on a cell. Save your CSS file and then reload the page; Figure 5.9 shows what you should see.

While the `vertical-align` property worked just fine (and looks sharp, thanks very much!), you can see that because every cell has a border, you can actually see the border of every cell, with a distracting gap between each. Quite frankly, this looks dreadful and not at all what you would expect in a table. Luckily, the designers of the CSS standard see things my way and have provided a style that removes this effect. So, you can apply this declaration to the entire table:

```
table {
    border-collapse: collapse;
}
```

Save and reload; you should find your table cells behaving properly now.

Figure 5.9

A table with a `border` property applied to all cells

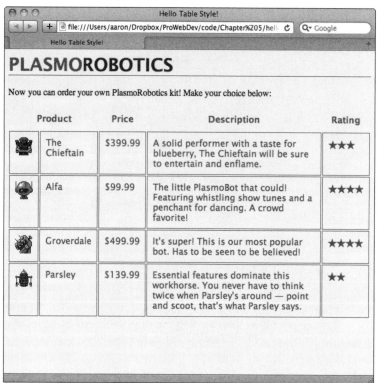

You've done some good work on those table cells, so let's see about improving the header cells, as they're looking quite plain. I sometimes like to give them a darker color to provide contrast over the table body. Add this style to your CSS file:

```
th {
    text-align: left;
    background-color: #336699;
    color: #FFFFFF;
    border-right: 1px solid #FFFFFF;
}
```

Here, you're overriding several defaults of the `th` element: You're aligning the text to the left instead of the default center, and you're changing the text color to white and adding a white right border because you're changing the background color to blue. This white border lines up with the column borders of the `body` cells.

Save and reload your page. This looks good, but take an extra-close look at the right edge of the last header cell. See how it doesn't quite line up with the right border of the body cells? That's because of the header cell's right border; you just can't see it because it's also surrounded by white.

To compensate for this unintentional effect, you have to apply a style specifically to that last header cell. This is where the class selectors come in handy. By applying a class tag to the final cell (recall, the code is <th class="last">Rating</th>), you can use the class selector to target just that cell. Type this as the next style:

```
th.last {
    border-right: 1px solid #336699;
}
```

By setting a border with the same color as the header cell, you effectively extend it by one pixel, thereby smoothing that right edge. See Figure 5.10 for a before-and-after comparison.

Figure 5.10

Fixing the right side of the header cell: before (left) and after (right)

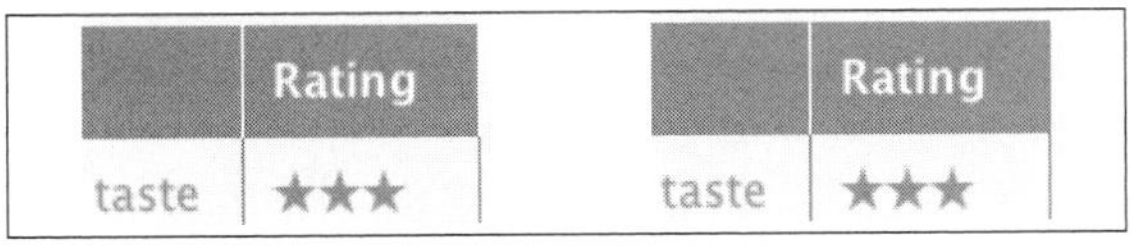

Am I seriously making a big deal out of one stray pixel? There are many people that wouldn't even notice this defect, so why waste your time on it? The answer comes down to quality. How much do you care about your product? That's not a rhetorical question. In the world of web development, precision counts; an indifferent pixel here and there can add up to a sloppy-looking site. And while the web is littered with sloppy sites, you can bet that their authors aren't around for long to profit from that kind of work. Don't be one of them!

Now that you have a fine-looking header row, let's return to the body cells for some final tweaking. As you'll recall, you created a two-column span for your Product header cell. The purpose of this was to provide a single header over two separate columns dedicated to the product: the name of the product and an image.

That appears to work well, but I'm not happy with the look of these two columns. I want the layout advantage of having the image in its own cell (by default, if the image shares a cell with the name, you'll run into a host of ugly layout issues — give it a try if you don't believe me), but I don't want it to look like I've got separate cells. The solution is to rid each cell of its adjoining borders.

From your newfound experience with your header cell's right border, you can likely guess the solution: You're going to apply a class tag to the image and product name cells and then style their borders away. Recall the HTML for the first two cells of the row:

```
<td class="image"><img src="images/bot1.gif" alt="The Chieftain"
    /></td>
<td class="name">The Chieftain</td>
```

To each of these cells (and you do the same for every row), you've applied the class `"image"` and `"name"`, respectively. Now you can target them with your selectors. In your style sheet file, add these rules:

```
td.image {
    border-right: none;
}
td.name {
    border-left: none;
    font-weight: bold;
}
```

For the image cell, you're specifying the right border (the one adjacent to the name cell) as `none`. Conversely, you eliminate the left border on the name cell (again, the one adjacent to the image cell). The result: no border between these cells, providing the illusion that they're the same cell, as shown in Figure 5.11.

Figure 5.11

The product cells give the illusion of being a single cell.

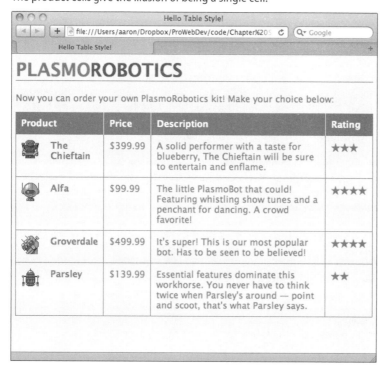

Before you leave table styling, I'd like to show you one more technique. You've probably seen tables that alternate row colors in order to make the tables easier to read. This is particularly useful when you have wide and long tables; the alternating row colors allow your eye to move across the row much more readily.

To accomplish this feat, you're going to apply styling to the `tr` tag. But because you can't apply the style to every row, you have to give each applicable row a `class` tag. That's why, for every second row in the HTML, I've added an `"alt"` class:

```
<tr class="alt">
```

Now you can add the final style to your CSS file:

```
tr.alt {
    background-color: #EEEEEE;
}
```

Save the CSS file and then reload the page in your browser; the page should look similar to Figure 5.12. Now you're cooking!

Figure 5.12

The final page, complete with alternating row colors

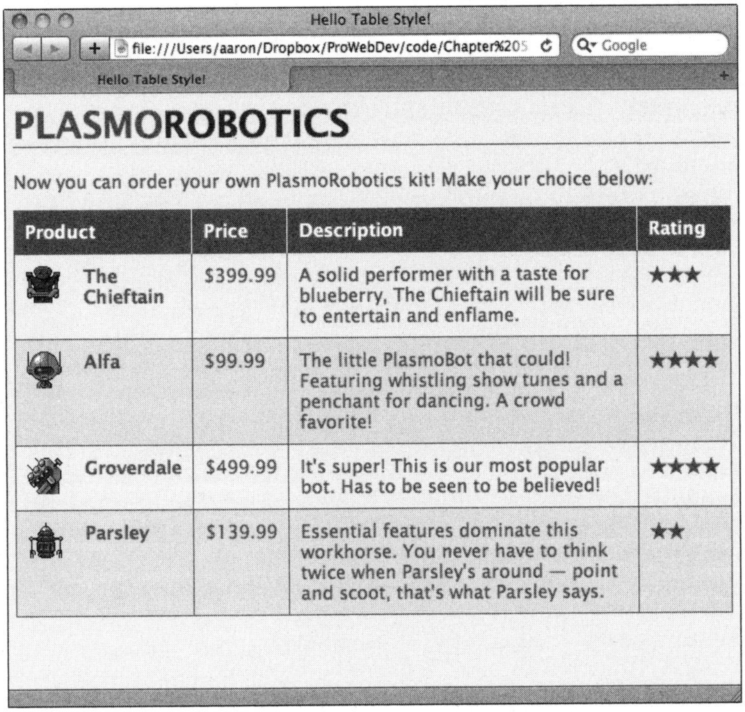

Styling forms

You've already seen how semantically built tables in HTML can be incredibly boring; the same is certainly true for forms. To see how CSS can add a dash of life to these tedious workhorses, you'll use the same form you created in Chapter 4. While this HTML file has the same fields as the previous form, I've made a few changes: I've created a link to the same style sheet I used in the table example, and I've added the h1 and p tags that make up the top part of the pages for the PlasmoRobotics site. The payoff here is what you get for free — instant style on the page background and these header elements.

Finally, I've added some styles around the individual form elements that will act as the hooks for the style declarations. To summarize:

- **Every line (the question and the form input) is surrounded by** p **tags to keep the lines separated.**
- **Every question is surrounded by a** label **tag.** This both increases the usability of the form (remember, clicking on a label activates its field) and lets you style the label, on which you'll hang the declarations of the question class.
- **Because the** input **and** select **tags are there, you don't need to frame them with anything; you can use selectors to target them exactly.** However, the Submit button is also an input, and that requires some additional styling; thus, you put an id attribute on that tag so you can target it.

Create a new file and then type this code:

```
<!DOCTYPE html PUBLIC "-//W3C//DTD XHTML 1.0 Strict//EN"
    "http://www.w3.org/TR/xhtml1/DTD/xhtml1-strict.dtd">
<html xmlns="http://www.w3.org/1999/xhtml" xml:lang="en"
    lang="en">
    <head>
        <title>PlasmoRobotics | Contact Us</title>
        <meta name="description" content="A page to describe HTML
basics." />
        <meta name="keywords" content="hello world, html, basics,
coding, fun" />
        <meta name="author" content="Aaron Vegh" />
        <meta http-equiv="Content-Type" content="text/
html;charset=ISO-8859-1" />
        <link rel="stylesheet" href="hellostyle.css" type="text/
css" />
    </head>
    <body>
        <h1>Plasmo<span>Robotics</span></h1>
        <p>Contact us today! Just fill out the form below:</p>

        <form action="submit.php" method="post" id="contact_form">

          <p><label for="name" class="question">Your Name</label>
```

```
        <input type="text" id="name" name="name" /></p>

        <p><label for="email" class="question">Your Email
Address</label>
        <input type="text" name="email" id="email" /></p>

        <p><label for="number" class="question">How many do you
need?</label>
        <input type="radio" name="drones" value="1-5"
id="one2five" /> <label for="one2five">1-5</label>
        <input type="radio" name="drones" value="6-10"
id="six2ten" /> <label for="six2ten">6-10</label>
        <input type="radio" name="drones" value="11+"
id="elevenPlus" /> <label for="elevenPlus">11+</label></p>

        <p><label for="features" class="question">What features
do you look for in a robot drone?</label>
        <input type="checkbox" name="features[]" value="cackle"
id="cackle" /> <label for="cackle">Evil Cackle</label><br/>
        <input type="checkbox" name="features[]" value="lasers"
id="lasers" /> <label for="lasers">Frickin' Lasers</
label><br/>
        <input type="checkbox" name="features[]" value="hat"
id="hat" /> <label for="hat">Go-Go Gadget Hat</label><br/>
        <input type="checkbox" name="features[]" value="toaster"
id="toaster" /> <label for="toaster">Built-in Toaster</
label><br/>
        <input type="checkbox" name="features[]" value="laundry"
id="laundry" /> <label for="laundry">Washing Clothes</label></p>

        <p><label for="purpose" class="question">You'll be using
your drones to</label>
        <select id="purpose" name="purpose">
            <option>Choose one...</option>
            <optgroup label="Recreational">
               <option value="fishing">Fishing</option>
               <option value="frisbee">Frisbee</option>
            </optgroup>
            <optgroup label="Industrial">
               <option value="welding">Welding</option>
               <option value="bedmaking">Bed-making</option>
            </optgroup>
        </select></p>

        <p><input type="submit" value="Send Form" id="submit" /></p>

    </form>
  </body>
</html>
```

Let's turn to your CSS file, `hellostyle.css`. When you come to the point where your CSS is supporting multiple pages, it can start to be difficult to know what style belongs where. That's why I try to partition my code with comments. *Comments* are lines of code that are ignored by the system; they're there only for your benefit. In HTML, they look like this:

```
<!-- This is an HTML comment; anything between these tags will be
     ignored. -->
```

And here's a comment in CSS:

```
/* This is a comment in CSS; anything between these symbols will
   be ignored. */
```

So, in the `hellostyle.css` file, you can currently see two groups of tags: those for any page (such as the `body`, `h1`, and `p` selectors) and those for the tables. So, prior to the start of the table's styling tags, I've placed this comment:

```
/* Styles for hellotablestyle.html */
```

And at the end of this code, at the bottom of the file, I've placed this comment:

```
/* Styles for helloformstyle.html */
```

Before you get into the CSS, I need to talk about the somewhat-complex realm of form styling. While there are no special form styles (as there are for tables, for example), there are significant differences in the way form elements can be styled depending on the browser. Simply put, some form elements are more amenable to styling than others, and how they receive their styling can vary; a certain amount of slippage between browsers should be expected.

Let's have a look at the form tags that you can expect to have the best luck with:

- **Text fields.** You can have good control over the appearance of text inside an `<input type="text">` field or a `<textarea>` tag. You can control the size and style of font, color, line height, and more. Text fields also respond to box model properties (padding, border, and margin), and you can set background colors. You can also set the width of these fields, but you can only set the height of a text area.

- **Select tags.** Drop-down menus are also quite amenable to styling, taking the same properties as text fields.

- **Check boxes and radio buttons.** You'll find yourself more limited with these elements; these controls are so small and well-defined that you would be advised to leave them in their default appearance anyway.

- **Buttons.** Both the `<input type="submit">` and `button` tags allow good control over appearance. Set fonts, colors, backgrounds, and positioning with impunity.

With great power comes great responsibility. It's worth noting at this point that users have to be able to recognize your form elements for what they are! If you go too far in styling your text boxes, for example, they may no longer look like text boxes. So, keep your styling subtle and tasteful.

You've now typed (or copied, perhaps, from the files on the website) the HTML and saved your document as `helloformstyle.html`. When you open it in your browser, you'll find a rather plain-looking form, as shown in Figure 5.13.

CROSS-REF
You can find the `helloformstyle.html` file on the website for this book:
`www.wileydevreference.com`.

Figure 5.13

The contact form without styling

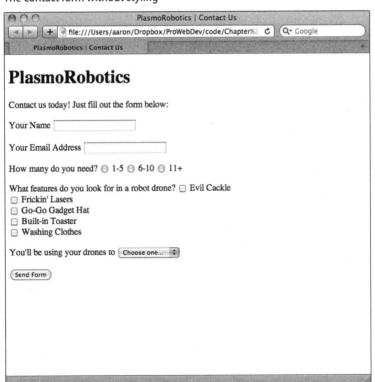

By now, most of your work is done, but you're going to dramatically change the look of this form with just four style declarations. As you create these statements, save and reload your page to study the effect these rules are having. In many cases, my values are arbitrary and completely subjective, so alter the amounts to your heart's content, and make sure you understand the consequences of your actions.

Let's start with the form. I could have used a `form` selector, but just in case there are other forms on the site being served by this style sheet, I gave it an `id`, which is a unique element in the scope of a page. Type this style rule:

```
#contact_form {
    border: 1px solid #336699;
    width: 550px;
    padding: 10px;
}
```

Here, you're giving the form a set width; this allows you to better control the appearance of the form and provides a neat outline to match the look of the site. The padding puts some space between the form elements and that border.

Now let's look at the individual questions of the form. A form looks its best when the elements are arranged in neat columns; the haphazard layout of the unformatted form is a real impediment to usability. To accomplish this, you'll use a new style called the *float*. This property takes a block-level element and pops it out of the regular flow of elements on the page. A float can either be to the left or right; all elements that neighbor the float flow around it. Traditionally, a float might be used for an image that sits within a block of text.

Here, you're going to set each question element to be the same width and then float it to the left margin. That way, the question element will look like a block sitting against the margin, with each one the same width. Their form elements within the same `p` tag will nestle up beside them. Here's the style declaration:

```
#contact_form .question {
    float: left;
    width: 250px;
    margin-right: 10px;
    text-align: right;
    font-weight: bold;
}
```

To improve readability, I've also provided some text formatting: aligning the question text to the right, bolding it, and using the `margin` property to open a small gutter between your two columns. If you refresh your page now, you'll see that the form is dramatically better.

The next style is pure aesthetics. You're going to style the `input` elements, so the type in the text fields is larger and the style of those elements better matches the site. But the elements still look like text fields:

```
#contact_form input, #contact_form select {
    font-size: 14px;
    font-family: "Lucida Sans", Helvetica, Arial, sans-serif;
    background-color: #dff3fe;
    border: 1px solid #336699;
}
```

The selector covers both the `input` and `select` tags, setting both the font attributes and some new colors.

When you reload at this point, you'll notice that in addition to the text fields and the pop-up menu, the Submit button has also changed. That's because the Submit button is also the product of an `input` tag, a fact that's always seemed odd to me. So, very often, you'll find that you need to treat this tag a bit differently. You'll do that now. While the appearance of the button is fine, I would like it to line up with the other form elements. Using the `id` attribute in the HTML file, I can target the button directly and then push it to the right:

```
#submit {
    margin-left: 260px;
}
```

The value for the `margin-left` attribute is derived from the width of the question element plus the 10-pixel gutter that you created.

Save and reload the page. Perfect? Not quite. That fourth question, with the series of check boxes, isn't flowing properly, as shown in Figure 5.14.

Figure 5.14

Problems with a list of check boxes

Can you tell what's happened here? The question element is floating, so the text flows around it. Remember, a floating element is like a block; its height is only as great as what's needed to contain the content. Perhaps the best way to fix this is to specify a more advantageous height. You could do this by adding an `id` attribute to this element, but for the sake of completeness, you'll do it by styling with an embedded attribute. In your HTML file, find this text:

```
<p><label for="features" class="question">What features do you
    look for in a robot drone?</label>
```

And change it to this:

```
<p><label for="features" class="question"
    style="height:100px">What features do you look for in a robot
    drone?</label>
```

The `style` attribute allows you to type any CSS declaration, and it will apply only to that tag. This isn't really that different from using HTML to format your document, so I don't recommend it.

Save and reload your page; you should now see an orderly, well-designed form, as shown in Figure 5.15. Very smart!

Figure 5.15

The completed form

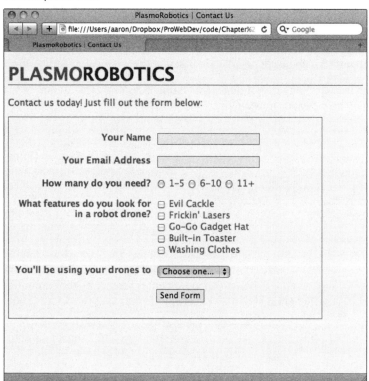

Perhaps you're asking yourself: Could a table have been used to lay this out? Absolutely. One of the strengths of table layout is its ability to arrange content in neat columns. But with CSS, you can do it in less code and with greater elegance.

You're done with forms and with the basics of CSS. It's time now to buckle up: You're going to use CSS to lay out entire pages.

Page Layout with CSS

What you've seen of CSS thus far has been impressive: the ability to globally style elements on any number of web pages by using easy-to-understand selectors. You have good control over the appearance of all page elements, and you can readily style tables and forms. And the good news is that all the features I've discussed so far will work fine in every browser.

But the picture grows a little cloudy from this point on because when it comes to using CSS to lay out pages, browser support becomes an issue. As I said at the outset of this chapter, the key approach is to follow the standards and then implement workarounds for the noncompliant browsers; after all, those crusty old browsers will disappear eventually.

Introducing the div tag

The key ingredient for CSS-based layout is an HTML tag that I haven't discussed yet: the `div` tag. This tag creates a division in your document; any content placed within a `div` tag represents a semantic unit. It's a block-level tag that's intended to have any formatting you choose.

By default, the browser treats a `div` similar to a paragraph tag, with multiple `div` tags taking up the full available width and stacking on top of each other. But when you start adding elements to `div` tags and style them correctly, you'll gain finer control over where content appears on a page.

But before you do that, you need to understand the structure of a web page so you know where the `div` tag comes into play. Figure 5.16 shows some popular web pages. All four of these designs are quite different; they have unique tasks to accomplish, and they appear to do them in very different ways, with varying degrees of success.

Figure 5.16

A selection of websites

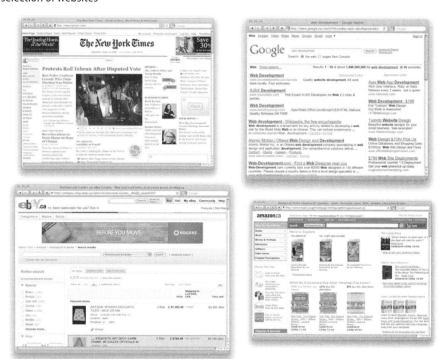

But if you were to disassemble these designs and highlight the areas where their main `div` tags are, you'd find that these sites would look very similar! Compare the sites in Figure 5.16 with an overlay of their `div`s in Figure 5.17.

All the sites have a top-level, page-spanning element that's traditionally known as the *header*. This usually contains the site's logo and sometimes the navigation, advertising, and other global links.

The rest of the page is divided into two or three columns. Some sites may take it further, dividing content within columns into more units (such as the right column on the *New York Times* site), but that doesn't affect the general layout.

There are too many sites out there to claim a catchall rule, but this layout is one of the most common types you'll find. And if you understand how to code a two- and three-column layout, you can do anything else.

Figure 5.17

Revealed: These sites share a similar layout.

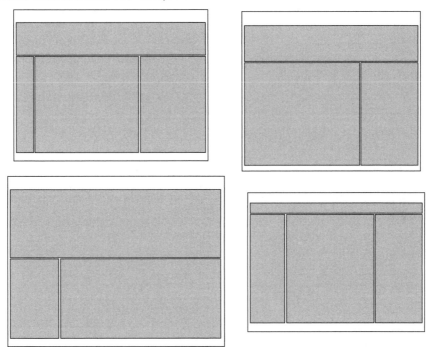

In the rest of this section, I'm going to demonstrate these different column layouts by using a very basic wireframe. Once you get these concepts down, I'll walk you through a detailed tutorial on creating a full-featured CSS-powered page.

Coding a two-column layout

You're going to start this lesson by writing the HTML that you'll be styling. You're going to love the simplicity of this code. Create a new document in your text editor and then type the following:

```
<html>
<head>
   <title>CSS Layout Playground | 2 Columns</title>
</head>
<body>
   <div id="header"></div>
```

```
        <div id="left_column"></div>
        <div id="right_column"></div>
        <div id="footer"></div>
    </body>
    </html>
```

You could start every document this way: Frame out your page by using `div` tags and then provide each `div` with an `id` attribute, which you'll use to style it. Once you're happy with the general layout, you can start filling in the sections.

For this exercise and the next, you'll embed your styles in the `head` tag. As you've done before, add a `style` tag between the `head` tags and then type your style rules there.

The header requires no special attention from a layout perspective, but you'll give it a few styles so you can see it on the page. You'll set a `height` in order for it to show up on the page when it doesn't have any content. You don't need to give it a `width` because a `div`'s default width is the span of the containing element — the window, in this case. You'll also set a background color and a bottom margin:

```
#header {
    height: 80px;
    background-color: #EEEEEE;
    margin-bottom: 10px;
}
```

Here's where the fun begins. You'll set the positioning characteristics for the left column `div`. To accomplish this, you'll apply a `float` value of `left`; this pushes it against the left side of the page, and all other content can flow around it. All floated elements should also have a width, so you'll set the column width at 250 pixels. Then, to put a gutter between this column and the right side, you'll add a 10-pixel right margin:

```
#left_column {
        float: left;
        width: 250px;
        margin-right: 10px;
        height: 300px;
        background-color: #999999;
    }
```

For the right column, you'll set a left margin value that pushes it to the right of the left column. The value of the left margin is equivalent to the width of the left column plus any padding, border, and margin it may have, so the left margin will be 260 pixels (the left column's width of 250 plus its 10-pixel margin). Without this margin on the right column, it would sit flush against the left margin of the page:

```
#right_column {
    margin-left: 260px;
    height: 300px;
    background-color: #DDDDDD;
}
```

Finally, you'll use the same technique for the footer as you employed for the header, with the only difference being the use of the top `margin` property to put some space between it and the columns above:

```
#footer {
    margin-top: 10px;
    height: 80px;
    background-color: #EEEEEE;
}
```

Save the file as `layout_playground_2col.html` and then view the page in your browser. You'll see different shades of gray highlighting the layout you've created, as shown in Figure 5.18.

C R O S S - R E F

You can find the `layout_playground_2col.html` file on the website for this book: `www.wileydevreference.com`.

Figure 5.18

The completed two-column layout

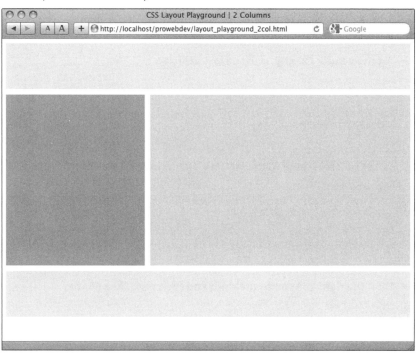

Coding a three-column layout

To do the three-column layout, you'll follow a similar principle. You'll float the left column to the left and the right column to the right, and you'll set the proper margins on the middle column.

The order in which the columns appear in the HTML is important on this one. Because floating elements are positioned based on the elements they follow, you can't place them after the main column as you might be tempted to try.

Create a new file and then type this code:

```html
<html>
<head>
    <title>CSS Layout Playground | 2 Columns</title>
</head>
<body>
        <div id="header"></div>
        <div id="left_column"></div>
        <div id="right_column"></div>
        <div id="mid_column"></div>
        <div id="footer"></div>
</body>
</html>
```

As before, you'll place your styles in the `style` tag in the document's `head`. Follow these steps:

1. **Set the header exactly as in the last exercise:**

```css
#header {
    height: 80px;
    background-color: #EEEEEE;
    margin-bottom: 10px;
}
```

2. **Float the left column to the left and then provide a width:**

```css
#left_column {
    float: left;
    width: 200px;
    height: 300px;
    background-color: #999999;
}
```

3. **Float the right column to the right and then provide a width:**

```css
#right_column {
    float: right;
    width: 200px;
    height: 300px;
    background-color: #DDDDDD;
}
```

4. **For the middle column, set the left and right margins so they're pushed between the other columns.** Again, take your total margin value from the widths and margins of those columns:

```
#mid_column {
    margin: 0px 210px 0px 210px;
    height: 300px;
    background-color: #d7d7d7;
}
```

5. **Style the footer the same as you did in the previous exercise:**

```
#footer {
    margin-top: 10px;
    height: 80px;
    background-color: #EEEEEE;
}
```

6. **Save this document as** `layout_playground_3col.html` **and then view it in your browser, as shown in Figure 5.19.**

Figure 5.19

The completed three-column layout

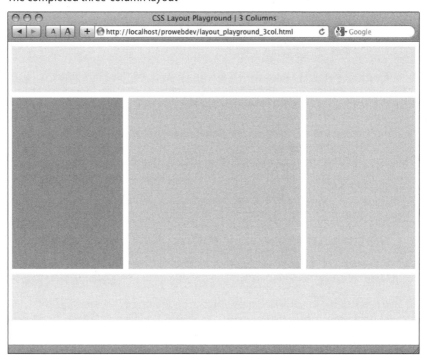

CROSS-REF
You can find the `layout_playground_3col.html` file on the website for this book: www.wileydevreference.com.

Fixed or flexible layout

The exercises you just completed are examples of *flexible* layout; regardless of the size of your browser window, the columns flow to fill it. This is achieved by setting a width for the floating columns but leaving it unspecified for the other column.

When a `div`'s width isn't provided, its width stretches to the width of its containing element; in this case, it's the width of the window — barring, of course, the margins placed on it to reveal the floating columns.

But a common layout technique is the *fixed* layout; no matter what size your browser window, the page contents remain the same width. There are good arguments for going either way in your own site design, but changing your mind couldn't be easier. Because the width of elements is set to its containing element, you need only drop a container atop them. So, to make your three-column layout a fixed width, use the following code:

```
<div id="wrapper">
        <div id="header"></div>
        <div id="left_column"></div>
        <div id="right_column"></div>
        <div id="mid_column"></div>
        <div id="footer"></div>
</div>
```

The `wrapper` tag contains the elements inside. Then, you can style that wrapper with a width, such as 960 pixels. You might also want to center the whole thing in the browser window instead of it being left justified. That code would look like this:

```
#wrapper {
    width:960px;
    margin: 0px auto 0px auto;
}
```

Those are enough gray boxes. Let's create a real web page now.

Creating an entire layout

In this example, you're going to lay out a page by using the techniques that you learned in Chapter 4 as well as in this chapter. The final result should look like Figure 5.20.

You can follow along by downloading the code from this book's website: www.wileydevreference.com. You'll find two files: `plasmo.html` and `plasmo.css`. I'll go through both files, calling out the important parts.

Figure 5.20

The completed page

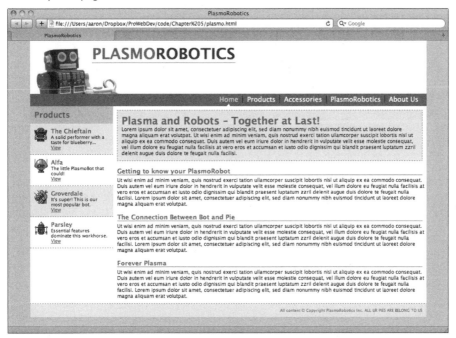

Setting up

The box model is the cause of some difficulty for new users, who not only find the principle difficult to pick up but who also run into unexpected behavior. In large part, this is because most elements are rendered with default margins. If you look again at the playground layouts you created in the last two exercises, you'll see that the header and columns are offset from the edge of the window; this is (for Safari, at least) evidence that the body tag has a 10-pixel margin. Different browsers may — and do — have their own rules.

One way to tackle this problem is to start with zero. So, when I create a new layout in CSS, I like to ensure that, by default, all elements have no padding, borders, or margins. To do this, you use the magic of the wildcard selector: an asterisk.

The top of my CSS file contains *global settings*, which form the basis for the rules to come. You set the background color for the page and default fonts:

```
*   {
    margin:0px;
    border:0px;
    padding:0px;
}
```

```
body {
    background-color: #CCCCCC;
}
h1, h2, h3, h4, li, p {
    font-family: "Lucida Sans", Helvetica, Arial, sans-serif;
    color: #336699;
}
```

Layout

The next task is to set up the layout. Your HTML code specifies a two-column layout: the `header`, `sidebar`, `main_content`, and `footer`. You'll style these `divs` by using the same techniques as in the previous exercise. Using a wrapper, you'll constrain the layout to 960 pixels and then center it on the page. For the header, you'll add an image to the background.

You're also going to set its positioning, which you'll need when you get to the header styles. There are two position styles: *relative* and *absolute*. When you use the former, you can move the styled element in any direction, relative to its default position. When you use the latter, you essentially pop the element out of the page flow, making its position relative to the top-left corner of the browser window.

As you can see in this case, you set the header's position to relative, but don't move it. Why not? Because an element that has position becomes its own coordinate space; if there's an element inside that's given absolute position, you can precisely control where it sits within its relatively positioned parent element:

```
#wrapper {
    width: 960px;
    margin: 0px auto 0px auto;
    background-color: #FFFFFF;
}
#header {
    height: 153px;
    position: relative;
    background-image: url('images/plasmobot.jpg');
    background-repeat: no-repeat;
}
#sidebar {
    width: 200px;
    float: left;
}
#main_content {
    margin-left: 210px;
}
#footer {
    margin-top: 10px;
    border-top: 1px dashed #336699;
    padding: 10px;
    background-color: #EEEEEE;
}
```

CROSS-REF
You can find the `plasmobot.jpg` file on the website for this book: `www.wileydevreference.com`.

Header and navigation

The navigation is part of the header in this file, and you use the `list` tag to render it in good semantic fashion. Note the classes added to the first and last elements. The first is to style the current page (notice that there's no hyperlink here), and the last is to let you remove formatting from the last list item.

See how the element containing the navigation has been positioned absolutely? This rule, combined with setting the `top` property, allows you to precisely drop the container holding the navigation where you want it. If the `header` tag wasn't positioned relatively, then this absolute attribute would be pressed right up against the browser window's left edge. Try it if you don't believe me!

Another advantage of using absolute elements comes when you see that they sit on top of other elements. This lets you stack elements on top of each other by using the positioning properties to overlap. Although not demonstrated here, there's a companion property called `z-index` that allows you to control the order in which stacked elements appear. This technique is commonly used on those fancy new Web 2.0 sites, which can't help but put badges all over their logos, usually with the big word Beta! inside.

Another common technique used here is the `ul` tag, which I've corralled into a horizontal group of items. While having a list of pages is semantically correct for navigation, its default appearance doesn't suit your page. But you can use the `list-style-type` property to first remove the bullets and then style the individual list items with the `float` property, bringing them in line. The rest of that list item rule provides a nice layout for those items — some breathing room and a line to separate them.

There's one more bonus trick here: To help indicate the current page in the navigation, I've created an image that sits on top of the navigation bar at a position that highlights the current page. In the HTML page, I give the image an `id` of `"nav_selected_home"`; you might imagine your CSS file would have a separate `id` for each page of the site, the only difference being its left position:

```
#nav {
    position: absolute;
    top: 125px;
    width: 960px;
    height: 25px;
    background-color: #666666;
    border-top: 2px solid #336699;
    border-bottom: 2px solid #336699;
}
#nav ul {
```

```
        list-style-type: none;
        float: right;
    }
    #nav ul li {
        float: left;
        padding-right: 10px;
        border-right: 1px solid #000000;
        margin: 2px 10px 0px 0px;
    }
    #nav ul li.active {
        color: #d7d7d7;
    }
    img#nav_selected_home {
        position: absolute;
        top: 20px;
        left: 475px;
    }
    #nav ul li.last {
        border-right: none;
    }
    #nav ul li a {
        color: #FFFFFF;
        text-decoration: none;
    }
```

Styling the header

Now you're into the header, which won't contain many surprises at this point. You'll use the same technique that you've used with the logo since the outset, but you're also going to position that h1 tag absolutely within the header div; this way, you can place the logo in a spot beside the robot's head:

```
    h1 {
        font-size: 36px;
        text-transform: uppercase;
        border-bottom: 1px solid #336699;
    }
    h1 span {
        color: #333333;
    }
    #header h1 {
        position: absolute;
        top: 10px;
        left: 150px;
    }
```

Styling the sidebar elements

The sidebar introduces you to some fairly complex nesting of tags. I created a series of `div` elements of the same class, which receive identical styling. It's interesting to note that you can lay out the elements within each product `div` by using the techniques that let you lay out a page. In this case, the image might be analogous to a sidebar column, and the two text elements beside it might be another column. In the same way, you apply a `float` to the image and then push the `h4` and `p` tags to the right by using a `margin-left` property. It works exactly the same:

```
#sidebar h3 {
    background-color: #C0C0C0;
    padding: 10px;
}
div.product {
    padding: 10px;
    background-color: #EEEEEE;
    border-bottom: 1px dashed #336699;
}
div.product.alt {
    background-color: #FFFFFF;
}
div.product img {
    float: left;
}
div.product h4 {
    font-size: 14px;
    margin-left: 40px;
}
div.product p {
    margin-left: 40px;
    color: #000000;
    font-size: 11px;
}
```

Remaining styles

The rest of the CSS file is simple formatting. I created a special `div` for the introduction to the page, and I've also styled the remaining headers and paragraphs, providing some white space and specifying the font size:

```
#introduction {
    padding: 10px;
    border: 1px dashed #336699;
    margin: 10px 10px 10px 0px;
    background-color: #EEEEEE;
}
```

```
#main_content h3 {
    font-size: 15px;
    border-bottom: 1px solid #336699;
    margin: 15px 10px 5px 0px;
}
#main_content p {
    font-size: 12px;
    color: #000000;
}
#footer p {
    font-size: 9px;
    text-align: right;
}
```

Solving Common Problems

To this point, it may seem that CSS layout is pretty straightforward. But at some point, you'll strike out on your own and run into unexpected issues. For those moments when it seems like there's no hope, I present a list of the most common problems that CSS users run into and their typical solutions:

- **Containing floats.** Take a look at the sidebar `div`s you worked with in the last exercise. The image was floated with the text alongside. Now, if the image had been taller than the text, it would have spilled over the `div`, creating a rather nasty effect. For a good explanation of the problem and how to solve it, visit `http://complexspiral.com/publications/containing-floats`.

- **Full-height columns with backgrounds.** Again in the previous exercise, notice that the sidebar content is shorter than the main column text. In many common layouts, that sidebar would have a background with a different color, and that sidebar would ideally run the entire height of the page. But a floated element is only as tall as its content; any background you apply would be clipped when that element ended. To solve this one, visit `www.alistapart.com/articles/fauxcolumns`.

- **The dreaded float drop.** When floating multiple elements on a page, you'll often want them to sit side by side. However, when you get the math wrong on the widths of the elements, the final element can drop below the others. This can also be caused by a bug in Internet Explorer 6. Read more here: `www.adobe.com/cfusion/communityengine/index.cfm?event=showdetails&postId=1081&productId=1`.

Speaking of Internet Explorer, ensuring that your layouts work in this browser can be a problem. Here are some common problems and techniques for solving them:

- **The double-margin bug.** In short, if you `float` an element to the left and also set its left margin, Internet Explorer 6 doubles that margin, wreaking havoc on your page. The solution is to add a `display:inline` rule to the element. You can read more about it at `www.positioniseverything.net/explorer/doubled-margin.html`.

● **The repeating content bug.** Sometimes, you'll find the characters from the last of a series of floating elements repeated below. This is particularly frustrating because there's absolutely nothing that provides a hint of the cause. In this case, it's often because of the presence of HTML comment tags between floating `div` elements. You can find more information at `www.positioniseverything.net/explorer/dup-characters.html`.

● **The three-pixel jog bug.** In certain situations, Internet Explorer bumps your content over by three pixels. When you have a floating element beside a non-floating element, there can be a subtle wrap effect. Sometimes, you may not even notice it, but in other cases, the jog can stick out like a sore thumb! There's a way around it though; go here to find out more: `www.positioniseverything.net/explorer/threepxtest.html`.

● **PNG transparency.** This isn't a bug so much as a limitation; with the PNG image format comes the ability to create powerful transparency effects that can really take your site's design to the next level. Unfortunately, image alpha isn't supported in Internet Explorer 6. However, there's a solution: a JavaScript file called `SuperSleight` that hacks Internet Explorer 6 to support this feature. You can get the script and read more about the issue at `http://24ways.org/2007/supersleight-transparent-png-in-ie6`.

● **Browser-specific CSS hacks.** As a finishing point on this topic, you may find that your CSS behaves differently in browsers in spite of your best efforts. There are so many ways for styles to interact that you can't afford the time to correct them anymore. Your client only cares that his or her site looks the same in any browser, and they don't care how it's done. For those situations, I use a JavaScript file called `CSS Browser Selector`. You can learn how it works and download it at `http://rafael.adm.br/css_browser_selector`.

There are other issues that can crop up too. If you run into a problem, your first step is to try to create a *test case*: a page that's as simple as possible in order to isolate the element that's the root of the problem. With this test case, you can go online and hopefully find help.

Summary

The study and practice of CSS is probably bigger than this chapter can hold. I began by describing the role of CSS as the means to provide style to simple HTML content. From there, I explained selectors and the general format of style definitions so you can both target and style specific page elements. We put these skills to work with a few examples before moving on to the use of CSS as a page layout mechanism. Finally, I described some of the ways you can get into trouble with CSS, along with some information on finding your way home.

With these essential skills in hand, you can both accomplish the layout in your imagination and dig your way out of trouble if and when it occurs.

JavaScript

Once derided as a "toy language," JavaScript has grown into a true force on the Internet. This has happened despite a pandemic of misunderstanding about the language regarding both its origins and its proper use.

First, despite the use of the word *Java* in its name, JavaScript has nothing to do with the Java programming language, except perhaps as a way for the new scripting language to achieve some cachet while Java was the hot new trend. JavaScript was invented by Netscape in the mid-1990s as a way for web authors to provide programmatic access to objects within a web page. Netscape bundled this language into their browser, and there was no going back. Microsoft included a similar language called JScript into Internet Explorer 3.0, and it was similar enough to the Netscape version that the community adopted it as a standard.

JavaScript has always had a bad reputation among programmers, who dismissed it as a poor cousin to "real" programming languages, such as C or Pascal. All that changed with the development of AJAX technology — Asynchronous JavaScript and XML — which put JavaScript at the center of a new wave of highly responsive, dynamic, and more desktop-like web applications. Suddenly, JavaScript was famous.

In this chapter, you're going to explore JavaScript and learn how to use it both to write simple applications as well as to manipulate elements on your web pages.

The Role of Client-Side Scripting

But first, we should take a step back and understand the difference between *client side* and *server side*. The web browser is the client, while the web server is the, uh, server. When the client requests a page from the server, that machine has the opportunity to process the request and send back specialized data through the use of various scripting languages, two of which I talk about in this book: PHP and Ruby. Server-side scripting is very powerful because it can readily incorporate information from databases or remote sources. However, the exchange requires a round-trip from the client to the server, causing the page to reload.

In This Chapter

The role of client-side scripting

JavaScript as a first programming language

Basic JavaScript syntax

Working with the Document Object Model

Common JavaScript techniques

JavaScript frameworks

Conversely, client-side technology happens entirely within the browser. Imagine a form that changed depending on the options selected — for example, when you choose your country of residence, the state menu might reload to reflect that country. This kind of interaction is much more immediate and more desktop-like, and reactions to user input are instantaneous. This is the power of client-side scripting.

JavaScript's role becomes even more pronounced thanks to AJAX; using this technology, the client-side script can actually make that round-trip to the server and seamlessly serve up the results without a page reload. This opens the door to a whole class of desktop-like applications.

Consider Google Maps, the general public's first introduction to AJAX technology, shown in Figure 6.1. Using a relatively seamless interface, Maps allows the user to drag maps around with his or her mouse; at the same time, as new parts of the map are dragged into view, those map pieces are downloaded as individual tiles.

Figure 6.1

Google Maps was the first major demonstration of AJAX technology.

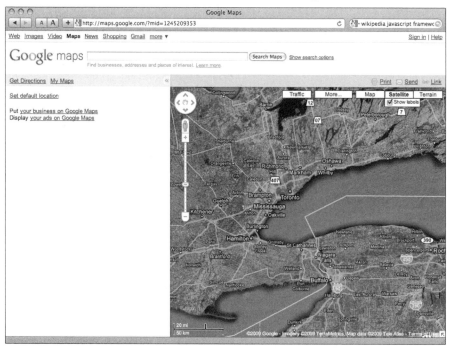

With JavaScript used in this way, the lines between client side and server side are blurred. Luckily, you're going to learn both in this book. First, you tackle JavaScript.

JavaScript as a First Programming Language

Getting started with JavaScript is very easy. Unlike with any other programming language, such as C, C++, Pascal, or BASIC, you don't need a *compiler* to convert your code into a binary application. Also, unlike a server-side scripting language such as PHP, Ruby, Python, or Perl, you don't need to set up a server or run a command shell to compose your code.

All you need to do with JavaScript is write a file like you would for HTML and then run it in your browser. In terms of barrier to entry, JavaScript qualifies as the best show in town.

Because JavaScript is based on the syntax of more-respected languages like C (and, yes, even Java), a novice programmer who takes up JavaScript as a first language is in a good position to delve into those more-advanced languages later on. A good foundation in JavaScript can also help you when you tackle PHP and Ruby later in this book.

CROSS-REF
For more on PHP, see Chapter 15. For more on Ruby, see Chapter 16.

Let's get a sense for what JavaScript is all about. In your text editor, create a new document and then type this code:

```
<html>
<head>
<title>First JavaScript</title>
</head>
<body>
    <h1>Hello, Adding Machine!</h1>
    <p>Enter a couple numbers to operate on.</p>
    <input type="text" size="5" id="t1" />
    +
    <input type="text" size="5" id="t2" />
    <input type="submit" value="=" onclick="calculate()" />
    <input type="text" size="5" id="answer" />
</body>
</html>
```

Save this file as `hellojs.html` in your Sites folder. Then, open your browser and view the file by visiting `http://localhost/hellojs.html`. You should see something similar to Figure 6.2.

CROSS-REF
You can find the `hellojs.html` file on the website for this book: `www.wileydevreference.com`.

Figure 6.2

The `hellojs.html` page

Everything in this code should be familiar to you if you've gone through Chapter 4, except for one tiny thing: Appended to the `submit input` element is an attribute you haven't seen before: `onclick`. This is a special JavaScript *event trigger* — that is, a piece of code that runs when a certain action occurs. In this case, when the `submit` (=) button is clicked, the function `calculate()` runs.

However, you haven't written that function yet. This is your first introduction to JavaScript.

In the `head` of your new HTML page, you're going to add a block of JavaScript code. This code is a *function* — a piece of code that executes from beginning to end when its name is called. When using JavaScript in HTML, you introduce it with the `script` tag. Type the following code immediately after the `title` tag in your HTML file:

```
<script type="text/javascript">
<!--
function calculate() {
   var t1, t2, answer;
   t1 = document.getElementById("t1").value;
   t2 = document.getElementById("t2").value;

   answer = t1 + t2;

   document.getElementById("answer").value = answer
}
//-->
</script>
```

Let's see what's going on here. After the `script` tag, you use HTML comment tags to wall off the JavaScript contained therein. This is a protective measure against browsers that deactivate JavaScript; in those cases, the raw code would appear in the browser, which probably isn't something you want happening. Note the closing comment tag; it's preceded with a JavaScript-style comment tag, so the HTML comment isn't interpreted as JavaScript. Make sense?

You then declare the function `calculate()`. Within the braces, the browser's JavaScript interpreter runs the following lines of code. It first sees the *declaration* of three variables: `t1`, `t2`, and `answer`. These variables represent the values that are added in the form you created.

The next two lines take care of getting the values from the text input fields. This is done by using a JavaScript function called `getElementById()`. Note how you used the `id` attribute on the text entry fields; this is done specifically so their values can be addressed by this function.

The next line takes care of the math; the `answer` variable is assigned the sum of the two terms.

Finally, the `answer` variable is placed into the final text field, again by using the `getElement ById()` function.

Now save the file and then reload your web page. Try typing **2** in the first field and **3** in the second field. Click the = button. Did you get 23, as shown in Figure 6.3?

Figure 6.3

Your first results of the `hellojs.html` file

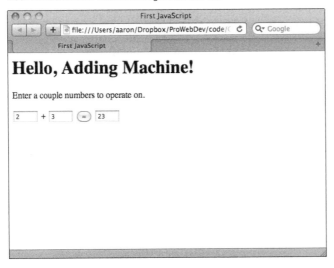

You just got snagged by a small technicality of JavaScript: It's a *typed language*. This means you sometimes need to tell the script that you're dealing with a number as opposed to a string of letters. By default, JavaScript treats text (yes, even numbers) from a text field as a string. In this case, you have to tell it otherwise.

Change this line:

```
answer = t1 + t2;
```

to this:

```
answer = parseInt(t1) + parseInt(t2);
```

Here, you surround each value with a call to a function: `parseInt`. This function takes an *argument* — the text value of those fields — and replaces it with an integer. Save and reload your page, and you should find that it now adds correctly.

This is pretty neat; you've used some basic text input boxes to create a program that adds two numbers. This is done entirely within the browser, with no intervention from the server.

Let's make it a little more interesting. Adding sometimes isn't enough, so you can create a program that lets you do any of the four major operations. First, let's modify the HTML a bit. Instead of the + sign between the two text fields, create another text field (the new code is in bold):

```
<input type="text" size="5" id="t1" />
<input type="text" size="1" id="op" />
<input type="text" size="5" id="t2" />
```

Now, here's where it gets interesting. This operator field is used to accept +, –, *, and / for addition, subtraction, multiplication, and division, respectively. If you're not familiar with the latter two symbols, these are the accepted keyboard substitutes for those operations and are used in every programming language. You'll declare the `op` variable alongside the others in the first line of the function, and you'll get the value of that variable right after you get the other terms for your equation. But how do you tell the code what operation to conduct on these terms? You use the `if...else` statement. Here's the complete new function, with the new code in bold:

```
function calculate() {
    var t1, t2, answer, op;
    t1 = document.getElementById("t1").value;
    t2 = document.getElementById("t2").value;
    op = document.getElementById("op").value;
    if(op == "+") {
        answer = parseInt(t1) + parseInt(t2);
    }
    else if(op == "-") {
        answer = parseInt(t1) - parseInt(t2);
    }
    else if(op == "*") {
        answer = parseInt(t1) * parseInt(t2);
    }
    else if(op == "/") {
```

```
    answer = parseInt(t1) / parseInt(t2);
}

document.getElementById("answer").value = answer
}
```

Think of it as a function call; the stuff inside the brackets is an argument to that function, and the function returns either `true` or `false`. So, in the first case, you ask `if` whether the value of `op` is + (the `==` symbol is an equality comparison). If so, then the code between the braces is executed, and the values are added. If not, the code moves on to the next statement. This continues until it either executes one of the blocks or runs through the complete `if` statement and does nothing. Save your file and then reload the browser. Try it with different operations.

There's quite a lot that still has to be done here. For example, someone could enter decimal numbers as terms and really mess things up. Or you could type the letter **P** instead of a mathematical operator, giving more undesirable results. As you'll learn, there are certain validations that need to be done to turn a proof of concept into a real-world application. But here's your introduction.

Now let's take a look at some of the building blocks of JavaScript.

Basic JavaScript Syntax

While JavaScript may be merely a scripting language, it has many of the same features as most popular programming languages. Later, when I cover languages like PHP and Ruby, you're going to see the same terms thrown around — and hopefully feel at home.

As you've already seen with the first JavaScript example program, the language deals with different *data types*. These are the ways the system recognizes various kinds of data. Table 6-1 shows the data types you'll deal with in JavaScript.

Table 6-1 JavaScript Data Types		
Type	*Example*	*Description*
Boolean	`true`	A logical `true` or `false` value used for testing the validity of statements
Null	`null`	An absence of value
Number	`3.14`	Any number without quotes

Object	`var func = function() {`
	`  alert('Function!');`
	`}`
		A language construct composed of functions and properties

String	`"The new iPhone 3.0 OS` `supports copy and paste."`	Any value surrounded by quotes or derived from a page's text field

As with any programming language, the code is composed of expressions. These individual, one-line statements are the commands to the interpreter, which translates your code into action. The simplest expression is a variable assignment, where, as in algebra, you create a variable and then assign a value to it:

```
var x, y;
x = 50;
y = 10;
```

Although not strictly required by all JavaScript interpreters, it's always good form to *declare* your variables — that is, specify them by using the `var` keyword — before using them. This helps you keep your variables organized and helps ensure that you don't overuse them; after all, every variable takes up a little memory. Take up too much, and you slow down the performance of your script.

It's worth noting that you should be more judicious in how you name your variables than I was in this example. While you can just use a single letter, you'll find your job as a programmer immeasurably easier if you give your variables descriptive names and reserve single-letter variables for small, incidental uses, such as for counters.

Alongside variables, you'll use any number of *operators*. These are the symbols that connect your statements and turn them into expressions. You've just seen the most important *assignment operator*: the equal sign (=). This places the result of the expression to its right into the variable indicated on its left.

There are other classes of operators. The two important ones you'll deal with now are the *arithmetic operators*, for performing mathematical functions, and the *comparison operators*, for comparing two statements. I've already described the mathematical operators; Table 6-2 shows the comparison operators.

Table 6-2 Javascript Comparison Operators

Operator	Example	Description
==	x == 24.1	Equals or is
!=	answer != 42	Doesn't equal
>	12 > 2	Greater than
<	2 < 12	Less than
>=	13 >= 12	Greater than or equal to
<=	12 <= 13	Less than or equal to

You'll start to use these operators in the next section, but there's one more data type that you need to consider first: the array.

Arrays

An array is a single variable that represents multiple values. It's like an old-fashioned card catalog drawer at the library; the name of the variable is on the little card outside the drawer, but you can open it up and pull out any card inside to get a different value.

Array values are easily created and sorted by their *index*. For example:

```
var cookieTypes = new Array();
cookieTypes[0] = "Chocolate Chip";
cookieTypes[1] = "Coconut Crunch";
cookieTypes[2] = "Pralines and Jam";
```

An individual array element is referenced by a number in square brackets. With arrays, the numbering always begins with zero. Once declared, you can reference the array as a whole with just the variable name or grab an individual value by appending the index in square brackets.

The language provides you with tools for using this array data in a variety of ways; you can iterate through the values and print them out into a list; you can search the array for a value provided by the user; you can sort the array values in different orders; and the list goes on.

Arrays are very powerful tools in programming, and you'll use them often. For now, let's look at another basic tool that you'll use in JavaScript: the control structure.

Control structures

One of the most basic features of a programming language is having the code decide on a course of action based on the given input. If statement A is `true`, then execute one code block. Otherwise, execute another code block.

The primary tool for controlling flow is the `if...else` statement. You've already seen this in action in the first example. It uses a general structure like this:

```
if (condition) {
    statements if true
}
else {
    statements if false
}
```

This can also be done without an `else`. The simple `if` statement simply executes a statement when its condition is `true`; otherwise, nothing happens. When you add the `else`, you add an alternative action. The statement code block is framed by braces. How you position them relative to your code is a matter of style; the style you see here — the opening brace ending the condition line and the closing brace on its own line after the statements — is my preferred style. Feel free to develop your own, but try to be consistent!

The other common control structure that you'll use in programming is the *loop*. A loop runs a block of code while a given statement continues to be `true`. The primary keyword for the loop is `for`. Here's the prototype for a `for` loop:

```
for ( starting expression; condition; next action ) {
    statements inside loop
}
```

While any of the three arguments within the `for` loop's brackets are optional, you'll find yourself using all of them most of the time. This might seem complicated now, but bear with me, and you'll find that it makes a lot of sense.

Before a `for` loop executes its code block, it needs to evaluate whether its conditions remain `true`. It begins with its starting expression (such as `counter = 1`) and then evaluates its condition (`counter < 10`). If that turns out to be `true`, the code block is executed. Finally, the next action is evaluated (`counter++`, which increments the counter by one). And back through the process you go.

Loops are a vital part of basic programming, and they go hand in hand with arrays, as you may be able to guess.

Creating a sample script

Let's put together everything you've learned in the last few pages into an example script. In this exercise, you're going to create a page that will provide a list of movies and allow you to rate them using one to five stars. As you rate each movie, your choice appears in a list. Figure 6.4 shows the final page in action.

Figure 6.4

The completed `movieratings.html` file

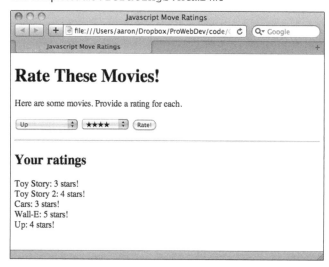

The HTML foundation

You start by writing just the HTML code that makes up your example. To keep this example simple, I'm dispensing with the niceties of proper xHTML and its validations; the focus here is on the JavaScript.

Start by creating a new text file and then typing the following code:

```
<html>
<head>
    <title>JavaScript Movie Ratings</title>
</head>
<body>
    <h1>Rate These Movies!</h1>
    <p>Here are some movies. Provide a rating for each.</p>

    <p><select name="movie" id="movie">
    </select>

    <select name="rating" id="rating">
        <option>&#9733;</option>
        <option>&#9733;&#9733;</option>
        <option>&#9733;&#9733;&#9733;</option>
        <option>&#9733;&#9733;&#9733;&#9733;</option>
        <option>&#9733;&#9733;&#9733;&#9733;&#9733;</option>
    </select>

    <input type="submit" value="Rate!" onclick="rate()" /></p>

    <hr />

    <h2>Your ratings</h2>
    <div id="ratings"></div>

</body>
</html>
```

An astute coder will notice that I've put nothing inside the first `select` tag set. You will soon; this element will contain the movies to be rated. Also, notice the final empty `div` tags under the header `Your ratings`. This spot is deliberately being kept empty because your script is going to fill this `div` with your ratings.

Incorporating arrays

You need one array to contain the movie titles and one to contain the ratings. Because arrays are indexed by number, you can match the number of the movie title to the number of the array for the rating. Thus, to set up your arrays, type the following code directly below the `title` tag in the `head` of your document:

```
<script type="text/javascript">
  <!--
      // create the array of ratings
      var ratings = new Array();

      // create the array of movies, and fill it
      var movies = new Array();
      movies[0] = "Toy Story";
      movies[1] = "A Bug's Life";
      movies[2] = "Toy Story 2";
      movies[3] = "Monsters, Inc.";
      movies[4] = "Finding Nemo";
      movies[5] = "The Incredibles";
      movies[6] = "Cars";
      movies[7] = "Ratatouille";
      movies[8] = "Wall-E";
      movies[9] = "Up";
</script>
```

The first line of code initializes the `ratings` array, creating a variable that you can refer to when it comes time to rate movies. Then, you create the `movies` array; this one contains ten items (in this case, the entire *oeuvre* of Pixar), with array index values from zero to nine. Remember, in programming, all arrays are indexed from zero.

Adding to your HTML foundation

With your `movies` array set, you can go back to your HTML and arrange to populate the `movies` select element. Between the empty `select` tags, type this code (new code is in bold):

```
<p><select name="movie" id="movie">
<script type="text/javascript">
<!--
   for ( i=0; i<movies.length; i++ ) {
      document.write("<option>" + movies[i] + "</option>");
   }
//-->
</script>
```

Here, you use a simple JavaScript `for` loop, which starts at the first index, loops until it reaches the final index (determined by the method `movies.length`), and then, for each index, writes out the HTML with the name of each movie in an `option` tag.

At this point, you do a sanity check to ensure that the work you've done to this point actually works. Save your file as `movieratings.html` and then load it in your browser. Check the movies pop-up menu; are the movies from your array listing correctly? If not, go over your code again and look for typos.

CROSS-REF

You can find the `movieratings.html` file on the website for this book: `www.wileydevreference.com`.

At this point, while you've got an array populating a pop-up menu on your page, you can't do anything with it yet. That, of course, is the purpose of that subtle event attribute on the sub-mit button: `rate()`.

Adding a function

The `rate()` function determines the movie and the rating and modifies the arrays appropri-ately. The following code follows your declaration of the `movies` array within the `script` tags in the `head` of your document:

```
function rate() {
    movieIndex = document.getElementById('movie').selectedIndex;
    ratingIndex = document.getElementById('rating').selectedIndex
    + 1;
    ratings[movieIndex] = ratingIndex;
    showlist();
}
```

The first two lines of the function simply determine the values for the `movie` and `rating`, respectively. They do this by using the `getElementById()` function to grab the value of the `select` elements; the method `selectedIndex` is appended to the selector in order to derive that value. For the `ratings` array, you can't just take the value of the index; you have to add one to that value to compensate for the zero-indexed array.

The next line of code modifies the `ratings` array, putting the rating at the index that matches the `movie` array value. Recall that you're taking advantage of the fact that arrays are numeri-cally indexed; for example, when you receive array element six for the movie, you know that you're applying a rating at index six for the movie *Cars*.

The final line of code calls another function: `showlist()`. This function displays the contents of the array in that empty `div` at the bottom of the HTML page.

Connecting functions and arrays

The `showlist()` function works by building a string out of the `movies` and `ratings` arrays. You have to be careful though; not every movie in that array will have a matching rating. So, you have to use an `if` statement to determine whether the movie is included in your list. After the `rate()` function, write this code:

```
function showlist() {
    var contents = "";
    for ( i=0; i<ratings.length;i++ ) {
        if ( ratings[i] != null ) {
```

```
        contents += movies[i] + ": " + ratings[i] + "
stars!<br/>";
    }
  }
  document.getElementById('ratings').innerHTML = contents;
}
```

You first create a new variable called `contents` and then initialize it with an empty string value. Then, you create a `for` loop that iterates through each element of the `ratings` array; you use the same technique as you did for the previous function.

Not every rating index will contain a value; you may have given only a rating for movie indexes one, three, and six. Thus, the `if` statement; you only add the values of movies that have ratings. You determine this by comparing the value of the current rating index with the value `null`. When they aren't equal (that is, when the rating index does have a value), execution proceeds within the code block.

Where a value exists, you use the `+=` assignment operator to append the movie title and rating to the `contents` variable. This happens for every index in the ratings array — thanks to the magic of the `for` loop.

Finally, your `contents` variable is complete. The last line of the function writes the variable out into the `ratings div` at the end of the HTML file.

Save the file and then view it in your browser. Wow — ratings!

There's only one problem. When you refresh the page, your valuable ratings information is lost. A real web application would interact with a server-side database, allowing you to store these values, perhaps save them with your stored profile, and even compare them to other users' ratings for the same movies. But for now, you've created something that works quite well as a way to provide a modicum of interactivity to your users.

Working with the Document Object Model

In the course of the exercises thus far, you've taken advantage of a powerful feature of JavaScript without naming it. That ends now. The Document Object Model, or DOM, is the mechanism in JavaScript that allows your code to access the various elements within an HTML document. You can use the DOM to get any element from a page and also write any element out. In this section, you examine how the DOM works.

From your study of HTML, you've likely surmised that page elements exist on the page in a hierarchy. An HTML tag contains `head` and `body` tags. Within the `head` tag is a `title` tag, perhaps some `meta` tags, and some `script` and `style` tags. The `body` tag can contain any number of `p`, `form`, `img`, `div`, and other tags that make up the content of the page. The DOM provides the JavaScripter with tools to manipulate the items in this hierarchy.

Because the DOM depends on a hierarchy, there needs to be a *root object*, the head honcho of elements. That's `window`; everything on the page descends from it. In fact, the `window` element is pre-eminent enough that it's usually assumed; your calls to various page elements could be preceded by the `window` statement, but when the current window is the context, it's not necessary.

The `window` contains a `document` object, which in turn holds the paragraphs, forms, images, and other items that make up the page.

As with CSS, you have to know the syntax for selecting individual items to act upon. There are three methods for identifying elements:

- **Dot-syntax.** This lets you choose individual elements by using certain arrays.
- **Tag.** This lets you select all tags of a specific type.
- **ID selection.** This lets you choose an individual named element.

The dot-syntax method

The first technique is named after the dots that separate the hierarchy of elements and is based on the fact that the JavaScript DOM creates arrays for `form` elements, `links`, `anchors`, and `images`. The best way to demonstrate this is to show some sample code:

```
<body>
    <h1>This is a header.</h1>
    <p>This is where you fill out a form.</p>
    <p>All fields are mandatory.</p>
    <form action="submit.php" name="signup_form" method="post">
        <input name="name" type="text" />
        <input name="email" type="text" />
        <input type="submit" value="Go!" />
    </form>
</body>
```

Once this page loads in your browser, the DOM loads up the `forms` array with the contents of the form. With that done, you can use a dot-syntax statement to get at any of its elements. For example, to put a new value in the `name` field, you can issue any of these statements:

```
document.forms[0].elements[0].value = "Your Name!";
document.forms['signup_form'].elements['name'].value = "Your
    Name!";
document.forms['signup_form'].name.value = "Your Name!";
```

Each of these techniques provides the same result. Because the `forms` array is numerically indexed, you can use the zero in brackets to indicate the first `forms` array. Within that array is another array of form elements; the `name` field is the first, so you can indicate it with the zero index.

The DOM also allows you to call items by their `name` attribute, which you can do either in place of the array index or simply by itself.

Perhaps a more proper way to write these lines would be to assign the element to a variable and then call a method:

```
var nameField = document.forms['signup_form'].name;
nameField.value = "Your Name!";
```

Again, this works too and makes for more readable — albeit longer — code. The style you choose is up to you.

The tag selection method

Sometimes, you might need to work with a related group of elements on a page, such as the cells of a table. Using the method `getElementsByTagName()`, you can provide a tag and then receive an array of matching elements back.

For example, you may want to make all text within `p` tags red to warn the user of an action just taken. You could do it this way:

```
var paras = document.getElementsByTagName("p");
for ( i = 0; i < paras.length; i++ ) {
    paras[i].style.color = "#FF0000";
}
```

This code takes advantage of JavaScript's ability to change the CSS styles of elements by using the `style` method and its various attributes. You'll look at this a little more in my final example.

The ID selection method

The final and most typical way of choosing page elements is by using the function `getElementById()`. It's so good that you've already seen it used several times in this chapter. Get to know it well because it will become your go-to method in your JavaScript bag of tricks.

As you've seen, `getElementById()` relies on your naming target page elements with an `id` attribute. That way, you can pick up exactly the right element every time — no hierarchies to traverse and no counting of page element arrays.

Here's an example. You'll often use JavaScript to dynamically hide and show elements on the page depending on user actions. You do this by creating `div` tags to contain the optional content. Take this code:

```
<a href="#" onclick="document.getElementById('flip2').style.
   display='block'">Show Flip2</a> |
<a href="#" onclick="document.getElementById('flip2').style.
   display='none'">Hide Flip2</a>
```

```
<div id="flip2" style="display:none">
   <p>This is content.</p>
</div>
```

By setting the `id` of the `div` to `flip2`, you can use the `getElementById()` method to target it and then use the `style.display` method to set its visibility.

Common JavaScript Techniques

To conclude my roundup of JavaScript, I'm going to demonstrate some common techniques that are particularly useful to web developers. These include:

- Passing form values to functions with `this`
- Validating form data
- Opening and closing windows
- Creating image rollovers
- Changing element styles

Passing form values to functions with "this"

My first example makes use of a special keyword in JavaScript: `this`. It's used as an argument in a function call to pass along the object making the call. Here's an example:

```
<input type="text" name="name" onfocus="flash(this)" />
```

In the receiving function, you can accept the field right away without having to select an element. This is useful when you want to provide an action for any number of elements that the user might interact with. The `flash()` function could look like this:

```
function flash(element) {
   element.style.backgroundColor = "#FFCC00";
}
```

You can imagine applying a function call like this to every text `input` element in your form to provide a little extra style. As an exercise, modify this `flash()` function to ensure that the currently chosen field remains the only one lit in yellow. (Hint: Look at the `getElementsByTagName()` function.)

Validating form data

This technique leads directly to the next example: validating your forms. For web developers, form validation is a very important topic. When I cover server-side scripting later in this book, you'll realize very quickly that your code will rely on the data entered in forms. If that data isn't what you expect, your code is going to do unexpected things.

JavaScript can really help with this. With form validation, you can write scripts that check the values that users enter before the form is submitted. Let's look at a simple form and then see how we might validate it and provide feedback.

Open your text editor and then type this HTML code:

```html
<html>
  <head>
    <title>Form Validation</title>
  </head>
<body>
  <h1>This is your form.</h1>
  <div id="error_reporter"></div>
  <form action="#" method="post" onsubmit="return
  validate(this)">
    <p>Name: <input type="text" name="name" /></p>
    <p>Email: <input type="text" name="email" /></p>
    <p>Age:
      <select name="age">
        <option>Choose...</option>
        <option>18-25</option>
        <option>26-40</option>
        <option>41-65</option>
      </select>
    </p>
    <p>Status: <input type="radio" name="status" value="great"
  /> Great
      <input type="radio" name="status" value="awful" />
  Awful</p>
    <p><input type="submit" value="Tell us!" /></p>
  </form>
</body>
</html>
```

Save this file as `formvalidation.html`. This form is ordinary enough, with the exception of one stray set of empty `div` tags. You'll use that set of tags to place any error messages that may occur. You've also placed an event trigger in the opening `form` tag, which makes use of the `this` keyword to pass the entire form to the function. The `return` keyword allows you to ensure that if the function doesn't pass your validations, it will prevent the form from submitting.

CROSS-REF

You can find the `formvalidation.html` file on the website for this book:
`www.wileydevreference.com`.

In the traditional space for it, you'll place the script that performs the validation. After the `title` tag, type this code:

```
<script language="text/javascript">
<!--
function validate(theForm) {
   var errors = "Errors:<br/>";

   // test the values
   if (theForm.name.value == "" ) {
      errors += "Please enter a name!<br/>";
   }

   if (theForm.email.value == "" ) {
      errors += "Please enter an email address!<br/>";
   }

   if (theForm.age.selectedIndex == 0 ) {
      errors += "Please choose an age!<br/>";
   }

   for ( i = 0; i < theForm.status.length; i++ ) {
      if (theForm.status[i].checked) {
         break;
      }
   }
   if (i == 2) {
      errors += "Please choose a status!<br/>";
   }

   if (errors.length > 12) {
      document.getElementById('error_reporter').innerHTML =
errors;
      return false;
   }
   else {
      return true;
   }
}
//-->
</script>
```

This validation script checks each form field in turn and uses various methods — depending on the kind of form element — to determine whether the user has entered a value. For the text fields, you simply take the value of that field and then compare it with an empty text string. If they're equal, then you've got an empty text field.

For the pop-up menu, there's no value property. Instead, you can use the selectedIndex property, which provides the index number of the chosen value. When that value is zero, it indicates that the first value has been chosen, which in this case is the value asking the user to choose an option.

The radio buttons are a little more complicated. Because they also don't supply a `value` property, you have to iterate through the radio buttons and determine if they've been checked. The technique you use to do this is the `for` loop. Each time through the loop, the value of `i` is incremented by one. The loop ends if a `checked` value is found, and the value of `i` is set to the index of the selected radio button. For example, after the loop is complete, if the value of `i` is two, then you know that the loop hasn't found a selected radio button.

The trick here is the use of the `errors` string. For each error found, that string will have the appropriate error message appended.

Finally, having gone through each validation, you need to determine whether an actual error was found. To accomplish this, you check the length of the `errors` string. You know that it will be 12 characters in length by default; this is the number of characters in the string when it's initialized. So, if the length is longer, then you know that there were errors. The `if` statement will check the length and, if there are errors, will dump the contents of the `errors` variable into the `div` tags you created in the `body` of the HTML document, also returning `false` to the form to prevent submission.

If there are no errors, you simply return `true`, and the form is submitted.

The functionality demonstrated here provides just the basics for form validation. You could nest `if` statements to check not just the presence of a value but that it matched certain requirements. For example, a `name` field probably shouldn't be allowed to contain numbers. Or through the use of regular expressions, you could validate the format of an email address.

Opening and closing windows

For my next trick, you'll see how to open and close windows by using JavaScript. This is a handy technique for moving the user to a sub-window, which might contain subsidiary content, such as a word's definition.

You use the `window` object to access the `open` and `close` methods. You start by opening a window from a hyperlink:

```
<a href="#" onclick="window.open('window2.html','','width=450,hei
    ght=400,resizable=yes,scrollbars=yes');">Open Window</a>
```

The `window.open` method takes three parameters:

- **The file to open.**
- **The name of the window.** This is optional and is rarely used.
- **The specifications of the window.** In addition to the width, height, ability to resize, and scrollbars, you can control the presence of the location bar, status bar, title bar, toolbar, and even the position of the window on the screen.

When it comes to closing a window, you can provide a hyperlink with the `window.close` method. You might put a line like this in the newly created window:

```
<a href="#" onclick="window.close()">Close window</a>
```

Happily, there are no parameters for this function call; the containing window simply goes away.

Creating image rollovers

I haven't spoken often about images in this chapter, but they clearly play a large role in the development of web pages. A common technique is the *rollover*, where the image changes as the mouse moves over it. This is often used in navigation bars to highlight the currently hovered link.

I've created two images for use in this exercise: an off image, which is the navigation item's regular state, and an on image, for use during the rollover.

CROSS-REF

You can find the `rollovers.html` file and the images for this code on the website for this book: **www.wileydevreference.com.**

The HTML is just enough to suit your needs:

```
<body>
    <img src="images/hover_off.jpg" name="hover"
    onmouseover="lightsOn('hover')"
    onmouseout="lightsOff('hover')" />
</body>
```

The entire page content is one image tag, but it's crammed with attributes. The first attribute is the name so this image can be identified in your script. Then come the event triggers: one for when the mouse hovers and another for when the mouse leaves. Each function passes the name of the image as its argument.

Now you need to write the JavaScript to support this. Rollovers need to move quickly; you don't want your user waiting while the new image downloads to the browser. So, you use a technique called *preloading*, which downloads and caches all the rollover images while the page loads:

```
<script type="text/javascript">
    <!--
    var rollOvers = new Array();
    rollOvers["hover"] = new Image(75,25);
    rollOvers["hover"].src = "images/hover_off.jpg";
    var rollOvers_on = new Array();
    rollOvers_on["hover"] = new Image(75,25);
    rollOvers_on["hover"].src = "images/hover_on.jpg";
    function lightsOn(img) {
        document.images[img].style.cursor = "pointer";
        document.images[img].src = rollOvers_on[img].src;
    }
```

```
function lightsOff(img) {
    document.images[img].style.cursor = "default";
    document.images[img].src = rollOvers[img].src;
}

//-->
</script>
```

You can see that I created two arrays: one to hold the off images (in this case, a single image) and another to hold the on images. The preloading occurs when you call `new Image()` and feed it a location via its `src` property. For each array, you provide the same image name: `hover`; I'm going to use that later to give you an easy way to swap images.

The `lightsOn()` function takes the name of the image and is called when the mouse rolls over. It turns the cursor into a pointer (as this image is usually going to be a hyperlink) and sets the `src` property to that of the on image array.

The `lightsOff()` function does the opposite, turning the pointer back to its default position and resetting the `src` property to its off state.

For every image in your navigation bar, you may have an entry in both the on and off arrays. Then, for each image, you would give it a unique name and pass that in your arguments to the switching functions.

Changing element styles

You've already seen this technique at work; you changed the color of paragraph text and switched the visibility of page elements on and off. As it turns out, the entire pantheon of CSS styles are available to the JavaScript DOM, allowing you to dynamically change styles on your pages.

The syntax for using this power is pretty simple:

```
document.getElementById('element').style.property = 'value'
```

The only caveat when it comes to getting and setting styles is in the naming. For example, the `background-color` property in CSS translates into `backgroundColor` in JavaScript. In fact, any CSS property with a hyphen in the name will appear in JavaScript without the hyphen and with the first letter of the second word capitalized. Table 6-3 shows a sample of the translation that occurs.

Table 6-3 Some CSS-to-Javascript Style Translations

CSS Style	JavaScript Style
background	background
background-color	backgroundColor
border, margin, padding	borderStyle, marginStyle, paddingStyle

CSS Style	JavaScript Style
float	cssFloat
font-family	fontFamily
list-style-type	listStyleType
margin-left	marginLeft

There are some oddballs in here. While JavaScript appears to adopt the `style` tag for most all-in-one declarations, it doesn't do so for the `background` property. When in doubt, consult the documentation for the language; `www.w3schools.com/htmldom/dom_obj_style.asp` is an excellent resource.

JavaScript Frameworks

If you've followed the exercises in this chapter, you've come to see that JavaScript is a very powerful language for manipulating elements on a web page. With a little imagination, you may find that there's much more that JavaScript can do. In this Web 2.0 era, JavaScript is used to provide real-time interaction with application servers and databases as well as animation effects that were once part of Adobe Flash technology. With the right techniques, you can use JavaScript to create web applications that have the feel and response of a desktop application.

However, you will have a hard time accessing these features with plain old JavaScript. Fortunately, groups of programmers have written *frameworks* — libraries of code — that you can use as the foundation for your project. By simply including a library of JavaScript, you can change the way you program the language, giving yourself easy-to-use tools to add a whole new level of sophistication to your websites.

Given the changes in the web today, it behooves you to learn about and gain competence in at least some of these frameworks. There are many out there to choose from — in fact, there's no way that I could cover them all — so I'm going to talk about two in particular: Prototype and Scriptaculous.

Prototype

The primary role of any framework is to make your life as a programmer easier. On this score, Prototype makes a compelling example. It sits on top of the JavaScript language, injecting its own unique syntax. This collection of *utility functions* and add-on methods makes it darn-near pleasurable to work with DOM elements. In this section, you'll take a look at what Prototype has to offer, and you'll see how the framework allows you to write less code.

To get started with Prototype, you need to download the library from the project's website. Visit `www.prototypejs.org` to download the latest version. Then, in the `head` of your HTML document, add a line like this:

```
<script language="javascript" src="js/prototype.js" type="text/
   javascript"></script>
```

You're now able to take advantage of Prototype's capabilities.

Utility functions

Perhaps the most important new function that Prototype offers is the `$()` construction. This is a replacement for the rather lengthy `document.getElementById()` method in regular JavaScript. Compare the two constructions:

```
var myId = document.getElementById('myId');
var myId = $('myId');
```

In fact, the `$()` method is so much terser that you wouldn't normally use it as I have here; rather than assigning the element to a variable, you could simply use the function call itself. For example:

```
$('myId').style.display = "none";
```

You'll find yourself using that syntax all the time in your Prototype-enhanced JavaScript.

Let's move on to another utility function that addresses a major shortcoming in the standard JavaScript DOM. While you can select collections of form elements, images, links, and anchors, you can't touch elements that belong to a given class. Prototype responds with the `$$()` construction. Using this function, you can grab all elements that belong to a certain class; use it just as you would in CSS, with the preceding period (`.`) to indicate the class name:

```
var fields = $$('.fieldValues');
```

What you get back is an array of the matching elements. You can combine these first two examples into a powerful piece of code that grabs just the elements within a specific parent container:

```
var fields = $('myList').$$('.fieldValues');
```

The `$$()` function also does more; you can grab any HTML tag you want with it, similar to the method `document.getElementsByTagName()`. But again, with the ability to target container IDs, you can make your selection more focused.

Arrays are a typing-intensive component in JavaScript, and Prototype has convenience methods to also help with those. In many ways, Prototype's implementation of array helper methods mirrors the Ruby language; this is no surprise, given that Prototype was originally developed as an adjunct to the Ruby on Rails framework! Although some of these constructions may take you by surprise, I urge you to try them in your own code; you'll learn to appreciate the elegance of this syntax.

CROSS-REF

For more on the Ruby language and the Ruby on Rails framework, see Chapters 16 and 17.

First up, here's an easy way to create an array:

```
var cities = $w('Toronto Ottawa Vancouver');
```

By separating your array elements with spaces, the $w() construction builds an array out of a single string. The method automatically creates numerical indexes for each value.

Once you've got an array, Prototype provides a number of helper methods to let you access those values. Instead of the lengthy for loop to step through the array elements, you can use the handy each method. Here's an example:

```
cities.each(function(city) {
    document.write(city + "<br/>");
});
```

This code block sends out the cities in your array, one per line.

One more handy utility method is the $f() construction. This method gets the value of a form element that has an id attribute. So, with a form containing a field such as this:

```
<input type="text" name="FirstName" id="FirstName" />
```

you can use this construction to pick out the value:

```
var firstName = $f('FirstName');
```

When you use Prototype's utility methods, you save a lot of time and energy. You also simplify your code, making it easier to understand later.

But there's more to Prototype aside from making your day-to-day code easier. It also provides capabilities that are difficult, if not impossible, with regular JavaScript. Let's look at some of those now.

Injecting class names

In traditional JavaScript, you're often called upon to change the styling of page elements. That's so passé; it's much more elegant to change the CSS class of an element and then let the proper technology do the styling work.

Prototype provides methods that both add and remove classes to elements. Let's say you had a list of items:

```
<ul id="list">
      <li onclick="highlight(this)">Item one</li>
      <li onclick="highlight(this)">Item two</li>
      <li onclick="highlight(this)">Item three</li>
</ul>
```

Each item in the list has an onclick event trigger. In the highlight() function, you have a single statement that adds a class to the li tag:

```
function highlight(element) {
    $(element).addClassName('red');
}
```

Here's an exercise for you: Given what you've learned about targeting tags inside an id container element, can you improve this function to turn off the other list items when one goes on? (Hint: Use $$() construction and the removeClassName('red') method call.)

Using the class this way, instead of the JavaScript style method, makes your code much leaner and easier to maintain.

Observation

Your final stop on the Prototype tour is a very powerful system called *observation*. Think of it as a passive event trigger. Instead of placing an event as an attribute of a page element, you can declare an observer to that element and then trigger a function when the action occurs.

The main benefits of observation are, again, simplified code as well as the ability to track events that are difficult to capture in regular JavaScript. There's also a final bonus: Prototype's event triggers are more compatible with browsers (yes, even Internet Explorer). Let's look at two examples of observation to get an idea of what it can do.

I'll start with the most basic event observation possible. Create an HTML element that you can observe, such as a hyperlink:

```
<a href="target.html" id="target">Click me now!</a>
```

Then, in the head of the document, write this JavaScript function:

```
<script type="text/javascript">
<!--
Event.observe(window, 'load', function() {
    Event.observe('target', 'click', function(){
        alert("Clicked!");
    });
})
//-->
</script>
```

The method Event.observe takes three arguments:

- **The ID of the target element.**
- **The event to observe.** This is like the attribute, except without the on. So, in place of onclick, simply use click.
- **The code to run when the event occurs.**

You can reference a separate function or, if the code is very short, you can run it in an *anony-mous function*, where you specify the `function` keyword and provide the actions, as I have shown here.

Why, you might wonder, are there two methods here? As you can see, your `click` target action is nested inside another method that waits for the window to finish loading. This parent method ensures that the elements that are required to run your intended observation are, in fact, present in the DOM. Try taking the window-loading observer out, and you'll find the code doesn't work!

Let's try a more useful example. Many applications that involve the use of the mouse rely on knowing the current mouse coordinates. With that information, you can know where the mouse is located and act accordingly based on the numbers. In your HTML document, create two text fields:

```
X: <input name="XPos" id="XPos" />
Y: <input name="YPos" id="YPos" />
```

Then, write this JavaScript:

```
<script type="text/javascript">
<!--
Event.observe(window, 'load', function() {
    Event.observe(window, 'mousemove', function(event) {
        $('XPos').value = Event.pointerX(event);
        $('YPos').value = Event.pointerY(event);
    });
});
//-->
</script>
```

When you load the file `prototype_test.html`, which is included on the website for this book (`www.wileydevreference.com`), you'll see the text fields update with the coordi-nates of the mouse location in real time.

Prototype is capable of much more, but I'll leave it aside for now and move on to the flashier side of JavaScript.

Scriptaculous

Think of Scriptaculous as Captain Kirk to Prototype's Mr. Spock. Spock is the analytic, procedural fellow upon whom the entire crew relies, including Kirk. But when it comes to putting on a spar-kling show, there's no one better than the Captain.

Scriptaculous relies on the solid foundations that Prototype provides. However, Scriptaculous creates the effects that steal the show: animation of elements, cool special effects, drag and drop, in-place editing, and more. As with Prototype, I can't cover all the features that this framework provides, but I can give you a quick tour as well as a feel for how easy it is to make some shiny things happen in your web pages.

The first step is to download and install Scriptaculous. It's available at one of my favorite URLs ever: `http://script.aculo.us`. Download the latest release and then move the entire group of files into your website directory.

Because Scriptaculous depends on Prototype, that file is also included. You're best off using the version of Prototype that comes with Scriptaculous to avoid any potential incompatibilities. Be sure to check the version number of your already-installed Prototype version (assuming you downloaded it in the last section) and then replace it with the new one if they're different.

Let's take a tour of Scriptaculous's most important features.

Sliders

While HTML provides a wide variety of form controls, one that is missing is the slider. You've seen this control in desktop applications on the Mac, such as in iTunes. Figure 6.5 shows the minimized iTunes application, displaying two sliders: one to control the volume and the other to control the playback time.

Figure 6.5

The iTunes application showing two slider controls

You can use sliders in your own application to let your users indicate a value between a given minimum and maximum. Using the Scriptaculous effects, you can get that value in real time and then act upon it instantly.

In my example page, you're going to use a custom image for the slider, which is composed of two parts: a `"track"` and a `"handle"`.

CROSS-REF

You can find the `scriptaculous_slider.html` file and the images in the code on the website for this book: `www.wileydevreference.com`.

Every page that you use in this part starts with two `include` statements for both Prototype and Scriptaculous. You can just assume that these lines are in every document:

```
<script language="javascript" type="text/javascript"
   src="prototype.js"></script>
<script language="javascript" type="text/javascript"
   src="scriptaculous.js"></script>
```

Start by writing the HTML for this example:

```
<h1>Choose a Value with the Slider</h1>
<div id="track">
   <div id="tool">
      <img src="images/slider_tool.png" alt="" />
   </div>
</div>
<p><input id="value" type="text" /></p>
```

I like to keep things simple. A `div` for the track will contain a `div` for the handle (which I name, alternately, the tool; or if I'm in a more precise frame of mind, grabby-thingy). This isn't without style, of course, so let's look at that code in the `head` of the document:

```
<style>
     #track {
         width:200px;
         height:5px;
         background-image: url("images/slider_track.png");
     }

     #tool {
         width:25px;
         height:25px;
     }

     #tool img {
         float: left;
         margin-top:-10px;
     }

     </style>
```

These CSS declarations do nothing more than position the elements on the screen. The important thing is that the dimensions of the track and the tool are registered because the Scriptaculous utility is going to use those values to work its magic.

Let's look now at the JavaScript that makes it work. This code is added after the HTML, still within the `body` tags. Note the use of the comment tags, as usual, to ensure compatibility with browsers that don't support JavaScript:

```
<script type="text/javascript" language="javascript">
   // <!--
```

```
    // horizontal slider control
    new Control.Slider('tool', 'track', {
      onSlide: function(v) { $('value').value = 'slide: ' + v },
      onChange: function(v) { $('value').value = 'changed: ' + v }
    });
    // -->
  </script>
```

As you've already seen in the use of Prototype, the core feature is a simple call to `Control.Slider`. This function takes three arguments: the ID of the tool, the ID of the track, and the function to call when the user does something to them. Also, like Prototype, the most common technique in that third argument is to use an anonymous function, giving the commands right there in the call.

In the case of the slider control, you're given a couple of events: an `onSlide` event, which provides data during the event, and an `onChange` event, which provides the difference between the starting and ending positions after the event has occurred. In both cases, you're simply taking the value of those events and putting them into the text field with the `value` ID.

Save the file and then view it in your browser. You should see something similar to Figure 6.6.

Figure 6.6

The completed slider test page

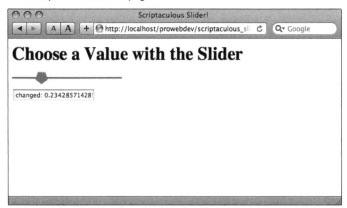

Animation effects

One of Scriptaculous's headline features is its animation library. Using very simple function calls, you can make elements move around the window, fade in and out, or fold into each other. There are many other effects too.

In this example, you use a couple of different effects at the same time to see how you can create terrific combinations. In the `scriptaculous_drawer.html` file, you have three different effects. The first effect displays some hidden text by using a slide animation. The second effect moves the text to the right. The final effect fades that text again.

CROSS-REF

You can find the `scriptaculous_drawer.html` file on the website for this book: www.wileydevreference.com.

The HTML is, as usual, simple enough:

```
<h1>Hide and Seek Text</h1>
<p><a href="#" onclick="Effect.toggle('toggle_text', 'slide');
    return false;">Now you see it...</a></p>
<div id="toggle_text" style="display:none">
    <div>
        You found me! Time to run...<br/>
        <a href="#" onclick="moveThisThing();return false;">Now you
    don't!</a>
    </div>
</div>
```

The first anchor tag has an `onclick` event trigger that performs your first animation. This Scriptaculous method takes two arguments: the ID of the element to be animated and the effect to be used; this toggle method lets you choose a slide, an appear, or a blind effect. Feel free to switch them out and choose your favorite.

The next block of code identifies the `div` that will be animated. Two items are of particular note here: First, that when you want an element to be made visible, its visibility must be established by using an inline CSS style (`style="display:none"`); you can't set this in an external style sheet.

The second note is about the nested `div` tag within the identified `div` container. This is a peculiarity of Scriptaculous in that it requires an animated element to be contained in a `div`; otherwise, you'll see certain jerky moves during the animation.

The final animation effects are being outsourced, as it were, by the call to the function `move-ThisThing()`. This is defined in the `head` of the document:

```
<script>
    function moveThisThing() {
        new Effect.Fade('toggle_text');
        new Effect.Move('toggle_text', { x: 200, y: 0, duration:
    1.0 });
    }
</script>
```

The fade effect simply reduces the opacity of the named element to zero. Meanwhile, the move effect repositions the named element according to the X and Y coordinates passed in, along with a duration in seconds.

While these two effects are executing one after the other, they do actually overlap in a very pleasing way; as the text block moves to the right by 200 pixels, it fades out of existence. Save this code and then run it in your browser, clicking the links to see the text move around. Pretty cool, isn't it?

Depending on what your application is doing with the animated elements, you can choose to reset the objects so they can be moved anew. However, in many cases, you move elements just once.

Scriptaculous has a large selection of visual effects; be sure to check their online documentation to reference them all and to see how they work. The principle of animated effects is that Scriptaculous provides the building blocks; how you put them together in your application is up to you.

Sortables

The final exercise for Scriptaculous is an easy way to sort groups of items. The sortables feature allows you to very easily convert any list of elements into a live, drag-and-drop collection of items that can be arranged in any order.

In the `scriptaculous_sortable.html` file, I've added some style to the list, but this is what the HTML looks like:

```
<h1>Arrange this list from best to worst!</h1>

<ul id="list">
   <li>Star Wars: Phantom Menace</li>
   <li>Star Wars: The Attack of the Clones</li>
   <li>Star Wars: Revenge of the Sith</li>
   <li>Star Wars: A New Hope</li>
   <li>Star Wars: Empire Strikes Back</li>
   <li>Star Wars: Return of the Jedi</li>
</ul>
```

CROSS-REF

You can find the `scriptaculous_sortables.html` file on the website for this book: `www.wileydevreference.com`.

Any *Star Wars* aficionado looking at this list would feel an immediate itch to re-sort it from best to worst; the default setting here is clearly incorrect! With just one Scriptaculous method call, you can provide this power; place this code directly below the list:

```
<script type="text/javascript">
   Sortable.create("list");
</script>
```

The call to `Sortable.create` only requires the ID of the target element; it's set to use a list by default, although if you really do need to use another type of element, you can specify it in the argument list.

Save the code and then run it in your browser. You can literally just click and drag on any given list item and move it to the correct position, as shown in Figure 6.7.

Figure 6.7

The completed sortable test page, showing the correct order

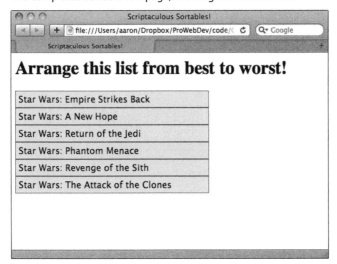

Summary

What you can't do at this point is save this information. In fact, while Scriptaculous and Prototype — and all of JavaScript, for that matter — have given you amazing abilities for manipulating elements on the page, once you click Refresh in your browser, it's all back to square one.

This is where server-side scripting comes to the rescue. When you get to that material, starting in Chapter 13, you'll start to see how to take advantage of various *persistence mechanisms*, which will let you save information from one page load to the next.

But for now, you've learned an amazing amount of JavaScript in a fairly brief time. This matches my credo for learning technology: Learn enough to be dangerous and then hone those skills as you use them in your work. With the skills you've picked up in the last three chapters, you can now credibly call yourself a front-end developer because you can build HTML-, CSS-, and JavaScript-powered sites.

Web Design

Design Concepts

The role of design in web development is often misunderstood. Design is not, as most people seem to believe, concerned solely with making things look good. More than that, design is a discipline that changes the way you interact with things — from websites to telephones to thermostats to cars. Anything man-made has been designed, whether intentionally or not. And, frankly, most things in life are poorly designed.

The goal of this part of the book is to teach you the principles that govern the design of websites. But design is a universal concept; after all, your work is always going to be intended for a human user. And whether that human is interacting with a hammer or your website, the same principles apply.

Consider an example of design working at its best. As a company, Apple has often been criticized for concentrating solely on the design of its products, referring only to their outward appearance — the look of the computer's case or the style of the operating system. But design goes much deeper than that; it's a part of the entire process of creating a product.

When Apple created the iPod, it was entering a market that was severely fragmented with many low-quality music players. Apple's solution focused on simplicity and ease of use. At every stage of the product's development, Apple asked: Is this feature absolutely necessary for a great user experience? The result was a product that did one thing very well. Users found the iPod easy to understand and something they could use right away. But even more important, the iPod's ability to sync via iTunes allowed users to manage their music more easily than ever before.

It was this consideration of the user of the product that made the iPod the smash hit it became. And that's the very core of design — making the product fit the user, not the other way around.

In this chapter, I'm going to deal with the mechanics of visual design: the principles that govern the discipline and the elements that are your tools for implementing it. The subject matter that I cover in this chapter is concerned with making things look good. This is ultimately your foundation for creating useful things, which I discuss in later chapters.

In This Chapter

Design sense isn't innate

The principles of design

The elements of design

Design Sense Isn't Innate

Most people regard design ability more as a genetic inheritance than a learned skill. To those people, designers have fashion sense or an eye for design that gives them their advantage. In other words, this design sense is thought to be innate.

I couldn't disagree more. Design is a discipline that works according to certain rules; just like a student can learn to write without learning the parts of speech, so too can a young designer intuit the principles of design without knowing what they're called. For the rest of us, the design parts of speech can open your eyes to a world that might have seemed the province of a separate class of person.

The objective of this chapter is that with the right tools at hand, you open your eyes to the design that's around you. From there, it's a quick step to developing your own visual design style.

The Principles of Design

Luckily for you, design as a field has been around for as long as humans have been representing ideas in image form; think of the earliest cave paintings. That's a long time in which to figure out what works and what doesn't. And those lessons in design have been codified into a number of working principles. Part rule of thumb and part neuroscience, these principles are a way of understanding how people view their world: what looks off and what feels right to the eye.

These are the principles that so-called born designers grasp intuitively, as they notice good design at an early age. If you're not one of these, this is your chance to learn. These principles aren't a complete accounting; rather, they're the ones most relevant to the field of web design.

Balance

Balance is the equilibrium that results when multiple objects are compared against each other, against the boundaries of the design, and against the horizontal and vertical axes. Balance is an important part of how you judge beauty; consider the human face, with a vertical line running down the center. An ideal face has the same elements on either side of that line. So too with an appealing visual design; elements that mirror each other have an intrinsic attraction.

Designers can manipulate balance to achieve different effects. Elements can be laid out equally from the center to create a restful feeling — this is *symmetrical balance*. But a common technique is to create tension by skewing the normal balance — this is *asymmetrical balance*. Often, a dominant element is skewed, with smaller elements placed around it. Figure 7.1 shows examples of both kinds of balance.

Figure 7.1

Examples of balance

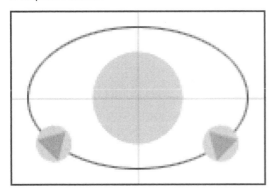

Symmetrical Balance

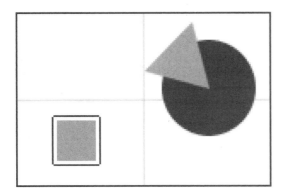

Asymmetrical Balance

Harmony

Harmony occurs where a number of elements share common traits but aren't identical. Harmony can be achieved by mixing and matching various properties, such as color, value, shape, texture, line, or size. When dissimilar elements are placed together with harmonious traits, you get an appealing combination. On your Mac, consider the three icons in the top-left corner of every window. They share the same size and shape, but they have different colors and symbols. Yet, it's visually clear that they belong together. See Figure 7.2 for other examples.

Figure 7.2

Examples of harmony

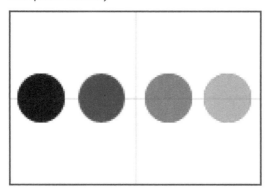

Harmony of Shape

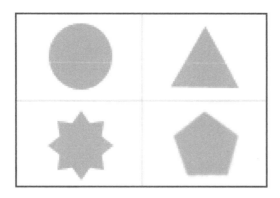

Harmony of Color/Value

Unity

Closely related to harmony is unity, which tells you about the ability of the eye to complete a composition, even when elements are missing. For example, recall Picasso's famous experiment with his painting of the bull. Through a series of drawings, he reduced the number of strokes necessary to evoke the image of the bull, bringing it down to its essential elements.

Unity can be achieved through a number of techniques, such as framing white space to evoke an image or element or creating a larger element from smaller pieces; these are known as *closure* and *proximity*, respectively. Figure 7.3 shows some examples of these techniques.

Figure 7.3

Examples of unity

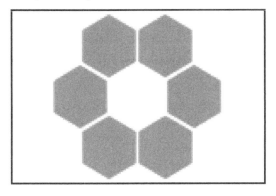

Unity by Closure

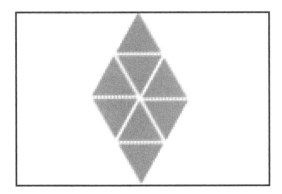

Unity by Proximity

Contrast

Contrast is a very common tool for increasing a composition's visual interest. This principle works best when somewhat similar or related objects are given dramatically different characteristics.

A light-colored object on a dark background, for example, gives that object the pop that the designer wants and says "Look here." As you can see from the examples in Figure 7.4, the most common use of this principle is to give a smaller object greater prominence.

Figure 7.4

Examples of contrast

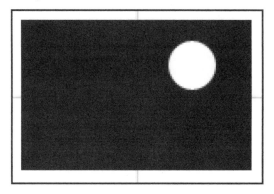

Contrast of Color

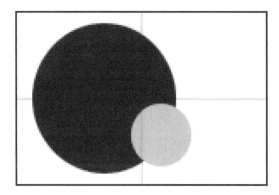

Contrast of Size

Repetition

Repetition is the principle that plays with the use of multiple similar elements. Used strictly, repetition brings order and calmness to a composition. Used with abandon, random repetition creates tension in a composition — the sense that something is missing or out of place. This technique is often used in patterns or in creating progressions — elements that change through each successive iteration. Figure 7.5 shows two kinds of repetition at work.

Figure 7.5

Examples of repetition

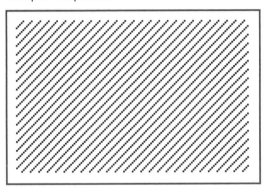

Repetition of Line

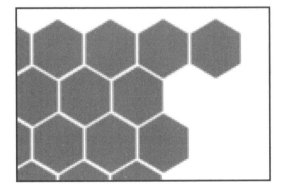

Repetition and
Randomness

Proportion

Proportion uses the difference in the size of elements to create visual effects. The designer can use the difference in scale between separate objects. Used properly, proportion can aid in the expression of perspective, as smaller objects recede into the distance. Objects of similar ratio can be applied in different sizes to establish a relationship between them. Consider an online photo gallery page, where thumbnails are the same ratio as the full-size image. See Figure 7.6 for examples of proportion.

Figure 7.6

Examples of proportion

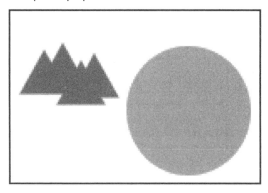

Proportion as
Perspective

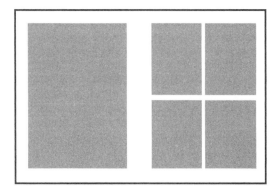

Proportion as
Relationship

Taken together, these principles of design form the building blocks of any composition. They can be used together or alone, in different combinations, and within different elements of an overall composition.

Now, let's take a look at the tools that a designer uses in applying these principles.

The Elements of Design

There's theory and then there's practice. In the latter category, I offer you the elements of design. These are the building blocks of any visual composition, so it's important to understand not only what they are but also the variations that are available. Along with each of these elements, I show examples of websites that employ them in clear ways.

Line

Lines and points are the most basic building blocks of design. Points have only a single location, but in groups, they provide the closure that the brain uses to create a relationship. Lines come in varying angles, thicknesses, and contours. The line can be used to create perspective in a composition, in groups to add visual weight, or to point to an important element of the design. The eye tends to follow a line, so it can be a powerful tool to both create interest and guide the focus of a composition. In Figure 7.7, the photograph on this home page is dominated by simple lines, serving two purposes: drawing your eye to the navigation and, in the white space, giving the logo greater visual weight.

Color

Color is a crucial element of any design and is also difficult to master. With the right color scheme, a design can be transformed from bland to dynamic or from frazzled to peaceful. Colors are powerful tools for influencing the overall mood of a composition; while you might instinctually recognize certain dominant trends — for example, that red is dynamic and green is restful — using them in the right combination is a skill that won't come easily. What follows are some principles of how color works to assist you in choosing schemes for your design.

Color can be defined along three axes:

- **Hue.** This is the name of the color. Blue, green, red, orange, and violet are examples of hues.
- **Saturation.** This is the amount of gray in the color. The lower the saturation, the more washed-out that color is; higher saturation leads to a richer, more vibrant color.
- **Value.** This is the lightness of the color, ranging from white at the lightest to black at the darkest.

Taken together, these three can define any color in the spectrum. This kind of color composition is referred to by its acronym: HSV.

Figure 7.7

The use of lines in a website composition

You may be familiar with a color wheel, which is a tool that shows the relationships between different hues given a set saturation and value. In my own practice, I use an application called ColorSchemer Studio, shown in Figure 7.8, to dabble with colors. The predominant feature of the program is a color wheel. ColorSchemer Studio costs around $50 and can be purchased from the Color Schemer website at www.colorschemer.com.

A color wheel is useful for determining harmonious color schemes:

- **Complementary.** These are two colors opposite each other on the color wheel. When placed together, these colors create a greater intensity. When mixed, these colors combine to create an overall decreased intensity.

- **Analogous.** These are two or more colors that are neighbors on the color wheel, creating similar hues in groups. Mixing these colors gives you combinations such as blue-purple or red-orange. In practice, a single color is dominant (to the point of being monochromatic), and an accent color is secondary.

- **Triadic.** These colors are matched by choosing three equidistant colors on the wheel, such as red-yellow-blue or purple-orange-green. Triadic combinations are popular because they provide strong visual contrast while still retaining harmony.

Figure 7.8

ColorSchemer Studio for the Mac

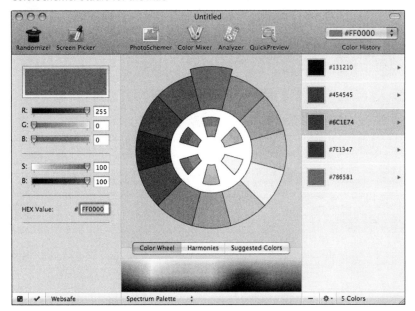

With a color wheel at hand, you can mix and match any of these color schemes or create your own by picking colors out at equidistant points on the spectrum. Although Figure 7.9 is shown in black and white, it was taken from a very colorful website that nonetheless follows a strict color discipline that harmonizes color very effectively.

To see it in full color, visit http://freedomtreefarms.com.

Figure 7.9

The Freedom Tree Farms site makes excellent use of vibrant color.

Shape

Like line, shape is a fundamental building block of any visual composition. Shapes can take any geometric form, although you most often talk about conventional shapes, such as squares, rectangles, circles, and the occasional triangle. Shapes can be rigid or contoured, dominant or recessive. They can be simple layout elements to delineate your written content or they can form the centerpiece of your design. On the website in Figure 7.10, the rectangle is used to create a visually interesting composition. While the credit card is the dominant element, the rectangle is present everywhere; it's the central theme of this design.

Figure 7.10

This site uses the rectangle as its dominant theme.

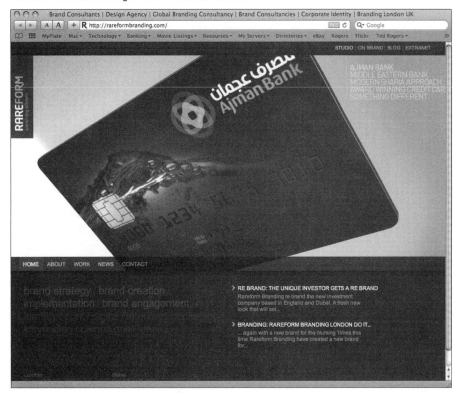

Texture

Within a shape, texture provides the visual interest by creating a surface appearance or a rough-ness. Texture lends your design a tactile element, which can be used to increase the realism of your composition. Conversely, the use of texture can point out how contrived the composition is; this is a technique used by many designers. In the example shown in Figure 7.11, the theme is of a postcard sitting on a desk. The background of the web page shows a fairly realistic ren-dering of wood paneling. It's close enough to the real thing that it enhances the fauxness of the composition, successfully substituting reality with a sense of camp.

Figure 7.11

A faux-wood texture provides visual interest — and just the right amount of camp — to a whimsical site.

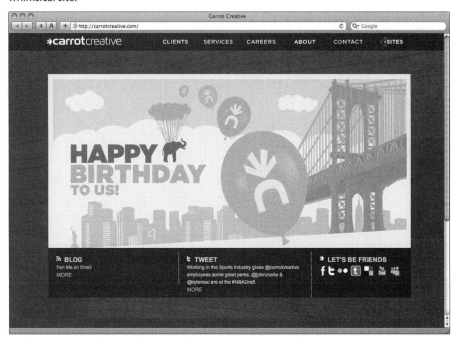

Value

I've already spoken about *visual weight*; this is the element that draws the eye to more dominant objects. The value of an element determines how much visual weight it has; the larger or darker an element is relative to the other elements in the design, the more likely it is to draw the eye. A common technique is to feature a single dominant element on a page to draw the eye there. Photography is a terrific tool in this regard; a color photograph draws the eye like a black hole takes in light. And if that photograph is of a young, attractive woman, so much the better; print publications have known for a long time that both men and women look at pictures of women. Figure 7.12 is a powerful example of a simple photograph that ensures that the viewer will look at the entire composition. The contrast of the subject against the black background only increases the value.

Figure 7.12

This site maximizes visual weight with a powerful color photo.

Type

The final element that I discuss here is perhaps the most difficult — yes, even more slippery than color. The use of type is a crucial part of communication because it's the visual form taken by words. Nowadays, there are probably more typefaces than there are colors, and they aren't nearly as readily categorized!

Let's start by defining some typographical terms:

- A *typeface* **is a particular style of type, also known as a *font*.** For example, this book is set in Arial, a typeface created by Microsoft to replace the classic (and far superior) Helvetica typeface.

- *Type size* **is expressed in varying units.** The *em* is equal to the width of that type-face's capital M character; the *point* is used in print publishing and is equal to 1/72 inch; and the *pixel* varies in size depending on the output medium.

- *Leading* **is the space between lines.** The default leading provided in any design program or in HTML is almost always too tight; most professionals widen that gap to create an easier reading experience.

- *Kerning* **is the distance between characters.** While modern typefaces and applications produce better kerning than ever before, some designers really get down to the character level, adjusting this space between letters.

- *Tracking* **is the uniform space between characters in a block of text.** While the kern can be adjusted for single characters, the tracking controls the space among all characters.

- **Justification describes the positioning of the text within a paragraph.** Left-justified text is the standard used in this book: a solid-left margin with a ragged-right margin. Right-justified text is the opposite. Centered text is often used in title elements. And for high concentrations of text — such as in newspapers and magazines — full justification provides solid left and right margins, adjusting the tracking automatically to make it fit.

- **There are two common kinds of typefaces: serif and sans serif.** Serif refers to the structural details (sometimes called "legs") that hang on to the ends of individual letters. Classic typefaces, such as Times and Palatino, use serifs. Modern-looking typefaces, such as Arial and Helvetica, are sans serif typefaces. Choosing between these styles is often the first step in judging the direction of your overall design.

- **Type can also be styled.** Most typefaces come in different *variants*. The standard typeface is known as the *roman* format; there's often also an *italic* format and a *bold* format.

Words can be the most powerful expression of design, serving as design elements, as shown in Figure 7.13. As a result, the choice of typeface is a crucial one.

Figure 7.13

Type can also be a visual element.

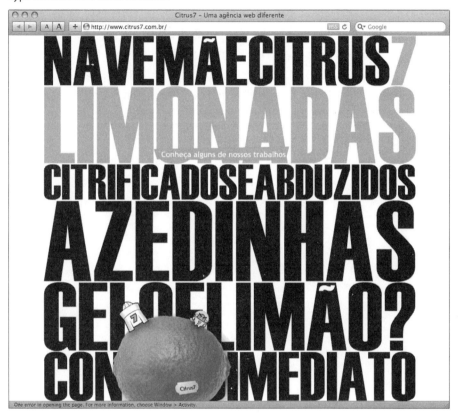

Summary

There's an old adage in the design community: "Amateurs borrow. Professionals steal." It implies that there's a great tradition among designers to build on each other's work. The best designers don't have a special gene. They are instead the most widely read, ceaselessly absorbing the work of others — not just in their immediate field but in any field where design is found.

A good web designer pays attention not just to the latest cool websites but also to the latest advances in industrial design, architecture, and new trends in interior design and even in the world of fashion. Design is everywhere; you simply need to look for it. When you do, you add to your own repertoire, which comes in handy when the client calls and asks for something that looks very professional — with just a hint of sass.

User Interface Design

Now that I've discussed the components that make up a visual design, you can turn your attention to a kind of design that's even more important — but often overlooked. User interface design is the practice of creating sites that aren't just easy on the eyes but are also easy on the brain.

Every website presents an *interface* to the person browsing it. That interface is the combination of the text, images, form elements, and other controls that make up the page. It's what the user interacts with to accomplish whatever they've come to your page to do.

There's nothing standard about the web; every site is uniquely designed, with its own look and feel. Unlike a car, for example, where the steering wheel, pedals, and dashboard are always positioned similarly, a website can position its elements pretty much anywhere. This novelty forces you to learn the ropes every time you visit a new site, which can lead to confusion, wasted time, and frustration. The practice of user interface design is to appreciate the elements that have become standard on the web and to ease the interaction between website and user.

As with the visual principles of design described in Chapter 7, there are also principles that govern user interface design. And if these principles sound like common sense, then you're on the right track to making your future websites more useable.

In This Chapter

Scanning and reading

Clear writing

A visual hierarchy

User testing

Scanning and Reading

The first principle of user interface design is understanding who the user is. *Users* represent the people who will visit your site, and they have this devastating knack for being human. Everything in the design of a website must be done with the knowledge that an imperfect, rushed, easily distracted person is going to be using the site.

In other words, you need to set aside your ego. Yes, you created a wonderful work of digital art. You labored over the positioning of every pixel, slaved over the art, and spent hours trying to get that JavaScript to work just so. But if the page doesn't serve the needs of that visitor — and quickly — then he or she might go elsewhere.

The first example of this seeming fickleness is in how users read on the web. Unfortunately, they read much less than you might assume.

Usability experts have done studies on this, attaching gizmos to people's heads and seeing what they're looking at on the screen while they browse. A web designer might expect a user to rove from the top of the page, admiring the fancy logo, to the navigation area before settling into a long, comfortable read of the text, line by line.

That designer would be sorely disappointed by the reality. Instead, users scan — browsing to a page, doing a quick visual take on the entire page's contents, and then deciding whether to stay or go. Their eyes move everywhere, appreciating nothing but absorbing everything. Within a second or two, the user has decided whether to stay or go.

How is that done? By using the visual cues that most web pages provide. A user spots blocks of content and labels them: navigation, ads, text, ads. Figure 8.1 shows a page from the Macworld website, as a user might see it within the first few seconds of arriving.

In his excellent book *Don't Make Me Think!* Steve Krug calls this process "satisficing": Users make their decisions based on first impressions and choose something adequate rather than optimal. They make the kinds of decisions that cost the least to make; after all, clicking the wrong link on a web page is an inexpensive mistake, so users opt to risk many errors rather than spending the time finding a perfect answer.

Compare this with your own experience. When you're online looking for information, do you carefully read every line on a page, consider your options carefully, and then click? Or do you fly to the closest answer that your eye alights upon? Time is short; you want the answer now.

The principle of understanding who the user is creates a lot of questions, and these questions should inform everything you do. Some of the other principles you should consider include the following:

- **Clearly delineate the sections of your page.** Make it obvious where the navigation, editorial content, and advertising areas are.
- **Write your text clearly and briefly.** Don't give the user unnecessary content to wade through to find an answer.
- **Make it clear where the user is on the site.** The process of satisficing generates a lot of errors; make sure the user can find his or her way back.

As an occasional writer myself, the most difficult lesson I've learned is that users don't read. Well, of course they do — but only as an endpoint in their browsing task.

Consider the activity of finding information on a particular topic, such as installing Postfix on Linux. You might start with Google and browse among the search results, scanning candidate pages, moving back and forth, and modifying your search parameters. Finally, you might find the page that helps you, and you settle in and read that article. But to get there, you've perhaps gone through a dozen or more pages.

Figure 8.1

A page on `Macworld.com`, as seen by a user

Usability dictates that unless you're writing a page destined to be one of those endpoints, you should shun text as much as possible.

Clear Writing

Text is the wheelhouse of the web; that's where the content always lies. So, it might seem counterintuitive to be told to make as little of it as possible. But there's no likelihood of text becoming an endangered species; the problem is, there's so much of it that text has become little more than space filler.

In fact, that's exactly what designers do when they mock up a website in Photoshop (which I cover in Chapter 12); they come up with something that looks great and place greeked text where the content goes. Figure 8.2 shows an example of this on a site that I worked on recently. The designer provided a Photoshop document that contained the complete site layout, with this standard filler text inserted where final text might eventually go.

Figure 8.2

A real-life design mockup with greeked text

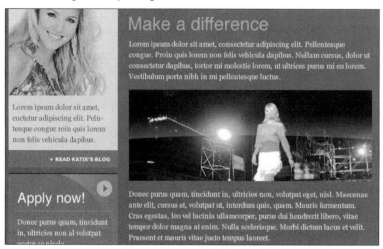

Designers understand that text provides a strong visual weight on a page, so they end up making decisions about how much text there should be in a given location, leaving it to others to come up with the text to fill it.

This is only the most ostensible path to text overload. Another is the unfounded need to guide site visitors. You often see this on a website's home page, in the so-called welcome text. Here's an example from a large international window-covering retailer:

```
[Company Name] is North America's leading manufacturer and
    retailer of custom-made window Blinds and Shades all at great
    factory-direct low prices.
Our products include, Wood and Faux Wood Blinds, Cellular and
    Pleated Shades, Roller and Roman Shades, Panel Tracks,
    Vertical and Horizontal Blinds, Woven Wood and Serenity Sheer
    Shading.
```

Interestingly, this block of text is tucked off to the side of the page, as if they secretly understand the value of it (that is, not very much!). Figure 8.3 shows the position of the text on this site — the identity of the site has been obscured to protect the innocent.

The text itself may appear innocuous enough, but that's the point; it's almost completely worthless as an aid to the site visitor. To have arrived here is to know that this site provides information on a variety of window coverings, and as you can see from the rest of the home page, there are plenty of more visible opportunities to show (rather than tell) what you can find here. What this text most readily accomplishes is to waste precious seconds as the user scans the text for useful information. Finding none, he or she may move on, getting much-needed drapery elsewhere.

Figure 8.3

Welcome text positioned on a leading window-covering retailer's website

There are plenty of places where text is necessary. Text is the primary means of showing a user where to go, but it needs to be written as briefly and clearly as possible.

The first principle of writing clearly is to keep it simple. Writing plainly eases understanding and ensures that visitors know what they're looking at without spending time thinking about it. Consider a few alternatives to the same link on a web page:

```
World of Beans
The Deal with Our Coffee
About Our Coffee
```

Each subsequent choice represents an increasingly clear picture of what the user will find on the other end of that link. When web developers decide to get cute with their text, they cause the visitor to stop for a moment and think, "I just want to find out about their coffee … does this World of Beans talk about that?" With the final option, there's no doubt.

While writing with clarity is important, it's also vital that you write with conciseness. That means packing in as much meaning as possible and in as few words as possible. By getting the message across with economy, you reduce the visual weight of the page and make it easier for the user to make the correct decision.

Think of the common newsletter signup message that appears on many sites. This is the sort of text that has to do a lot of work — after all, getting a visitor to give up their email address is no easy task! The key is to communicate the benefits of doing so as quickly as possible. Here's one example from a leading online shoe retailer:

```
Join our email list for exclusive deals and special offers.
```

This is an excellent example. It contains the well-known keyword "join," which establishes that this is a subscription. It also spells out the benefits very clearly: You'll receive "exclusive deals and special offers," which implies that you'll be an insider — very compelling. My favorite part is the form that accompanies this text: a single text field for your email address. They ask for nothing more, so it's readily apparent that signing up isn't an onerous process.

I would improve this signup process by providing a link to an endpoint, where the visitor could optionally learn more about the newsletter, including how it looks, what information it contains, how often to expect it, and an assurance that he or she can unsubscribe at any time. Yes, that's a lot more text, but remember that with an endpoint, users can get the information they're seeking. In this example, there's actually quite a bit left in doubt. In a well-designed site, clear writing would show the bare minimum required to perform an action and optionally answer any potential questions. In the practice of web development, this is known as the confluence of breadth and depth. The best sites cultivate both breadth and depth by letting users see as much as possible while also letting them drill down for greater detail. With clear writing, it's much easier to make this practice work.

A Visual Hierarchy

As I've already mentioned, it's important for the scanning user to know what he or she is looking at when he or she comes to your web page. If the user can't establish the kinds of content being offered, he or she will have a hard time drilling further into your page to determine where to go next.

Newspapers solved this problem ages ago. Pick up any local daily, and you can see how visual elements are grouped in a clear *visual hierarchy*; the most important stuff is at the top, and the less-important stuff is further down. Techniques such as the use of photos, the size of headlines, and the positioning of elements on the page all contribute to the message of what's most important. Just as they established their practice in print, newspaper websites are the best examples to show this technique. See Figure 8.4 for the local daily where I live.

Just as with the previous example, you can readily parse what sections accomplish what tasks. The very top is reserved for advertising, and your eye readily slides right on by. (Shh! Don't tell that to the advertisers!) The search and navigation area is contained in the next level down. Below this is the dominant visual element: the headline article, with a large headline type size and a huge photograph.

Figure 8.4

The *Toronto Star* home page

It's also important that related elements be grouped together. On this newspaper home page, less important news articles are in the same visual space as the main headline; this proximity denotes a relationship. In fact, this proximity trick is commonly misused to display advertising, as shown in Figure 8.5. If you respect your users more than your client or boss, don't do this.

The practice of sliding ads into the user's field of view is a transparent trick and one that breaks the covenant of trust with your users. Ads belong in their own space, if they must be used at all. Editorial space should be reserved for editorial content only.

By the same token, the visual hierarchy also determines where elements should appear for the designer. If you think of the site header as the global container element, consider the elements within as children — in a hierarchical sense. Figure 8.6 shows how elements on a page can be grouped in a hierarchy. The contents of these nested boxes can be whatever your site deals with: articles and sub-elements in a news story, products and related items on a shopping site, or categories and additional navigation on a general information site.

Figure 8.5

A news story on the MSNBC website includes an advertisement within the body of an article.

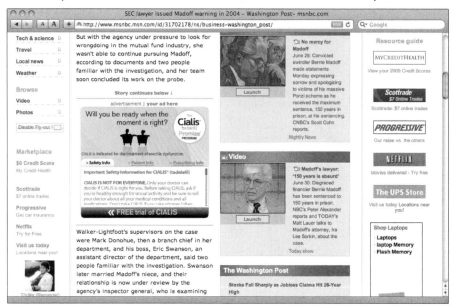

Figure 8.6

A diagram showing visual hierarchy

When you preserve the order of elements on a page, your site becomes that much more accessible for your users. But there's more you can do. What follows are some tips for making your page as comprehensible as possible for your users.

Make links look like links

The advent of Cascading Style Sheets (CSS) has made it easy to make text hyperlinks look like anything, including the body text around them. Sound crazy? It happens all the time. Or the link is made subtly different from the text — just enough to make you wonder if that's what it is. In Figure 8.7, I show two links. While the second line shows the default blue, underlined link style, the first line shows a link style that has no underline and a color slightly lighter than the surrounding body text.

While CSS provides the power to make these kinds of changes, the results of usability testing show that people are far more likely to recognize a link when it's blue and underlined. At the very least, give your links an underline to separate them from the rest of the text.

Figure 8.7

Link styles in text: the top link isn't as obvious as it should be.

Separate elements with white space

Professional designers understand the intelligent use of *white space* — areas of the composition that don't contain content. White space provides a break for the eyes and helps separate content in the visual hierarchy. It's not necessarily white in color either; white space is just an area that doesn't contain anything.

The eye gravitates toward designs that give it room to breathe. There are a number of ways to increase white space in your design:

- **Space between paragraphs.** You can apply a margin-bottom property in CSS to increase the space between paragraphs of text.

- **Space between columns of text.** When you float columns of text beside each other, increase the margin size between them. I often use 10 pixels as a minimum.

- **Space around text.** Apply a padding property to your elements in order to increase space around them.

- **Space between lines of text.** More space between lines — the leading — makes text more readable. Use the `line-height` property to set this spacing.

Figures 8.8 and 8.9 show a before-and-after view of a web page: the first without good use of white space and the second with good use of white space. Note the difference between the flow of the text and the headlines when these elements aren't crowded together.

Figure 8.8

A web page without good use of white space

Figure 8.9

A web page with good use of white space

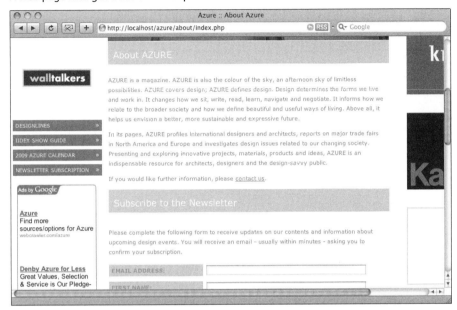

Know the steps to accomplish a task

One of the more difficult tasks for you as a web developer is putting yourself in the user's place. When a user is expected to perform a given task, you need to figure out exactly what the steps are in that task and find ways to optimize it as much as possible.

The classic search box is a great example. Perhaps you've seen a search box that has the features shown in Figure 8.10.

Figure 8.10

Website search: the worst-case scenario

I call this search box the worst-case scenario. If you were to encounter this feature, how would you accomplish the task of, say, searching for widgets? You would need to follow these steps:

1. **Click in the text field.** The default text labeled Search doesn't go away.

2. **Select and delete the default text.**

3. **Type the search term** widgets.

4. **Use the pop-up menu to select the type of search.** Is it a product, a feature, an accessory? Take a moment to think about that.

5. **Click the Go button or simply press Return to begin the search.**

If it looks like a lot of steps to you here, imagine how the user feels when he or she performs them! And then imagine him or her making a mistake and having to return to repeat the exercise. Figure 8.11 shows a more ideal search box.

Figure 8.11

Website search: an improved interface

In this example, you make the website do more of the work, relieving the user of the onerous details. Here, the steps to complete the process are fewer:

1. **Click in the text field.** The default text automatically disappears, thanks to a JavaScript action.

2. **Type the search term** widgets.

3. **Click the Go button or simply press Return to begin the search.**

The second method cuts down on the number of steps for the user and, in so doing, reduces the chance of the user making an incorrect decision.

Perhaps the most important improvement to this design is the removal of the choice of what type of search is to be made. This is the sort of decision that can be presented to the user after the search has been made, perhaps by showing the results broken down by those criteria.

If you follow this principle in all the elements of your web design, you can dramatically increase how easily your users interact with your pages. It might seem like a small thing, until you add up all the wasted time and frustration that you cost your users, especially multiplied by all the pages you put in front of them. The key idea here is to always be mindful of the work you're asking your user to do when you create a feature on your site.

Navigation

Websites aren't like places in the physical world. In your day-to-day life, you can keep track of where you are by any number of visual cues: the position of the sun, the distant walls in your neighborhood Walmart, or the signs on the highway.

But on a website, there's no inherent structure to show where you are. The page you're viewing at any given time is just a virtual piece of real estate — one among billions. The vast scale of the Internet means that there's a great chance of getting lost — either within the network itself or, most importantly, on your website.

That's where good navigation comes to the rescue. Like sign posts at the end of the aisle in a grocery store, navigation tells you not only what you can find but where are you now. Consider the navigation bar shown in Figure 8.12. This bar styles the current page (Footwear) differently, making it clear that this is where you're currently located.

Figure 8.12

Navigation that shows the user's current location

Another handy tool for navigation is the use of the Home link. No matter where the user is on your site, he or she should always be able to get back to where he or she began. A Home link is a simple way to get there.

N O T E

A very common convention in websites is to use the site's logo as the link to the home page. While this works on many sites, you shouldn't count on using only the logo as the way to the home page. Always provide users with an explicit link to get back to square one.

For sites that have depth and breadth, using a style of navigation called *breadcrumbs* can be a very powerful way of both communicating to a user his or her current location and giving him or her a way to step back. Figure 8.13 shows a breadcrumb tool at work.

Figure 8.13

Breadcrumb navigation provides a more accurate location within a section of the site.

Once again, doing some extra work developing your site's navigation ensures that the user has an easier time on your site.

User Testing

There are many theories about what makes a site more useable. The principles presented thus far are the result of a lot of study in this field, where real people are observed using real websites. But there will certainly be times in your web development career where a client or boss will ask you to implement something you feel to be wrong. While you might respond by exchanging opinions based on your feelings without empirical evidence, the more productive response is to propose *user testing*.

User testing may sound like a big deal, but it couldn't be simpler. I conduct user testing on my websites all the time: I call my wife over and ask her to try something or ping a friend via an instant messenger and have him or her navigate a chain of pages.

There's a myth out there about user testing that suggests an expensive lab, with lab-coat-wearing experts behind one-way glass, banks of video cameras, and suave, overpaid handlers coaching the subjects through an intricate series of tests. Yes, these scenarios do exist, but you can really get the same information from something far less formal and far more common.

Problem spotting

Consider a hypothetical website. How many functional and user-related errors might there be in such a system before it's released? This number can range from a handful to scores depending on the complexity of the system. While the developers of the system are responsible for catching these bugs, they're frequently too close to the system to see them. By bringing in people who have never seen the system before, you open that system up to new eyes, which inevitably spot things you hadn't noticed.

The beauty of user testing is that when it comes to finding qualified subjects to test with, *unqualified* is exactly what you're after. You want someone who's naïve to the system and who hasn't seen it before. And except for in very specialized cases, that person can be anyone: the guy sitting next to you in a coffee shop, your mailman, or your precocious niece. Any one of them could look at your site, be asked to perform the most basic task with it, and provide a useful response.

In fact, the more informal your testing, the better, as you're more likely to do it. The first test might reveal some show-stopping bugs — the kind that prevent the user from going any further in the process, such as a link that goes to the wrong location. But along the way, the user may uncover other gaffes — things that you've done that might have made sense to you at the time but which confound the user's expectations.

When you do enough testing, you reveal the bugs in your site. The more you do, the more problems you spot.

Testing methodology

Once you've decided to conduct user testing and once you've found a friend or two with some spare time, how do you conduct the actual test? I find it best to keep things simple. Start with the most basic task that a user might do on your site and then instruct your subject to perform that task: "Starting from the home page, find information on a skateboard."

Then, sit back, let the test subject work, and keep your mouth shut. This is the most important part. You may be tempted to direct the test subject in a certain way, but you don't want to interfere with the process. Every hesitation and incorrect click is data for you, and you should be taking copious notes. Some people even hook up a video camera and record this session, although you don't have to go that far.

While the test subject is performing the task, encourage him or her to vocalize his or her thoughts. This is user-testing gold. You might hear a variety of statements that shed light on what he or she is thinking while viewing your site: "Hmm. I'm looking for a way to get to skate-boards. I don't see anything in the main part of the page, so let's look at the navigation. Okay. Products. I'll click that. All right, now I see a bunch of different categories. Ah, Skateboards. I'll click that. Now I see a list of skateboards. Which one do I choose? It's just a bunch of names. There are descriptions, so I'm scanning over them. Ah, I'll just choose this one randomly."

This kind of running dialogue is a way for you to find out both what the user is thinking and what problems he or she is running into. In this example, several useful bits of information are revealed: If skateboards are important, why can they only be reached through the navigation bar? Then, while the user had no trouble finding them after clicking on the Products link, there was no way to guide his or her selection of a particular board. A theory might suggest adding pictures to this page so the user would have something to compare them with. This would lead to a re-test to determine whether that change paid off with a quicker response.

Summary

Enhancing the usability of your websites increases the chance that they'll succeed at what they're doing. If you follow common-sense rules about what makes websites easier to navigate, people are more likely to stay and discover what you have to offer. But with user testing, you can find the data that supports the principles outlined in the first part of this chapter. As long as you do it as economically as possible, you can put together enough impressions that your site design can't help but be improved.

Search Engine Optimization

Among web developers, those who practice Search Engine Optimization (SEO) are most closely compared to used-car salesmen. And no wonder: There are many misunderstandings about this sector and plenty of money to be made. Unfortunately, a lot of companies have taken advantage of people's naïveté — as well as weaknesses in search engines — to artificially boost the popularity of some websites.

You won't find that kind of talk here. SEO is a legitimate and powerful tool for increasing the likelihood of your website being found. With the millions of sites out there, you need every advantage you can get. In this chapter, you explore not only ways to improve your site's visibility online but also ways in which you can bring in more traffic.

The Dominance of Google

There can be no doubt about it: When it comes to search engines, Google is the king. According to comScore's 2008 Digital Year in Review, Google ended with 63.5% of the search market. But even more telling, Google represented 90% of all the growth in search during 2008. Put another way: Google is already huge and still growing faster than anyone else.

Google's PageRank technology is no doubt a large part of its success. This is an algorithm that parses all the web pages out there to find relevant pages in fractions of a second. This can't be overstated: Those pages are almost always the ones that are closest to what you want. This high degree of relevance is what makes Google so powerful. It's also the nut that your website has to crack.

So, when I talk about SEO, I'm almost always going to mean Google Optimization because that's where most of your traffic is coming from. Despite that, much of what I discuss here will help you with other search engines.

In This Chapter

The dominance
of Google

PageRank and the art
of relevance

HTML optimizations

Google tools

PageRank and the Art of Relevance

Relevance is a loaded term. Of course your site is relevant to you, but is it going to be important to anyone else? It all comes down to content. What can users get on your site that they can't get elsewhere? Are you blogging with a degree of intellect and wit unmatched by anyone else? Do you have a database of exclusive information? Do you sell a unique line of products?

Whatever your site is about, Google uses a seemingly simple process for determining how relevant it is. Popularity is determined by two factors: the number of websites that link to yours (which can be thought of as a vote) and the popularity of those sites (how many sites link to them).

PageRank is the metric; it judges the relevance of a site on a score from zero to ten. As a result, different votes have different weights depending on whom the website belongs to. If my website is linked from `apple.com`, this link would be worth much more than a link from `chucks-gadgets.net`. That's because Google's algorithm assumes that a popular site is more likely to lend my site credibility.

So, the key to boosting your PageRank score is to do one thing well: Get other sites to link to you. I talk more about how to do that later, but for now, it's important to understand how PageRank works and to see the inherent problems that can arise from this system. Because the fortunes of a website may live or die based on its placement in Google's search results, that site's PageRank is a crucial metric. Some companies have set up unsavory practices to artificially increase their popularity. The most common sort is the *link farm*, a massive cluster of made-up websites that look, to a search engine, like related content but whose sole purpose is to link to the source site. To human eyes, of course, a link farm site is utterly phony, as shown in Figure 9.1.

Google's exact formula for determining PageRank is more complicated than is described here, and it's a proprietary formula known only in part. I do know that it's constantly tweaked to overcome those who are trying to abuse the system in ways similar to these sites. So, one could make the argument that link farms aren't even that successful in boosting PageRank because Google's been aware of this practice for many years.

It's much better to contribute to the Internet rather than clutter it up. If you're taking the time to create a website, do it for the right reasons; add to the discourse, not to the noise. Google naturally rewards the former over the latter.

Figure 9.1

A typical link farm site

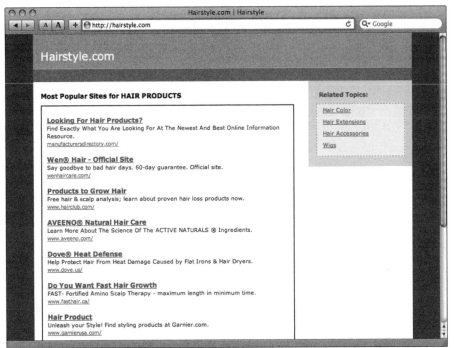

HTML Optimizations

Because search engines are machines, they take a very analytical approach to scanning your site. Because websites are coded by people, there are often mismatches between what you write and what the website reads. Using several optimizations in your code, however, can ensure that your site does well in the search engines' scanners.

While all search engines have a different algorithm, they do have one property in common: They have to scan all the pages on the web. This is done with a software agent called a *spider*. It moves through the web, gathering up all the pages. Google's spider scans the entire web repeatedly; the more popular the site, the more frequent the scan.

The spider software basically copies all the text within your site, following all the hyperlinks to ensure it gets all the pages. It stores those pages on the search engine's servers and processes the pages based on the text it finds. So, what can you do in your code to ensure that the spiders find the right content?

Meta tags

I talked briefly about `meta` tags in Chapter 4 but without going into much detail about their significance. These are the tags that provide information about a page: the type of content it includes and the keywords that should lead search engines to it. There are many `meta` tags, but only a few are relevant to search engines.

The first one I discuss isn't technically a `meta` tag, although it's still a big player in search engine results. The `title` tag is the main headline for your page; it appears in the browser's title bar, and it's the heading in the site's search engine results listing. Figure 9.2 shows an example for the Apple website; match the `title` tag as seen in that site's HTML code (shown by choosing View ⇨ View Source in Safari) to the text that appears in the title bar of the window.

Figure 9.2

Demonstrating the `title` tag on an Apple web page

The contents of the HTML `title` tag should be concise and accurate. My rule of thumb is to use the name of your company or site as well as a very brief description of the page. This means you'll have a different `title` tag for every page on your site. This not only makes it clearer for users browsing your site but also really helps your site to pop in Google search results. Let's use Apple as an example again — after all, they're consistently one of the top ten most-visited sites on the Internet, so they're doing something right! In this example, a Google search for pages on `apple.com` yields a list, with every page given a concise, relevant title, as shown in Figure 9.3.

Figure 9.3

Great use of the `title` tag in `apple.com` search results

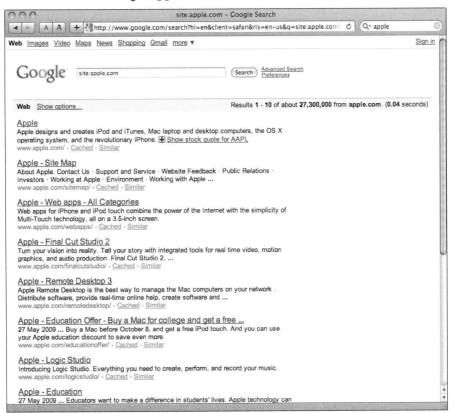

Every page has the company name, a hyphen, and a brief description of the page content. Do the same, and you won't go wrong.

Two other `meta` tags bear examination. The first is the `description` tag. The content placed inside this tag appears in Google's search results beneath the title. If you look closely at Figure 9.2, you can see the `description meta` tag in action in the source code. Then, if you look at the first result in Figure 9.3, you can see that very same text below the title.

Just like the `title` tag, it's important to write an accurate, concise description of the page. Not only does this information appear in search results, helping browsers find your page, but the information is also indexed and ranked by Google to help determine relevance to the search query.

The tips that I provided in Chapter 8 — about clear, concise writing — also apply here. You have perhaps a sentence or two to describe the content of your page, so it must be to the point. Here are a couple ways to do it.

For a site selling cameras:

```
<meta name="description" content="We offer digital SLR and
    compact cameras from Canon, Nikon, Sony, Minolta, and Konica.
    All cameras are sold with our 100% money-back guarantee."/>
```

For a home renovation business:

```
<meta name="description" content="Commercial and residential
    contracting and renovations for homes and businesses in
    Chicago, Schaumberg, Naperville, and Orland Park. We
    specialize in insurance repair."/>
```

For a music-based social networking site:

```
<meta name="description" content="Sign up to share your music
    collection! Tell us about your unique taste in music, and
    discover new artists and songs."/>
```

As you can see, there are no slogans or empty-headed marketing phrases — just the facts.

The last `meta` tag that I talk about is the `robots` tag. While you generally want search engines to index your site, there may be cases where you don't want pages to appear in Google's (or other sites') search results. For example, sites that are in development for your clients should be available publicly but not indexed by search engines. Others maintain blogs that they don't want indexed, preferring to keep their content to a small circle of friends and family. The format of this tag is like other meta tags:

```
<meta name="robots" content="noindex, noarchive" />
```

The `meta` tag takes multiple values. As Table 9-1 shows, Google recognizes these values:

Table 9-1 Meta Robot Tag Values

Value	Description
noarchive	Don't archive the site, and don't make it available as a cached page.
nofollow	Don't follow links from this page.
noindex	Don't index the page.
noodp	Don't use text from dmoz.org — a Yahoo!-like directory of sites; also known as the Open Directory Project — to provide a title or snippet for this site.
nosnippet	Don't show a snippet (normally the description meta tag contents) when showing the site in search results.
unavailable_after:[date]	Remove this page from the search results after the specified date and time. Use this date format: unavailable_after: 25-Aug-2009 15:00:00 EST.

NOTE

If you're familiar with meta tags, you may be wondering where the keywords tag is in this discussion. As it happens, that tag isn't used by Google or other popular search engines. The reason? You can most likely blame the SEO abusers; in an attempt to enhance their search results, they were spiking that keywords tag with all kinds of inaccurate information to the point of making it useless. Instead, search engines rely on the content of those pages as a whole, parsing keywords out of them.

Page structure

Because machines are responsible for parsing your site, you see better results when your code is machine-friendly. This is a big reason for the wide adoption of the xHTML standard, which packages your HTML in an XML document format. When your page validates correctly, an xHTML document is more readily understood by the search engines than your average HTML page.

The first step, then, is to ensure that your code validates against the document type that you're using.

CROSS-REF

For more on validating code, see Chapter 4.

Next, you want to ensure that you're writing clear, semantic HTML. This is tagging that describes the kind of content being used. Recall again the advice from Chapter 4: Code for what the content is, not for what the content looks like.

Following this principle can help you with search engines. Use the standard tags that HTML makes available to describe your content. For example, here's a way to write valid xHTML that doesn't take good advantage of semantic markup:

```
<p class="header">World of Widgets</p>
<p>Take your pick of these widgets:<br/>
Widget Alpha<br/>
Widget Delta<br/>
Widget Gamma</p>
```

To a search engine, this text looks like two paragraphs. Instead, use heading and list tags to specify the kind of content you're using:

```
<h1>World of Widgets</h1>
<p>Take your pick of these widgets:</p>
<ul>
    <li>Widget Alpha</li>
    <li>Widget Delta</li>
    <li>Widget Gamma</li>
</ul>
```

That code looks better and tells a search engine what kind of content your page contains. Also, while not shown in this example, the div tag is a major boon for search engine parsing and shows a huge advantage over the previously used table tag for layout. After all, a table tag tells Google that tabular data is being displayed, while a div tag specifies a discrete section of content. If Google comes across your table-based layout expecting to see financial data, it's going to be a bit flummoxed when it simply sees generic content instead. With a div tag, Google sees distinct page elements that can be more readily parsed for their content.

Keywords

While you've already seen that the meta tag isn't used by search engines, that doesn't mean you can't take advantage of the power of meta tags to increase your site's visibility. By keeping in mind the words and phrases that best evoke the core message of your page, not only will you write better web copy, but you'll also help the search engines index the page.

In Chapter 8, I espoused the virtues of writing less copy. In this chapter, I'm going to espouse writing better copy. To begin with, try making a list of the single words and phrases that you feel are best associated with your page — and, more to the point, which keywords you think may be used to search for your site. If you already have text content, you can start there. For example, consider this partial list of keywords for a manufacturer of windows and doors:

```
Windows, windows and doors, tax credit, energy tax credit,
    federal energy tax credit, energy efficient windows, energy
    efficiency tax credit, economic stimulus package, tax credits,
    energy efficiency, federal income tax, federal tax credits
```

This site places a strong emphasis on the government incentives being offered for reducing energy costs. That message is also loud and clear in its main body copy, sparse though it may be:

```
The Tax Credit Guarantee
Only from [company name]
Get a tax credit up to $1500
Learn More
```

The words "windows" and "doors" are everywhere else on the page, but the main text is all about tax credits. It's no mistake that the phrase is used twice in the same block in an attempt to increase the emphasis.

In many cases, websites use graphical elements to communicate, and a picture of text can't be parsed by search engines. There are a couple of ways around this. First, make use of the image's `alt` attribute. That attribute is there to either describe in words the image being used or to repeat the text that the image represents if the image fails to load. For example:

```
<img src="/images/button_special.gif" alt="Special Offer" />
```

A second way is to include commented text around the image, especially in cases where the image is a large one that contains a fair amount of text. And feel free to include the same kinds of tags you might use if you were marking up text normally.

```
<!--
<h1>Fun and Games</h1>
<p>Get started with a <a href="chess.html">chess game</a> or <a
    href="checkers.html">a checkers game</a>.</p>
-->
```

All of this, of course, is a way to get around the extremely limited type offerings that are available to web developers. But if you can stay with the offerings available to all browsers, then the best option is to layer text on top of an image. This combines the appeal of a visual design with the efficacy of text, as shown in Figure 9.4.

By exposing the search engine to plain text as much as possible, you'll have a better chance of getting your page found by searchers.

Figure 9.4

Using plain text on an image

Hyperlinks

Hyperlinks are the currency of the web. Google uses them to determine the relevance of web pages. If you think of links as money, then the site that receives the most links is the richest site of all and reaps all the rewards — that is, the most visitors.

There are two kinds of hyperlinks: those that link to pages within your own site and those that link to other sites. You need to use both to have a well-balanced, credible website.

Search engines give weight to links that contain relevant text. Unfortunately, many sites eschew this principle and instead write their links like this:

```
<p>To learn more about air conditioners, <a href="ac.html">click
   here!</a>.</p>
```

When a search engine spider comes along, it looks at the text in between those a tags and draws no conclusions about the relevance of the link. Instead, try this:

```
<p>Learn more about <a href="ac.html">air conditioners</a>.</p>
```

As a bonus, the text is shorter! Any opportunity to cut down on the amount of text online is a win in my book. When you take this principle to its logical conclusion, you can create text that's rich in links, both within your site and to other sites.

The key here is to not overwhelm your visitor with links. There are a couple ways you can tell when you've gone too far. First, when you pick a keyword to make into a link, make sure you do it just once; there's nothing more annoying than seeing a paragraph full of links that go to the same destination. Second, don't put too many links in your copy — perhaps one or two per paragraph. Of course, that's just a guideline; you should be able to judge by viewing the visual weight of the links in your text. An example of a good amount of linking comes from one of my favorite websites, A List Apart, shown in Figure 9.5.

Figure 9.5

A good example of link frequency, from the A List Apart website

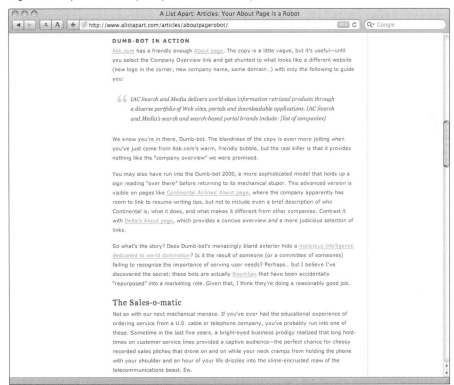

This example tends toward the heavier side in the hyperlink department, but it has good reason: The copy is talking about a number of external web pages and linking to them to provide examples. If your link density is greater than this, make sure you have cause for doing so.

Links provide a way for search engines to see what sites are worthwhile, matching your link destination with the actual text doing the linking. But when you link to external sites, you're giving that site the vote for relevance, right? What benefit is that to your site? As it turns out, both the giver and the receiver benefit in Google's algorithms. The point of the relevance game is to create a virtuous circle of sites that link to each other in a so-called *web of relevance*. As a result, a site that links to other sites both promotes the other sites and suggests that its site is also relevant.

There's one other benefit to linking externally. Smart web developers monitor the source of incoming links (by using tools that I describe next). When they see links coming from your site, they may investigate what you've said about them. Very often, there's a good reason to provide a link back, further cementing the bond between your sites.

This is exactly the kind of relationship that the best search engines reward. Valuable, relevant content that contributes to the community always receives links and climbs in search results.

Google Tools

Google offers a number of tools for web developers, which help them improve and monitor their sites. I'm going to talk about two tools in particular: Google Webmaster Tools and Google Analytics.

Google Webmaster Tools

Google provides terrific insight into how it sees your site with its free Google Webmaster Tools (GWT). You can sign up for these tools at `www.google.com/webmasters`. Once you're registered, you're asked to add a website to your account. You can add as many sites as you want.

Before the tool provides you with information, it has to verify that you're the owner (or, more typically, the controller) of the site in question. The best way to accomplish that is by using a special `meta` tag that GWT provides. Simply save and upload your home page with that `meta` tag, click Verify, and you're done. Figure 9.6 shows the verification page for one of my sites.

Once the tool has had a chance to index your site, it can provide you with information on four data points:

- **Top search queries.** This shows the top ten search queries that led to your site.
- **Links to your site.** This shows the pages and sites that link to your site.
- **Crawl errors.** This shows the problems that the Google spider encountered while indexing your site.
- **Sitemaps.** This is the list of sitemaps that you have on your site.

The top search queries show what terms were typed in Google that resulted in your site appearing in the search results. This is invaluable information for determining the keywords that are effective in finding your site. Also, if there are keywords that you think should be there, this is how you find out! Go back to your HTML to add more of those keywords to your copy.

Links to your site show how people are getting to you. The most common (at least for me) path is denoted as the "/" method — the root path — which means that people came to your site directly. By investigating the More link, you'll be surprised by the number of sites that link to yours. It's always worth studying this list for similar sites that have linked to you. If you find an appropriate candidate, consider adding a link back to them from your site.

Figure 9.6

The Google Webmaster Tools site verification page

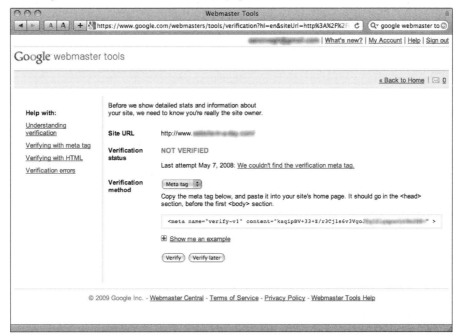

Crawl errors show where Google had trouble accessing your pages. The most common error is "not found," where it followed a link to a page that doesn't exist anymore. If you investigate further, you'll find the specific pages that weren't found as well as the source page that likely contains an out-of-date link.

The final pane here is the Sitemaps list. This isn't a sitemap in the traditional sense of a web page that links to all the pages on the site. The sitemap standard is a way to tell Google what pages are on your site in a rigorous, machine-readable way. This is particularly valuable when you have pages that Google may have difficulty accessing, such as those generated dynamically. A sitemap is simply an XML file; you can write it yourself and then upload it to the root of your web directory.

Here's a simple example of a sitemap file. You can use this format yourself to tell Google where to find it:

```
<?xml version="1.0" encoding="UTF-8"?>
<urlset
  xmlns="http://www.google.com/schemas/sitemap/0.84"
  xmlns:xsi="http://www.w3.org/2001/XMLSchema-instance"
  xsi:schemaLocation="http://www.google.com/schemas/sitemap/0.84
```

```
                    http://www.google.com/schemas/sitemap/0.84/sitemap.xsd">
        <url>
         <loc>http://www.widgets.com/about/contact.php</loc>
         <lastmod>2009-02-20T01:00:00-07:00</lastmod>
         <changefreq>yearly</changefreq>
         <priority>0.3</priority>
        </url>
        <url>
         <loc>http://www.widgets.com/index.php</loc>
         <lastmod>2009-02-20T01:00:00-07:00</lastmod>
         <changefreq>weekly</changefreq>
         <priority>1.0</priority>
        </url>
        <url>
         <loc>http://www.widgets.com/blog.php</loc>
         <lastmod>2009-02-20T01:00:00-07:00</lastmod>
         <changefreq>weekly</changefreq>
         <priority>0.3</priority>
        </url>
        <url>
         <loc>http://www.widgets.com/products/index.php</loc>
         <lastmod>2009-02-20T01:00:00-07:00</lastmod>
         <changefreq>daily</changefreq>
         <priority>0.5</priority>
        </url>
        <url>
         <loc>http://www.widgets.com/services/index.php</loc>
         <lastmod>2009-02-20T01:00:00-07:00</lastmod>
         <changefreq>yearly</changefreq>
         <priority>0.5</priority>
        </url>
      </urlset>
```

The XML document opens with a `urlset` tag, which contains a few attributes specifying the namespace and schema location for this document type. You can copy the entire contents of the `urlset` tag.

What follows are the individual page references. For each page that you include in the sitemap, you must have `<loc>`, `<lastmod>`, `<changefreq>`, and `<priority>` tags. The last-modified tag tells the search engine when the document was changed, while the change-frequency tag suggests how often this content is updated in the future. Different time spans help Google schedule scans of this page appropriately. The priority is a decimal between 0 and 1 and is your own measure of how important this page is among others on the site. For example, you might give the home page a 1 and your copyright page a 0.

Sometimes, I have jittery clients who insist that their site make it into Google's search results as soon as humanly possible. While the structure of Google makes these promises impossible, adding their pages explicitly to the Google index by using a sitemap is a way to make my clients happy. Just remember to keep that sitemap up to date as the site changes!

Google Analytics

Just a few years ago, website analytics was an industry dominated by high-priced players, charging hundreds of dollars a month to provide statistics on who visited your site and what they did while there. But with the advent of the free Google Analytics tool, anyone with a website can view almost everything he or she needs to know about the site's performance, with the help of beautiful, easily readable graphics, as shown in Figure 9.7.

Figure 9.7

Google Analytics' main Dashboard page

To use Google Analytics, you need to have a Google account, just as with Google Webmaster Tools. Visit http://analytics.google.com to sign up. Once you've done this, you can set up a website profile by following these steps:

1. **On the Overview page, click the Add new profile link in the top-right corner.** The Create New Website Profile page, shown in Figure 9.8, appears.

2. **As you're creating a profile for a new domain (as opposed to one that already has Analytics tracking), leave the first section for the profile type as is and then type the name of the domain.** You're shown a tracking code for this domain, as shown in Figure 9.9. You need to ensure that this code is on every page that you want to track on your site. In short, it should be on every page. There are two versions of the tracking code: the new version and the legacy tracking code. Use the new version.

3. **Select all the JavaScript code in the New Tracking Code box and then paste it into your web pages directly above the closing** `</body>` **tag.**

4. **When you've finished copying and pasting code, click the Finish button.**

Figure 9.8

The Create New Website Profile page

Figure 9.9

The Tracking Code page

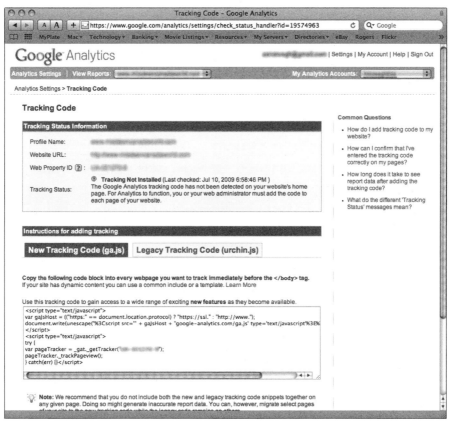

Once the tracking code is installed, you can see the profile on the main Dashboard page. If you want to verify that the code is installed and that the system is gathering data, click the Edit link in your profile listing. There's a brief status message on the top right of this page. If you're checking it right after setting up the profile, it should say Tracking not installed, followed by a Check status link. When you click that link, the system confirms that the code is installed, as shown in Figure 9.10.

This is the point where instant gratification tapers off. You must now wait at least 24 hours for Google Analytics to gather data before the data appears in the report. Let's look at those reports now to get an idea of what Google Analytics can do for you.

Figure 9.10

The system confirms that the code is installed.

Before you start exploring the Google Analytics interface, keep an eye on the applicable time frame. This is located in the top-right corner of the report screens. It defaults to the last month, counting back from the current date. For any numbers that you examine in Google Analytics, ensure that you understand that they're for the dates indicated. If you want to use a different time frame, simply choose it from the pop-up menu.

The Google Analytics interface is divided into four major groupings of functionality:

- **Visitors.** You can view the number of visitors by day as well as the number of page views, time onsite, bounce rate (percentage of visitors who leave after looking at one page), and more. You can drill-down into the numbers here to discover the operating systems, browsers, screen resolutions, and languages used while visiting.

- **Traffic sources.** You can see where the traffic to your site is coming from. Some of your traffic will come from direct sources — people typing the name of your site into the location bar. Other sources include referring sites: other sites that link to yours as well as search engines, such as Google. This section of the system shows specific sources, ranked by the number of links that are sent your way. You can also view the search keywords that are used to find your site.

- **Content.** You can see the most popular pages on your site. The pages that receive the most traffic are listed here, and you can also see the most popular entrance pages — the pages most often landed on by new visitors — as well as the exit pages — where they leave. You can also view a site overlay, showing the number of clicks on every hyperlink throughout the site.

- **Goals.** You can set up goals to determine whether visitors are reaching certain parts of your site. For example, you may have a registration form. If a completed form is worth something to you — say, having a registered user on your site has a dollar value — you can establish that form's thank-you page as the goal. When that page is visited, you have met a goal, and with a dollar value attached, you can readily determine how much money your site is generating.

Take some time to explore the functionality that Google Analytics makes available. As a web developer with clients, I often use this tool to determine how their sites are faring. My clients also appreciate receiving the reports that Google Analytics generates; every report includes an Export function that generates a PDF or spreadsheet document, ready to send to anyone who wants it.

Summary

The use of the techniques of Search Engine Optimization (SEO) goes a long way toward making your site more relevant, both to search engines and, ultimately, to users. Although SEO has been abused by some companies and individuals looking to make a quick profit, I prefer to regard SEO as a way to contribute to the usefulness of websites across the Internet.

Wireframe Basics

W eb development can be a complicated business; as soon as you add more people into the mix, the complications increase exponentially. Every person involved in the process brings their own expectations and ideas to the table. Once you spend any time building websites, you discover that there are as many ways to build one as there are developers.

There's an adage in the industry: The later in the job you get, the more expensive it becomes to make changes. Consider a situation where you're building a site for a client. You may start by designing the site in Photoshop (see Chapter 12). If the client wants something to look different at that point, it's relatively painless. But once you've exported those Photoshop documents to a group of images, a single change may mean that you have to re-export images, which could become more time-consuming as the project progresses.

Also consider the case of creating any kind of dynamic capability in JavaScript. If you've just spent several hours creating an animated navigation menu, that's not the time for the client to provide initial feedback! Unfortunately, this advice comes from hard-learned personal experience.

The purpose of the *wireframe* — also known as the prototype — is to visually communicate your intentions to the client as early as possible in the process. Ideally, you want this communication to occur as quickly and efficiently as possible. That's why there are a variety of wireframing techniques available; this chapter will explain which to choose depending on your situation.

Wireframe Fidelity

The first decision you need to make when considering a wireframe is its *fidelity*. Fidelity refers to how close to the final product it will be. There's a range of options, from the lowest fidelity (a scrawl on a napkin) to the highest (a semi-functional website).

Low fidelity is faster, cheaper, and easier than high fidelity. However, it requires some imagination on the part of the client to bridge the gap between what you're showing and how it translates to the final product. That's why, with a low-fidelity wireframe, I'm very careful to convey the purpose of the document:

- The wireframe doesn't convey any sense of the final site's look and feel.

- The wireframe may show the navigational structure of the site; for example, showing the pages in a hierarchy.

- The wireframe may show a process, such as the basic steps to complete an action.

- The wireframe may show the kinds of content that will be required; for example, an image, a headline, and a teaser text block.

Determining the amount of fidelity for your wireframe is a matter of understanding your client. To that end, I've put together a list of questions you might ask. And in the finest tradition of teen-girl magazines everywhere, I've set it up in the form of a quiz. For each of the following questions, the answers range from 1 (strongly agree) to 5 (strongly disagree). When you're done, add up the numbers. Let's get started!

The client:

____. Has a strong grasp of technology

____. Has demonstrated experience navigating a variety of websites

____. Is the only decision-maker

____. Has explained what he or she wants in clear language

The website:

____. Is relatively straightforward in terms of requirements

____. Is relatively small in size

____. Makes light use of advanced features, such as JavaScript or server-side scripting

Compare your number to the following ranges:

- **7–12.** You and your client are dealing with a small site, and you're probably on the same page. Talk it out, maybe sketch an idea or two on some notepaper, and you're set.

- **13–18.** There might be some sweat on your brow as you think about this one. Pull together a list of the requirements as you understand them, draw some wireframes, and make sure you're seeing eye to eye before proceeding.

- **19–25.** The site is probably more than you can keep in your head at one time. Break it down into pieces to deal with them individually. Wireframe the most important parts. Get the client to sign off on the wireframe and then keep it in a safe place.

- **26–30.** This is becoming a challenge. Perhaps you don't have a good understanding of what your client wants or maybe what he or she wants isn't very straightforward. This could be a terrific opportunity, but the need to understand the requirements is much greater. If low-fidelity wireframing doesn't do the job, go to a higher fidelity. There's probably much more at stake here, so you need to get it right.

- **31–35.** Run for the hills! Ask yourself if the worst-case scenario is something you can realistically handle. If so, then spend some quality time with the client, and assuming the money is there, prepare a high-fidelity wireframe. If not (and, yes, this happens), you may want to pass on this opportunity. Better now than later.

The key is to know the lowest-fidelity wireframe that you can get away with. Go too low, and you can have an expensive and embarrassing misunderstanding down the road. Go too high, and you might find yourself doing a lot of work for insufficient reward.

Types of Wireframes

These are the types of wireframes that I've used over the years, ranging from lowest to highest fidelity. You may have also heard of other types; this list isn't exhaustive. Instead, I'm presenting a range of options to cover the difference between waving your hands enthusiastically and building the entire site. The goal is to pick the style that allows your client to "get it."

The sketch

This is the classic pen-and-paper method. Maybe your paper is a beer coaster, or a napkin, or graph paper. I keep a pad on my desk and sketch ideas on that. This is the easiest way to communicate anything visual; a simple sketch is great because nobody seriously expects it to resemble the finished product, so clients can suspend their judgment and focus on what matters.

A proper sketch is just that: devoid of as much detail as possible, offering just the essentials. If you're new to sketching, then a great way to discipline yourself is to use the fattest marker in your possession. I have a Sharpie marker with two ends: a fat pointed tip and a smaller beveled tip.

The key feature of the fat marker is the constraint of detail; you can't get fancy with it. So, instead of providing fine detail and spending time thinking of the text you want to use, you instead go for the largest, most significant items. Figure 10.1 shows the sort of sketch that eschews detail, instead giving the 20-foot view — perhaps if you were standing 20 feet away from the real site, this is what you'd see.

The purpose of the simple sketch is to communicate a single idea: the overall layout of a site's elements, the rough guess of the relative size of elements, or a guide to a conversation. The sketch is often done with the client to help explain the concepts that you're talking about. In other situations, it can be used to give you a rough idea of the functionality of a page.

Figure 10.1

A simple sketch with a fat Sharpie marker

The sitemap

I often deal with clients who want more of a site than they realize. While talking about their site, they may try to downplay the scope of the job — after all, they don't want to spend a fortune! But as you start to get a sense of what they need, you might find yourself dealing with a site larger than you expected.

In other situations, I've dealt with clients who are fixated on page count. "How many pages can I get for this much money?" is a common (albeit worrying) question. As you'll learn in the later chapters on web application development, *page count* is a fairly meaningless term in the era of dynamic content and page templates; instead, it's more useful to talk about discrete pieces of functionality.

In both of the situations I've described here, a *sitemap* can be a valuable tool for both you and the client to establish the scale of the job at hand. While this may be a literal sitemap — in the sense of showing little square boxes with the lines connecting them representing hyperlinks — it can also be used to show areas of functionality.

In a recent job, the first scenario I described came to pass. The client said that he wanted a fairly modest new site. But the more we talked about it, the more significant the site became. Consequently, my language about the scope of the job changed to include phrases such as "a lot of work" and "some effort." When the client kept using the more modest language to describe the site, I knew that we had a potential communication issue.

So, when I submitted my estimate, it included a sitemap to show the various pieces of functionality at play. Each box in this sitemap isn't a single page but, rather, a group of pages that are responsible for that discrete functionality: There's a store product catalog, a blog, a list of content-managed links to external sites, a retail locator, and a content-managed FAQ, as shown in Figure 10.2. That's aside from the static content, which is a much simpler matter (outlined in gray on the left side).

Figure 10.2

A sitemap detailing areas of functionality, not individual pages

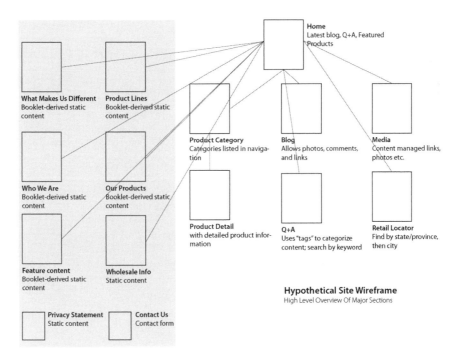

Once the client saw this sitemap, it became very clear that he was dealing with something more significant than he had thought, which justified the price that I was proposing.

This example isn't to say that you can't use a sitemap in its more traditional sense; you certainly can. That style of sitemap is useful where you have a mostly static website — that is, a site that's built and maintained in HTML. When such sites grow to a certain size, it's useful to lay them out on a piece of paper. Clients love this because it provides a useful bit of documentation when you create the site — and it doesn't hurt to have it on-hand when the client wants to add more pages and has forgotten your initial plan.

The page-level prototype

Some jobs are large enough or complicated enough that a sitemap or sketch isn't adequate. As you step up the chain of fidelity, you come to what I call the *page-level prototype* — a page-by-page layout of the site. Using very simple shapes and generic text blocks, I lay out a paper-based representation of the site — one page at a time. As you might imagine, this can be a fairly labor-intensive process. But the result is certain to make very clear how the user will move through the site and how certain kinds of functionality might work.

For another recent client, I was tasked with building an e-commerce site to sell promotional clothing. Through our discussions, I gained the clear impression that my client's expertise was in selling, not web development. As a result, I felt that a high-fidelity wireframe would alleviate her concerns about the site I intended to build.

What follows is a series of pages that I assembled for this client. Figure 10.3 shows the first page, which is a traditional sitemap.

Figure 10.3

The sitemap for an e-commerce site

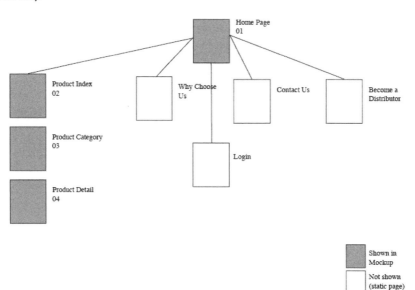

In this wireframe, I didn't lay out every page; the static pages were simple enough that my client didn't need them drawn out. But the e-commerce process was another matter: How would users navigate the product catalog, and how would they make a choice for adding an item to their cart? The pages that appear in this wireframe, as shown in Figure 10.4, are colored blue in the sitemap.

The home page — and subsequent pages — are a clearly generic representation of a website; there's no attempt at design. In this iteration, the home page shown in Figure 10.5 denotes the promotional areas, editorial content, and the navigation that will lead the user to the product catalog.

Figure 10.4

The home page in the wireframe

Home Page 01

Wireframe Developed by Innoveghtive Inc

The catalog shows the categories of products that are available on the site. As you can see, there's a fair amount of fictional text; this isn't meant as the real thing (in fact, there would end up being no less than nine categories). For the left sidebar, shown in Figure 10.6, there's a navigation list showing all the same category names. This will be used in subsequent category detail pages.

On this page, I'm showing the products that appear within the category. Each product has a small thumbnail image, along with the name of the product. The left-hand sidebar shows the current category highlighted; the user can click any category name to view those products. When you click on any of these items, you go to the product detail page, as shown in Figure 10.7.

Figure 10.5

The product catalog page

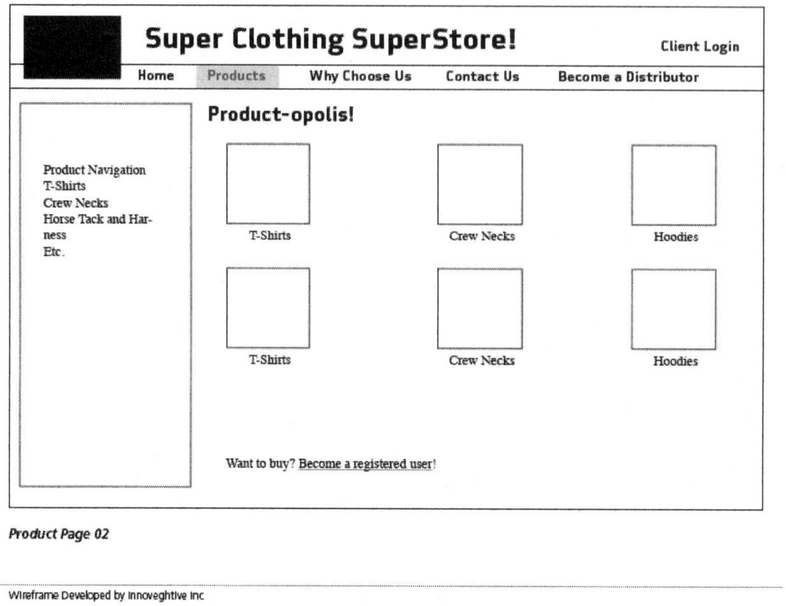

Super Clothing SuperStore!

Client Login

Home | Products | Why Choose Us | Contact Us | Become a Distributor

Product-opolis!

Product Navigation
T-Shirts
Crew Necks
Horse Tack and Harness
Etc.

T-Shirts   Crew Necks   Hoodies

T-Shirts   Crew Necks   Hoodies

Want to buy? Become a registered user!

Product Page 02

Wireframe Developed by Innoveghtive Inc

Figure 10.6

The category detail page

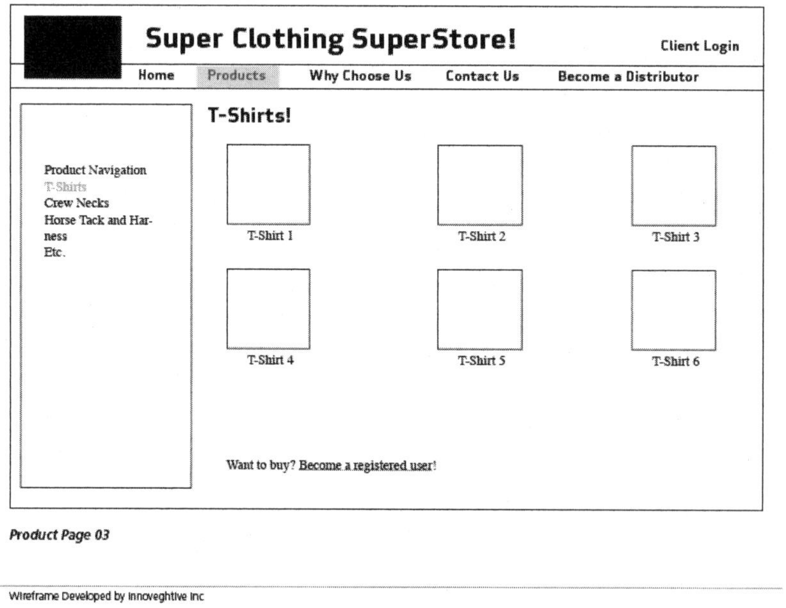

Super Clothing SuperStore!

Client Login

Home | Products | Why Choose Us | Contact Us | Become a Distributor

T-Shirts!

Product Navigation
T-Shirts
Crew Necks
Horse Tack and Harness
Etc.

T-Shirt 1   T-Shirt 2   T-Shirt 3

T-Shirt 4   T-Shirt 5   T-Shirt 6

Want to buy? Become a registered user!

Product Page 03

Wireframe Developed by Innoveghtive Inc

Figure 10.7

The product detail page

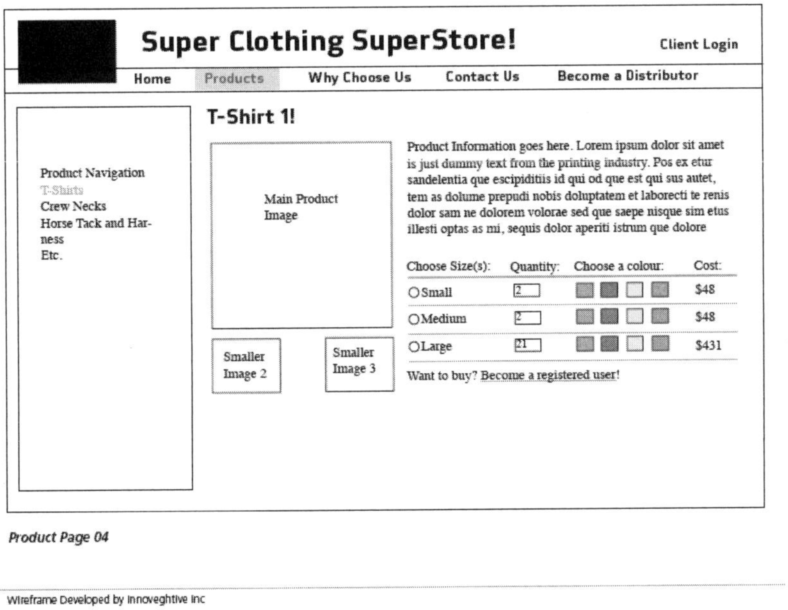

Product Page 04

Wireframe Developed by Innoveghtive Inc

The product detail page provides a view of the actual product. The contents include a large image and a number of thumbnail images (clicking on the small image shows the larger version). One of the challenges for this page is determining how a user selects a product with the vectors of size, quantity, and color. When the user makes a selection, the price updates with the per-unit price multiplied by the quantity.

The client got a very clear impression of the user experience after seeing this wireframe. It helped give the client peace of mind and enabled me to execute the job with a lot more confidence.

The clickable prototype

At the highest level of fidelity is the clickable prototype. This is the next thing to building the actual site. Using HTML and CSS and perhaps some very simple images, you can build a working site. The most common use for a clickable prototype is for sites that are quite large. With an actual working website, the client can literally click through it, determining the relationship of pages to each other and getting a feel for the scope of the job.

The clickable prototype is the most expensive type of wireframe to produce because it takes the most time and effort to complete. For a recent proposal to a very large client, I produced a clickable prototype that encapsulated about one-quarter of the site's content; it totaled close to 100 pages! The purpose of this wireframe was to demonstrate to the client my understanding of the relationship between all the different content areas. I knew the client wanted a section on

News, a section on Events, and a section on Downloads. But how did they fit together? What links would take you to a particular page from, say, the home page?

With the clickable wireframe, you can propose those links in a very tangible way. And although it's difficult to set up, once you've created the framework, making changes is very simple. For example, if a client decides that links should happen in a different way than you envisioned, you can easily make the changes in HTML.

One of the most challenging aspects of creating a clickable prototype is overcoming the perception of clients that you're delivering a final product. Surely, if you can click on a link and move to different pages, then this is what the live site will be like. And given that the clickable prototype is purposely lacking in any graphic design elements, they may be disappointed because it will look like a very boring website!

As I said from the outset, when delivering any wireframe to a client, it must come with stern warnings against expecting look and feel to be determined at that stage. That's why the best wireframes are the ones that are as basic as possible.

In the following examples, I'm going to show some pages from the wireframe that I did for that client, starting with the home page shown in Figure 10.8.

Figure 10.8

The clickable wireframe home page

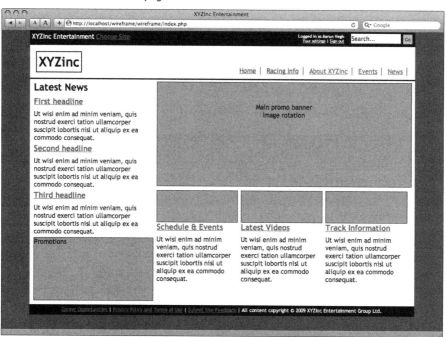

The click-through shown in Figure 10.9 is designed to be as un-designed as possible. Where images might appear, you use featureless gray boxes. The main site navigation is simple and text-based. There are very few text styles and no fancy JavaScript. In other words, it's just the facts. While there's a hint of layout present here, the emphasis is on functionality.

While a clickable wireframe is great for showing how text-based pages can look and connect, it's also useful for graphical pages, as shown in Figure 10.10. Without showing any actual content, the wireframe can show the layout and behavior of a page that's purely an interface.

Figure 10.9

The clickable wireframe postings page

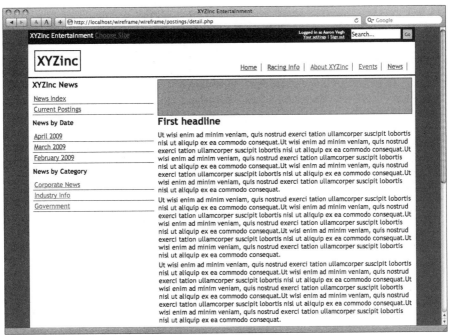

Figure 10.10

The clickable wireframe gallery page

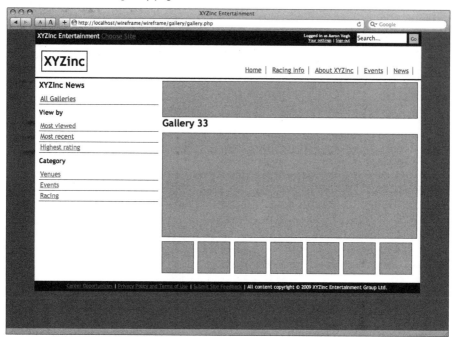

Wireframing Tools

When it comes time to put together your wireframe, you need to pick the right tool. Luckily, web developers using Mac OS X can choose from a variety of tools for creating wireframes. The tools range from the complex to the basic, but they're definitely different depending on the end result you're after. As it happens, I have all these tools in my Applications folder.

OmniGraffle

The Omni Group is one of the oldest developers for Mac OS X — they shipped OmniWeb, the first web browser available for the platform. You'll find their flagship product OmniGraffle at their website: `www.omnigroup.com`.

At its core, OmniGraffle is a charting tool; it's the Mac's answer to Visio from Microsoft. It features a powerful, easy-to-use interface for making a variety of diagrams, including sitemaps and web page interfaces.

OmniGraffle's built-in ability to create flowcharts also lets you easily put together hierarchies of pages into sitemaps. You can draw lines connecting pages together; if you want to move the pages later, the lines follow.

One of OmniGraffle's most attractive features is its extensible Stencil support. Stencils are templates that provide shapes that you can add to your layouts. I use the WebFlow stencil set (available at `http://graffletopia.com/stencils/265`), which provides nice-looking web page icons to accommodate a variety of uses, as shown in Figure 10.11.

Figure 10.11

Using the WebFlow stencil in OmniGraffle

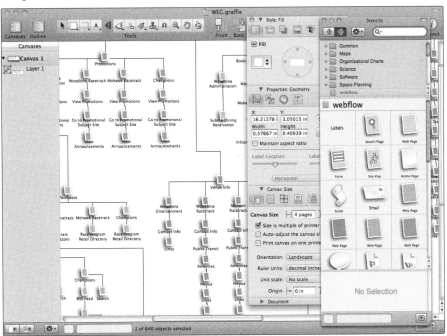

With OmniGraffle's ability to draw a variety of shapes and add text, you can also use it to create mockup web pages.

While OmniGraffle is available in both Standard and Pro editions, the former should provide more than enough features for your wireframing needs.

Adobe InDesign

Available either alone or as part of the Adobe Creative Suite (at version four as of this writing), Adobe InDesign is a page layout application. Although I've been using it for years to assemble print publications, from newspapers to brochures, it's also very handy for assembling both sitemaps and page mockups.

InDesign — as well as QuarkXPress, the other page layout heavyweight on the Mac — offers powerful layout tools that enable you to create virtually any kind of prototype you desire. Because I use InDesign in my own work, I tend to use it disproportionately over the other programs mentioned here. I use it to create simple sitemaps, page mockups, and explanatory (or process) diagrams. Figure 10.12 shows a diagram for a process that I laid out for a client, allowing site visitors to register for travel logistics services.

Figure 10.12

A diagram created in Adobe InDesign

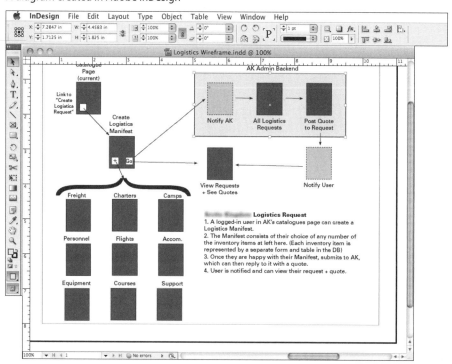

For other examples of InDesign layouts, look back at Figures 10.2 through 10.7.

Adobe Photoshop

While the other tools described here are good for creating approximate mockups of sites, Photoshop, the flagship creative tool from Adobe, can readily create true-to-life renderings of websites. With its ability to create highly accurate, photo-quality renderings, Photoshop isn't an ideal prototyping tool, as it encourages the development of fine detail. But for situations where you're ready to give your client a clear look at everything — layout, look, and feel — Photoshop is the best tool you can use. Figure 10.13 shows a visual mockup of a recent site project.

Figure 10.13

A mockup created in Adobe Photoshop

CROSS-REF
For more on Photoshop, see Chapter 12.

Using text editors

A text editor is the ideal tool for creating a clickable wireframe, just as it is for creating your websites. The right text editor is the web developer's most potent weapon; try them all and then keep the one that works best for you. I use TextMate, which is shown in Figure 10.14.

Figure 10.14

The TextMate text editor

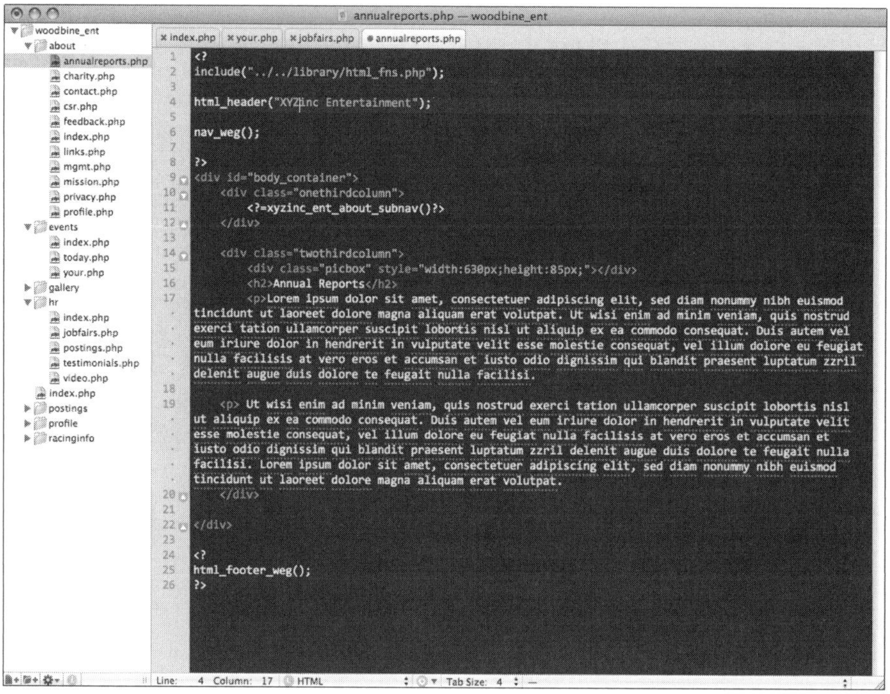

Summary

Wireframing is the art of giving your client just enough detail to state your intentions, without taking a lot of time. Deciding on the right wireframing method is as important as wireframing itself. In this chapter, I talked about the very basic wireframe: the sketch. Moving up from there, you can employ increasing degrees of detail — all the way to a clickable prototype developed in simple HTML.

I concluded by talking about the variety of tools you might use on the Mac to actually create your wireframes; it's a decision that owes itself as much to your comfort level as to the desired level of detail. But once you have the right prototype in your client's hands, you'll be that much closer to determining the requirements for the job.

The Grid

Those who are new to website design often start with a blank canvas — that proverbial white page. Just as it is for writers, that emptiness can be daunting to web designers. You may have things to put on that page, but where do you put them?

For new designers especially, the best tool that I know of is the grid. A grid provides much-needed balance and alignment to your web page designs. The use of grids actually predates the web; designers have been using them for as long as there have been publications. But nowhere is this more evident than in a newspaper. Figure 11.1 shows the front page of the *Los Angeles Times*.

At the heart of the grid is the column. On this newspaper web page, the layout is divided into six columns. With the *Los Angeles Times*, the designers take no chances, placing vertical lines between those columns to make the distinction even clearer. In grid-based designs, you often notice the use of vertical and horizontal lines to separate elements.

The columns of the grid serve as a guide as well as a way to cleanly present content in an organized fashion. Text is most easily read in short line lengths, so the newspaper's narrow columns make the reading experience easier. Along the way, those columns form the backbone of the entire publication's design. Using the principles of the grid, newspaper designers are able to quickly lay out an attractive, easy-to-navigate page while still meeting their daily deadlines.

In This Chapter

Lay out the grid

Grid tools and techniques

The same is true for web-based layouts. Once you create your grid, you dramatically cut down on the time that you need to spend when you implement new visual elements.

While the grid originated in the print world, it's actually easier to apply to the web. After all, unlike in print, the only dimension you control on the web is the horizontal one. That is, you know how wide your site will be, but you have no control over how tall it will be. Even on a static website, where you're coding the content manually, your text can be rendered very differently on different platforms, in different browsers, and by different users — depending on the available installed fonts — thereby eliminating any control you might have over the height of the page.

Let's take a look at a grid that's applied to a web page. MODx is a content management system for the web; its site, shown in Figure 11.2, is a good example of the application of the grid.

Figure 11.1

The front page of the *Los Angeles Times* newspaper

SATURDAY, NOVEMBER 21, 2009

Los Angeles Times

latimes.com

State ekes out a rise in jobs

But unemployment in California still climbs as more seek work.

ALANA SEMUELS

California employers added workers to their payrolls in October for the first time in more than a year, but the state's unemployment rate ticked higher as more job seekers entered the labor pool amid hopes that companies are finally hiring again.

The state gained 25,700 jobs last month, marking the first time it has added workers since April 2008. Government, financial activities, education and health were among the sectors posting gains, probably with the help of the massive federal stimulus package, analysts say.

But the jobless rate continued to inch up, as the positions added couldn't keep up with the expansion of the labor force. Unemployment statewide hit a fresh post–World War II high of 12.5%, from a revised 12.3% in September, the California Employment Development Department said Friday.

Prospects for job growth in key recession-battered industries, meanwhile, remain weak.

"Job losses are decelerating, but I don't think we'll see a sustained recovery in California until we begin to see job growth in construction and manufacturing," said Stephen Levy, di-

[See **Jobs**, Page A18]

Stimulated
Net gain or loss of jobs in California each month

Oct. 2009
25,700

Source: California Employment Development Department
Los Angeles Times

As an island slowly dies, so do its people

ROBYN DIXON
REPORTING FROM
ANJANDOBO, MADAGASCAR

Foreigners have come to Anjandobo village, a cluster of wooden huts on the desolate red dust of southern Madagascar. They've come — outsiders.

The sean are sweating. They wear hats and carry cameras and plastic bottles of water.

The sun exhausts the nearby four journalists and a group of aid workers from UNICEF and the World Food Program. Everyone bristle under rocks. There's little shade.

A small Anjandobo child watches the scene with their

water bottles.
"I'm thirsty."
"No water," replies the child's mother.

Her younger toddler chimes in. "I want to drink water."
"No water," the mother repeats, matter-of-fact.

Madagascar's rainfall has decreased 10% in the last 50 years, and its temperature has risen 10%.

— The World Bank

The spiny forest that once grew everywhere is a memory not much mourned here. It was a tangle of spectacular trellis-like trees with reaching, spiky arms, full of thorns and terrible.

[See **Madagascar**, Page A30]

TAKING IT TO THE RINK

Siena Moyer, 2, of Stevenson Ranch is lifted into the air by her mother, Gina, after the opening ceremony for Downtown On Ice, an outdoor skating rink at L.A.'s Pershing Square. It will be open every day through Jan. 18.

MEL MELCON Los Angeles Times

Cancer testing: What could it hurt?

A lot, actually. The downside of screening can even be fatal.

KAREN KAPLAN

It seemed like a good idea at the time.

In 1984, Japan began screening the urine of 6-month-old infants for neuroblastoma, the most common type of solid tumor in young children. The test was simple and could show signs of cancer long before clinical symptoms arose.

Hundreds of infants went through the ordeal of diagnosis and treatment, but it didn't reduce the number of tumors, including deadly ones, found later. Almost none of the tumors caught by screening turned out to be dangerous — and more of the screened children died from complications of surgery and chemotherapy than from the cancer itself.

In 2004, health officials ended the program.

The United States is grappling with the same type of

problem today. After decades of focus on the upside of cancer screening, public health experts are increasingly reevaluating the wisdom of administering routine cancer-screening tests to millions of asymptomatic people.

Though screening certainly saves lives, recent studies make

it clear that it also leads to biopsies, surgeries, chemotherapy and radiation — even some deaths — that otherwise would not have occurred.

That screening has a downside is not easy to accept, as evidenced by the furor over this week's recommendations from the U.S. Preventive Services

Task Force that most women wait until age 50 to start routine mammograms, and then get them only every other year.

Though the decision was based on new scientific evidence that many more women are harmed than helped by annual tests starting at age 40, it

[See **Screening**, Page A27]

TEST OF NERVES: Professional dancer Jonathan Roberts and Dawn Chmielewski do their routine for the audience before the "Dancing With the Stars" broadcast.

ADAM LARKEY ABC

COLUMN ONE

Her feat in strappy heels

Reporter steps into a crash course in ballroom dancing

DAWN C. CHMIELEWSKI

Eight hours of practice and an utter lack of common sense have brought me here, poised to descend 19 steep steps to the ballroom floor of "Dancing With the Stars."

I lean heavily on a backstage railing, by-perceptibling, and await the cue. Outwardly, I have undergone the transformation from entertainment reporter to salsa dancer, ready to perform before a live audience in a strappy heels and a zebra dress with a plunging neckline and beaded fringe that sways with every teetering step.

Inside, I am a knot of anxiety.

I ask my professional dance partner, Jonathan Roberts, whether he'd be able to carry me down the stairs should I faint. He laughs and says there's a bucket at the bottom in case I feel sick.

As the audience begins to applaud, Roberts takes my hand and we make a grand entrance. Mercifully, the lights blind me to the 720 people seated in Studio 46 in the Fairfax district — and to the panel of three judges who will evaluate my performance. Paulina and all.

Host Tom Bergeron greets us onstage and asks: "What possessed you to do this?"

It started as a dare.

[See **Dancing**, Page A14]

SENATE READIES FOR KEY HEALTH VOTE

Democrats expect to clear a major hurdle today that would open the bill to debate after Thanksgiving recess.

NOAM M. LEVEY
REPORTING FROM WASHINGTON

After negotiating critical last-minute commitments, Senate Democratic leaders on Friday stood on the verge of achieving the necessary 60 votes to begin debate on the most expensive healthcare legislation to go before the Senate in nearly half a century.

Nebraska Sen. Ben Nelson, who had been among three Democratic holdouts, announced that he would back an all-important procedural vote set for today that would allow the chamber to take up the wide-ranging bill unveiled this week by Senate Majority Leader Harry Reid (D-Nev.).

Democratic leaders also expect Sens. Blanche Lincoln (D-Ark.) and Mary L. Landrieu (D-La.) to support a cloture vote on the so-called motion to proceed, although the two lawmakers have not formally announced their plans.

With the backing of those three senators, Democratic leaders would be all but assured of clearing the procedural hurdle, a key step if Congress is to send President Obama a healthcare bill by the end of January, as party leaders hope.

Republican lawmakers have put up a steady effort to make it more difficult for conservative Democrats to vote to open debate, casting this parliamentary move as a referendum on the healthcare bill itself.

"This vote is something we need to look at as a vote that's not some sort of . . . a procedural vote," Sen. Judd Gregg (R-N.H.) said on the Senate floor.

[See **Healthcare**, Page A21]

Fox benches voice of Clippers
Remarks on Iranian player lead to suspension. SPORTS, C1

Genetic bias law
New job and health insurance protections take effect. NATION, A20

Activist dies
Tommy Jacquette, 65, advocated tirelessly for Watts. OBITUARIES, A31

Complete Index A2
California A3–A18
Nation A20
World A26
Obituaries A31

Weather Page: Mostly
sunny. L.A. Downtown: 68/52. BUSINESS, B8

Printed with soy inks on partially recycled paper.

Figure 11.2

The MODx website

Note the visual alignment of the elements on this site. There's a degree of harmony on this page, which comes from the site's adherence to a grid. Figure 11.3 shows the site again, with the columns highlighted.

The MODx site employs a 12-column grid. Each column has a 10-pixel *gutter* — the space between columns. Twelve is a great number because it's evenly divisible by six, four, three, and two. You can put together three groups of four columns, four groups of three, or six groups of two. You can also mix and match the columns by using uneven groupings to create visual tension in the composition.

A well-designed grid is the backbone of a solid website. The following section shows you how to build a grid.

Figure 11.3

The MODx website, with the grid highlighted

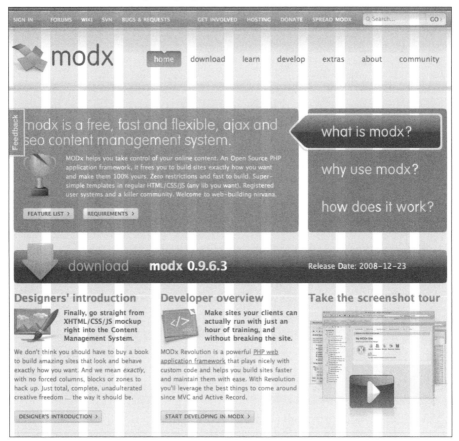

Lay Out the Grid

The first step in building a grid for your site is choosing the width. While the limitations of designing for the web reduce the choices available to you, this is a decision that depends not only on the realities of screen size but also on the content that will be driving your site.

In most cases, however, your decisions are based on screen size. In 2009, most of my work still revolved around the theory that you should design for screens with a resolution of 1024 × 768 pixels. This is the standard resolution found in older computers. Nonetheless, there are enough of these computers around that you have to support them.

At this point, you may be asking, "What about flexible layouts?" There are two approaches to layout. The *fixed* layout specifies an exact width for the site design; when you alter the size of the browser window, the content width remains the same. But a *flexible*, or *liquid*, layout uses percentages instead of pixels to determine width. In such a layout, the width changes as the browser window moves, filling the space.

Although there can be good reasons to use a flexible layout, I'm a strong advocate of the fixed variety. For a designer, a fixed layout provides a constraint that makes it easier to control the look and feel of the site; you know where every element will sit relative to its neighbor. And flexible layouts produce too many variables when you consider the wide variety of screen sizes available: Will it be too cramped on an 800 × 600 display? Ridiculously wide on a 1920 × 1200 display? I have enough to worry about with my design! You'll find that most sites that are professionally done rely on fixed widths. Unless you see a compelling reason to do it otherwise, I recommend giving yourself a break and putting your foot down on the width!

Now, given the limitation of a 1024-pixel screen width and the fact that you want to design for a fixed-width site, you're left with few options. When you account for the browser *chrome* (the browser's window and window elements, including scrollbars), you can probably count on having somewhere between 950 and 970 pixels of width. Anything wider spills past the window boundaries, and anything narrower is too narrow on larger screen sizes.

As it happens, a width of 960 pixels is a perfect number for grid design. If you divide it by 12, you get 80 pixels; divide it by 16, and you get 60 pixels. Figures 11.4 and 11.5 show these two grids as they would appear in a Photoshop file.

Figure 11.4

A 12-column grid with a 960-pixel width

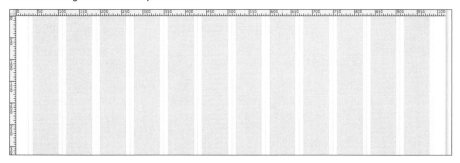

The grids shown here are buffered by gutters, typically 10 pixels on each side. The columns can be grouped into larger sets of two, three, four, six, eight, or more, which helps to constrain and ground your design.

However, you shouldn't follow the grid approach at all costs. As you saw in Chapter 7, breaking with the established approach lends visual interest and tension to a composition. Similarly, when you have a well-ordered grid layout, the one item that pops out will draw the eye.

Figure 11.5

A 16-column grid with a 960-pixel width

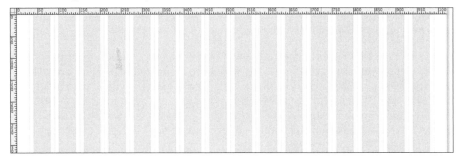

Let's take a quick look at some popular sites that employ a grid layout. Newspaper sites offer great examples that demonstrate the use of grids, and *The New York Times* is one of the best, as shown in Figure 11.6. This is an interesting example because they use a 24-column grid, essentially halving the column width from the standard 12-column, 960-pixel-width layout. This technique clearly gives them more choices at layout time.

Figure 11.6

The *New York Times* website, which uses a 24-column layout

What kind of Mac user would you be if you didn't consider the Apple site? In my opinion, this is one of the best-designed sites on the web; its intelligent use of the grid is just one of the many things that it does right. `Apple.com` uses a 960-pixel-width layout with a 12-column grid. In Figure 11.7, note that the main content features a 2-8-2 column configuration, but there are elements that also transcend those boundaries. It's safe to say that having established a strong grid, the designers have played with the model to achieve great visual effects.

The Starbucks website is another great example. Its 960-pixel-width layout is again divided into 12 columns. Are you noticing a pattern here? Some of the most professional, best-designed sites on the web begin with this very basic constraint. In Figure 11.8, you can see how the central broadcast area spans the entire width, while the featured elements underneath are sitting exactly on the borders of the columns.

The next time you design a site, do what the pros do: Use a grid.

Figure 11.7

The Apple product page for the Mac, featuring a 12-column layout

Figure 11.8

The Starbucks website, featuring a 12-column layout

Grid Tools and Techniques

The web offers many ways to take advantage of the grid in your layout. Here are some of the ones that I use to assist me in my design work.

960.gs

I think of the website 960.gs, shown in Figure 11.9, as the home of web-based grid design. Nathan Smith, a UI expert based in Dallas, Texas, set out to simplify the way that designers build websites. On this site, you'll find not just a repository of websites that use grid-based design (complete with hideable guides to actually show the columns within their screenshots) but also a set of tools to assist the designer — both for rapid prototyping and for production use.

Figure 11.9

The 960.gs site

Smith makes available a set of template files for use in a variety of applications, including Photoshop, OmniGraffle, InDesign, and others. There's also a CSS framework, which provides a set of pre-designed styles that you can use to build grid-based, multicolumn websites. I personally don't use the framework very often in my own work, but the templates in Photoshop are very handy indeed. My favorite aspect of the template is how it provides for flexible margins, with 10 pixels on each side of every column. The site can be found at `http://960.gs`.

Gridmaker

Gridmaker lets you interactively construct grids of varying size and column density and then export them out to Photoshop. It's a Flash-based application, and it works very well. However, the best feature is a plug-in, which you can download and install in your local copy of Photoshop. With the plug-in installed, you can create a new document in Photoshop and then run Gridmaker, shown in Figure 11.10, from the Window ⇨ Extension menu. Set the specifications of your grid, and the plug-in automatically creates it for you on a transparent layer, ready to guide you in your layout.

This is an excellent tool because it helps to create a wide variety of grids, unlike what's on offer at 960.gs. However, 960.gs provides the template that includes guides as well as Gridmaker's background colors. As you saw in Chapter 7, those guides are very handy tools for snapping objects into the right place.

You can get Gridmaker at `www.grafikk.co.uk/gridmaker`.

Figure 11.10

The Gridmaker plug-in running in Photoshop CS4

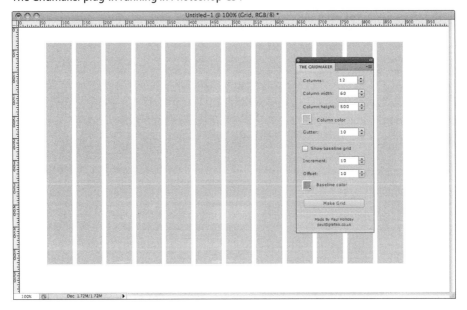

Fluid 960

If you want to really play with the grid, there's no better place than Stephen Bau's Fluid 960 Grid System. Building on Nathan Smith's work, the Fluid 960 template is a tool that you can play with both in the browser and by downloading the file set. The browser-based version is a beautifully designed template with simple elements that cover the gamut of any web page design.

Using the Fluid 960 elements, you could readily mock up a great-looking wireframe, complete with dynamic animation effects, as shown in Figure 11.11. Another great feature of this tool is its ability to use either a flexible layout or a fixed layout; if you prefer flexible layouts, this is a great resource.

You can find the Fluid 960 Grid System at `www.designinfluences.com/fluid960gs`.

Figure 11.11

The Fluid 960 Grid System

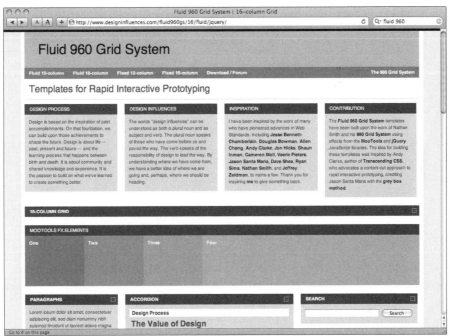

960 Gridder

I've saved the coolest tool for last. The 960 Gridder is a JavaScript-based *bookmarklet*, which is a bit of code that's saved in a bookmark. You place it in your browser's Bookmark bar; then, whenever you run across a website that has a grid layout, you click the bookmarklet, and you see a highlighted overlay showing the columns, as shown in Figure 11.12.

The 960 Gridder (available from `http://gridder.andreehansson.se`) only works effectively with websites that have a 960-pixel width — hence, its name. But you can set the number of columns that are highlighted as well as the gutters and the color of the highlight. Once activated, you can click the tab on the right side to set a number of options. Once you try it out with a few sites, you'll develop a better understanding of how sites are assembled to respect the grid.

Figure 11.12

The 960 Gridder bookmarklet at work

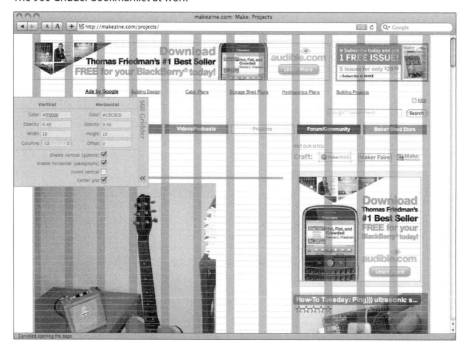

Summary

The grid is an indispensable tool for a web designer. It provides the stable foundation on which you can build the most professional-looking layouts. While naïve designers may chafe at the restrictions of a grid, the constraints it provides are actually very liberating; the examples of some top-flight websites shown in this chapter should prove that you can do your best work within a grid.

Photoshop 101

When you buy a Mac, it comes with pretty much everything you need to be a web developer; grab yourself a free text editor and an open-source file transfer client, and you're good to go. But when it comes to actually designing a website, there's nothing that can beat Adobe Photoshop. And it's definitely not free.

In this chapter, I'm going to start off by justifying why you need Photoshop to build websites. With that done, I show you how to use it. In the right hands, Photoshop gives you the ultimate power to build a website from your — and your clients' — imagination.

Unfortunately, power isn't cheap. A brand-new Photoshop CS4 (at the time of this writing, CS5 had not yet been released) license will set you back a cool $700. Yes, you can definitely find it for less: Search Google, and you can find prices under $500. And who knows? With the power of eBay or Craigslist, you may find yourself with a real deal on a recent version.

But there's no doubt about it. I've been building websites for 12 years, and I haven't run into anyone who doesn't use Photoshop. Designers pass around PSD files like office workers lob DOCs. If you work with anyone else in this business, you need to read their documents.

The good news is that Photoshop is a brilliant program that gives you the freedom to create anything you want. Here's a brief list of Photoshop's top features:

In This Chapter

Photoshop basics

Saving for the web

- **Bitmap image editing.** Photoshop is, first and foremost, a tool for manipulating the individual pixels in an image. This is called *bitmap editing*. Contrast this with *vector editing*, which treats objects as points in space. The web is a bitmap world, while vectors are predominantly used in print. That's why print designers use Adobe Illustrator.

- **Layers.** Other applications have adopted layers, but Photoshop provides the most power here. Layers allow you to stack objects in a very intuitive way: The more layers you create, the better control you have over your composition. You can organize your layers into groups and even nest groups for better organization. When the number of layers grows into the dozens or hundreds, you'll appreciate this feature.

- **Nondestructive editing.** Photoshop provides a number of ways to alter objects without changing them: You can use *layer styles* to provide drop shadows or outlines without affecting the layer contents; you can use a *layer mask* to easily crop out the part of the layer you want to appear; and you can use an *adjustment layer* to apply an image effect onto the layer beneath it. The benefit is that you can make potentially risky changes to your design and easily revert or alter the effect to suit your taste.

- **Transformation tools and adjustments.** You can slice, skew, distort, rotate, and free transform objects into all kinds of shapes. You can also manipulate the colors to your heart's content as well as adjust the contrast, opacity, and gamma of an object.

- **Slicing and saving for the web.** Using the Slice tool, you can segment your composition into pieces that Photoshop can save out as individual graphics, ready for assembly in your HTML code.

There's also a galaxy of third-party tools that tie into Photoshop — filters, special effects, automation tools, and more — to enhance Photoshop's usefulness for different purposes.

Photoshop Basics

Photoshop is too big to cover in just one chapter, so I'm going to focus on the process of creating a web page design by using Photoshop. Along the way, I describe the features that matter most to you as a web designer. So, boot up your copy of Photoshop to follow along!

N O T E

Are there alternatives to Photoshop? If you still can't justify the expense, then there are up-and-coming replacements available on the Mac. Advancements in the Mac OS have given independent developers the foundation they need to build full-featured image editors, and several have recently appeared on the market. The top three on this list are Acorn, from Flying Meat Software (`www.flyingmeat.com/acorn`); Pixelmator (`www.pixelmator.com`); and Iris, from Nolobe Software (`http://nolobe.com/iris`). You can't beat the prices for these programs compared to Photoshop, but they don't have all the features of Photoshop either.

Photoshop Elements is also an option if you're looking to get image editing on the cheap. While originally geared for retouching photos, this little sibling to Photoshop has come a long way, with many features that you'll find in Photoshop, such as layers and effects. The interface is more simplified, so not everything that you see here in regards to Photoshop will be immediately apparent. But for less than $100, you may have a worthy and affordable alternative.

Creating a document

The first step in starting your new website design is to create a new document. In Photoshop, choose File ➪ New. The New dialog box, shown in Figure 12.1, opens.

The dialog box asks you to specify a size for the document. Because you're designing for the web, you should use pixels as your measurement unit and 72 dpi (dots per inch) as your resolution, which is the standard for computer displays. Photoshop includes a number of size templates; choose the Web preset and then pick a size from the pop-up menu. Because you're designing a standard site with a 960-pixel width, the 1024 × 768 template is fine. There's no need to title the document at this point. When you're done, click OK. Your new window, as shown in Figure 12.2, appears.

Figure 12.1

Photoshop's New dialog box

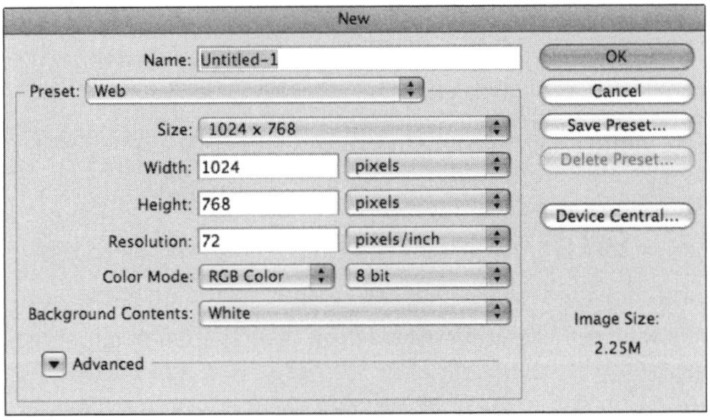

This is a good time to talk about the parts of the Photoshop interface. As you can see in Figure 12.2, there are quite a few panels in Photoshop; those are the small sub-windows that contain tools and contextual information. While some people dislike panels — particularly in such abundance — there's no better way to ensure that you have the most relevant tools at your disposal, given the large feature set available to you. With time and practice, you'll have little trouble finding the panel that you're after.

The prime panel, as it were, is the Toolbar. This is the narrow strip located against the left edge of the screen. These are the tools that you'll use to compose and edit your images. Each tool in the list has a letter in parentheses next to it: This is the keystroke you can use to activate that tool. Photoshop has a vast array of keyboard shortcuts to quickly accomplish the actions you do the most. Running from top to bottom, the tools are:

- **The Move tool (v).** Used to move objects that are currently selected
- **The Marquee tool (m).** Used to draw rectangular or elliptical selections around areas of the composition
- **The Lasso tool (l).** Used to draw arbitrary, magnetic, or polygon-shaped selections

- **The Magic Wand tool (w).** Used to select areas of similar color
- **The Crop tool (c).** Used to draw areas to be cropped out of the main image
- **The Eyedropper tool (i).** Used to sample a color from part of the image
- **The Healing Brush tool (j).** Used to correct blemishes and red-eye in photographs
- **The Brush tool (b).** Used to paint on the image
- **The Clone Stamp tool (s).** Used to duplicate image elements by using brushstrokes
- **The History Brush tool (y).** Used to brush by using the History layer stack
- **The Eraser tool (e).** Used to delete portions of the current layer
- **The Gradient tool (g).** Used to create color gradients
- **The Blur tool (r).** Used to blur parts of the current layer
- **The Dodge tool (o).** Used to selectively lighten or darken (burn) parts of a layer
- **The Pen tool (p).** Used to draw Bézier paths for complex selections or a vector-style drawing
- **The Text tool (t).** Used to insert text into your composition
- **The Direct Selection tool (a).** Used to select paths created by the Pen tool
- **The Shape tool (u).** Used to create a variety of shapes, including lines
- **The 3D Rotate tool (k) and the 3D Orbit tool (n).** Used to manipulate three-dimensional objects
- **The Hand tool (h).** Used to move the canvas if the window is too small to contain it
- **The Zoom tool (z).** Used to zoom in or out of your composition

There are two more items at the bottom of the Toolbar: the foreground/background color selectors and the Quick Mask toggle.

There's also the Options bar, which is just below the menus. This is a contextual zone; it changes depending on the tool you have selected. In many cases, the defaults are what you need (the Marquee tool, for example, is almost always square and free-form; but, if necessary, you can set it to always select at certain dimensions).

On the right side are more panels. The most important of these is the Layers panel. By default, a new document contains just one layer: Background. The icons along the bottom of this panel allow you to create new layers, layer groups, layer masks, and adjustment layers as well as set layer styles. You'll also make frequent use of the Text panel (the capital A) and the Info panel (the lowercase i). You'll get a chance to use these panels as you move through the design exercise later in this book.

Figure 12.2

The Photoshop window and interface

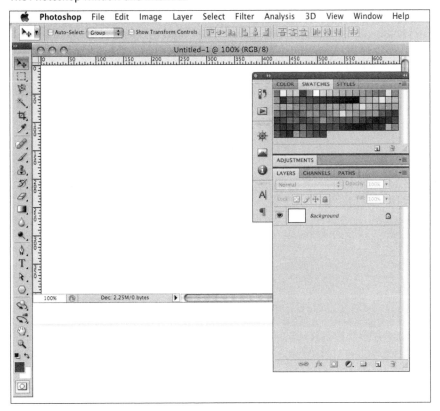

Laying out the grid

As you'll recall from Chapter 11, the grid is an important foundation for any design. While you could create columns in a grid by using guides in Photoshop (with the Rulers showing — ⌘+R reveals them — simply drag a guide out of the ruler region), it's a time-consuming task. If you downloaded the templates from 960.gs, you have what you need; inside that package is a 12-column template for Photoshop (see Figure 12.3). Open that package and then immediately choose File ➪ Save As so you don't overwrite the original template. Name the file `Site Template.psd`.

The grid template provides you with both guides (the blue lines) and column markers (in red). While the columns provide a visual cue, the guides serve a practical purpose in Photoshop: Objects snap to them. Give it a try: With the Marquee tool, draw a selection starting right up against one of those guides. Now try drawing a different selection, but begin it a few pixels from the guide. You'll find that your selection snaps right to the guide. The same is true for objects: If you create a square with the Shape tool and then use the Move tool to move it, you'll find that it snaps to those guides.

While the grid template is usually very handy for helping create your objects, you may find that the guides get in the way. You can either hide the guides by pressing ⌘+; (semicolon) or turn off snapping by pressing ⌘+Shift+; (semicolon).

Figure 12.3

The 960.gs 12-column grid template

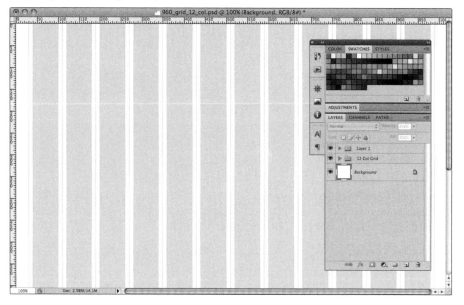

The grid template comes with two layer groups; the one labeled 12 Col Grid contains the red column markers — click the disclosure triangle beside the name to reveal those layers. The other layer group, Layer 1, is a placeholder for your own work. You can delete this set if you want by dragging it to the trash can icon at the bottom of the Layers panel.

For your site design, you begin by setting a background color for the document. Click the background color square in the Tools panel (by default, it's white) and then use the Color Picker to choose a neutral shade of gray, as shown in Figure 12.4.

Figure 12.4

The Photoshop Color Picker window

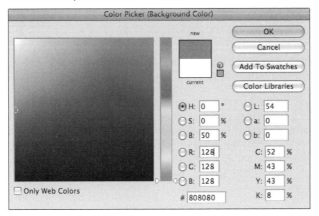

When that's done, make sure the Background layer is selected in the Layers panel and then choose Edit ⇨ Fill. Choose Background Color as the fill contents, as shown in Figure 12.5, and then click OK. If that seems cumbersome, there's a great keyboard shortcut: To fill any selected object with the background color, press ⌘+Delete. To fill with the foreground color, press Option+Delete.

Figure 12.5

The Photoshop Fill dialog box

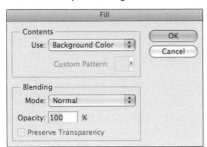

Next, you create the background for the content area of the site. First, create a new layer by clicking the New Layer icon in the Layers panel. You can double-click the layer name to rename it if you want. With that layer selected, choose the Shape tool. Then, in the top contextual Toolbar, choose the square shape. Also make sure that the Fill Paths mode is selected; this is the third of the first set of three icons.

Create a white background for the content area. Use the foreground color picker to choose white and then use the Shape tool to draw a rectangle from the inside-left margin of the left column to the inside-right margin of the right-most column. Figure 12.6 shows the tool selections and where that background should sit relative to your guides.

Now you can apply a layer style. With the white background layer selected, click the fx icon in the Layers panel; from the pop-up menu that appears, choose Drop Shadow.

The Layer Style window appears. Take a look around; the entire suite of layer styles are here, including Inner Shadow, Glows, Embossing, Overlays, and Stroke. The best way to get to know these tools is simply to play with them. For now, I'm using the Drop Shadow style to give the background a shaded effect so the white really pops off the background. With the Preview option turned on, you can see the effect in real time as you change values, as shown in Figure 12.7. You may want to turn off guides (⌘+;) to get a better look at it.

Figure 12.6

Creating your content background by using the Shape tool

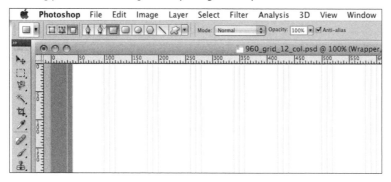

Figure 12.7

The Drop Shadow Layer Style window

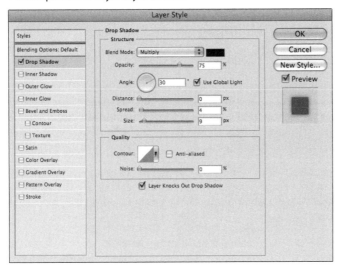

Creating a logo

Let's create a logo. In the Layers panel, create a new layer group by clicking the folder icon.
Double-click the new group and then rename it Logo. Next, choose the Text tool and then click
in the top-left corner of the white area. The contextual Toolbar at the top changes to provide a
variety of text-related icons: font pop-up menu, size, alignment, color, and more. Type in the
name of your company, and style the text the way you want, as shown in Figure 12.8; it works
just like any word processor.

Figure 12.8

Creating text

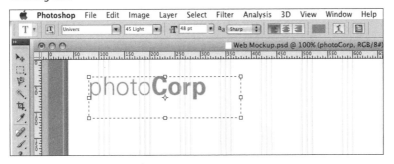

When you're done editing, choose the Move tool. Now, a text-only logo is okay, but you can do better. Let's give that logo a swoosh.

Create a new layer in the same Logo group. Use the Shape tool, but this time, choose an ellipse. Select a good foreground color and then draw an ellipse that encompasses your logo. Then, press V to get your Move tool back. To create the swoosh, you're going to select it, move the selection, and then delete the unneeded portion of the ellipse.

First, ⌘+click the thumbnail that appears in the Layers panel. This selects the contents of that layer, putting a selection marquee around your ellipse. Then, press m to activate the Marquee tool. You can then drag the selection off the ellipse without moving the ellipse. Move the selection up and to the left and then press Delete to erase the selected portion of the ellipse. You should end up with something similar to Figure 12.9.

To deselect the marquee, press ⌘+D. You now have a layer that contains just a swoosh. With your Move tool, you can push it around until it's positioned nicely relative to the wordmark. If you like, you can also move the swoosh underneath the word: Just drag the swoosh layer below the text layer in the Layers panel.

You might also want to rotate that swoosh to make it more dynamic. You can do this by choosing Edit ➪ Free Transform. You see anchors appear around the swoosh; using those anchors, you can grow or shrink the swoosh (hold down the Shift key to constrain it to its original ratio), but if you move your cursor away from the selection, you can also rotate it. Give the swoosh some play until you find an effect that pleases you. One possible outcome is shown in Figure 12.10.

Figure 12.9

Creating a swoosh by moving a selection marquee

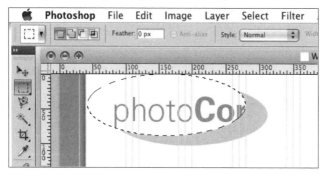

Figure 12.10

The finished logo

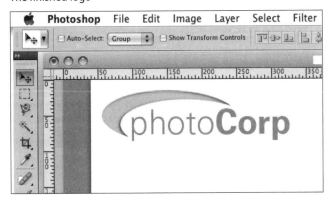

Creating navigation

The next step is to set up a navigation bar. One of the more common navigation styles is the tab layout; individual sections are represented in a folder tab metaphor. The front-most tab has a slightly different appearance than the others around it. You'll create a set of navigation tabs that display both behaviors.

Start by creating a new layer set; call it Navigation. With that set selected in the Layers panel, create a new layer by pressing ⌘+Shift+N, which allows you to also name the layer. This layer is the tab's bottom border, which is the foundation for the tab metaphor.

Make sure that your guides are turned on and that Snap is active (choose View ➪ Snap). Then, using the Marquee tool, draw a selection that spans the entire white region of your site — about 30 pixels in height. If you use the Info panel, you can watch the pixel dimensions as you draw the marquee.

With your selection made, you'll use the Gradient tool to create a nice blend from your site's primary color to white. I'm using the same color that I employed in the logo (it's lime green, if you must know!). The Gradient tool — press g on the keyboard to activate it — provides a number of different gradient styles, which are accessible through the contextual panel at the top of the screen. The colored pop-up menu lets you choose the foreground and background colors of the gradient, and these default to the current foreground and background colors. You're going to choose the second option in that pop-up: the foreground color to transparent (the transparent one has a checkered background).

The next group of controls governs the style of the gradient; make sure the Linear Gradient is selected. You're now ready to draw your gradient within your selected area. The Gradient tool is a simple line-drawing mechanism: The beginning of the line represents the foreground color, and the endpoint represents the background color. The space between is the blend between the two. In this case, with a green foreground color and the background set to transparent, draw with the Gradient tool from the top of the selected area to the bottom of it — a 30-pixel line. You should end up with something similar to Figure 12.11.

Figure 12.11

The gradient of the tab navigation's bottom border

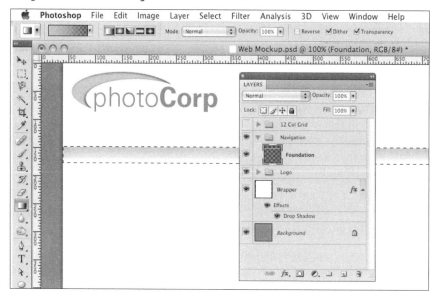

Now, because your shape is graduating into transparent, you can't tell that you've actually succeeded yet because it looks like you've created a color-to-white gradient. Later, you'll put a photograph under it, and you'll see the transparency in action.

For the next step, you'll create an actual tab. Create a new layer and then name it Tab. Then, select the Shape tool and choose the Rounded Rectangle shape. This shape produces a rectangle with rounded corners, which will help with that tabbed look. Further to the right, you find a text entry for the corner radius; I prefer something small like three pixels, but you can choose what feels right for you.

Before you draw the rectangle, look at the Options bar to the left of the shape options. There are three options for the type of shape to be drawn. Choose the third option, Fill Pixels; this option draws the shape directly on the layer. The other options create a new Shape Layer or a new Path, respectively.

Again, you can watch your Info panel as you draw the rounded rectangle for the tab. Mine is 125 pixels × 33 pixels — you're going to clip off those bottom three pixels in a moment. Once the tab is drawn, you can use the Move tool to adjust it so it sits on top of the bottom border.

TIP

With the Move tool, you can either move objects around by using your mouse or nudge them by using the cursor keys. The cursor keys move objects one pixel at a time; when modified with the Shift key, they move ten pixels at a time.

The rounded rectangle you've just drawn has rounded corners on the top and bottom. You only want the rounded corners on top. So, using the Marquee tool, select the bottom three pixels of the tab (you'll select more if you set your radius to something higher) and then delete them.

Figure 12.12 shows the tabs before and after the deletion. First, draw your selection around the bottom of the tab, ensuring that it's wide enough to span the tab and is three pixels tall. Then, press the Delete key to erase the selected portion from the layer. For fine work like this, it helps to zoom in to the tab: Hold down spacebar+⌘ (if you use ⌘+spacebar, you activate Spotlight on your Mac and annoy yourself to no end) and then click the tab until it fills your screen.

Figure 12.12

Deleting the bottom portion of the tab

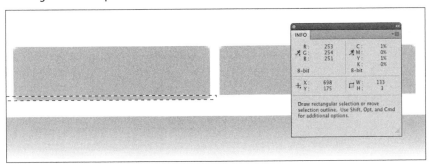

With the bottom of the tab perfectly flat, move it to the bottom border so it sits right on top — the solid color of the tab blending with the top of the border gradient. This is the active tab. Now you'll create the others. Fortunately, you don't have to create the tab rectangle again; you can just copy it.

With the tab layer selected, use the Move tool and press the Option key while you drag to the right. As you do, a new copy of the tab appears. When you let go of the mouse, you see that a new layer has been created called Tab copy. Use the Move tool to position it properly next to the first tab.

Because this tab is supposed to represent an inactive state, you need to change its color. The easiest way to do that is to ⌘+click the thumbnail image in the Layers panel; you should see the marching ants appear around the second tab. You can now fill it with a new color or gradient; I'm opting for the latter. Choosing a dark-gray foreground and white background, I create a gradient that lightens toward the top.

When you're happy with the look of your inactive tab, replicate it for as many tabs as you need. A standard site might have five such tabs, as shown in Figure 12.13, so let's go with that.

What's missing here? Text. Press t on your keyboard to activate the Text tool and then draw an area on top of your active tab to create a text box. Then, from the Options bar at the top, you can choose your typeface, style, size, and color. I chose Univers Bold, 16 point, in the same gray that I used for the inactive tabs. That made a good contrast with the active tab color.

Figure 12.13

Completing the tab layout

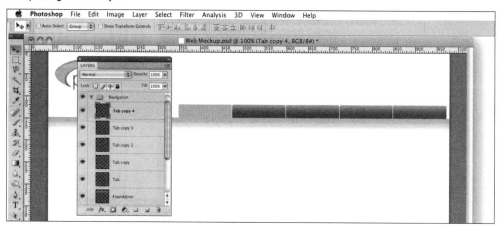

Choose the Move tool when you're done with the text and then adjust its position to sit in the middle of the tab. You can now replicate this text so you have fewer specs to adjust: Hold down the Option key while moving the text box to create a copy. Now you can use the Text tool again to highlight the text and change its color to a light gray. Then, replicate this text label to the rest of the inactive tabs. You can create labels for each of the tabs now, as shown in Figure 12.14.

For the final step, you should create an active state for every tab. First, make a copy of one of the inactive tabs and then move it over the top of the first Home tab; name that tab's layer Home inactive. Then, make four copies of the active Home tab, and name their layers appropriately. Ultimately, you should have colored and gray versions of all five tabs.

During this time, you should take note of two items of relevance in the Layers panel:

- **Order counts.** Items higher in the Layers panel sit on top of lower items. You can move layers up and down the list with your mouse. It's always a good idea to organize this list as much as possible so you can find the layer later and to simplify the layering of your composition. Therefore, each tab state should be grouped together.
- **You can show and hide layers.** There's a tiny eye icon for each layer. Click the eye, and the layer disappears. This is very useful now, as you'll want to hide the active states for four out of the five tabs and the inactive state for the first tab.

When you're done, your Layers panel should look similar to Figure 12.15.

That's one sharp piece of web navigation. Let's move on to the main event for your home page.

Figure 12.14

Applying text labels to the tabs

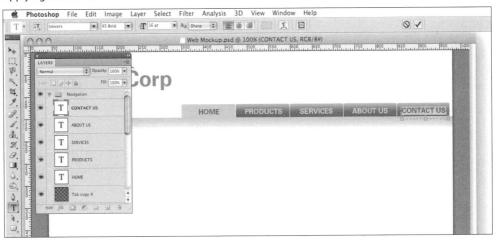

Figure 12.15

The Layers panel showing navigation

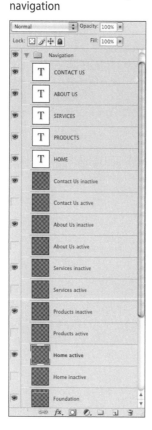

The broadcast area

It seems every agency or industry professional that I've worked with has a different name for it: the "main banner"; the "home promo box"; the "big thingy there." The most recent term I hear is *broadcast area* — the foremost promotional unit of the site. It's typically a highly visual block that contains some text to describe the core principle of the site or to show the most important promotion. This is what's going to catch the visitors' attention when they arrive, so it needs to be engaging.

There's nothing more engaging than a good photograph, so you'll go to the web and grab one. There are a variety of terrific sources of professional, royalty-free artwork: iStockphoto (`www.istockphoto.com`), Can Stock Photo (`www.canstockphoto.com`), and stock.xchng (`www.sxc.hu`) are some of my go-to sites. The latter offers a surprisingly good selection of free images, which I like to use for low-budget or proposal designs.

Create a new layer group and then call it Broadcast. Then, once you find an image that you're pleased with, you can open it in Photoshop and, with the Move tool, drag it right onto your web composition. If it's a full-sized image, it should appear on your document much larger than your viewable area. You might need to zoom out (hold down spacebar+⌘+Option to get the negative magnifying glass and click until you're able to see the entire image) and then use the Free Transform tool (⌘+T) to resize the image. Hold down the Shift key to constrain the ratio of the image as you pull in from any corner. If the guides aren't on, activate them so your image snaps to them. When you've adjusted the image to fit the width of your content area, press Return to lock in your transformation.

Depending on where in the layer levels you've placed it, your newly dropped image is likely sitting on top of other elements in your page, as shown in Figure 12.16.

Figure 12.16

The newly dropped image, obscuring other elements

The only constraint on this layer's location in the stack is that it should be beneath the navigation group. That way, the transparent bottom border will blend into this photograph. Now you need to clip this photo to a reasonable size. A typical broadcast area spans the entire width of a page, but to provide some room for more content below, you don't want this unit to be too tall, forcing users to scroll too much. So, you can settle for a height of about 350 pixels.

To make life easier for yourself, click your mouse in the top ruler bar (if the ruler isn't showing, press ⌘+R) and then drag a guide down to align with the top of the navigation's bottom border. You'll draw your selection from this line.

With the image layer now selected, use your Marquee tool to draw a selection that's the total width of the content area and 350 pixels high (remember, use the Info panel to watch your numbers!). If you aren't happy with the region of the photo that you selected, press ⌘+D (deselect) and try again.

Now here's the fun part: The area that you selected is what you want to keep, so you need to invert the selection. Press ⌘+Shift+I, and your selection is reversed, highlighting everything on this layer except what you chose. Now press Delete. You now have a nicely cropped photograph directly beneath your navigation area, as shown in Figure 12.17.

Figure 12.17

The completed broadcast photo

But your work here isn't done yet. This is where you might put some text to explain the company's purpose, vision, or novel use of doughnut holes. You're going to create a text area: a semi-transparent panel with some text.

In the same layer group as your image, create a new layer called text area shape. Then, using the Shape tool (again, making sure that Fill Pixels is selected in the Options bar), choose a rectangle and a white foreground color. Use the column guides to allow yourself a three-column width. My final rectangle is 240 × 290 pixels on the right side of the image.

Now, a pure-white block is somewhat jarring, so you tone it down a little by reducing the opacity; a handy little slider at the top of the Layers panel allows you to do this. Taking it down to 75% achieves a suitable effect with the image I have (your results may vary). With that done, I'll add some text supplied by the (yes, fictitious) client.

It doesn't hurt to add some visual accents. I added a new layer to draw a 1-pixel key line beneath the photo, and I added a stroke inset to the broadcast area's text box. Can you figure out how to do that last effect? Make a selection of the box and then look for the Select ⇨ Modify submenu. You can stroke a line by choosing Edit ⇨ Stroke.

The final broadcast area is complete. See Figure 12.18 for the results.

Figure 12.18

The final broadcast area

Main content area

With the broadcast area taken care of, it's time to move on to the content of your home page. This space is often used to provide featurettes that lead further into the site. For each of your site's ultimate content areas, a promotional box can highlight that feature.

This is an opportunity to showcase a little bit of editorial content, presented in a clean arrangement. In this design, you'll use four promotional units and arrange them precisely by using the 12-column grid layout. As you did with the navigational tabs, you'll create the first one and then duplicate it multiple times, giving you the foundation of the design while letting you change just the parts that are different.

The first step, as always, is to create a new layer group. I've called mine Promo boxes. This layer group will contain a group for each box, so you'll create the first group right now; I called mine Promo 1. Then, create a new layer within that group. You'll use this layer to draw the box's background shape.

Click the Shape tool and then choose the rectangle from the contextual menu. With a white foreground color, draw a rectangle that's 220 pixels × 170 pixels from the far-left margin of the content area to the right side of the third column. Remember, the 12-column grid gives you four 3-column-wide boxes. The grid guides provide you with a 10-pixel gutter in between them.

For visual interest, I'm drawing the promo box to sit just a bit on top of the broadcast area. And to make the white box visible, I'm applying a drop shadow by using the layer styles. Because you're butting up against the side of the white content area, which also has a drop shadow, you might notice an inconsistency in the darkness of the shadow; that happens because you now have two shadows overlapping. You can minimize this problem by reducing the opacity or size of the promo box's drop shadow. But, ultimately, when it comes time to slice and export this design to individual images, you'll clip the side of this box and thus remove this hazard in your final web page. Figure 12.19 shows the drawn promo box.

Figure 12.19

The promo box background

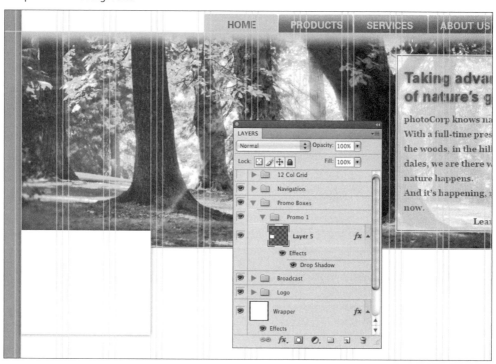

A small thumbnail image really helps set off a promotional unit like this. I grabbed a set of free icons for the Mac, which are available in PNG format, to make this area more interesting.

NOTE
Recall from Chapter 4 that PNG is a file format that provides full transparency. This allows you to place even shaded elements on top of others to achieve some slick new effects.

In this case, the PNG image sits just above the top of the promo box, again providing some more visual interest. With the Text tool, type some content. The final box, shown in Figure 12.20, is ready for duplication.

Figure 12.20

The completed first promo box

Just as you can duplicate layers, you can move and duplicate layer groups. In the Layers panel, select the Promo 1 group. Then, holding down the Option key, drag horizontally in the image window, creating a new layer group identical to the first. Place it 10 pixels to the right of the first box, using the guides to assist you. Then, repeat the process to create the third and fourth boxes. At the same time as you're Option+dragging, hold down the Shift key to constrain the move to the horizontal axis. This ensures that your boxes line up.

When I completed my duplication process, I discovered that the promo boxes were too close to the broadcast area's text content box. If you have the same problem, you can easily move the promo boxes down by selecting the Promo Boxes group and then using the Move tool. After holding the Shift key and pressing the down arrow a few times, you'll have the right layout.

You may also want to change the position of the broadcast area's text box. Although my text box fit within the grid when I originally placed it, the box now seemed unbalanced compared to the four promo boxes below. The solution is to make that box wider, spanning the distance between the middle columns of the last two promo boxes. This also requires that you adjust the width and size of the text inside that box to fit properly.

With that accomplished, you can now address the final three promo boxes. Get some more images, and replace the ones currently occupying these boxes. The final result, shown in Figure 12.21, combines unique text and icons for each box.

Figure 12.21

The completed promo box set, with the adjusted broadcast text area

Final touches

At this point, your design is mostly complete, and all major page elements are there. Although a designer often examines his or her work pixel by pixel during the entire process, now is the time when you're most likely to step back and ask: Does this work? Very often, I've come this far in a design and abandoned it. However, for a mockup going to a client, this one will suffice. All that remains is the inclusion of some of the basic elements that make up any web page, such as a footer and perhaps some widgets at the top.

Figure 12.22 shows the final composition as it heads to the client. Use the File ⇨ Save for Web & Devices command to export the entire image as a JPEG (which makes it easier for your client to open). I cover this feature in more detail shortly. This is what you'll send, while keeping your many-layered composition in the PSD format.

Figure 12.22

The finished design

You'll get feedback, of course, and this is the best time to get it. Once you go through a few iterations with the client, you're then ready to actually build the website. And that's also where Photoshop comes in handy.

NOTE
The completed Photoshop document used in this exercise is available on this book's website: `www.wileydevreference.com`. Go grab it to compare your results with what I've done.

Saving for the Web

With the help of the Slice tool and the Save for Web feature of Photoshop, you can make short work of turning your static composition into a functional web page. Let's take a look at that process now.

The Slice tool is your primary tool for exporting your image. Taken as a whole, your composition isn't worth much. It needs to be split into the individual components that make up the page. Think of a slice as a permanent selection; it establishes a zone of the image that will be exported when you use the Save for Web feature.

The Slice tool is comprised of two separate pieces of functionality: The default tool creates slices, while the Slice Select tool allows you to both choose slices and alter their size. These tools are hidden under the Crop tool (press C to select the Crop tool and then press Shift+C to toggle through the modes until the Slice tool is selected).

Once the Slice tool is chosen, you can draw rectangles around the regions you want to export. There are *active slices* — that is, those that you draw — and *inactive slices*, which Photoshop assumes based on the areas that you've left unselected. While standard practice dictates that you should explicitly cordon off every area of your composition, you don't strictly need to.

For example, in the design you created, you may want to manually export most page elements (by selecting them with the Marquee tool and then copying and pasting them into a new document) and slice just the navigation, as you might anticipate those items changing more frequently. For this exercise, however, you will slice the entire composition.

There are some rules to keep in mind as you decide where to make your slices:

- **Keep the background separate.** Think about how you'll build this page in HTML and CSS. The background of the white panel sitting on a gray background is represented by its own `div` tag, so you want to capture it separately. My preferred method for a situation like this is to take a 1-pixel-tall snapshot of the white, drop shadow, and gray background, spanning the entire width of my document. You can then set that image as the background of the `wrapper div` (see Chapter 5 for a refresher if you need it).

- **Think square.** If you think about the individual components of a page as boxes piled on top of each other (from the top of the page moving down), then you'll be of the right mindset to slice your image. Make your slice of the logo sit evenly beside the background above the navigation tabs; that's one level in the stack, spanning the width of the page. Then, capture the level that contains the navigation tabs. Repeat this process for each component on the page.

- **Don't capture HTML text.** For elements that you intend to represent in your HTML code, don't let them appear in your images. For example, the search field and button should be removed from that slice (use the visibility icon in the Layers panel to temporarily de-activate them while you make your export).

- **Know when to go manual.** Some elements aren't appropriate for capture with the Slice tool. The GO button for the search box is much more easily selected and exported manually. The promo boxes running below and on top of the broadcast area have drop shadows, which disappear if you run a hard-edged slice alongside them. Instead, manually select them and export to a new image, saving them as PNG files, which will retain the drop shadow along with its transparency.

Figure 12.23 shows the results of my slicing on this document. For clarity's sake, I have hidden the elements that won't be exported with my slices: the search feature, the broadcast area text, the promo boxes, and the footer text.

Figure 12.23

The design with slices and exportable content displayed

Also, notice the difference between the active slices — the ones I drew — and the inactive slices. The inactive slices have a light-gray index number, while the active slices appear with a dark-blue index number.

NOTE

Watch those slice index numbers. If you don't have Snap turned on, you could easily overlap slices or leave tiny unseen gaps between them. This will lead to unexpected results when you export the slices, so make sure you've got snapping turned on.

You're ready to export your slices. Choose File ⇨ Save for Web & Devices. You see the Save for Web & Devices dialog box, as shown in Figure 12.24.

Figure 12.24

The Save for Web & Devices dialog box

There's quite a bit of functionality crammed into this window. There's even a toolbar to help you work with your slices. By default, you have the Slice Select tool chosen. You can use that tool to click your slices and then use the image export options on the right side of the window to set the parameters for that slice. By default, every slice is exported with the same characteristics, although you can also set different specs depending on the slice.

Here's how to choose an image format:

- **GIF.** This format is ideal for simple images that use few colors. GIF is *lossless*, which means that it saves out a faithful rendering of your image by using a limited color palette. GIF also provides a very basic transparency setting, where individual pixels can be either fully transparent or opaque.

- **JPEG.** For images that contain many colors, such as a photograph, JPEG provides the best results by compressing the image data. This results in some artifacts in the image, but you can control the amount of compression to provide the best compromise. JPEG has no transparency features.

- **PNG.** For images that have lossless compression and also require full transparency, PNG is the way to go. The resulting images are larger in file size, but you have no other option when your image needs a soft drop shadow or other partial transparency.

The best way to become familiar with these formats is to play with them; try different export settings, and observe the compromise between image quality and file size. The exported size for the selected slice or image appears in the bottom-left corner of this window, along with an estimated download time by using the ever-popular 56K modem. It won't take long for you to grow comfortable with your options.

When you have finished with your image settings, click the Done button. You're presented with the Save Optimized As dialog box, shown in Figure 12.25, which also includes some powerful features.

Figure 12.25

The Save Optimized As dialog box

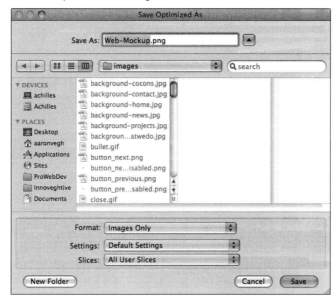

When you have multiple images being saved at the same time, Photoshop creates a folder named `images` at your chosen save location and fills it with the file name you choose, appended with the index number of each slice.

Below the file area of this dialog box are three options:

- **Format.** By default, Photoshop saves your images, along with an HTML document that lays them out. Unless you're looking for something quick and simple, avoid this option and head straight to Images only.

- **Settings.** Here, you can change the naming convention of the files that are saved. There are many options contained within this dialog box, but you'll typically use the default state.

- **Slices.** Here, you have three options: You can save all the images (including the inactive ones); all user images (that is, those that you've drawn); or selected images (which you can select by using the Slice Select tool in the Save for Web dialog box).

The last option is particularly compelling. While you may save most of the composition just once, your navigation, for example, might be output several times. By choosing just those slices in the Save for Web dialog box by holding down the Shift key while clicking for contiguous slices or the Command key for a noncontiguous selection, you can export just those images. This is also handy for naming them; because you'd save two states for each tab (active tabs are green, while inactive tabs are gray), you can set all tabs in one state, export them with the file name `navigation_off.gif`, and then repeat for the on position.

When you're ready, click the Save button, and your images are saved to the folder of your choice, as shown in Figure 12.26. You're now ready to build your web page.

Figure 12.26

The results of the Save for Web operation

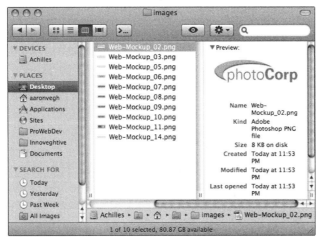

Summary

Photoshop is an incredibly powerful tool and should be in the hands of every web professional. Although I could only offer the basics here, you'll find that playful exploration will reward you; the more time you spend with the program, the more likely you'll stumble upon that amazing visual treatment that separates your work from that of others. Every designer seems to have his or her own signature style, and you'll no doubt develop your own.

Server-Side
Development

Principles of Server-Side Development

Up to this point, everything you've learned in this book about creating websites has been focused on front-end development. By front end, I'm referring to activity that takes place within your local web browser. When given a batch of HTML, CSS, and JavaScript, your browser converts that code into a visual layout. The web server, which is responsible for delivering that code, is little more than a file server in this kind of exchange.

But we're living in the twenty-first century. The whole point of the Internet is to provide dynamic content, interacting with other hosts on the web, and sharing the content that you generate with the rest of the world, your coworkers, or even just yourself — all from different devices.

The technologies that make this possible are considered back end because they sit on the web server on the other end of your Internet connection.

Because web servers are always on, they can be reached by any client at any time. With the use of programming languages that can pull information from both the client and any other source online, a web application can deliver dynamic content that brings customized information to a client, no matter where he or she is. This relationship is shown in Figure 13.1.

This part of the book teaches you the basics of web application development. This chapter covers the general principles of back-end development and examines the available technology options. Then, it covers the MySQL database server, which is used to store the information that you'll call upon in most of your web apps. The remaining chapters of this book will look at two popular programming languages — PHP and Ruby — with a particular focus on Ruby as the means to develop cutting-edge web applications.

For now, let's make sure you understand exactly what a web application is and how it works.

In This Chapter

Deconstructing
a web application

The PHP language

Ruby on Rails arrives

Installing the software

Figure 13.1

How a web application moves information

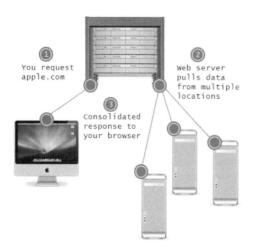

Deconstructing a Web Application

In your traditional front-end-only website, the web server is little more than a glorified file server; it receives requests for pages and dutifully passes them along. As a web developer, you simply use an FTP client to access that remote server and place the files that you want on the server.

Web applications place more emphasis on the web server. Instead of simply serving up static web pages, a properly configured server can process specialized requests from the client, which can include any kind of data. It can act on that request in dynamic ways — that is, an application can respond to a request uniquely and in ways determined at runtime. It can also pass back a customized web page for ultimate display on the client side.

You've already become familiar with the Apache web server (review Chapters 1–3 to refresh your memory). Although by default Apache only passes along the documents you request, you can add modules that give it the ability to process scripts, written in a variety of programming languages. In other words, the web server can get involved in the processing of the files.

The first language that had widespread appeal for programming web applications was Perl. For those accustomed to other languages, Perl can look a tad awkward. But for the first time, developers found themselves able to accept user input, do something interesting, and reply with a customized HTML page.

In the traditional Perl web application, the scripts were consigned to a special directory: `cgi-bin`. The `cgi` stands for *common gateway interface*; this is a protocol for communicating with web servers. The `bin` is short for *binary*, which implies that Perl scripts are like applications.

Let's consider a basic example: One of the most common early techniques for a server-side application was the form mailer. You've seen this before: A contact form on a web page invites you to fill out your email address and write a message. On the back end, a script takes your form input and then creates and sends an email to a specified recipient.

In the days of Perl-based CGI scripts, the HTML form's `action` attribute would point to a script in the server's `cgi-bin` directory (`formmail.cgi`, perhaps). That script would collect the form data (for example, the name, address, email, and message) and then send it all out in an email. The script might then assemble some HTML, perhaps a confirmation message, to return to the browser.

It may seem difficult to imagine, but this kind of capability was seen as The Future; by easily allowing people to write web-based applications, it would only be a matter of time before everything was on the web and desktop applications would be eliminated! There was a whole industry built around network computers that relied on the Internet for its applications and data storage. Of course, reality came crashing in: The Internet wasn't fast enough! Nobody wanted his or her personal data stored online. And the network computer industry, such as it was, went away.

But the interest in web-based applications only grew. While they weren't going to replace desktop programs anytime soon, always-on web-based applications had their place. And new technologies were (and are) continuing to be developed that made it easier to build feature-rich, fast, and secure applications.

The PHP Language

While Perl has its loyal following, it was the development of the PHP scripting language that truly put the power of web application development into the hands of the people. While both are derived from the popular C programming language, PHP was designed to have a cleaner syntax and a shorter learning curve, and — most importantly — it could be embedded within HTML pages.

PHP was designed to be a transparent part of the web application development process. The PHP module is easily included in the Apache configuration file. Once done, the server can suddenly process pages that have a `.php` extension. Then, while you're writing HTML code in your page, you can enclose PHP within a set of special delimiters — the `<?` and `?>` tags — and that code is executed on the server.

Today, the popularity of PHP is widespread. There's virtually no hosting service that doesn't provide the language on its systems, ensuring that you have the ability to run your application anywhere. Even Windows servers usually include PHP; the language has been ported to every existing platform.

PHP also enjoys broad support for a wide range of technologies. Because most web developers use PHP, you'll find features either built into the language or available as easily used add-ons that can interact with technologies such as:

- **Database servers.** These include MySQL, PostgreSQL, and even Microsoft SQL Server.
- **Curl.** This is used for programmatically interacting with remote resources, such as files and web pages.
- **XML.** This is used for creating and managing structured data.
- **Remote APIs.** These are used for interacting with services as diverse as ecommerce payment gateways and Flickr.

There's much more that PHP can do, and I touch on several of these capabilities in Chapter 15. For now, though, let's examine database servers more closely. While PHP and other languages are adept at pushing data around, you also need a place to store it. Databases are the prime means to do so, and MySQL is the most popular.

If you look back at Figure 13.1, you see a typical web transaction referring to other servers to get their response. Imagine a site like `www.apple.com`, which is one of the most popular sites on the web. It has server farms located in different parts of the world. These farms are collections of web and database servers that respond to requests coming in by the thousands per second. While the web server handles the request, a database server acts as the repository for any information that needs to be added to the response. These servers can be either different machines (as in the case of Apple) or a piece of server software running on the same physical machine as the web server (the most likely situation in your case).

Just as PHP is the most popular scripting language, MySQL is the most popular database server. Like PHP, MySQL is free, easy to learn, and available everywhere. In fact, there's even a term for the combination of all these technologies: *LAMP*, short for Linux, Apache, MySQL, and PHP.

When you put these pieces together, you have the foundations for whatever web application you want to build. Consider some of the sites you know that are built on this platform:

- **Digg.com.** The most popular social news aggregation site
- **WordPress.** The most popular blog and content management system
- **Facebook.** The most popular social networking site
- **Yahoo!.** One of the largest search engines
- **YouTube.** The most popular video-sharing site
- **Wikipedia.** The world's largest encyclopedia

If the technology is good enough for these guys, you can use it too.

Ruby on Rails Arrives

PHP is great — but it does have its drawbacks. Developers have been griping about PHP for as long as the language has been around, and their issues with it are intimately tied with the reasons for its success. The two biggest concerns with PHP are its sloppy results and security holes.

As you'll discover when I cover PHP in Chapter 15, you can begin working with it very quickly, without fully understanding how the pieces fit together. The code that results from this kind of approach tends to be untidy, utilitarian, and difficult to maintain. My hand is guiltily going up here too; I've written a lot of code that just gets the job done and which I dread having to look back on when the client wants changes later on.

In fact, as you become more experienced with web development, you'll come to appreciate the difference between code that you wrote well and code that you hacked together. For code that you wrote well, you actually look forward to working with it; you know where everything is, it makes sense, and adding new features is a sensible and almost automatic process. For code that you hacked together, you approach it with a sense of dread. Before you can even think of where to add the new feature, you have to sort out how it works in the first place. And you often find yourself fixing bugs that you discover along the way.

Take it from someone who's been there: You will write both kinds of code. But for the vast majority of PHP projects out there, there's no standard technique for writing code. One developer might look at another's code and fail to make any sense of it. And even more critical, it's very easy to miss implementing the checks needed to ensure the security of your application.

A web application can be a very complicated thing; it has to handle any number of standard features, such as user creation, authentication, form handling, data input validation, database access, content management, and more. If you're writing it in PHP, you have to invent these components every time you write a new application. And every implementation will be somewhat different than others.

This is where a framework comes in handy. It's a collection of code that you can call upon to handle oft-repeated tasks. Developers often build their own libraries of code, perhaps tweaking them over time to improve them (for example, a chunk of code to talk to the database or a way to validate form data).

Frameworks are a way to formalize these libraries, and some are bigger than others. But perhaps the most successful framework is Ruby on Rails.

Most people have never heard of Ruby, which is a programming language like PHP. Until the Rails framework came along, it was actually pretty obscure. But when web developer David Heinemeier Hansson chose Ruby as the foundation for his new framework, it became a huge hit.

Rails is a very comprehensive framework. It couples the advantages that Ruby brings to programming (true object-oriented programming) with a design pattern that's fully exploited by the framework. Using Ruby on Rails, you're given the means to create almost any web application with very little effort.

Using frameworks in general and Rails in particular gives you three benefits:

- More stable, secure code
- Code that's easier to maintain and extend
- A methodology for writing applications

In this book, my recommendation is simple: Use PHP for applications that you need to create quickly and Rails for your major projects.

CROSS-REF
For more on using Ruby as well as Ruby on Rails, see Chapters 16 and 17.

Installing the Software

Before you move on to the next chapter, you need to make sure that all the components that I'm talking about are installed and working properly. So, right now, you're going to install and configure the PHP module for Apache, the MySQL database server, and a complete Ruby on Rails development environment.

Installing PHP

Every modern Mac already comes with a version of PHP installed; however, it isn't active in Apache yet. For Mac OS X 10.6 Snow Leopard, the operating system ships with PHP version 5.3.0. Follow these steps to activate and test PHP:

1. **Open the Apache configuration file in your favorite text editor, using administrative privileges.** As a TextMate user, my preferred way to do this is by issuing the following command in Terminal:

   ```
   $ sudo mate /private/etc/apache2/httpd.conf
   ```

   Recall from your earlier study of the command line that `sudo` grants the user administrative privileges (so you can save the file when you're done editing it). The `mate` command is TextMate's command-line client and simply opens the provided file in the graphical editor.

2. **Find the** `LoadModule` **directive for PHP.** It's already there in the file (around line 115 in Snow Leopard) on a line preceded by a hash (#), as shown in Figure 13.2. The hash is a comment indicator, which means this line is ignored.

Figure 13.2

The commented-out PHP `LoadModule` directive in Apache's configuration file

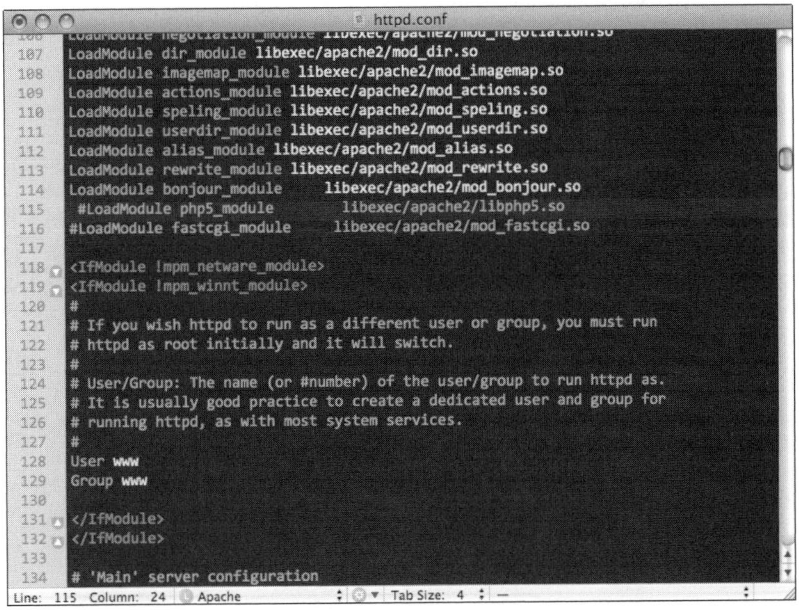

3. **Erase the hash at the beginning of the line, save the file (you're asked to type your password), and then close it.** Apache is now ready to process PHP files. But you need to ensure that the PHP configuration file is available (it isn't by default). Snow Leopard comes with a default file that you can simply rename so it's picked up when Apache loads.

4. **Type this in Terminal:**

```
$ sudo mv /private/etc/php.ini.default /private/etc/php.ini
```

5. **Restart Apache.** You can go to the Sharing preference pane in System Preferences to toggle the web server. Or you can be a real command-line expert and do it from Terminal:

```
$ sudo apachectl restart
```

It's time to test your new PHP installation. Create a new text file called `test.php`. Type this code in that document:

```
<?php phpinfo(); ?>
```

Save this document in your `Sites` directory. Then, visit that page in your browser; if you set up the alias to your Sites directory (as described in Chapter 1), it will be `http://localhost/test.php`. You should see something similar to Figure 13.3.

Figure 13.3

The PHP information page

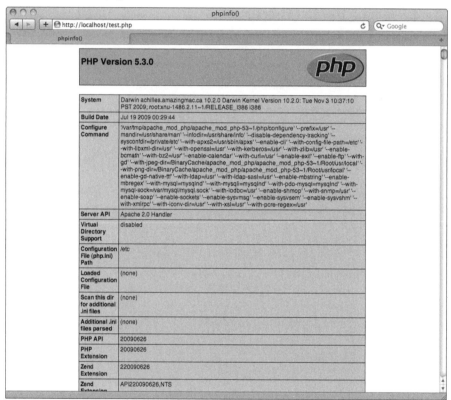

When you're done with `test.php`, trash it. As you can see, it provides a great deal of information about your computer. While this file isn't a terrible threat on your `localhost`, being mindful of security is always important.

Installing MySQL

In the Linux world, you often acquire MySQL in two separate components: the server and the client applications. On the Mac, you can get both in a single package. The easiest way to install the database is by downloading an install package from the MySQL site. Unfortunately, it's not the easiest thing to find. Follow these steps:

1. **Visit** `http://dev.mysql.com/downloads`**.** You see a table showing two versions of MySQL; you're interested in the Community Server edition (MySQL offers a commercial product for large businesses).

2. **Click the Download link above the left-hand column.** You're taken to a long list of operating systems and platforms.

3. **Click the Mac OS X (package format) link to view the complete list.**

4. **Choose the package that most closely describes your OS and hardware.** If you have an Intel Core 2 Duo chip, then you can use the 64-bit version of the software; otherwise, choose plain x86 for your OS version or, if you're still using a G5, get the PowerPC version.

5. **Once you've decided on a build, click the Pick a Mirror link.** You're asked to register.

6. **If you decide not to register, click the No thanks, just take me to the downloads! link.** You see a list of servers that are close to you.

7. **Choose a server by clicking either the HTTP or FTP link to download in either format.** It doesn't really matter which you choose.

That's a lot of steps to simply get the software! But it gets easier. Once you have the package, it turns into a standard Mac installer. Open the disk image and then launch the installer package inside, as shown in Figure 13.4 — it's named `mysql-5.1.41-osx10.5-x86_64.pkg` in this case.

Figure 13.4

The MySQL package installer

This is the standard Mac installer application; Figure 13.5 shows the first screen. Simply agree to each step, type your password when asked, and then the installation begins.

When the installation is complete, run the other installer package in this disk image; the `MySQLStartupItem.pkg` file installs a prefpane in your System Preferences application. With it installed, the MySQL server starts up automatically when you boot your Mac.

Figure 13.5

The MySQL installer

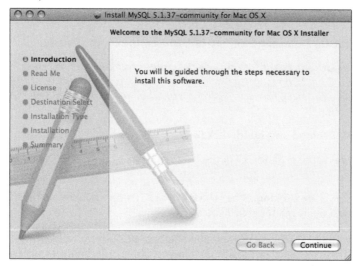

A server is all well and good, but you need a client to interact with it. Although there are a number of clients available — a few examples include free web applications (such as PHPMySQL) and desktop applications (such as Sequel Pro) — none provide the power and fidelity of the command line. And if you intend to use SSH to access remote servers, you need to use the command-line tools there too.

However, there are two configuration changes to make before you can do that. First, you need to put the MySQL application directory in your shell's `PATH` variable; this allows you to provide only the name of the application rather than its full path. The second configuration is the setting of passwords for the root MySQL user. Follow these steps:

1. **In Terminal, execute this command:**

```
$ echo 'export PATH=/usr/local/mysql/bin:$PATH' >>
  ~/.bash_profile
```

This command appends a directive to your `bash_profile` file, which helps configure your shell. This directive places the MySQL directory into your `PATH` variable. So, now, instead of typing the command **/usr/local/mysql/bin/mysql**, you can simply type **mysql**.

2. **Set the password for your MySQL root user:**

```
$ mysqladmin -u root password NEWPASSWORD
```

Replace NEWPASSWORD with your password of choice. You don't see any response from this command; it just works.

With those two items taken care of, you should be able to type in the command **mysql -u root -pYOURPASSWORD** (that's right, there's no space between the password switch, -p, and the actual password) and find yourself inside MySQL's command environment, shown in Figure 13.6.

Figure 13.6

The MySQL command-line client

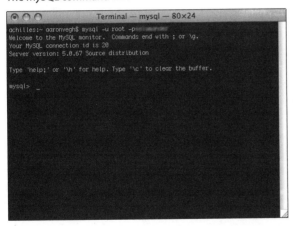

That's it! You can just type **exit** and then press Return to get out of this client. I talk more about the MySQL client in Chapter 14.

Ruby on Rails installation

Just like with PHP, Mac OS X 10.6 Snow Leopard comes with both Ruby and Rails built in. This makes your life considerably easier. The only problem is that the shipping version of Rails is probably out of date. You should run the following commands to update your installation — or just to confirm that you're up to date.

```
sudo gem update --system
sudo gem install rails
sudo gem update rake
sudo gem update sqlite3-ruby
```

These commands all interact with the gem system; think of it as an apt-get for Ruby components. The first command updates the system itself. Then, you install the latest version of Rails. You finish with the updating of two vital components: the rake build tool and the Ruby SQLite database component.

The execution of these commands can take awhile, so be patient. Once they're complete, you can try setting up a new Rails project. In Terminal, change directories to your home directory's Sites directory and then execute this command:

```
$ rails testproject
```

You should see a long list of files appear before Terminal returns, as shown in Figure 13.7.

Figure 13.7

Output from the rails command

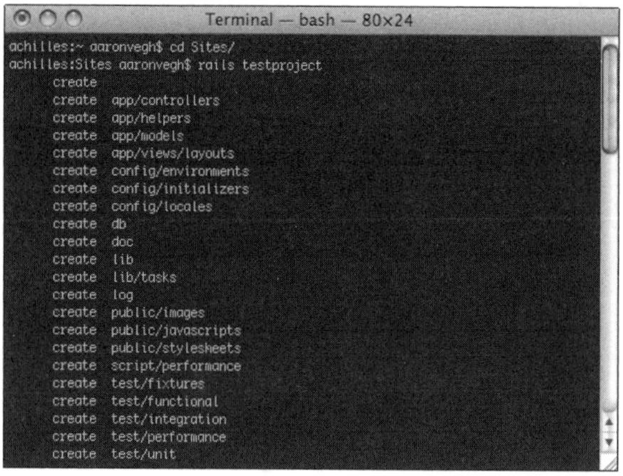

Now type **cd** in the new testproject directory that was created and then execute this line:

```
$ script/server
```

You should see some text appear about Booting Mongrel. Now switch to your browser and then type the URL **http://localhost:3000**. You should see a page similar to Figure 13.8.

Congratulations! You've got a working Ruby on Rails installation. You can press Control+C in Terminal to stop the web server and put it aside until you get to Chapter 16.

Figure 13.8

The Rails welcome page

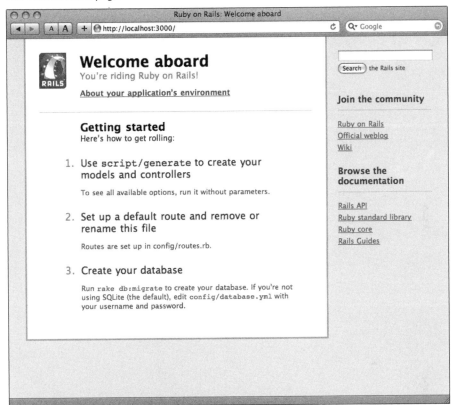

Summary

I've laid the groundwork for the final chapters of this book. Understanding the principles of how web applications are put together should help as you work through the pieces that make them function in the following chapters. And with the guide to installing those pieces, you should be ready to go when it comes time to learn about them. In fact, that's where you are right now: You start with the MySQL database server.

MySQL Database Server

W e all need a place for our stuff. This is true for homeown-
ers, kids with too many toys, and web application developers. For the latter crowd, we have a database server.
This is a piece of software that allows you to store data in and,
perhaps more importantly, pull data from a database.

You can think of a database as a spreadsheet; the vertical columns
represent the kinds of data that you'll store — such as Name,
Address, and Phone Number.

There are also horizontal rows, which make up an individual database record. Each row contains *fields*, which store the information
that belongs to each column — such as P. Sherman, 42 Wallaby
Way, Sydney, and 800-333-4332. Put it all together, and you have a
complete database of contact information.

Perhaps this doesn't sound that incredible. After all, spreadsheets
have been around for ages, and people have long been using them
to store things such as contact information. But MySQL and other
similar systems also use *relationships*, which make a database very
powerful.

A *relational database* allows you to create multiple tables of information and then link them together in many different ways. For
example, you might have different addresses for each person. So,
one table would contain the names, while a second table might
contain the addresses. This relationship is shown in Figure 14.1.

This model shows two tables. You might imagine one record for
each person, with multiple possible records for addresses, such as
one for home and another for work. With a relational database, you
can connect these tables together very easily.

In This Chapter

MySQL basics

Getting data into
and out of tables

Getting relational

MySQL utilities

Figure 14.1

A database table relationship: people and addresses

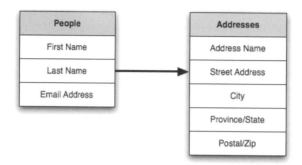

MySQL Basics

As it happens, the relational database we'll use is MySQL. It's a free, open-source server that's quite pervasive on web servers, so a competence in this database will mean you'll always have a place to put your data.

In this chapter, you're going to use the MySQL command-line client to connect with the server and create databases and the tables that compose them. Then, I'm going to show you different ways of putting information into a table and getting it out. You finish your tour of MySQL with a description of some of the utilities that make working with MySQL even easier.

Creating a database

Assuming that you followed the setup steps in Chapter 13, you should now have a working MySQL installation on your Mac; if not, it's imperative that you have MySQL up and running to fully appreciate the discussion in this chapter.

When dealing with the command-line client, you always activate MySQL the same way: by typing your username, password, and, if you have one, a database name. Your command might look like this:

```
achilles:~ aaronvegh$ mysql -u root -pmyfunkypassword mydatabase
```

Substitute your own password and database name here, and note the lack of a space between the -p switch and the actual password.

If you're uncomfortable with your password being on full display on the command line for anyone nearby to see, you can omit it:

```
achilles:~ aaronvegh$ mysql -u root -p
Enter password:
Welcome to the MySQL monitor. Commands end with ; or \g.
Your MySQL connection id is 232
Server version: 5.0.67 Source distribution
Type 'help;' or '\h' for help. Type '\c' to clear the buffer.
mysql>
```

When you type your password at the prompt (on line 2), you're granted access to the client environment, as shown by the `mysql>` prompt.

Let's start by creating a new database. In the exercises that you'll follow in this chapter, you're going to keep track of baseball teams. Of all sports, baseball is known for its ability to generate mountains of data. I'm not going to go into extreme depth in the example here, but I cover enough to give you a basic knowledge of how database tables work together.

In your client program, execute this command to create your new database:

```
mysql> create database baseball;
Query OK, 1 row affected (0.35 sec)
```

MySQL always returns a status message from your queries. Note how it says `1 row affected;` because everything in the system is in a database, even your databases are in a database. You've just added a new database to the database table. Make sense?

Execute this command to see all the databases:

```
mysql> show databases;
+--------------------------+
| Database                 |
+--------------------------+
| information_schema       |
| baseball                 |
| mysql                    |
+--------------------------+
3 rows in set (1.67 sec)
```

Every MySQL installation comes with two databases set by default: `mysql` and `informa-tion_schema`. These databases govern the inner workings of the system, so you don't need to concern yourself with them. As you can see, the `baseball` database is listed there, ready for you to get to work. If you happen to be using a different database and want to switch to the new one, that's simple enough:

```
mysql> use baseball;
Database changed
```

This wasn't necessary in this case (when you create a database, it becomes the selected one automatically), but there's no harm in executing the command again.

Setting up users

Before you begin moving data in and out of your new database, I should spend a moment discussing the rather important topic of user management. The way you have things set up right now, there's just one user: `root`. Just like under Unix, `root` is the super user. And also like under Unix, you don't want to be `root` all the time! Creating a user specifically for a given database is a sensible precaution, as it minimizes your exposure should that user's credentials be hacked.

The first step I take after creating a new database is assigning a user to it. MySQL provides a command called `grant` to take care of this. It accepts the name of the user (either a new or existing user will suffice), and if it's a new user, you can also define a password.

The `grant` syntax requires that you provide a series of *privileges* — essentially, you must define what this user can do with the database. Table 14-1 shows a list of possible privileges.

Table 14-1 MySQL Privileges	
Privilege	*Context*
ALL [PRIVILEGES]	Server administration
ALTER	Tables
ALTER ROUTINE	Stored routines
CREATE	Databases, tables, or indexes
CREATE ROUTINE	Stored routines
CREATE TEMPORARY TABLES	Tables
CREATE USER	Server administration
CREATE VIEW	Views
DELETE	Tables
DROP	Databases or tables
EVENT	Databases
EXECUTE	Stored routines
FILE	File access on server host
GRANT OPTION	Databases, tables, or stored routines
INDEX	Tables
INSERT	Tables
LOCK TABLES	Tables
PROCESS	Server administration
REFERENCES	Databases or tables

Privilege	Context
RELOAD	Server administration
REPLICATION CLIENT	Server administration
REPLICATION SLAVE	Server administration
SELECT	Tables
SHOW DATABASES	Server administration
SHOW VIEW	Views
SHUTDOWN	Server administration
SUPER	Server administration
TRIGGER	Tables
UPDATE	Tables
USAGE	Server administration

Each privilege in this table includes the context in which it's used; the tables context refers to privileges that apply to managing data in tables. This is the one you're going to be concerned with the most, followed closely by the server administration context, which governs general system maintenance features.

In the interest of providing the least amount of exposure to security risk, this is the sort of grant statement that you might run for a database being put into production use:

```
mysql> grant delete, insert, select, update on baseball.* to
    baseballer identified by 'g0j@ys';
Query OK, 0 rows affected (0.26 sec)
```

The privileges provided in this statement are the minimum required for a user to manage a database that has already been configured, ideally by the root user. These actions are the most essential database operations — what are commonly referred to as the CRUD operations: Create, Read, Update, Delete. Provide anything else, and you may be granting them too much freedom.

This statement also grants those limited privileges to every table in the baseball database (again, the asterisk is used as the wildcard to select all). Finally, you identify a username, and because it's a new user, you add identified by g0j@ys to assign a password.

Try it! Type **exit** to leave the MySQL command client and then sign in with your new credentials:

```
achilles:~ aaronvegh$ mysql -u baseballer -pg0j@ys baseball;
Welcome to the MySQL monitor. Commands end with ; or \g.
Your MySQL connection id is 3
Server version: 5.0.67 Source distribution
Type 'help;' or '\h' for help. Type '\c' to clear the buffer.
mysql>
```

You can test your new user in both good and bad ways. Here's a session to show both:

```
mysql> select first_name from players limit 2;
+------------+
| first_name |
+------------+
| Alex       |
| Derek      |
+------------+
2 rows in set (0.01 sec)
```

This is correct; you have granted the ability to run `select` statements to `baseballer`. Now let's try something prohibited:

```
mysql> drop table players;
ERROR 1142 (42000): DROP command denied to user
    'baseballer'@'localhost' for table 'players'
```

Zing! Just what you wanted — a polite but firm reprimand.

Creating tables

With a database created, it's time to configure the individual tables. But before you can do that, you need to sit down and figure out what your database is going to contain. With databases, as with any application, a good plan up-front can save you a lot of headache during development.

At this point in the process, I usually draw out a *schema*: a written representation of the database tables and their relationships. With this information laid out, I can ensure that I have all the pieces that I need in order to put my database together.

For this draft of your database, you're going to use the schema shown in Figure 14.2.

Your database needs three tables: `teams`, `players`, and `games`. Each table will have a list of *fields*, the individual types of data that you're going to track. Each field in Figure 14.2 is followed by the data type in parentheses. In this schema, I'm using a combination of regular text-based strings (known in MySQL as a *varchar*), whole numbers (called *integers*), and decimal numbers (called *floats*). There's also a date field, which uses the surprisingly named *date* data type.

Tables 14-2, 14-3, and 14-4 show the different data types that you can use in MySQL.

Each of these numerical types is *unsigned* by default; that is, they're assumed to be positive numbers. If you want to account for negative numbers, you can specify each of these as *signed*. This cuts the range of your values in half in order to provide for the negative values. For example, a `signed tinyint` has a value range of -126 to 127, while the `unsigned int` has a value range of 0 to 256.

Figure 14.2

The baseball database schema

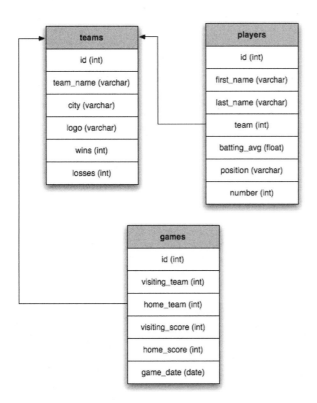

Table 14-2 MySQL Numerical Data Types

Data Type	Description
bigint	The king-size 8-byte integer stores a value up to 18,446,744,073,709,551,615. You probably won't need this large of an integer.
double	An 8-byte number with a floating decimal point
float	A 4-byte number with a floating decimal point
int	The standard 4-byte integer stores a value up to 4,294,967,295. This is the one I generally use for everything, as you're unlikely to notice a performance difference by using a smaller version.
mediumint	A 3-byte value that stores a number up to 16,777,215
smallint	A 2-byte value that stores a number up to 65,535
tinyint	A 1-byte value that stores a number up to 256. Use this for values that you know will never exceed this amount, such as a count of balls and strikes for an at bat.

Table 14-3 MySQL String Data Types

Data Type	Description
longtext	A string with a maximum length of 4,294,967,295 characters (about 858,993,459 words)
mediumtext	A string with a maximum length of 16,777,215 characters (about 3,355,443 words)
text	A string with a maximum length of 65,535 characters (about 13,000 words)
varchar(size)	A string of letters and numbers ranging in length from 0 to 255

While text-based fields can hold traditional written text (such as field names and blocks of text), the larger string fields, such as `mediumtext` and `longtext`, can hold much more than even the largest novels. These fields are traditionally used to hold binary data, such as images or other files. If those files grow large, they can easily require these larger data types. For example, a 75KB ZIP file on my desktop right now contains over 66,000 characters, which would be too many for a `text` data type alone.

This isn't usually a problem I run into because while some developers favor storing binary data in databases, I prefer to use a simple file path instead, letting the file system of the server do the storage of the binary data. This is why, for the `logo` field in the `teams` table, I've used a simple `varchar` data type; it's just going to contain the name of the image file.

Table 14-4 MySQL Date Data Types

Data Type	Description
date	A 3-byte representation in the format of YYYY-MM-DD
datetime	An 8-byte representation in the format of YYYY-MM-DD HH:MM:SS
time	A 3-byte representation in the format of HH:MM:SS
timestamp	A 4-byte representation in the format of YYYYMMDDHHMMSS. Because it's only a 4-byte number, the maximum year it can handle is 2037.

Finally, the `date` data types provide different options for the various kinds of time you want to capture. However, do note the byte size of these types; the `timestamp` in particular is somewhat dangerous if you anticipate your application still being used some 30 years from now.

Now that you know what data types you can use for your tables, it's time to actually build them. To do so, you employ MySQL's `create table` command.

Type this on your command line to build the `teams` table:

```
mysql> create table teams (id int auto_increment primary key,
    -> team_name varchar(255),
    -> city varchar(255),
```

```
        -> logo varchar(255),
        -> wins int,
        -> losses int);
Query OK, 0 rows affected (0.00 sec)
```

The format of this command takes advantage of a neat trick in MySQL's command client: Commands are terminated with a semicolon (;). In order to visually separate my table creation command, I can press Return to put each field on its own line, and MySQL continues the prompt.

Let's look at each part of this command. After naming the table you want to create, you open a parenthesis and start naming the fields, followed by their data type. The first field, id, is a special case; this is the field that provides the unique identifier for each record. So, you use two special keywords for this one: auto_increment, which tells the database to give a unique number to each record, and primary key, which tells the database that this field will be the one that's used to differentiate this record from all others in the table — it must be a unique value.

The remaining fields are provided with a name and data type. For the varchar types, I'm also providing a size value, which lets me add a full 255 characters for these fields. If you wanted to be more conservative, you could judge that the team_name field might never need more than, say, 50 characters and then use that value instead. But if some super-long team name isn't being saved in the database, you're going to have a hard time tracking down the cause of that bug. It's much better, in my opinion, to sacrifice some very cheap memory and hard disk space for the sake of possible time savings in the future.

With your final field defined, you close the parentheses and finish with the semicolon. MySQL gives you the feedback that your query was good, and you're in business. Let's build out the rest of the tables now. Type these commands in Terminal:

```
mysql> create table players (id int auto_increment primary key,
    -> first_name varchar(255),
    -> last_name varchar(255),
    -> number int,
    -> team int,
    -> batting_avg float,
    -> position varchar(255));
Query OK, 0 rows affected (0.01 sec)
mysql> create table games (id int auto_increment primary key,
    -> visiting_team int,
    -> home_team int,
    -> visiting_score int,
    -> home_score int,
    -> game_date date);
Query OK, 0 rows affected (0.00 sec)
```

When you're done, you should be able to see the results of your handiwork. To see the tables in your database, execute this command:

```
mysql> show tables;
+-------------------+
| Tables_in_baseball |
+-------------------+
| games             |
| players           |
| teams             |
+-------------------+
3 rows in set (0.00 sec)
```

And if you want to check the specifications on any table that you've created, try this command:

```
mysql> describe games;
+---------------+---------+------+-----+---------+-------------+
| Field         | Type    | Null | Key | Default | Extra       |
+---------------+---------+------+-----+---------+-------------+
| id            | int(11) | NO   | PRI | NULL    |auto_increment
| visiting_team | int(11) | YES  |     | NULL    |             |
| home_team     | int(11) | YES  |     | NULL    |             |
| visiting_score| int(11) | YES  |     | NULL    |             |
| home_score    | int(11) | YES  |     | NULL    |             |
| game_date     | date    | YES  |     | NULL    |             |
+---------------+---------+------+-----+---------+-------------+
6 rows in set (0.01 sec)
```

Getting Data into and out of Tables

Creating tables is fun, but they're not worth much without any information. That's where MySQL's insert command comes in handy. Here's an example:

```
mysql> insert into teams set team_name="Blue Jays",
    city="Toronto", logo="bluejays.jpg", wins="75", losses="87";
Query OK, 1 row affected (0.01 sec)
```

The insert command takes your table name and, after the set keyword, a series of field-value pairs. You don't need to supply every field name, so if you want to supply a field later, you can do that (I'll show you how).

Let's see what you've accomplished. The select command lets you see what's in a database table, and it's your primary means of getting data out of MySQL. Here's a basic usage that gets the job done:

```
mysql> select * from teams;
+----+-----------+---------+--------------+------+--------+
| id | team_name | city    | logo         | wins | losses |
+----+-----------+---------+--------------+------+--------+
|  1 | Blue Jays | Toronto | bluejays.jpg |   75 |     87 |
+----+-----------+---------+--------------+------+--------+
1 row in set (0.00 sec)
```

This command should be pretty clear, but that asterisk? It's a wildcard character, which matches all records. When you have a few more records in your database, I'll show you some more tricks with the `select` statement. Let's do that now: Type the following commands to add the American League East division to your database:

```
mysql> insert into teams set team_name="Yankees", city="New
    York", logo="yankees.jpg", wins="103", losses="59";
Query OK, 1 row affected (0.06 sec)
mysql> insert into teams set team_name="Red Sox", city="Boston",
    logo="redsox.jpg", wins="95", losses="67";
Query OK, 1 row affected (0.00 sec)
mysql> insert into teams set team_name="Rays", city="Tampa Bay",
    logo="rays.jpg", wins="84", losses="78";
Query OK, 1 row affected (0.00 sec)
mysql> insert into teams set team_name="Orioles",
    city="Baltimore", logo="orioles.jpg", wins="64", losses="98";
Query OK, 1 row affected (0.00 sec)
```

When you're done, you should have a table that looks like this:

```
mysql> select * from teams;
+----+-----------+-----------+-----------------+------+--------+
| id | team_name | city      | logo            | wins | losses |
+----+-----------+-----------+-----------------+------+--------+
|  1 | Blue Jays | Toronto   | bluejays.jpg    |   75 |     87 |
|  2 | Yankees   | New York  | yankees.jpg     |  103 |     59 |
|  3 | Red Sox   | Boston    | redsox.jpg      |   95 |     67 |
|  4 | Rays      | Tampa Bay | rays.jpg        |   84 |     87 |
|  5 | Orioles   | Baltimore | orioles.jpg     |   64 |     98 |
+----+-----------+-----------+-----------------+------+--------+
5 rows in set (0.00 sec)
```

Look at that first column in the `select` results. The `id` is a field that you never specify. Recall from your `create table` commands that you used the `auto_increment` keyword. Here it is at work; for every new record created, the system advances the `id` number to the next available integer. This ensures that each record remains unique. You'll also discover that this unique ID is the basis of your table relationships: You're going to use that ID number to connect a record in one table with a record in another.

With some information in your database table, you can now do a few more things with your `select` statement, as shown in the following examples.

To select records that match a particular criterion, you can append a `where` clause to the statement:

```
mysql> select * from teams where city="Toronto";
+----+-----------+---------+--------------+------+--------+
| id | team_name | city    | logo         | wins | losses |
+----+-----------+---------+--------------+------+--------+
|  1 | Blue Jays | Toronto | bluejays.jpg |   75 |     87 |
+----+-----------+---------+--------------+------+--------+
1 row in set (0.00 sec)
```

The `where` clause works with operators other than the equal sign. Let's see who the real contenders are in this league:

```
mysql> select * from teams where wins > 90;
+----+-----------+----------+-----------------+------+--------+
| id | team_name | city     | logo            | wins | losses |
+----+-----------+----------+-----------------+------+--------+
|  2 | Yankees   | New York | yankees.jpg     |  103 |     59 |
|  3 | Red Sox   | Boston   | redsox.jpg      |   95 |     67 |
+----+-----------+----------+-----------------+------+--------+
2 rows in set (0.00 sec)
```

You can also connect multiple `where` clauses together to increase the accuracy of your request:

```
mysql> select * from teams where wins > 80 and losses < 80;
+----+-----------+-----------+-----------------+------+--------+
| id | team_name | city      | logo            | wins | losses |
+----+-----------+-----------+-----------------+------+--------+
|  2 | Yankees   | New York  | yankees.jpg     |  103 |     59 |
|  3 | Red Sox   | Boston    | redsox.jpg      |   95 |     67 |
|  4 | Rays      | Tampa Bay | rays.jpg        |   84 |     78 |
+----+-----------+-----------+-----------------+------+--------+
3 rows in set (0.00 sec)
```

Sometimes, you'll want a *fuzzy search*, where you want to find a partial text string within a field. The MySQL keyword `like` is ready to serve; in this case, the query will find team names that start with R:

```
mysql> select * from teams where team_name LIKE "R%";
+----+-----------+-----------+-------------+------+--------+
| id | team_name | city      | logo        | wins | losses |
+----+-----------+-----------+-------------+------+--------+
|  3 | Red Sox   | Boston    | redsox.jpg  |   95 |     67 |
|  4 | Rays      | Tampa Bay | rays.jpg    |   84 |     78 |
+----+-----------+-----------+-------------+------+--------+
2 rows in set (0.00 sec)
```

You substitute the `like` keyword for the equal sign; you can then use the `%` character as a wild-card to match any subsequent characters. This character can be placed before or after your target text; I often use this technique to search for a single word or phrase within a large text field. An example of this might be `select * from table where bio like "%keyword%";`.

You can control the order of the results by specifying an `order` clause. For text fields, this sorts by alphabetical order; for numerical strings, it sorts by numerical order (surprise!). Here are a couple examples:

```
mysql> select * from teams order by city;
+----+-----------+-----------+-----------------+------+--------+
| id | team_name | city      | logo            | wins | losses |
+----+-----------+-----------+-----------------+------+--------+
|  5 | Orioles   | Baltimore | orioles.jpg     |   64 |     98 |
|  3 | Red Sox   | Boston    | redsox.jpg      |   95 |     67 |
|  2 | Yankees   | New York  | yankees.jpg     |  103 |     59 |
|  4 | Rays      | Tampa Bay | rays.jpg        |   84 |     78 |
|  1 | Blue Jays | Toronto   | bluejays.jpg    |   75 |     87 |
+----+-----------+-----------+-----------------+------+--------+
5 rows in set (0.00 sec)

mysql> select * from teams order by losses desc;
+----+-----------+-----------+-----------------+------+--------+
| id | team_name | city      | logo            | wins | losses |
+----+-----------+-----------+-----------------+------+--------+
|  5 | Orioles   | Baltimore | orioles.jpg     |   64 |     98 |
|  1 | Blue Jays | Toronto   | bluejays.jpg    |   75 |     87 |
|  4 | Rays      | Tampa Bay | rays.jpg        |   84 |     78 |
|  3 | Red Sox   | Boston    | redsox.jpg      |   95 |     67 |
|  2 | Yankees   | New York  | yankees.jpg     |  103 |     59 |
+----+-----------+-----------+-----------------+------+--------+
5 rows in set (0.00 sec)
```

The second example shows a use of the `desc` keyword to modify the `order` clause. By default, sorts are ascending: from A to Z and 0 to 9. The `desc` keyword flips that around: Now I know that the hapless Orioles are the worst team in the American League East. As a Jays fan, I take some heart in this.

For every query thus far, you've returned all the database fields in the table by using the asterisk wildcard. Of course, you don't have to do that; instead, you can specify the fields you're interested in. Let's put it all together in one statement and get the essential data out of this table:

```
mysql> select team_name, wins from teams order by wins desc;
+-----------+------+
| team_name | wins |
+-----------+------+
| Yankees   |  103 |
| Red Sox   |   95 |
| Rays      |   84 |
| Blue Jays |   75 |
| Orioles   |   64 |
+-----------+------+
5 rows in set (0.00 sec)
```

There's also a way to *alias* field names. You might do this if the field names you gave are more machine-friendly than human-friendly. For example, I used the field name `team_name` in order to be most specific. But perhaps you want to return the field name as just `team`. Here's how you do it:

```
mysql> select team_name as team, wins, losses from teams;
+-----------+------+--------+
| team      | wins | losses |
+-----------+------+--------+
| Blue Jays |   75 |     87 |
| Yankees   |  103 |     59 |
| Red Sox   |   95 |     67 |
| Rays      |   84 |     78 |
| Orioles   |   64 |     98 |
+-----------+------+--------+
5 rows in set (0.00 sec)
```

You can also limit the number of records you get back from your query. In some cases, you may have a large database but only want to see a sampling of the records. Other times, you may expect to receive only one match from your query but want to limit it to be sure. In this example query, I'm going to return every team that has more than 60 wins but limit it to the top two teams:

```
mysql> select * from teams where wins > 80 limit 2;
+----+-----------+----------+-----------------+------+--------+
| id | team_name | city     | logo            | wins | losses |
+----+-----------+----------+-----------------+------+--------+
|  2 | Yankees   | New York | yankees.jpg     |  103 |     59 |
|  3 | Red Sox   | Boston   | redsox.jpg      |   95 |     67 |
+----+-----------+----------+-----------------+------+--------+
2 rows in set (0.00 sec)
```

The commands in this section are almost all you should need to get data into and out of a MySQL table.

Updating and deleting rows

But what happens when you want to change information in a table? This is where the `update` command comes in. It works like a combination of the `insert` and `select where` statements. Let's see how it works when you give the Yankees the record they deserve:

```
mysql> update teams set wins="59", losses="103" where id="2";
Query OK, 1 row affected (0.01 sec)
Rows matched: 1  Changed: 1  Warnings: 0
mysql> select * from teams where id="2";
+----+-----------+----------+-----------------+------+--------+
| id | team_name | city     | logo            | wins | losses |
+----+-----------+----------+-----------------+------+--------+
|  2 | Yankees   | New York | yankees.jpg     |   59 |    103 |
+----+-----------+----------+-----------------+------+--------+
1 row in set (0.00 sec)
```

It's important that you remember to use the `where` clause here! Without it, the statement would change every row in the table with your update criteria. Take it from someone who did that to an in-production application during a peak-use period. We learn best from the most painful experiences.

The `where` clause works the same way as the clause in a `select` statement, so you could update a set of rows based on having a certain number of wins, for example, or using the `like` keyword based on the presence of text in a fuzzy search.

```
mysql> update teams set team_name=concat(`team_name`,"*") where
    wins > 90;
Query OK, 1 row affected (0.00 sec)
Rows matched: 1  Changed: 1  Warnings: 0
mysql> select * from teams order by wins desc;
+----+-----------+-----------+-----------------+------+--------+
| id | team_name | city      | logo            | wins | losses |
+----+-----------+-----------+-----------------+------+--------+
|  3 | Red Sox*  | Boston    | redsox.jpg      |   95 |     67 |
|  4 | Rays      | Tampa Bay | rays.jpg        |   84 |     78 |
|  1 | Blue Jays | Toronto   | bluejays.jpg    |   75 |     87 |
|  5 | Orioles   | Baltimore | orioles.jpg     |   64 |     98 |
|  2 | Yankees   | New York  | yankees.jpg     |   59 |    103 |
+----+-----------+-----------+-----------------+------+--------+
5 rows in set (0.00 sec)
```

This query does something new: It uses a built-in MySQL function — `concat()` — to *concatenate* the items provided in the attached arguments. This way, I can use the existing field contents and then append the asterisk used in listings to indicate a team that has clinched its division.

So much for updating a table. Now you might want to delete rows from a table. The `delete` command comes in handy here, and it works in the same way as a `select` statement: Provide the criteria, and it deletes what matches. This is a very dangerous statement because it acts instantly and without mercy. In almost all cases, I recommend that you use only the primary key field of a table as the criteria for your `delete` statement. Let me give you a couple examples.

To use `delete` the right way, you refer to the existing database table and get rid of one troublesome team:

```
mysql> delete from teams where id="2";
Query OK, 1 row affected (0.00 sec)
mysql> select * from teams;
+----+-----------+-----------+--------------+------+--------+
| id | team_name | city      | logo         | wins | losses |
+----+-----------+-----------+--------------+------+--------+
|  1 | Blue Jays | Toronto   | bluejays.jpg |   75 |     87 |
|  3 | Red Sox*  | Boston    | redsox.jpg   |   95 |     67 |
|  4 | Rays      | Tampa Bay | rays.jpg     |   84 |     78 |
|  5 | Orioles   | Baltimore | orioles.jpg  |   64 |     98 |
+----+-----------+-----------+--------------+------+--------+
4 rows in set (0.00 sec)
```

The primary key is ideal because you know that the query can affect only one row. Where you can get into trouble is when you want to delete rows that match certain criteria. This statement also works:

```
mysql> delete from teams where losses > "80";
Query OK, 2 rows affected (0.00 sec)
mysql> select * from teams;
+----+-----------+-----------+------------+------+--------+
| id | team_name | city      | logo       | wins | losses |
+----+-----------+-----------+------------+------+--------+
|  3 | Red Sox*  | Boston    | redsox.jpg |   95 |     67 |
|  4 | Rays      | Tampa Bay | rays.jpg   |   84 |     78 |
+----+-----------+-----------+------------+------+--------+
2 rows in set (0.00 sec)
```

Did you mean to delete two teams? Perhaps not, but there's no way to get them back. Much better and safer to issue two `delete` statements based on the `id` field. You've been warned.

I've now covered those CRUD operations I mentioned earlier. If you stopped reading this chapter now, you'd have 90% of what you need to use MySQL — and good for you! But my editor has generously granted me more room to discuss that which will make you more comfortable with MySQL, and I'm going to take advantage of it.

Changing tables

The first problem you might run into when managing your database is the need to alter your database tables. Yes, people are people, and change is a part of development. Look at my original database schema from Figure 14.2. Wouldn't it make sense to include the league and division for each team? It definitely would. For this task, you'll use the mighty `alter table` command. Of all the MySQL commands, this one — at least to me — is the biggest workhorse, covering a wide gamut of functionality.

In this case, you're going to use `alter table` to add two new columns. Here's how it works:

```
mysql> alter table teams add column(league varchar(255), division
   varchar(255));
Query OK, 2 rows affected (0.09 sec)
Records: 2  Duplicates: 0  Warnings: 0
mysql> describe teams;
+-----------+--------------+------+-----+---------+-------------+
| Field     | Type         | Null | Key | Default | Extra       |
+-----------+--------------+------+-----+---------+-------------+
| id        | int(11)      | NO   | PRI | NULL    |auto_increment
| team_name | varchar(255) | YES  |     | NULL    |             |
| city      | varchar(255) | YES  |     | NULL    |             |
| logo      | varchar(255) | YES  |     | NULL    |             |
| wins      | int(11)      | YES  |     | NULL    |             |
| losses    | int(11)      | YES  |     | NULL    |             |
| league    | varchar(255) | YES  |     | NULL    |             |
| division  | varchar(255) | YES  |     | NULL    |             |
+-----------+--------------+------+-----+---------+-------------+
8 rows in set (0.00 sec)
```

Note the syntax of the `add` keyword; it takes the same arguments that you used in the `create table` command, with the field name and the data type. The new columns are added to the end of the list.

Now you can use the `update` command to give all the teams in the current table the right information:

```
mysql> update teams set league="American League",
   division="East";
Query OK, 2 rows affected (0.00 sec)
Rows matched: 2  Changed: 2  Warnings: 0
mysql> select city, league, division from teams;
+-----------+-----------------+----------+
| city      | league          | division |
+-----------+-----------------+----------+
| Boston    | American League | East     |
| Tampa Bay | American League | East     |
+-----------+-----------------+----------+
2 rows in set (0.00 sec)
```

You can also change the specifications for a column. Let's say, for example, that instead of storing a file path in the `logo` field, you wanted to store the binary image data. Clearly, a simple `varchar` isn't going to be adequate. You can use `alter table` again to change the field specification:

```
mysql> alter table teams modify logo longtext;
Query OK, 2 rows affected (0.01 sec)
Records: 2  Duplicates: 0  Warnings: 0
mysql> describe teams;
+-----------+--------------+------+-----+---------+--------------+
| Field     | Type         | Null | Key | Default | Extra        |
+-----------+--------------+------+-----+---------+--------------+
| id        | int(11)      | NO   | PRI | NULL    |auto_increment|
| team_name | varchar(255) | YES  |     | NULL    |              |
| city      | varchar(255) | YES  |     | NULL    |              |
| logo      | longtext     | YES  |     | NULL    |              |
| wins      | int(11)      | YES  |     | NULL    |              |
| losses    | int(11)      | YES  |     | NULL    |              |
| league    | varchar(255) | YES  |     | NULL    |              |
| division  | varchar(255) | YES  |     | NULL    |              |
+-----------+--------------+------+-----+---------+--------------+
8 rows in set (0.00 sec)
```

You can also use `alter table` to drop a column altogether. Let's say that you don't want to have a logo field anymore:

```
mysql> alter table teams drop logo;
Query OK, 2 rows affected (0.00 sec)
Records: 2  Duplicates: 0  Warnings: 0
mysql> describe teams;
+-----------+--------------+------+-----+---------+--------------+
| Field     | Type         | Null | Key | Default | Extra        |
+-----------+--------------+------+-----+---------+--------------+
| id        | int(11)      | NO   | PRI | NULL    |auto_increment|
| team_name | varchar(255) | YES  |     | NULL    |              |
| city      | varchar(255) | YES  |     | NULL    |              |
| wins      | int(11)      | YES  |     | NULL    |              |
| losses    | int(11)      | YES  |     | NULL    |              |
| league    | varchar(255) | YES  |     | NULL    |              |
| division  | varchar(255) | YES  |     | NULL    |              |
+-----------+--------------+------+-----+---------+--------------+
7 rows in set (0.00 sec)
```

Finally, you can drop tables altogether, completing the cycle from create, to use, to destroy.

```
mysql> drop table teams;
Query OK, 0 rows affected (0.00 sec)
```

Getting Relational

Now that you know how to manage data in database tables, it's time to learn about the true power of relational databases. To get started with this, you need to load up your database with some good example data. The `baseball.txt` file contains the commands that will create all three tables shown in Figure 14.2 and will then populate them with data. You can just cut and paste the `insert` statements right into Terminal or restart your database completely with the included `create table` statements.

CROSS-REF

You can find the `baseball.txt` file on the website for this book: www.wileydevreference.com.

When you've done your import, your `teams` table should look like this (I've left out the `logo`, `league`, and `division` columns to fit the width of this page):

```
mysql> select id, team_name, city, wins, losses from teams;
+----+------------------+---------------+------+--------+
| id | team_name        | city          | wins | losses |
+----+------------------+---------------+------+--------+
|  1 | Yankees          | New York      |  103 |     59 |
|  2 | Red Sox          | Boston        |   95 |     67 |
|  3 | Rays             | Tampa Bay     |   84 |     78 |
|  4 | Blue Jays        | Toronto       |   75 |     87 |
|  5 | Orioles          | Baltimore     |   64 |     98 |
|  6 | Tigers           | Detroit       |   86 |     77 |
|  7 | Twins            | Minnesota     |   87 |     76 |
|  8 | White Sox        | Chicago       |   79 |     83 |
|  9 | Indians          | Cleveland     |   65 |     97 |
| 10 | Royals           | Kansas City   |   65 |     97 |
| 11 | Angels of Anaheim| Los Angeles   |   97 |     65 |
| 12 | Rangers          | Texas         |   87 |     75 |
| 13 | Mariners         | Seattle       |   85 |     77 |
| 14 | Athletics        | Oakland       |   75 |     87 |
| 15 | Phillies         | Philadelphia  |   93 |     69 |
| 16 | Braves           | Atlanta       |   86 |     76 |
| 17 | Marlins          | Florida       |   87 |     75 |
| 18 | Mets             | New York      |   70 |     92 |
| 19 | Nationals        | Washington    |   59 |    103 |
| 20 | Cardinals        | St. Louis     |   91 |     71 |
| 21 | Cubs             | Chicago       |   83 |     78 |
| 22 | Brewers          | Milwaukee     |   80 |     82 |
| 23 | Astros           | Houston       |   74 |     88 |
| 24 | Reds             | Cincinnati    |   78 |     84 |
| 25 | Pirates          | Pittsburgh    |   62 |     99 |
| 26 | Dodgers          | Los Angeles   |   95 |     67 |
| 27 | Rockies          | Colorado      |   92 |     70 |
| 28 | Giants           | San Francisco |   88 |     74 |
| 29 | Diamondbacks     | Arizona       |   70 |     87 |
| 30 | Padres           | San Diego     |   75 |     92 |
+----+------------------+---------------+------+--------+
30 rows in set (0.01 sec)
```

Here's the `players` table (I've omitted the `batting_avg` column to fit this page):

```
mysql> select id, first_name, last_name, number, team, position
    from players;
+----+------------+-----------+--------+------+----------+
| id | first_name | last_name | number | team | position |
+----+------------+-----------+--------+------+----------+
|  1 | Alex       | Rodriguez |     13 |    1 | 3B       |
|  2 | Derek      | Jeter     |      2 |    1 | SS       |
|  3 | Mike       | Lowell    |     25 |    2 | 3B       |
|  4 | Dustin     | Pedroia   |     15 |    2 | 2B       |
|  5 | B.J.       | Upton     |      2 |    3 | CF       |
|  6 | Akinori    | Iwamura   |      1 |    3 | 2B       |
|  7 | Marco      | Scutaro   |     19 |    4 | SS       |
|  8 | Aaron      | Hill      |      2 |    4 | 2B       |
|  9 | Adam       | Jones     |     10 |    5 | CF       |
| 10 | Melvin     | Mora      |      6 |    5 | 3B       |
+----+------------+-----------+--------+------+----------+
10 rows in set (0.00 sec)
```

Finally, here's the `games` table. Note that I've used alias names in the `select` query to give me shorter column names so as to fit this page width:

```
mysql> select id, visiting_team as visitors, home_team as home,
    visiting_score as vscore, home_score as hscore, game_date from
    games;
+----+----------+------+--------+--------+------------+
| id | visitors | home | vscore | hscore | game_date  |
+----+----------+------+--------+--------+------------+
|  1 |        4 |    2 |      2 |      3 | 2009-08-29 |
|  2 |        8 |    1 |      0 |     10 | 2009-08-29 |
|  3 |        3 |    6 |      3 |      1 | 2009-08-29 |
|  4 |       26 |   24 |     11 |      4 | 2009-08-29 |
|  5 |       18 |   21 |      4 |     11 | 2009-08-29 |
|  6 |       30 |   17 |      7 |      4 | 2009-08-29 |
|  7 |       16 |   15 |      9 |      1 | 2009-08-29 |
|  8 |        9 |    5 |      5 |      3 | 2009-08-29 |
|  9 |       25 |   22 |      3 |      7 | 2009-08-29 |
| 10 |       12 |    7 |      3 |      0 | 2009-08-29 |
| 11 |       19 |   20 |      4 |      9 | 2009-08-29 |
| 12 |       23 |   29 |      0 |      9 | 2009-08-29 |
| 13 |       27 |   28 |      3 |      5 | 2009-08-29 |
| 14 |       14 |   11 |      4 |      3 | 2009-08-29 |
| 15 |       10 |   13 |      4 |      8 | 2009-08-29 |
+----+----------+------+--------+--------+------------+
15 rows in set (0.00 sec)
```

The first thing you might wonder after looking at the `games` table is, how can a human understand this? That is, in fact, the point; in most cases, you won't be interacting directly with ID numbers to tie database tables together. You'll use a programming language, such as PHP or Ruby on Rails, to accomplish this. But it's critical that you understand the principles behind the magic that those programming languages give you.

In the `games` table, the second and third columns are intended to store the ID numbers of records from the `teams` table. So, in the first row, the visitors are ID 4; that's the Toronto Blue Jays. They're playing a team with an ID of 2 in the `teams` table; that's the Boston Red Sox. And with the rest of that row, you can see that the Red Sox won, 3–2, on August 29, 2009.

Why not just put the name of the teams in the visitors and home columns? Why do this lookup? The beauty of relational databases is that you can have a single record for an *entity*. In this case, you only want to have one record for each baseball team. If you'd used the team name Montreal Expos to keep track of every game played, there'd be a lot of work to do once they moved to Washington, D.C., to become the Nationals. With a single record, you can make the change in one place, and the ID number stays the same. This is the art and science of database schema design; you must understand the essential entities that make up your application and then model them appropriately.

MySQL can help you do the work of tying IDs to team names by using the power of the `join` statement. This is an adjunct to the `select` command, allowing you to tie two tables together based on a common ID field. In your case, you can use a `join` to replace one ID field's contents with its text-based equivalent from the source table. Let's try it out with a practical example. Of the games listed in your database, which ones did the visitors win, and what were the scores?

```
mysql> select games.id, concat(teams.city, " ", teams.team_name)
    as vteam, visiting_score as vscore, home_score, game_date from
    games join teams on teams.id=games.visiting_team where
    visiting_score > home_score;
+----+---------------------+--------+------------+------------+
| id | vteam               | vscore | home_score | game_date  |
+----+---------------------+--------+------------+------------+
|  3 | Tampa Bay Rays      |      3 |          1 | 2009-08-29 |
|  4 | Los Angeles Dodgers |     11 |          4 | 2009-08-29 |
|  6 | San Diego Padres    |      7 |          4 | 2009-08-29 |
|  7 | Atlanta Braves      |      9 |          1 | 2009-08-29 |
|  8 | Cleveland Indians   |      5 |          3 | 2009-08-29 |
| 10 | Texas Rangers       |      3 |          0 | 2009-08-29 |
| 14 | Oakland Athletics   |      4 |          3 | 2009-08-29 |
+----+---------------------+--------+------------+------------+
7 rows in set (0.01 sec)
```

Read that `select` statement carefully. The first part is very familiar to you now; you're choosing the fields you want (by using the `concat()` function to put together the city and team name fields) from the `games` table. Then, you have your `join` statement. The clause `join teams on teams.id=games.visiting_team` is the key to making this work; you need to connect the contents of the `visiting_team` column with the `teams` table's `id` column.

Finally, you set the condition for the results; the visiting team's score must be higher than the home team's.

`Join` statements can be complicated, so don't worry if this looks overwhelming. You can often work around the need to use joins in your programming code, but if this does make sense, you'll have a lot more power in your web application development.

Play around with these tables, and get used to selecting information based on other tables. Here are some examples to get you started.

You might want to find all New York Yankees players in the database:

```
mysql> select id, first_name, last_name, position from players
    where team = 1;
+----+------------+-----------+----------+
| id | first_name | last_name | position |
+----+------------+-----------+----------+
|  1 | Alex       | Rodriguez | 3B       |
|  2 | Derek      | Jeter     | SS       |
+----+------------+-----------+----------+
2 rows in set (0.00 sec)
```

You might want to see which teams have players in the database. And because there may be multiple players per team (which there are), you'll use the MySQL function `distinct()` to show you the results just once per team name:

```
mysql> select distinct(team_name) from teams join players on
    players.team=teams.id;
+-----------+
| team_name |
+-----------+
| Yankees   |
| Red Sox   |
| Rays      |
| Blue Jays |
| Orioles   |
+-----------+
5 rows in set (0.00 sec)
```

You may also want to know just how many players are in the database. The command-line client provides the number of records after every query, but when you want to use the database through another language, this is the kind of query you send:

```
mysql> select count(*) from players;
+----------+
| count(*) |
+----------+
|       10 |
+----------+
1 row in set (0.00 sec)
```

There's plenty more that you can do with this database. Investigate the MySQL documentation on its website (`http://dev.mysql.com/doc/`), play around with various queries, make mistakes, and have fun!

MySQL Utilities

I'm going to wrap up my discussion of MySQL by investigating two programs that accompany the MySQL client program and that make life easier when interacting with the server. These programs are `mysqladmin` and `mysqldump`. The first lets you administer databases directly from the command line, and the second lets you create single-file duplicates of your database for quick and easy transport.

The workflow is pretty straightforward. When I create a website, I do so on my Mac. When it's time to move the site to the remote production server, I need to package up the database on my Mac and then upload it to the server. I can do the complete operation from the command line. Let's step through the process.

First, I export my database by using `mysqldump`:

```
achilles:~ aaronvegh$ mysqldump -u root -prootpasswd baseball >
    baseball.sql
achilles:~ aaronvegh$ ls -l b*
-rw-r--r--  1 aaronvegh  staff  6462 31 Aug 21:57 baseball.sql
```

The `mysqldump` command starts up just like the `mysql` command-line client; it takes the username and password, followed by the database name. Then, the angle bracket redirects output to a file that you name. Once complete, the file is found in the current directory.

The next step is to move the file up to the remove server. You might recall from Chapter 3 that you use `scp` to accomplish this:

```
achilles:~ aaronvegh$ scp baseball.sql aaron@vegh.ca:~/baseball.
    sql
baseball.sql                          100% 6462     6.3KB/s   00:00
```

With the file on your remote server, you can switch to `mysqladmin` to create the database on that machine:

```
achilles:~ aaronvegh$ ssh aaron@vegh.ca
Last login: Sun Aug 30 23:12:22 2009 from bas3-
    toronto02-1279545643.dsl.bell.ca
[aaron@cl-t030-220cl ~]$ mysqladmin -u root -prootpasswd create
    baseball
```

The `mysqladmin` command is just like the others you've worked with; type your credentials and then issue the keyword. In this case, you issue a `create baseball` command to set up the new database. The command doesn't return anything except a fresh prompt. If you already have this database on the server, you may want to replace it altogether, so use a delete statement in front:

```
[aaron@cl-t030-220cl ~]$ mysqladmin -u root -prootpasswd drop
    baseball
Dropping the database is potentially a very bad thing to do.
Any data stored in the database will be destroyed.
Do you really want to drop the 'baseball' database [y/N] y
Database "baseball" dropped
```

You can follow this command with your create command, ignoring the intimidating warning.

Now's your chance to populate the empty database with your local export:

```
[aaron@cl-t030-220cl ~]$ mysql -u root -prootpasswd baseball
    < baseball.sql
```

This is the mysql command client being used in shell mode; you pass in the database file, and it returns you to a new prompt without going into the execution environment. Note the direction of the angle bracket; it shows that data is passing from the file to the mysql command.

If you've a mind for scripting, then you can appreciate the beauty of this operation. The MySQL utilities are ready-made for automation with a shell script; they take their arguments right on the command line, and they don't return anything on success.

Summary

MySQL is an amazingly powerful relational database system that's also very easy to use. While some of the examples in this chapter might have seemed labor-intensive, when you get into web application programming, you're going to see how the relational data is connected. The database is the backbone of your web application, so understanding how it works is critical to what follows — using it with programming languages, such as PHP and Ruby.

PHP Introduction

You have finally come to the last section you need in order to be a well-rounded web developer. I've covered the complete spectrum of skills to this point — from managing your own server, to the techniques of front-end website construction, to design, to databases. The only skill left to learn is the most powerful: back-end development.

As I discussed in Chapter 13, I'm going to cover both PHP and Ruby as back-end scripting languages. While both are capable options for the development of complete and robust web applications, my experience has taught me that Ruby on Rails makes the most powerful large-scale application environment and will help you create a complete application more quickly, with fewer bugs and better maintainability.

Having said that, PHP remains a terrific language. It's broadly supported on most web hosts, it's easy to learn, and, for smaller tasks, it gets the job done with aplomb. In this chapter, I'm going to discuss the basics of using PHP: how it works as a language and how it works in the context of a web application, passing data between pages. You're also going to see how to use PHP to interact with MySQL so you can both save to and recall data from your MySQL server.

The examples in this chapter won't be overly robust — just enough for you to understand the principles at work and to imagine how to use the language to power larger applications.

In This Chapter

Your first PHP application

Basic PHP syntax

Creating a PHP application

Your First PHP Application

First off, I'm going to assume that you have PHP working and that you've confirmed it by following the steps from Chapter 13. If you can view the phpinfo() script output, then you're ready to begin.

Do you remember the calculator example from learning JavaScript in Chapter 6? You're going to see how you would implement that in PHP.

Create a new file in your text editor and then type in the following code:

```html
<html>
<head>
<title>First PHP</title>
</head>
<body>
    <h1>Hello, Adding Machine!</h1>
    <p>Enter a couple numbers to operate on.</p>
    <form action="hellocalc.php" method="post">
    <input type="text" size="5" name="t1" />
    +
    <input type="text" size="5" name="t2" />
    <input type="submit" value="=" />
    <input type="text" size="5" value="" />
    </form>
</body>
</html>
```

Save the file somewhere in your home folder's `Sites` directory; I created a `prowebdev` directory there for these files. Call the file `hellocalc.php`. Now go to your friendly neighborhood browser and open `http://localhost/prowebdev/hellocalc.php` (or whatever your path is — just make sure it's done through `localhost`!). You should see something similar to Figure 15.1.

Figure 15.1

The `hellocalc.php` file

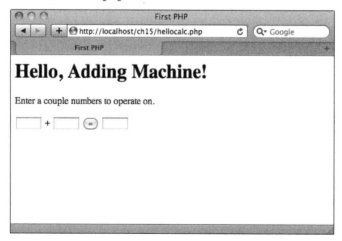

This should look familiar to you from Chapter 6. But the code is different, and those differences reflect the way that these languages approach receiving and acting upon user input. The difference is that one is client side (JavaScript), while the other is server side (PHP). Recall from the JavaScript example that you didn't use the form tag; after all, you weren't submitting data to a server. Instead, you had an onclick handler that triggered a JavaScript function contained in the same file.

If you look closely at the form tag, you'll see that it's calling the same file as the one you just wrote. Believe it or not, you're going to do the same thing with your PHP example as you did with the JavaScript example; the script that does the calculating will be in the same file.

As of now, there's no PHP present in this code. But with the .php appended to the file name, the web server would have passed it through the PHP interpreter. Let's give it something to do this time. Alter your code to the following (changes are shown in bold):

```php
<?
   if(isset($_POST["t1"])) {
      $t1 = $_POST["t1"];
      $t2 = $_POST["t2"];
      $answer = $t1 + $t2;
   }
   else {
      $t1 = "";
      $t2 = "";
      $answer = "";
   }
?>
<html>
<head>
<title>First PHP</title>
</head>
<body>
   <h1>Hello, Adding Machine!</h1>
   <p>Enter a couple numbers to operate on.</p>
   <form action="hellocalc.php" method="post">
   <input type="text" size="5" name="t1" value="<?=$t1?>" />
   +
   <input type="text" size="5" name="t2" value="<?=$t2?>" />
   <input type="submit" value="=" />
   <input type="text" size="5" value="<?=$answer?>" />
   </form>
</body>
</html>
```

CROSS-REF

You can find the `hellocalc.php` file on the website for this book: `www.wileydevreference.com`.

The first thing you need to address about PHP is the use of these *delimiter tags*: the opening `<?` and closing `?>` tags are the signal to the PHP interpreter that its contents need to be processed. Those tags are known as the *short tags* because they're so brief. There's also a classic opening tag — `<?php` — which you'll find used by default on any server that supports PHP. If you're writing a PHP application for an unknown server (or one that can be run on any server), you should use the long tag. I'll touch on one gotcha related to the long tag in a moment.

I've placed the PHP script at the top of the file, above the HTML content that will be rendered by the browser. Technically, I could place that PHP script anywhere within the PHP code. The only constraint is that this script generates values that are used in the HTML form; the lines of code that produce those values must be before those lines.

Let's go through the script to see how it works. The first thing you need to do is ascertain whether the page is loading for the first time or with the values from the form beneath this code. The way to tell the difference is to inspect the POST variables; this is the mechanism that PHP uses to provide access to the data sent through a form. I'll cover this in more detail later, but for now, just understand that when a script is submitted, it automatically creates a series of variables inside a special array named $_POST. You test one value of that array to see if it's there. If it is, execution will move into the `if` statements; otherwise, execution will move into the `else` statement. This is almost identical to the way things are done in JavaScript.

A variable in PHP is declared with a dollar sign ($). Unlike in JavaScript, you don't have to declare variables up front. Also unlike JavaScript, variables in PHP are *untyped*, which means that it knows the difference between a number and a string without your having to tell it. This is one of the reasons why PHP is so easy to learn, as it takes away this layer of complexity.

The first part of the `if` statement pulls the values from the form beneath this code. The name attributes of the form fields are the same as the variable names found in the $_POST array. This is done automatically by the PHP interpreter; if you ever find data not appearing as you would expect, check that the name field in your form matches the variables in your script. The script ends by adding those two numbers together and then placing the value into a variable called $answer.

The `else` statement — the statements of which are run if this form is loading for the first time — sets those variables to empty values. This is done in order to give you a way to populate those fields for a first run. If you didn't set the variables, an attempt to access them within the form would result in a warning right inside the text field. It looks like this:

```
<br /> <b>Notice</b>:  Undefined variable: t1 in <b>/Users/
   aaronvegh/Sites/prowebdev/ch15/hellocalc.php</b> on line
   <b>23</b><br />
```

NOTE

Have you just tried removing the `else` block from your code and not seen this warning? That may be because your version of PHP isn't configured to display warnings. By default, the version of PHP that comes on the Mac is set to show errors only. Later in this chapter, I show you how you can manage changes to your PHP configuration, including the display of errors and warnings.

Fortunately, the `undefined variable` error is easily diagnosed; set the variable before you use it!

Having written a script that pulls values and assigns them to variables, the fun part is using them. Within your form, you've added some value attributes. These attributes are populated in PHP by using the quick output operator: `<?=`. Unfortunately, this operator only works with PHP's short tag. If you use the long tag, then you have to use the `echo` command instead. An example might look like this:

```
<input type="text" size="5" value="<?php echo $answer?>" />
```

That's the only problem when it comes to choosing which tag to use. I prefer the short tag and will use that going forward.

With that done, save the file and then reload your browser. You should find that it adds anything you submit to it, as shown in Figure 15.2, including float values. Your JavaScript version would have failed on you with those. Again, PHP just knows what to do.

Figure 15.2

The completed calculator application

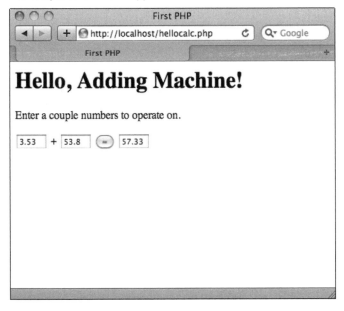

But there's one distinct advantage to the way JavaScript does things: It runs its calculations without refreshing the page. For your PHP calculator to work, your client (the web browser) needs access to the server (your instance of Apache). Although processes occur quickly and are local in your current configuration, you need to accommodate for the fact that your client and server are sometimes located on either side of a slow, unreliable network connection: the Internet.

So, it's fair to say that this particular application — a calculator where the rules are set and unchanging — would make a far better JavaScript application than a PHP one. But fear not: There are many areas where the reverse is true and where the best applications use both technologies. You'll be glad you learned both.

Basic PHP Syntax

You've already seen two of PHP's strengths: It's untyped, and its code runs within HTML. You'll find scripts that use a small amount of PHP to provide a value or two, and you'll find massive code bases, with many files composed of thousands of lines of script.

Like JavaScript, PHP is a language made up of expressions; you declare variables, assign values, and perform operations on them in a procedural manner. Each line of code builds on the work before. Variables in PHP are defined with a $ sign and don't need to be declared before using them:

```
$myCar = "Hyundai Tucson";
```

Every line of code is terminated by a semicolon, and any text value that you assign to a variable must either be enclosed in quotation marks or derived from another function call or variable. Numbers can be enclosed in quotation marks if you like; it's optional, as the interpreter will do the right thing in both cases.

Operators

Operators, as in JavaScript, are the engines of a language; they take the variables and then perform the necessary actions. Also as in JavaScript, there are mathematical operators, assignment operators, comparison operators, and logical operators. Tables 15-1 to 15-4 show these operators, including an example for each.

Table 15-1 PHP Mathematical Operators

Operator	Description	Example	Result
+	Addition	x = 2; y = 1; x+y	3
−	Subtraction	x = 2; y = 1; x−y	1
*	Multiplication	x = 4; y = 2; x*y	8

Operator	Description	Example	Result
/	Division	x = 4 ; y = 2 ; x/y	2
%	Modulus (division remainder)	x = 10 ; y = 8 ; x%y	2
++	Increment	x = 5 ; x++	6
--	Decrement	x = 5 ; x--	4

These are the basic mathematical operations that you'll perform on numbers. The final three may be new to you; the modulus operator calculates the remainder after a dividing operation, which is handy (for example) when you want to determine if a number is even or odd. The increment and decrement operators are also handy for easily moving values up or down, although they can be replaced with a standard operator: x = x + 1 is the same as x++.

Table 15-2 PHP Assignment Operators

Operator	Description	Example	Result
=	Simple assignment	x = 5	5
+=	Increment assignment	x = 5 ; x += 2	7
-=	Decrement assignment	x = 5 ; x -= 2	3
*=	Multiply assignment	x = 5 ; x *= 2	10
/=	Divide assignment	x = 5 ; x /= 2	2.5
.=	Concatenation	x = 2 ; x .= 2	22
%=	Modulus assignment	x = 5 ; x %= 2	1

Of these operators, you'll almost certainly find yourself using the simple assignment the most; like the decrement and increment mathematical operators, these operators make your code briefer. In this book, I default to using the simple assignment, as it makes the code more expressive and readable.

Table 15-3 PHP Comparison Operators

Operator	Description	Example	Result
>	Greater than	x = 2 ; y = 1 ; x > y	true
<	Less than	x = 2 ; y = 1 ; x < 1	false
==	Is equal to	x = 2 ; y = 2 ; x == y	true
!=	Is not equal to	x = 2 ; y = 2 ; x != y	false
<=	Less than or equal to	x = 2 ; y = 1 ; x <= y	false
>=	Greater than or equal to	x = 2 ; y = 1 ; x >= y	true

Comparisons perform much of the work in determining program flow. The == operator is an operator for which I mentally substitute the word "is." The value on the left is not equal to the value on the right; they're the same: x is y. Don't confuse this with the simple assignment operator, which makes the left have the same value as the right. Yes, I do that sometimes.

Table 15-4 PHP Logical Operators

Operator	Description	Example	Result
&&	and	x = 2; y = 0; (x > 0 && y < 5)	true
||	or	x = 2; y = 0; (x > 0 || y < 5)	true
!	not	x = 2; x != 5	true

You'll use these operators when you have multiple conditions to consider in your program flow.

Arrays

Every language needs a set of container classes — those structures in which you can store multiple values and represent them with a single variable name. Both JavaScript and PHP share the same concept: Arrays are indexed collections of values. They're very flexible and powerful data structures. Mastering arrays is a critical part of learning any language — and no more so than in PHP.

Creating an array is a simple enough task: Call the `array()` function and then provide the needed values:

```
$cars = array("Lumina", "Caravan", "Corolla", "Taurus",
    "Silverado");
```

The items you provide are put into an array named $cars, and each value is given an index number, starting from zero. So, if you wanted to pull a particular car out of this array, you would call on the index number:

```
$thisCar = $cars[1]; // assigns "Caravan" to $thisCar
```

You can also create your own indices, effectively turning the array into a hash (a concept formalized in Ruby, as discussed in Chapter 16):

```
$thisCar = array("Make"=>"Toyota", "Model"=>"Corolla",
    "Year"=>"2009");
```

And instead of using an index number, you call on the key to get the value:

```
echo "My current car is a " . $thisCar["Make"];
```

Arrays can be very powerful when they become multi-dimensional. So far, you've seen two-dimensional arrays, which contain two pieces of data. You can add a third dimension by making the value of an item also be an array:

```
$myCars = array (
    array("Make"=>"Honda", "Model"=>"Civic", "Year"=>"1998"),
    array("Make"=>"Toyota", "Model"=>"Corolla", "Year"=>"2005"),
    array("Make"=>"Hyundai", "Model"=>"Tucson", "Year"=>"2008")
);
```

I've tried to format this code to make it easier to understand. Within the opening array, I've created three individual `array()` calls, so `$myCars` is an array containing three arrays!

Each of these arrays is reachable by an index number. If you want to get at a particular value, you might do this:

```
echo "My first car was a " . $myCars[0]["Make"] . " " .
    $myCars[0][ "Model"];
```

PHP provides many functions for working with arrays, including operations that let you sort, add, remove, search, and count values. By the time you're done here, you'll use arrays to perform all kinds of operations.

Control structures

Aside from assigning values to variables, controlling a program's execution through control structures is a major component of programming.

if…else

Just as with JavaScript, the most important control structure is the *if…else* construction. Its syntax is identical to that used for JavaScript:

```
if (condition) {
    statements if true
}
else {
    statements if false
}
```

Here's a practical example:

```
if ($myCar["Model"] != "Corolla") {
    echo "Not a Corolla!";
}
else {
    echo "My Corolla!";
}
```

You don't need an `else` statement; a single `if` can be evaluated, and any other condition will simply cause the enclosing code to be passed over. Conversely, there's an addendum to the `if...else` construction that includes multiple `elseif` statements; this allows you to catch any number of conditions, such as:

```
if ($myCar["Model"] == "Civic") {
    echo "My Civic!";
}
elseif ($myCar["Model"] == "Corolla") {
    echo "My Corolla!";
}
elseif ($myCar["Model"] == "Tucson") {
    echo "My Tucson!";
}
else {
    echo "Not my car!";
}
```

Strictly speaking, a final `else` statement isn't necessary. But your code will be more bug-proof if you can account for any user input — including where data is typed that isn't in your array.

Some developers find the `if...elseif...else` construction a little wordy, so PHP provides a tidier technique called `switch`. It looks like this:

```
switch ($myCar["Model"]) {
    case "Civic":
        echo "My Civic!";
        break;
    case "Corolla":
        echo "My Corolla!";
        break;
    case "Tucson":
        echo "My Tucson!";
        break;
    default:
        echo "Not my car!";
}
```

You can't argue with its compactness, and it's definitely expressive; you can readily see what this code does. But I find that I don't use `switch` very often, perhaps owing to its syntax being different from PHP code. It simply looks out of place in my code, so I'm less inclined to use it.

There's one more format that `if...else` comes in: the *ternary* format (ternary means three parts: the condition, the `true` statements, and the `false` statements). It's an extremely brief format and, like the `switch` statement, it feels a little out of place. But occasionally within my HTML code, I find this format very attractive:

```
<?
$light = "on";
$text = ($light == "on") ? "I can see!" : "Hey, who turned off
    the lights?";
echo $text; // returns "I can see!"
?>
```

In the ternary format, a variable takes the result of testing the condition (in brackets) followed by a question mark. The matching condition executes the first statement, with the alternate statement following the colon.

This makes for some pretty concise code, although, again, it's different from most PHP code.

For and foreach

While some control structures help you execute code based on logical comparisons (such as `if`), others are *enumerators*, helping you move through collections of data. The `for` structure is the most common of these; you'll find something like this in most languages. It has the following syntax:

```
for (starting expression; condition; next action) {
    statements;
}
```

The `for` structure takes three arguments: The initial state of the loop is expressed. Then, the second argument is executed; if it returns `true`, then the third argument is run. Here's a practical example:

```
for ($x = 1; $x <= 10; $x++ ) {
    echo $x . "<br/>";
}
```

If you were to run this code, you'd see the numbers one through ten displayed, one per line, in your browser.

The `for` statement is pretty useful in the case of arrays that are numerically indexed. As you'll recall, an array is composed of values that are paired with an index key that increments from the number zero. So, if you had an array of cars — such as the one I described for multi-dimensional arrays — and wanted to display the model year of each car, you might do this:

```
for ($x = 0; $x < count($myCars); $x++) {
    echo $myCars[$x]["Year"] . "<br/>";
}
```

The variable `$x` stands in for the index of the array, while each round of the `for` loop increments to the next array.

As it happens, moving through arrays is so useful that PHP provided a structure for exactly that scenario: the `foreach` loop. All you have to do is pass it to the array you want to move through. Here's the syntax:

```
foreach (array as key=>value) {
    statements;
}
```

The `foreach` loop arguments can optionally specify only the value, which you would do if the array were numerically indexed. So, instead of the `for` statement above, you could more easily express it this way:

```
foreach ($myCars as $mc) {
    echo $mc ["Year"] . "<br/>";
}
```

That's not too bad. But here's where it becomes challenging. With multi-dimensional arrays, you might find yourself wanting to nest enumerators. Here's how you would do that:

```
foreach ($myCars as $mc) {
    foreach($mc as $key => $value) {
        echo $key . ": " . $value . " ";
    }
    echo "<br/>";
}
```

Using the array that I gave you previously, this code would output the following:

```
Make: Honda Model: Civic Year: 1998
Make: Toyota Model: Corolla Year: 2005
Make: Hyundai Model: Tucson Year: 2008
```

You'll be putting this knowledge into practice in the next section.

Passing data between pages

Part of what makes a server-side language worth having is its ability to facilitate the passage of data from the user on one page to a response on another.

A classic example might be a website's logon form; you must type a username and password to use a special area of the site. A server-side script needs to receive the information entered, decide whether it's legitimate, and provide a page that responds appropriately. So, how does a server-side script get that information from the user?

That's what this section is all about. You're going to examine the four ways that information can be passed between pages. In general, those methods are:

- GET variables, which pass the data from one page to another, embedded within the link
- POST variables, which pass the data from one page to another, as part of the HTTP headers
- SESSION variables, which store the data in a file on the server, specifically for that user, that lasts for the browsing session
- COOKIE variables, which are stored on the user's computer and can last for as long as you like (assuming the user doesn't remove the file)

Let's try these out. In the following exercise, you're going to create four files — one to demonstrate each of these techniques. Start by creating a new text file and then typing this code:

```html
<html>
<head>
<title>PHP Passing Data</title>
</head>
<body>
    <p><a href="page2.php?name=Aaron">Let's start moving some
    data!</a></p>
</body>
</html>
```

Save this file as `page1.html`. You can give this file an extension of `.html` because there's no PHP code within it. Instead, you're linking to a PHP file via a standard anchor tag. And it's here that you pass a GET variable; by appending an argument to the end of the URL, starting with a question mark, you can pass any value that you want (feel free to substitute your own name). This format is a property of HTTP, which PHP takes advantage of. You could also pass multiple values by separating them with ampersands. For example:

```html
<a href="page2.php?name=Aaron&color=blue">Click here</a>.
```

CROSS-REF

You can find the `page1.html` file on the website for this book: `www.wileydevreference.com`.

Let's see how you receive the variables on the other side. Create another text file and then type this code:

```php
<html>
<head>
<title>PHP Passing Data</title>
</head>
<body>
<?
    $name = $_GET["name"];
```

```
?>
    <form action="page3.php" method="post">
    <p><?=$name?>'s favorite color: <input type="text"
   name="color" size="15" /></p>
    <input type="hidden" name="name" value="<?=$name?>" />
    <input type="submit" value="Continue" />
    </form>
</body>
</html>
```

You'll save this code as `page2.php`, exactly as advertised in the hyperlink on the first page. Here's the key line for taking the value from the first page:

```
<?
    $name = $_GET["name"];
?>
```

CROSS-REF

You can find the `page2.php` file on the website for this book: `www.wileydevreference.com`.

Within the PHP tags, you create a new variable and assign it the value from the `$_GET` array. This is an array created when the server detects `GET` variables; it sets the keys as the variable name and the value as the, uh, value.

Once you have the variable set with the value from the last page, you can demonstrate that you have it by using it. Within the form that you set up to capture another variable, you can echo out the name:

```
<p><?=$name?>'s favorite color: <input type="text" name="color"
    size="15" /></p>
```

This field is also within a `form` tag that you created. Note the `method` attribute; it's set to send the data by `POST`. You can also send form contents by using `GET`, but you'll generally prefer `POST`.

Why is `POST` better? For an answer, go ahead and load `page1.html` in your browser. It should look like Figure 15.3. It's not much to look at, but when you click the link, you get `page2.php`, as shown in Figure 15.4.

Figure 15.3

The page1.html file

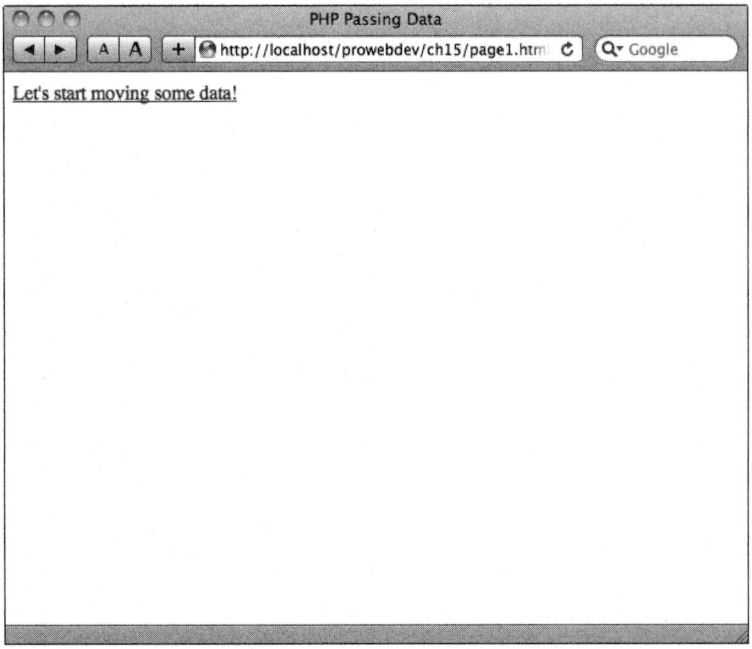

Let's start moving some data!

Figure 15.4

The page2.php file

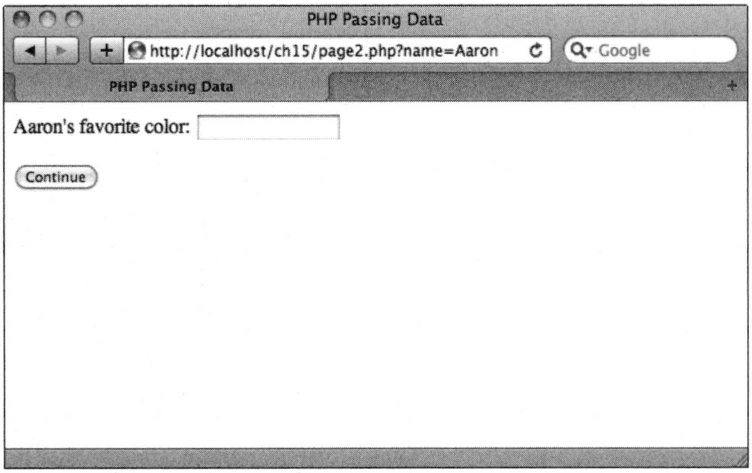

Aaron's favorite color: [_____]

Continue

And here you can see what makes a GET a GET. The URL that you see in the location bar includes the argument that you passed. Want to see how to hack a web page? Change the URL from Aaron (or whatever you had) to Bob. Reload the page. Suddenly, you've got a new name, as shown in Figure 15.5! Any user could do this. Imagine if, instead of a harmless first name, you were using this method to pass a user ID number. Change the ID number, and your user might be able to edit someone else's record. This is probably not behavior that you want to allow in your application.

Figure 15.5

If you change a GET argument, your page also changes.

That's why I can only recommend using GET variables for unimportant matters, such as passing the current state or trivial situations like this one.

For passing data a little more securely, you'll use a POST array, and that's how you move data between the second and third pages.

As you can see in the form on page2.php, you're collecting a single field from the user: his or her favorite color. But because you want to send both the name and the color, you need to use a hidden field. This places a particular value within the set of data that moves on with the form while hiding it from the user.

Let's move on to page3.php. Create a new text file and then place this code inside:

```
<?
session_start();
?>
<html>
```

```
<head>
<title>PHP Passing Data</title>
</head>
<body>
<?
    $_SESSION["name"] = $_POST["name"];
    $_SESSION["color"] = $_POST["color"];
?>
    <p>Welcome, <?=$_SESSION["name"]?>! Your favorite color is
    <span style="color:<?=$_SESSION["color"]?>"><?=$_
    SESSION["color"]?></span>.</p>
    <p><a href="page4.php">Sessions are transitory. Let's keep
    your choice for longer.</a></p>
</body>
</html>
```

CROSS-REF

You can find the `page3.php` file on the website for this book: `www.wileydevreference.com`.

Capturing data from a POST variable is virtually identical to getting it from a GET variable. But in this example, you're going to transfer the data right into SESSION variables — normally, you would just create regular variables to hold these values.

A SESSION variable is data stored on the server, and it remains for as long as the user is in the current session. A *session*, in this case, is the time the same browser window is open. You could navigate to a different website and come back to find your session still in place. But if you close the window, the session closes.

Sessions are activated by issuing a command at the very top of any file that you intend to use it with:

```
<?
    session_start();
?>
```

This must be the first line of your PHP file — before any other data is sent to the browser. Once that's done, you can create new entries in the $_SESSION array; simply supply the key (variable name) that you want. In this case, you've created two variables: one for the name and one for the color.

To demonstrate that the data has arrived, you use it in the page content, and in this example, you set a CSS style to the color chosen. This won't work if your color choice is exotic, but for the colors that CSS does recognize, you'll have a fetchingly colored word to end the sentence, as shown in Figure 15.6.

Figure 15.6

The `page3.php` file

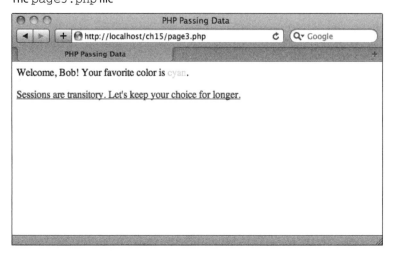

The final element on this page is a hyperlink to `page4.php`. This link doesn't pass any data, either through the link in a GET variable or through the headers via POST. Instead, it relies on the data residing in the SESSION array. Open one more text file and then type this code:

```
<?
session_start();
setcookie("pwd_name", $_SESSION["name"], time()+60*60*24*30,
    "/");
setcookie("pwd_color", $_SESSION["color"], time()+60*60*24*30,
    "/");
?>
<html>
<head>
<title>PHP Passing Data</title>
</head>
<body>
    <p>Welcome, <?=$_COOKIE["pwd_name"]?>! Your favorite color is
    <span style="color:<?=$_COOKIE["pwd_color"]?>"><?=$_
    COOKIE["pwd_color"]?></span>.</p>

</body>
</html>
```

Once more, because you're using SESSION variables on your page, you need to begin with a call to `session_start()`. Then, you have your calls to a new function, `setcookie()`. This function creates a cookie for you, which is used to store data on the user's computer.

The function prototype looks like this:

```
setcookie(cookie_name, cookie_value, expiry, path);
```

The first two arguments are pretty straightforward. The `expiry` argument uses the PHP function `time()`, which provides the current time in seconds since the Unix epoch began (that's January 1, 1970). To this number, you can add any number of seconds in order to set the expiry time. Here, you set it for 30 days, using the convenience of multiplication (60 seconds × 60 minutes × 24 hours × 30 days).

Finally, you provide the path `/`, which designates the root directory as the relevant path for this cookie. In other words, this cookie is relevant for any page in this domain. That's generally how you want to set your cookies anyway.

Save this page as `page4.php` and then reload your browser. Something untoward occurs, as shown in Figure 15.7.

You receive error messages in your code. The complaint is that you're using variables from the `$_COOKIES` array, but they haven't been set yet. But you just set them! As it happens, PHP doesn't have access to `COOKIES` variables until the next page load. Go ahead and refresh the page, and you should see everything displaying correctly, as shown in Figure 15.8.

Figure 15.7

The `page4.php` file, loading for the first time

Figure 15.8

The `page4.php` file, loading for the second time

This time, the page has access to the COOKIES array and is able to show the variables. The lesson here? In this case, you could have used the SESSION array values to display data in the page content. Let's recode `page4.php` to give you some protection from such gaffes (the new content is in bold):

```php
<?
session_start();
setcookie("pwd_name", $_SESSION["name"], time()+60*60*24*30,
    "/");
setcookie("pwd_color", $_SESSION["color"], time()+60*60*24*30,
    "/");
if(isset($_COOKIE["pwd_name"])) {
    $name = $_COOKIE["pwd_name"];
    $color = $_COOKIE["pwd_color"];
}
else {
    $name = $_SESSION["name"];
    $color = $_SESSION["color"];
}
?>
<html>
<head>
<title>PHP Passing Data</title>
</head>
<body>
    <p>Welcome, <?=$name?>! Your favorite color is <span style=
    "color:<?=$color?>"><?=$color?></span>.</p>

</body>
</html>
```

CROSS-REF

You can find the `hellocalc.php` file on the website for this book: `www.wileydevreference.com`.

Sometimes, you might find yourself wanting to troubleshoot cookies on your development Mac. If you're using Safari, you can quickly take a look at all the cookies on your computer by choosing Safari ⇨ Preferences and then clicking the Security tab. Click the Show Cookies button to see the complete list, as shown in Figure 15.9. Use the Spotlight filter to find the one you're after, providing a keyword for the domain, the name, or the value.

Figure 15.9

Looking for stored cookies in Safari

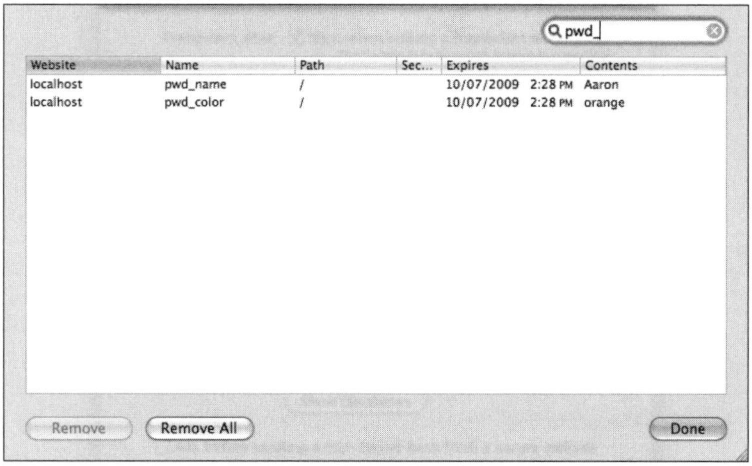

If you're a Firefox user, you can find cookies by choosing Firefox ⇨ Preferences and then clicking the Privacy tab. There, you'll find a hyperlink that says remove individual cookies.

You have now learned how to pass information from page to page in PHP. Before you move on, let's look at another critical element of PHP's power: writing your own functions.

Writing functions

So far, you've only seen very simple code in your PHP scripts. But when you have larger blocks of code, you may want to organize them more effectively. You may also need to execute certain blocks of code numerous times. By writing your own functions, you can make your code leaner, easier to read, and more flexible.

Unsurprisingly, writing your own functions works just like it does in JavaScript. Here's an example:

```
<?
function myFunction(arg1, arg2) {
    do stuff;
}
?>
```

A function may or may not return a value. Here's an example of a function that does, including how to use it:

```
<?
$answer = addThis(3, 5);
function addThis(arg1, arg2) {
    return arg1 + arg2;
}
?>
```

The variable $answer would end up with a value of 8 in this case. You can make arguments optional if you want by providing them with default values:

```
<?
function favoriteColor($color = "blue") {
    echo "My favorite color is " . $color . ".";
}
favoriteColor("red"); // "My favorite color is red."
favoriteColor(); // "My favorite color is blue."
?>
```

This function is also noteworthy in that it doesn't return a value; instead, it does some work itself by echoing text to the browser.

Including code

As your projects grow in size, you'll find it useful to organize your code into separate files. Families of functions can exist together in one file, and you can use the `include()` function to bring them into your current file.

One of the most powerful features of PHP is its ability to let you easily template websites. Imagine you're writing code for a large site using just HTML. All the pages share a lot of similar code: the header area, the footer area, and many other reusable components of the interface. Now, having implemented this similar code on every page, what happens when you have to make a change? You have to laboriously search for and replace text in every affected file.

In these cases, it would be useful to have those chunks of code encapsulated in PHP functions, which you could call on for a particular page. That way, you'll have one set of code to change, and it will be reflected immediately everywhere you use it. Let's give it a try.

Create a new file and then type the following code:

```
<?
function html_header($title = "Fancy Website") {
?>
    <html>
    <head>
    <title><?=$title?></title>
    </head>
    <body>
<?
}
function html_footer() {
date_default_timezone_set("America/New_York");
?>
    <div id="footer">
        <p>All content &copy; copyright <?=date("Y", time())?>
    MyCo. Inc.</p>
    </div>
    </body>
</html>
<?
}
?>
```

Save this file as `html_fns.php`. This is a file that I create for most of my PHP jobs — a place where I put functions that specifically generate template HTML. Right now, it contains two functions: one for the top part of a website and another for the bottom.

CROSS-REF

You can find the `html_fns.php` file on the website for this book: `www.wileydevreference.com`.

Let's see what happens when you put them to work. In a new text file, type this code:

```
<?
include("html_fns.php");
html_header();
?>
<h1>This is our home page</h1>
<p>And it's very useful!</p>
<?
html_footer();
?>
```

Save this file as `home.php`. The `include()` function call takes a relative file path; that is, one that uses Unix-like path conventions to find the file in question. Because both `home.php` and `html_fns.php` are in the same directory, you don't need to use any directory-traversing notation.

CROSS-REF
You can find the `home.php` file on the website for this book: `www.wileydevreference.com`.

Often, however, you might place your library of HTML-generating code into a separate directory. In that case, your call might look like this:

```
include("library/html_fns.php");
```

This call would find a folder named `library` in the same directory as `home.php` and point to the destination file inside of it. Or perhaps you need to include a file that's a directory level above the one doing the calling:

```
include("../library/html_fns.php");
```

The Unix-derived `../` notation takes you up a level in the directory hierarchy.

One way to think of the `include()` function is as a way to transport the contents of the included file into the present file. So, the functions `html_header()` and `html_footer()` are now in the same scope as the rest of the code in `home.php` — just hidden out of sight.

Go ahead and load `home.php` in your browser. You should see something similar to Figure 15.10.

Figure 15.10

Your PHP script, compiling generated HTML

If you were to view the source code of this page, you'd find that all the pieces have been put together in the order specified in your `home.php` file:

```html
<html>
    <head>
    <title>Fancy Website</title>
    </head>
    <body>
<h1>This is our home page</h1>
<p>And it's very useful!</p>
<div id="footer">
    <p>All content &copy; copyright 2009 MyCo. Inc.</p>
</div>
</body>
</html>
```

Now, when that corporate takeover occurs, rather than going through the site page by page to change MyCo. Inc. to Galacticorp LLC, you can just go to your template code and make the change once. After all, you'll have more important things to worry about — such as your job.

Creating a PHP Application

You've learned a lot about PHP. Now, let's put that together with your knowledge of MySQL and make a real, honest-to-goodness web application.

This application is going to let you use a web-based interface to track baseball teams, players, and games, exactly as they were laid out in Chapter 14. In the process, you'll see how to organize code for a working web application and how to get data into and out of a MySQL database. This is going to be pretty intensive and hands-on, and I strongly encourage you to follow the code very closely, typing it in as I provide it here. If you have any problems, the complete source code and associated files are located on the website. In fact, you may want to go get those files now so that you'll have the images that I used for this project.

CROSS-REF
You can find the files for the Baseball! application on the website for this book: `www.wileydevreference.com.`

Drafting the Baseball! application

The application is fairly simple in scope: You want to track baseball teams, players, and games. The application gives you liberal control over those tables, allowing you to view records, add new records, and edit and delete records. These functions might be considered *administrative* features because you're exercising total, direct control over records in a database. This application might serve as a password-protected back end of a website, which might show selected portions of this data to the public user. I'll leave it to your imagination to determine how this data might be used, but I can provide some hints:

- **Provide an RSS feed of game results.** Once you know how to pull data out of a database, you can provide it in any format, including RSS's brand of XML.
- **Data-mine the information.** This allows users to parse the raw data that you provide, build reports that show players with the top batting averages, or calculate the standings within each division.
- **Build a fantasy baseball league.** Using the raw data as the foundation, you could let users create their own team rosters and then track their players' stats throughout the season.

And the list goes on.

Let's take a look at what you're aiming for. The Baseball! application consists of three main screens — one each for managing games, players, and teams — as shown in Figures 15.11, 15.12, and 15.13.

Figure 15.11

The completed games screen for the Baseball! application

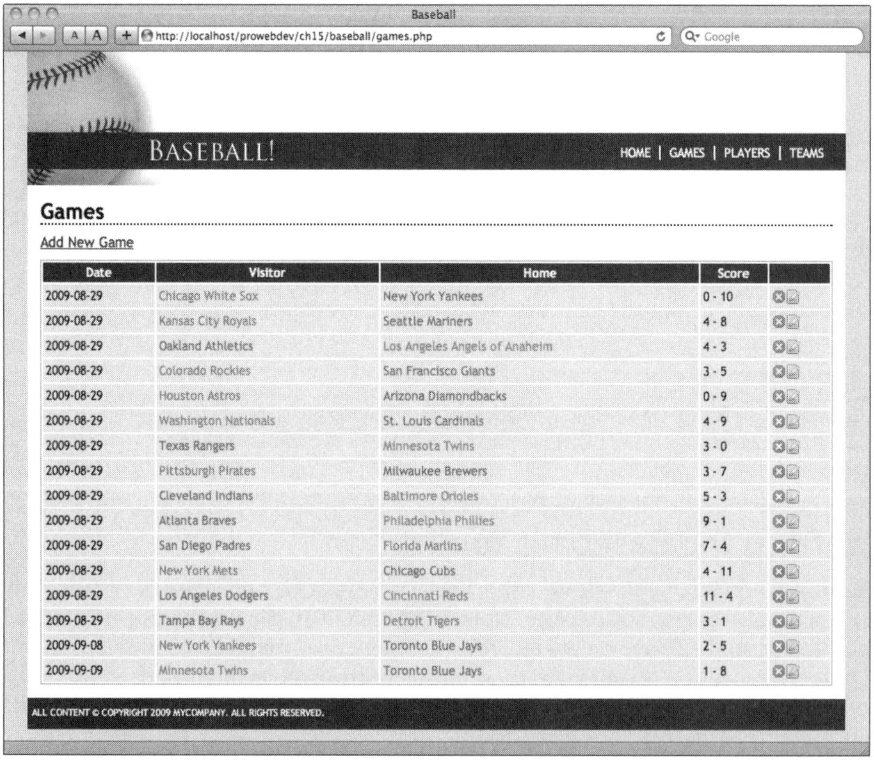

Figure 15.12

The completed players screen for the Baseball! application

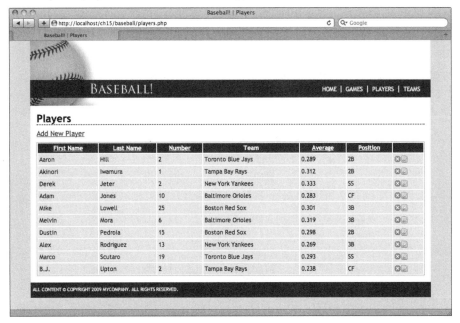

You'll build this application incrementally, starting with the task of organizing your code. Because PHP code is somewhat unruly, you have to lay out your code in a logical way, lest the project become unmanageable.

My technique involves separating the logical functions of the application into their separate domains. To start this project, create a folder called `baseball`, and inside that, create the following folders:

- `admin`. This contains pages that let you edit individual records.
- `controllers`. This contains scripts that change records without showing a user interface.
- `images`. This one is self-explanatory. You can copy the images from my online files into this folder.
- `library`. This contains common code used in all pages, such as the CSS file, the scripts that generate HTML, and any JavaScript files required.

Figure 15.13

The completed teams screen for the Baseball! application

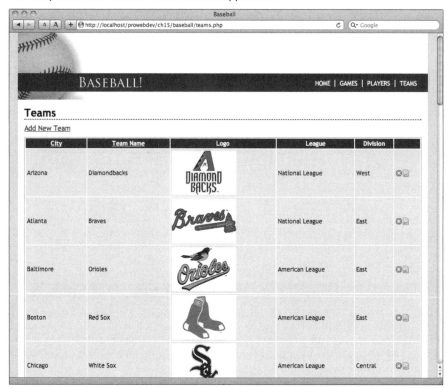

Alongside these folders are the main pages for the site: `index.php`, `games.php`, `teams.php`, and `players.php`. If this were part of a larger site, I might recommend placing these files within the `admin` folder and then placing that folder's contents behind a logon form. In this case, the small scale of this example application forces me to leave that task as a homework assignment for you.

NOTE

How would you create a password-protected site? A very simple technique might involve receiving a username and password and then matching them against a single acceptable value. If there's a match, you can set a `SESSION` variable noting that a user is accredited. For every page that you want to protect, place an `if` statement around the complete page; if that session variable isn't correctly set, return them to the logon page. For more-complex situations, you can check a MySQL database for a selection of usernames and passwords. The techniques shown in building the Baseball! application will put you on the right track.

Writing the template code

The first steps that I take when building a web application are to put together the visual look and feel for the site. That means designing and assembling the HTML to represent it. While the results of this code will end up in a PHP script that I reserve for generating template code, I often start by creating a complete page the old-fashioned way: in a single HTML file.

Regardless of how you put together your template code in this case, I'll show you the final result. Create a new text document and then name it `html_fns.php`. You'll write the code for two functions: one each for the header and footer that will appear on every page:

```php
<?
function html_header($title) {
    ?>
    <!DOCTYPE html PUBLIC "-//W3C//DTD XHTML 1.0 Transitional//EN"
        "http://www.w3.org/TR/xhtml1/DTD/xhtml1-transitional.dtd">
    <html xmlns="http://www.w3.org/1999/xhtml" xml:lang="en"
    lang="en">
    <head>
        <title>Baseball! | <?=$title?></title>
        <meta http-equiv="Content-Type" content="text/
    html;charset=ISO-8859-1" />
        <link rel="stylesheet" href="<?=$GLOBALS["root"]?>library/
    baseball.css" type="text/css" />
        <script language="javascript" src="<?=$GLOBALS["root"]?>lib
    rary/application.js" type="text/javascript"></script>
    </head>
    <body>
        <div id="wrapper">
            <div id="header">
                <ul>
                    <li><a href="<?=$GLOBALS["root"]?>index.
    php">Home</a></li>
                    <li><a href="<?=$GLOBALS["root"]?>games.
    php">Games</a></li>
                    <li><a href="<?=$GLOBALS["root"]?>players.
    php">Players</a></li>
                    <li class="last"><a href="<?=$GLOBALS["root"]?>tea
    ms.php">Teams</a></li>
                </ul>
            </div>
            <?
            if(isset($_GET["message"])) {
                ?>
                <p id="message"><?=strip_tags($_GET["message"])?></p>
                <?
            }
            ?>
    <?
}
```

```
function html_footer() {
    ?>
            <div id="footer">
                <p>All content &copy; copyright <?=date("Y",
        time())?> MyCompany. All rights reserved.</p>
            </div>
        </div>
    </body>
    </html>
    <?
}
?>
```

The file html_fns.php goes inside the library folder. This should look pretty familiar to you from earlier in this chapter, and there's little here to surprise you. Well, except for two little things.

The first is a new function call named strip_tags(). You use this function to process any user input; it removes any scripting tags, including HTML, from the input. This is a measure against crackers, who might use input fields to inject code that might hijack your application or even your server. While strip_tags() isn't a completely foolproof solution, it provides a reasonable level of protection; ensure that you use it on any data that comes from a form in your applications.

The other new code is that little bit of PHP code that precedes every hyperlink. In front of every link to another page, I've placed the code <?=$GLOBALS["root"]?>. Just like the $_POST, $_GET, $_SESSION, and $_COOKIE arrays, $GLOBALS is available to take any variable value that you'd like to use on any page in your project.

On a page that you'll create momentarily, I define that variable to provide a file path to this project on the web server. This wouldn't normally be needed if your site were sitting on the root level of a web server (in that case, every path could simply be preceded by a / to start from the root); but as this project is in development, it's nested among other folders on my server. I need a quick way to control where the folder is sitting so that when it changes, the links in my site don't break. In template code, this is even more important; I don't know what level of the page hierarchy the calling page will be in, so linking relatively won't work.

Let's move to that page now. If you recall the discussion of including files, you might imagine that if you were to habitually include many files on every page, it might become difficult to manage. That's why I like to create a single clearinghouse for included files. I put it in the library folder, and I call it includes.php. Create a new text file and then type this code:

```
<?
session_start();
$GLOBALS["root"] = "/prowebdev/ch15/baseball/"; //change to suit
    your web directory
include("html_fns.php");
// database housekeeping
mysql_connect('localhost', 'root', 'password');
mysql_select_db('baseball');
?>
```

Every page on the site is going to begin with a call to include this file, so you're now able to use SESSION variables by executing session_start() at the top of this file. This automatically makes the $_SESSION array available to you.

Then, you have the declaration of the $GLOBALS["root"] variable. The value of this variable may be different in your case, so change it to suit your needs.

After that, you can include other files that might be part of your project. In this case, I have just one: the html_fns.php page that you just created. Others could also be included in this spot.

Finally, something new: The MySQL functions listed here prepare your code for the interactions with the database by first connecting to the server and then selecting the database. These commands need to be run before running any queries, so this is the perfect place to put them.

Before you continue, take the CSS file from my project archive and then place it in the library folder. If you're still learning CSS, take some time to scan the file and see how it works with the HTML that you're writing.

It's time to create your first public-facing PHP page. Open a new text document and then type this code:

```
<?
include("library/includes.php");
html_header("Home");
?>
<div id="bodycontent">
    <h1>Welcome to the Baseball Tracker!</h1>
    <p>You can keep track of your favorite sport here.</p>
    <p>Manage:</p>
    <ul>
        <li><a href="games.php">Games</a></li>
        <li><a href="players.php">Players</a></li>
        <li><a href="teams.php">Teams</a></li>
    </ul>
</div>
<?
html_footer();
?>
```

As a web application home page, it leaves a lot to be desired. But let's keep things simple in order to clarify what's happening here. As promised, the first statement is your call to the includes.php file, which, as you've seen, combines all the required pieces of your project together. With that call made, you have access to sessions as well as to the functions inside html_fns.php, and your database is ready to go.

The call to html_header() includes an argument for the title tag of the page; if you check back to the header template code, you see where this argument fits in. The rest of this page is basic HTML, followed by the call to html_footer(), which tidies the page up.

Save this page as `index.html` and then open it in your browser. You should see something similar to Figure 15.14.

If you don't see something like this, then you should check a couple of places:

- **Did you set the path correctly for the** `$GLOBALS["root"]` **variable?** If it's not set right, the path to your images and CSS files will be broken and the page will look like generic HTML.
- **Did you add the images and CSS file for this project from the website?** Make sure the contents of my `images` folder are inside the `images` folder in your project. Do the same for the `baseball.css` file going into the library folder.

Make sure you have this working before you move on; if your links between files aren't working, then nothing is going to work correctly for the rest of this project.

Figure 15.14

The home screen for the Baseball! application

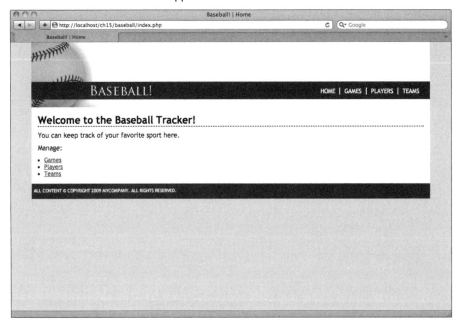

Managing games

The first screen that you'll work with is the Games screen. This page displays the contents of the games table in your MySQL database, which you set up in Chapter 14. You can also add new games as well as edit and delete existing games in the database.

Open a new text file and then type this code:

```
<?
include("library/includes.php");
html_header("Games");
?>
<div id="bodycontent">
    <h1>Games</h1>
    <p><a href="#" onclick="reveal_form('newgame');">Add New
    Game</a></p>

    <div class="data_entry" id="newgame">
        <form action="controllers/game_add.php" method="post">
        <table>
            <tr>
                <th>Date</th>
                <th>Visitor</th>
                <th>Home</th>
                <th>Score</th>
                <th></th>
            </tr>
            <tr>
                <td><input type="text" name="date" /></td>
                <td><?= team_selector("visiting_team", null)?></td>
                <td><?= team_selector("home_team", null)?></td>
                <td>Visitors: <input type="text" name="visiting_
score" size="3">, Home: <input type="text" name="home_score"
size="3"></td>
                <td><input type="submit" value="Add Game" /></td>
            </tr>
        </table>
        </form>
    </div>

    <table>
        <tr>
            <th>Date</th>
            <th>Visitor</th>
            <th>Home</th>
            <th>Score</th>
            <th></th>
        </tr>
        <?
        $result = mysql_query("select * from games order by game_
date");
        while ($row = mysql_fetch_array($result, MYSQL_ASSOC)) {
            ?>
            <tr>
```

```
            <td><?=$row["game_date"]?></td>
            <td><?=color_team($row["visiting_team"],
    $row["visiting_score"], $row["home_score"])?></td>
            <td><?=color_team($row["home_team"], $row["home_
    score"], $row["visiting_score"])?></td>
            <td><?=$row["visiting_score"]?> - <?=$row["home_
    score"]?></td>
            <td>
                <form action="controllers/game_delete.php"
    method="post" onsubmit="return confirm('Really delete?');">
                    <input type="hidden" name="id"
    value="<?=$row["id"]?>" />
                    <input type="image" src="images/cancel.png" />
                </form>
                <form action="admin/game_edit.php" method="post">
                    <input type="hidden" name="id"
    value="<?=$row["id"]?>" />
                    <input type="image" src="images/page_edit.png"
    />
                </form>
            </td>
        </tr>
        <?
    }
    ?>

    </table>
</div>
<?
html_footer();
?>
```

This is a fair amount of code, but as you type it, notice how most of it is fairly simple HTML. Let's go through this section by section. You start here exactly as you did with index.php: by calling includes.php and calling the header function. You then start this page's content. The first block of code is there to capture new games. The form is contained within a div tag that's set to be hidden in your HTML — note that the div has both a class (where the CSS attribute display:none is set) and an ID, which is used to point to it in the Document Object Model (DOM).

CROSS-REF
For more on the DOM, see Chapter 6.

You should actually pause here and write the JavaScript that will reveal this form when the user clicks the Add New Game link. This code goes in the application.js file inside your library folder:

```
function reveal_form(form) {
    document.getElementById(form).style.display = "block";
}
```

This is really basic JavaScript, changing the passed-in ID of the form to a visible element. Save that file and then let's get back to studying the code.

The form to create a new game is set up in a table with both a header row and a row for input. Now, among these fields, you'll see some simple text input fields but also two calls to a PHP function called team_selector(). The rest of this form is simple enough, but you need to sidetrack into that function for a moment before continuing.

You want this function to output an HTML select tag that contains the name of every team, and you need to have it there for both the visiting and home teams. Furthermore, when it comes time to edit an existing record, where the team is already selected, you need a way of telling this code what the currently chosen team is, so the corresponding option tag has it set. Thus, your call to team_selector() takes two arguments: the name of the field and the currently selected team (if there is one).

I wrote this function into the html_fns.php file. At the bottom of that file, add the following code:

```
function team_selector($name, $current) {
    ?>
    <select name="<?=$name?>">
        <?
        if(!isset($current)) {
            ?>
            <option>Choose a team...</option>
            <?
        }
        $teams = mysql_query("select id, team_name, city from teams
order by city");
        if(!$teams) {
            echo "Failed to run query! " . mysql_error();
        }

        while($row = mysql_fetch_array($teams)) {
            if(isset($current) && $row["id"]==$current) {
                $selected = " selected";
            }
            else {
                $selected = "";
            }
            ?>
            <option value="<?=$row["id"]?>"<?=$selected?>><?=$row["c
ity"]?> <?=$row["team_name"]?></option>
            <?
        }
        ?>
```

```
        </select>
        <?
  }
```

This function begins by opening up a `select` tag with the name that you pass in as the first argument. In this case, it has the names `visiting_team` and `home_team` for the two times it's called in your `games.php` file.

Now you need a way for this pop-up menu to show a default prompt if this is being used with a new form. You do that by using the PHP function `isset()`, which checks whether a variable exists. When you pass in the value `NULL` for the second argument, you effectively nullify the variable, causing `isset()` to return `false`. As I use it here, I negate the `isset()` condition by prepending the logical `NOT` character `!`. So, the statement might read, "if the variable `$current` is *not set*...."

Once the prompt is dispensed with, you run your very first MySQL query! The PHP function `mysql_query()` takes a standard SQL command, exactly as you learned it in Chapter 14. In this case, I'm taking only the fields that I'm interested in using; if you want, you can select all by using the asterisk wildcard.

The proper thing to do when running a query like this is to check that it succeeded. This is simple enough: Using an `if` statement, you can check whether the variable exists; if not, then you can send a message to the user.

You have every expectation that this will work, of course, so let's proceed with the script. The next part is the most crucial, and the pattern you see here is repeated in most places that you get information from a MySQL database.

Using a `while` statement, you assign all the rows returned from the database query — one at a time. The `while` statement runs the contents of its loop for each row returned. The PHP function `mysql_fetch_array()` passes an array to the assigned variable `$row`, letting you work with the values one at a time. Each time `mysql_fetch_array()` is run, it advances the array pointer, passing back each new row in the array without your intervention. It's an elegant, simple way to move through a database result set.

The work of this loop is pretty straightforward: You simply want to output a `select` tag's `option` tag for each row. Within that tag, you provide the value of the team and then display the team name that will appear on your page. The complicated parts of this code are about deciding whether you have a `$current` value. If so, then you'll add the text `" selected"` (note the space) into the variable `$selected`. Otherwise, that variable will contain nothing.

So, when you output the `option` tag, it indicates whether it's selected.

Save this file and then return to `games.php`.

Below the form that lets you add a new game, you want to display a table that shows all the existing games in the database. The rest of the page sets that up. Now that you've seen the way you retrieve data from the database — by using a combination of the `while` loop with the `mysql_fetch_array()` function — this should look fairly familiar.

Each run of the loop produces a table row on the page. Within each cell of the row, you output the correct field from the database. To make things a little more interesting, I have applied a function to the name of the team. This function, `color_team()`, outputs the name of the team for you, coloring the text red or green depending on whether it's the loser or winner of the game.

When writing a function, you have to think about what information it needs to accomplish its task. In this case, you have to provide three arguments: the team at issue, the score they earned, and the score their opponent earned. With that, you can determine whether your team won or lost and then act accordingly.

I also placed this function in `html_fns.php`. Add this to the bottom of that file:

```php
function color_team($team, $us, $them) {
    if($us > $them) {
        // winning team! Color green
        echo "<span style='color:green'>".team_name($team)."</
span>";
    }
    elseif($them > $us) {
        // losing team! Color red
        echo "<span style='color:red'>".team_name($team)."</span>";
    }
    else {
        // tie? No, we're using this for nonscoring purposes.
        echo team_name($team);
    }
}
function team_name($id) {
    $team = mysql_query("select team_name, city from teams where
    id=". $id);
    return mysql_result($team, 0, 'city') ." " . mysql_
    result($team, 0, 'team_name');
}
```

As promised, the `color_team()` function takes the scores and then compares them. If the current team has the higher score, you return the name of the team colored green. Otherwise, the team is colored red. I'm also using the default state of the `if…else` syntax to provide a third option. If there's no scoring information, the function will output the team name without color. You'll make use of this later.

Because you're providing just an ID number as the team, you can't simply output that in this function. Instead, you have to use a couple lines of code to interrogate the database and return the team name. Because this is a separate piece of functionality that might be useful elsewhere in the code, I separated that into its own function, `team_name()`. It simply takes a team ID number and then echoes back the team name formatted with its city.

This function also introduces another means of getting information out of MySQL: the `mysql_result()` function. For queries from which you only expect to receive one row, using `mysql_result()` provides a quick and easy way to get at specific fields. Its argument list isn't immediately apparent from this usage, so here it is:

```
mysql_result(result_data, row, field)
```

The first argument is the variable that's filled by your call to `mysql_query()`. That variable is an array, so because you're dealing with only one row returned from your query, you can call the first array row in the second argument, which is zero (remember, all arrays are indexed starting from zero). Finally, you specify the field name in quotation marks. Boom! Instant field data.

The `team_name()` function concatenates the city and team name into one string and then outputs it to the browser.

The final piece of code on `games.php` provides the editing controls. These are done by using two forms: one to provide a delete control and another to provide an edit control.

You could have used a simple hyperlink to provide these items. This is what that might look like:

```
<a href="controllers/game_delete.php?id=<?=$row["id"]?>"><img
    src="images/cancel.png" /></a>
```

But in this situation, you encounter an important security issue. Using a hyperlink places the ID of the game record in the URL, using the `GET` syntax. By revealing the way your application works, a malicious user could readily enter any ID number and start deleting records at random!

Hence, the use of the forms. Embedding the logic in a `POST` variable hides it from the user; placing the ID in a hidden field ensures that the right information is passed along to the target script, and the casual user is none the wiser. Could this be more secure? Definitely: An enterprising hacker could look at your source code and piece things together. But this is a reasonable compromise that secures your code in most situations.

That should do it for this page! With the file saved, open it in your browser; you should have a page that looks similar to Figure 15.11. Each record has a pair of icons at the end of each row; these allow a user to delete and edit that record.

Of course, you're not done yet. While you can look at the data, you can't do anything with it. There are three directions to take now: You need to write the code that lets you add a new record provided by the Add New Game form; you have to delete records; and you have to show an editing screen for existing games.

Adding controllers

Let's start with the new game handler. For scripts that only interact with the database — in this case, scripts that add new records, update existing records, and delete records — I refer to these as *controllers* and put them into their own folder. These scripts aren't loaded in the browser; they will, however, take the data from a page, do their work, and forward you to a result page. I like this technique because it clearly compartmentalizes the code and, with a good naming convention, makes it easy to find the code you need to change in the future.

Create a new text file and then type this code to save the data from the Add New Game form:

```
<?
include("../library/includes.php");
// collect values from form
$date = strip_tags($_POST["date"]);
$visiting_team = strip_tags($_POST["visiting_team"]);
$home_team = strip_tags($_POST["home_team"]);
$visiting_score = strip_tags($_POST["visiting_score"]);
$home_score = strip_tags($_POST["home_score"]);
$insert = mysql_query("insert into games set game_date=STR_TO_
    DATE('".$date."', '%Y-%m-%d'), visiting_team='".$visiting_
    team."', home_team='".$home_team."', visiting_
    score='".$visiting_score."', home_score='".$home_score."'");
if($insert) {
    header("Location: ../games.php?message=New game created!");
}
else {
    header("Location: ../games.php?message=Game insertion
    failed!");
}
?>
```

After the obligatory `include()` call, you collect the values from the form into local variables, taking the opportunity to sanitize each piece of form data by using the `strip_tags()` function.

With those variables set with the form data, you can put together a MySQL query that inserts the data into a new record. For queries that insert data, the assigned variable, `$insert`, receives only a `true` or `false` value depending on success or failure.

Your next step is to test that variable; if the data was successfully inserted into the database, you use the PHP function `header()` to change the location of the page to your original `games.php` page. The `header()` function allows you to insert any HTML header command, but I only ever use the `Location` header.

You can only send an HTML header if no data has been sent to the browser yet. If you echo anything to the browser prior to the call to `header()` or even if PHP outputs an error to the screen beforehand, `header()` returns an error. That's what makes this call so useful for a controller file, which outputs nothing to the screen and simply does its work before moving back to a regular page.

Save this file as `game_add.php` inside the `controllers` folder. Now give it a try: Click the Add New Game link on `games.php` and then create a player record. Once you click the Add Game button, the page should appear to reload right away, with your new game added and a little bonus message saying that the game has been inserted. If not, go back and double-check your code; typos are your enemy.

So much for adding a game. Let's write another controller to let you delete a game. Create a new text file and then type this code:

```
<?
include("../library/includes.php");
$del = strip_tags($_POST["id"]);
$query = mysql_query("delete from games where id='".$del."'");
if($query) {
    header("Location: ../games.php?message=Game deleted!");
}
else {
    header("Location: ../games.php?message=Game not deleted!");
}
?>
```

This file works almost exactly like the game_add.php controller; it's a smaller file because you only have one variable to deal with. Once more, you check the result of the query to MySQL and then send back a message to games.php accordingly.

Save this file as game_delete.php inside your controllers folder. Load up games.php and then try deleting the game you just added. Just like when you add a game, the page should appear to simply reload, with one less game and a message indicating the game has been deleted.

The final page leading off this one is the one that lets you edit records. This is code that presents an interface for users to interact with, unlike the other two files, so you'll place it within the admin folder. Open a new text file and then type this code:

```
<?
include("../library/includes.php");
$id = strip_tags($_POST["id"]);
$game = mysql_query("select * from games where id='".$id."'");
html_header("Edit Game");
?>
<div id="bodycontent">
    <h1>Edit Game</h1>

    <form action="../controllers/game_edit.php" method="post">
        <table>
            <tr>
                <th>Date</th>
                <td><input type="text" name="game_date"
    value="<?=mysql_result($game, 0, "game_date")?>"/></td>
            </tr>
            <tr>
                <th>Visiting Team</th>
                <td><?=team_selector("visiting_team", mysql_
    result($game, 0, "visiting_team"))?></td>
```

```
        </tr>
        <tr>
            <th>Home Team</th>
            <td><?=team_selector("home_team", mysql_result($game,
0, "home_team"))?></td>
        </tr>
        <tr>
            <th>Score</th>
            <td>Visitors: <input type="text" name="visiting_
score" size="3" value="<?=mysql_result($game, 0, "visiting_
score")?>"><br/>
                Home: <input type="text" name="home_score"
size="3" value="<?=mysql_result($game, 0, "home_score")?>"></
td>
        </tr>
        <tr>
            <td colspan="2">
                <input type="hidden" name="id" value="<?=$id?>" />
                <input type="submit" value="Update" />
                  <a href="../games.php">Cancel</a>
            </td>
        </tr>
    </table>
</form>
</div>
<?
html_footer();
?>
```

After the `include()` call, you take the only variable you need for this file: the ID number of the record you want to edit. Then, you can use that ID number to send your query to the database for that single database record, placing the result into the `$game` variable.

The rest of the page is pretty straightforward. Your form lets you see every field in the row, and each field has a value attribute populated by using the information from the database. Just as you've already seen, for a result set consisting of a single record, it's easiest to use the `mysql_result()` function, pulling the single field from the row.

Also, for the first time, you're seeing the `team_selector()` function — which you wrote back when you created `games.php` — handle an existing record. In those two calls, you pass in the selected team as the second argument so your function can use that as the chosen value in the pop-up menu of all teams.

Before you leave this page, there's one more item to point out. Alongside the submit button, you type a hidden field that contains the ID number of this game record. You'll need that to pull the right record from the database in the following script.

Save this file as `game_edit.php` inside the `admin` folder. Now load up `games.php` and then click the edit icon on any row. You should see a page similar to the one in Figure 15.15.

Figure 15.15

The Edit Game screen for the Baseball! application

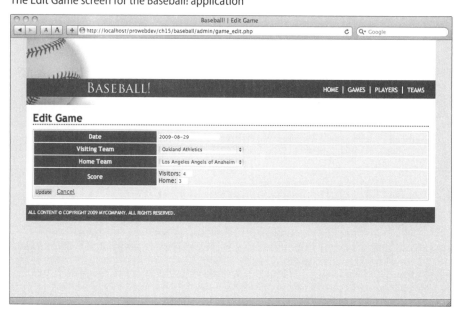

You're almost done. The last script you need to write will handle the changes made to this form. Open a new text file and then type the following code. It should look pretty familiar to what you've already done in the `game_add.php` script:

```
<?
include("../library/includes.php");
// collect values from form
$id = strip_tags($_POST["id"]);
$date = strip_tags($_POST["game_date"]);
$visiting_team = strip_tags($_POST["visiting_team"]);
$home_team = strip_tags($_POST["home_team"]);
$visiting_score = strip_tags($_POST["visiting_score"]);
$home_score = strip_tags($_POST["home_score"]);
$insert = mysql_query("update games set game_date=STR_TO_
    DATE('".$date."', '%Y-%m-%d'), visiting_team='".$visiting_
    team."', home_team='".$home_team."', visiting_
    score='".$visiting_score."', home_score='".$home_score."'
    where id='".$id."'");
if($insert) {
    header("Location: ../games.php?message=Game updated!");
}
else {
```

```
        header("Location: ../games.php?message=Game update failed!");
    }
    ?>
```

A few subtle differences exist between this script and the one you wrote to add games. First off, you collect the ID number of the database row because you're dealing with an existing record. Then, the MySQL query is different because you're updating rather than inserting (remember to add the " ' where id=' " phrase!). Finally, the message to the user on completion indicates an update rather than a new record.

Save this file as `game_edit.php` in the `controllers` folder. You've now finished all the features related to the games database table. You can view, create, delete, and edit games. Go ahead and test it now to make sure everything works properly.

Completing the application's roster

I don't have the space in this chapter to take you through the rest of this application in as much detail. However, there are some important pieces of functionality that will come in handy for you, so I'll cover them here.

The essential structure of the other sections is virtually identical to the games page. Both the players and teams pages feature a table of the database contents, along with a form to create a new record, and controls to delete and edit those records. These pages are written in the same way that you did for the games page, and you can improve your knowledge of these principles by getting them to work yourself.

But there are a few techniques that I'd like to further describe.

First, the players page provides a mechanism to sort the data in the table. By default, the players table loads by sorting the players alphabetically by their last name. But most table headings are also hyperlinks; clicking those links will reload the table to sort by that heading. Let's see how that works.

The table that displays the players has a header row in the HTML that looks like this:

```
<tr>
    <th><a href="players.php?sort=first_name">First Name</a></th>
    <th><a href="players.php?sort=last_name">Last Name</a></th>
    <th><a href="players.php?sort=number">Number</a></th>
    <th>Team</th>
    <th><a href="players.php?sort=batting_avg">Average</a></th>
    <th><a href="players.php?sort=position">Position</a></th>
    <th></th>
</tr>
```

Each column heading, with the exception of the `Team` heading, has a link back to the same page. But they each have a `GET` argument, assigning the database field name to the `$sort` variable. When that variable is passed in, you can use it to dictate how you pull data from the database. At the top of this page, right after the `include()` call, you have the following code:

```
if(!isset($_GET["sort"])) {
    $sort = "last_name";
}
else {
    $sort = strip_tags($_GET["sort"]);
}
```

Here, you can see the trick: On an initial page load, you assign the field `last_name` to the `$sort` variable. Otherwise, you take whatever is passed in the GET variable (recalling the security threat of any publicly available data input, you screen it with `strip_tags()` again).

Therefore, that `$sort` variable has a value no matter what. So, when it comes time to pull your data from the database, you can use it as part of your query:

```
$result = mysql_query("select * from players order by ".$sort);
```

There you go — instant sorting.

The other feature I'd like to demonstrate in more detail is apparent on the Teams page. There, you're allowing for the uploading of images. This is the sort of functionality that you'll want to include in many of your applications, and it's not too difficult to manage with PHP.

The Add New Team form includes a field that lets you select an image file from your hard disk. Let's take a look at how to prepare your form and then how to handle the file when the form is submitted.

Every PHP form that allows for the uploading of files must have two distinct elements: a form attribute called `enctype` and a hidden field specifying the maximum file size. Here's what it looks like:

```
<form action="controllers/team_add.php" method="post"
    enctype="multipart/form-data">
    <input type="hidden" name="MAX_FILE_SIZE" value="1000000" />
```

The `enctype` attribute must be set to `multipart/form-data`; this is an HTML requirement that prepares any server for data that includes binary data in addition to the normal text that a form would produce.

The hidden field must be the very first form element. The value that you provide for the MAX_FILE_SIZE is expressed in bytes; in this case, I'm allowing for the upload of files up to about one megabyte in size. In reality, the logo files that I've included with this project are mostly less than 10KB.

Then, your file `input` tag is one you may not have seen yet:

```
<td><input type="file" name="logo" /></td>
```

Take note of the name of this field, as you'll use it in the script that handles this form's contents. Let's go there now — to the controller that takes this form data and puts it in the database. But first, you have to make sure the image that's uploaded is stored in a folder on your server.

To handle an uploaded file, you take three basic steps:

- First, specify the directory where the file will be saved.
- Then, create a string that contains the complete file path of the uploaded file.
- Finally, move the file from the temporary upload buffer to the file path.

Here are those three steps in code:

```
$uploaddir = '../images/logos/';
$uploadfile = $uploaddir . basename($_FILES['logo']['name']);
if (move_uploaded_file($_FILES['logo']['tmp_name'], $uploadfile)) {
```

The variable `$uploaddir` points to a folder called `logos` inside your `images` folder. Then, you create a new variable called `$uploadfile` that appends the name of your file to that path. You get that file name by accessing a special `$_FILES` array, which contains any files you've uploaded. It's a multi-dimensional array that begins with the name of your file field and has a number of characteristics:

- `$_FILES['userfile']['name']`. The original name of the file on your computer.
- `$_FILES['userfile']['type']`. The mime type of the file, as provided by the browser; for example, `image/jpeg`.
- `$_FILES['userfile']['size']`. The size of the file, in bytes.
- `$_FILES['userfile']['tmp_name']`. The temporary file name under which the file is stored on the server.
- `$_FILES['userfile']['error']`. The error code associated with the file upload, if one occurs.

The final step of the process is to move the uploaded file into your directory of choice. When I write this code, I place it inside an `if` statement in order to make the rest of this file depend on whether the file is copied. A file upload can readily fail, almost always because of a permission error. The destination directory needs to be writable by the web server.

CROSS-REF

For more on permissions, see Chapter 2. For more on the Apache user, see Chapter 3.

To complete your `team_add.php` controller, add the name of the uploaded file to the database, along with the rest of the fields. The `mysql_query()` statement looks like this:

```
$insert = mysql_query("insert into teams set team_name='".$team_
    name."', city='".$city."', logo='".basename($_FILES['logo']
    ['name'])."', division='".$division."',
    league='".$league."'");
```

So, the image file goes to a directory on your server while the name goes in the database. Then, whenever you want to use that image file, such as on the `teams.php` page, you can call it like this:

```
<td><img src="images/logos/<?=$row["logo"]?>" /></td>
```

There's one more thing you need to do to ensure that file uploads run smoothly: verifying that the correct behavior occurs when a record is being updated. In that case, you can't guarantee that an image is being replaced. Therefore, before you go through all the trouble of dealing with the `$_FILES` array and moving the uploaded file, you have to test whether a file has been uploaded in the `team_edit.php` controller file. As you're already acquainted with the `$_FILES` array, you know what will happen in this situation. Here's the relevant code from the controller:

```
if($_FILES["logo"]["size"] > 0 ) {
```

You know that if the size of the uploaded file is greater than zero, well, you've got a file. You can then process it exactly as you did in the first file.

As in the case of any `if` statement, you have to account for both the `true` and `false` conditions; when a file isn't uploaded, you need to prepare a series of statements that takes into account whether or not the image is there. Try to write this code yourself, and refer to the source files that I provide if you have a problem.

Summary

This was a very arduous chapter. I covered the very basics of the PHP scripting language, and I took you right through to a complete web application by using MySQL. It's a lot of ground to cover, and if you've made it this far, I'm proud of you.

But don't rush it. Take your time with this material; if you didn't completely understand some parts, don't be afraid to go back and look at them more closely. Once you see the patterns in this code, you'll be able to handle a number of different scenarios in your own applications.

As you leave PHP and step into Ruby on Rails, you should keep this technology's idiosyncrasies in perspective. As you were typing this chapter's web application, you may have found it somewhat labor-intensive. There's a lot of boilerplate code in a PHP application like this. Keep that in mind as you learn Rails, and you'll understand the advantages of that framework for large projects.

You're in the home stretch now. If you stopped reading this book right now, you could be content to know that you've got all the skills you need to be a web developer. But if you take the next step of using Ruby on Rails, you'll be that much better equipped to handle the big jobs. That'll make you a better developer in the long run.

16

Ruby Introduction

U ntil fairly recently, Ruby was a very obscure language with little exposure outside of Japan, the home of its creator. In fact, were it not for the development of the Rails web application framework, it's probably fair to say that you would have never heard of Ruby. It's very fortunate for everyone that Rails came along though; Ruby is a beautiful language, and as I hope you discover, it's a delight to write in.

In this chapter, I'm going to introduce you to standard Ruby, touching on the same topics that I covered with the other languages in this book. Once you have some understanding of how the Ruby language works, you'll see how its unique features are put to work in the construction of the Rails framework.

While JavaScript and PHP are very similar, you'll find that you have to slightly adjust your thinking to appreciate Ruby. The chief difference lies in the purpose of each language. While JavaScript and PHP were developed explicitly for web applications, Ruby was designed to be a general-purpose scripting language.

While it borrows many features from C, Ruby features a pure object-oriented design. You may have heard of object-oriented programming (OOP), which I distinguish from procedural programming (the kind that you've been doing up to now). In Ruby, every variable is an object, and they contain all the methods that can be used on them.

Let's practice using Ruby. In Mac OS X, Ruby 1.8 comes installed and ready to use. Open Terminal and then type the command **irb**; this is the *interactive Ruby* shell, with the >> prompt to start your programming:

```
achilles:~ aaron$ irb
>>
```

Here are a couple examples. In the first example, the message is printed three times. Type each of these three lines into your new command shell, pressing Return after each line:

```
>> 3.times do
?> print "Hi!"
>> end
Hi!Hi!Hi!=> 3
```

16 ▶ In This Chapter

Understanding object-oriented code

Your first Ruby application

The Invoicr application

The shell returns with the result of your expression: three greetings to the world of Ruby! Note that the number has the method `times` attached to it with a period. In Ruby, methods are called on objects using this *dot syntax*. The object is known as the *receiver*, and you can think of the method as the *message* being sent to the receiver. If the object understands the message, the command executes.

Here's another example. Numbers are objects in Ruby, and you can call any method that the object has in its arsenal. You can easily check those methods at any time by calling `methods` on any object. Try this in your shell:

```
>> 3.methods
=> ["%", "odd?", "inspect", "prec_i", "<<", "tap", "div", "&",
    "denominator", "clone", ">>", "public_methods", "object_id",
    "__send__", "instance_variable_defined?", "gcdlcm", "equal?",
    "freeze", "to_sym", "*", "ord", "+", "extend", "next", "send",
    "round", "gcd", "methods", "prec_f", "-", "even?", "taguri",
    "singleton_method_added", "divmod", "hash", "/", "integer?",
    "downto", "dup", "to_enum", "taguri=", "instance_variables",
    "to_r", "|", "eql?", "rdiv", "size", "id", "instance_eval",
    "truncate", "~", "to_i", "singleton_methods", "to_yaml_style",
    "modulo", "taint", "zero?", "times", "numerator", "instance_
    variable_get", "frozen?", "enum_for", "display", "instance_
    of?", "^", "method", "to_a", "rpower", "+@", "-@", "quo",
    "instance_exec", "type", "**", "upto", "to_f", "<", "step",
    "protected_methods", "<=>", "between?", "==", "remainder",
    ">", "===", "to_int", "nonzero?", "pred", "instance_variable_
    set", "coerce", "to_yaml", "respond_to?", "kind_of?", "floor",
    "succ", ">=", "prec", "to_yaml_properties", "to_s", "<=",
    "fdiv", "class", "private_methods", "=~", "tainted?", "__
    id__", "abs", "untaint", "nil?", "chr", "lcm", "id2name",
    "power!", "is_a?", "ceil", "[]"]
```

Don't worry about what these methods mean; as you gain expertise in Ruby, you'll be happy to know that these are here for when you forget which methods apply. See later in this chapter for a way to use documentation to discover the meaning of any method.

As you continue to learn Ruby, you'll find the `irb` shell to be a great place to try out concepts and make sure things work as you expect before using them in larger applications.

Understanding Object-Oriented Code

Let's take a closer look at what object-oriented code is all about. In a standard procedural language, such as PHP or JavaScript, you're creating a series of instructions that are evaluated in order. This works fine for smaller code bases but can become quite inconvenient when your project grows to thousands of lines of code. While procedural languages have mechanisms that allow you to organize your code into separate functions or files, the arrangement of those files and how you put them together is entirely up to you.

With an object-oriented language, the syntax determines how your program works. An object is a way for you to model real-world things in your program. You give an object both *properties* — such as `size`, `color`, or `smell` — and *methods* — such as `fold`, `convertToRGB`, or `freshen`. Together, this *state* and *behavior* make up the definition of an object.

This language is actually easier than it sounds, as you'll see in the following real-world example.

Your First Ruby Application

As I've mentioned, Ruby isn't primarily intended for the web; it's a general-purpose scripting language that has been proven well-suited for the Rails framework. To get up to speed on Ruby, you'll use a combination of the `irb` shell and scripts that you'll write in a text editor. For your first application, you'll write a script.

CROSS-REF

For more on Ruby on Rails, see Chapter 17.

Open your text editor of choice, create a new document, and then type the following text:

```ruby
#!/bin/ruby
class Dice

  def initialize(sides)
    @sides = sides
  end

  def roll
    1 + rand(@sides)
  end

  def sides
    @sides
  end

end
d = Dice.new(6)
print "Random roll of our #{d.sides}-sided die: #{d.roll}\n"
```

Save this file as `dice.rb`. Take note of where you save it so you can then run it in Terminal:

```
achilles:~ aaron$ ruby ~/Desktop/dice.rb
Random roll of our 6-sided die: 4
```

CROSS-REF
You can find the `dice.rb` file on the website for this book: `www.wileydevreference.com`.

So, how did that work? In your code, you define a *class*. This is the formal name for an object in Ruby. In the language, an object is actually just an *instance* of a class. So, let's define your new `Dice` class. The `def` keyword is used to write a method, and methods can take arguments in parentheses (just like in the other languages you've studied in this book). Every class can use the preset `initialize` method, which is always called whenever a new instance is created with the `new` method. In your `initialize` method, you want to set the number of sides to the dice. The `sides` instance variable is a property of the `Dice` object and should be set at the time of creation.

The next method that you'll create is the `roll` method. Its purpose should be obvious: You use Ruby's built-in `rand` function to pick a number between 1 and the number of sides.

Finally, you'll create one more method to return the value of the `sides` property. This kind of method is called an *accessor* method because it provides access to the value of the property. Note the efficiency of the language here; in Ruby, the last declared variable in a method is automatically returned, so there's no need for a `return` keyword.

This ends the `Dice` class definition. You can immediately start using it by invoking the class name with the `new` method and supplying the number of sides as a parameter. In this case, the variable `d` becomes an instance of the `Dice` object, giving you access to its properties and methods. All you do is print a line of text that incorporates a couple return values from the class: the `sides` method and the `roll` method. The rather peculiar syntax of the hash and curly braces (# and {}) is a Ruby device for inserting variables into strings. Ruby also supports a JavaScript-like syntax using plus signs:

```
print "Random roll of our " + d.sides + "-sided die: " + d.roll +
    "\n"
```

However, you'll probably prefer the more concise hash (#) format.

Spend a few moments to make sure you understand how this example works as well as the relationship between the class definition and its use as an instance. This is the most powerful distinction of object-oriented programming, and you'll find that Ruby takes full advantage of this pattern, incorporating it into everything that you'll do.

Ruby syntax

Much of Ruby's syntax is borrowed from the C language (which should be familiar to you as a PHP or JavaScript programmer) and also takes conventions from Smalltalk, Ada, and Lisp — languages you may not have heard of before. Ruby is an *interpreted language*; like PHP and JavaScript, its written commands are converted into actions by a special program. This is the opposite of a *compiled language*, such as C, which turns your code into a stand-alone, executable file.

Like PHP and JavaScript, data types aren't strictly enforced; for example, the interpreter determines whether a variable is a string or number (and like PHP, there are tricks in the code to help the interpreter figure that out!).

Variables

Let's start with variables; these are the items that hold values in Ruby, as in any other language. There are several different variable types, and the differences between them have to do with their scope — that is, where and how they can be used:

- *Local variables* **begin with a lowercase letter and can be used only in the current scope, such as a method or script.** Examples include `myFirstCar` and `letter`.

- *Constant variables* **begin with an uppercase letter and are used to declare a value once for the duration of a program.** Examples include `Car` and `Alphabet`.

- *Instance variables* **begin with an @ character and are used to store an attribute of a class instance.** You'll see in the previous `Dice` example that an instance variable is used to hold the number of sides in the object. Other examples might be `@color` and `@locale`.

- *Class variables* **begin with two @ characters (@@).** They are used to store values that can be used in any instance of a class. If your dice were always supposed to be white, then you might declare a class variable `@@color`, which you could then invoke within any instance of that class. Other examples might be `@@model` and `@@writingTool`.

- *Global variables* **begin with a dollar sign ($), and these variables can be used anywhere in your script.** As with any other language, the use of global variables is rarely a good idea, so if you find yourself using one, pause and ensure that you're doing it for the right reasons. Examples include `$wheels` and `$planet`.

Operators

The operators that allow you to evaluate expressions in a language are fairly standard; the tables used in Chapter 15 for PHP are equally relevant in Ruby (see Tables 15.1 to 15.4). The difference, however, is that in Ruby, operators are implemented as method calls. Consider the expression a+b. While your experience with other languages would suggest that the addition operator is its own discrete language unit, in Ruby, it's actually a method of a. Need proof? Try this in Terminal, running an `irb` session:

```
>> a = 1
=> 1
>> b = 2
=> 2
>> a.+(b)
=> 3
```

Start by assigning a value to the variables a and b. Now, instead of just adding them together as I did here, I invoke the addition method, passing in the variable b as a parameter. This syntax is highly unconventional for math operations, but it's a strict interpretation of how Ruby views operators. So, how does a standard math operation work? By employing some syntactic sugar (a convenient syntax that reduces typing for programmers), the language allows you to call a method with or without the dot and with or without the following expressions in brackets. So, of course, standard algebra works just fine:

```
>> a+b
=> 3
```

Container classes

While PHP and JavaScript are limited to just one container class — the array — Ruby features two. The array is, of course, the staple of any language, allowing you to store any value you want within a numerically indexed group. The other Ruby collection type is called the *hash*. It's a set of paired *keys* and *values*.

Actually, if you think back to your experience with PHP, you might recognize that an array there could be like either a Ruby array or a Ruby hash. That's quite true. However, Ruby formalizes that difference rather than letting a programmer choose a style.

Let's start with arrays. In Ruby, it's very easy to create a collection of objects; type the following code in `irb`:

```
>> clients = ["John Major", "Randy Bachman", "Louis Davies"]
=> ["John Major", "Randy Bachman", "Louis Davies"]
```

By naming a variable and placing your values in a comma-delimited list within square brackets, you automatically create an array. Just as in other languages, the values of the array are indexed from zero, and you can reach the values by picking out a particular index value:

```
>> clients[0]
=> "John Major"
>> clients[2]
=> "Louis Davies"
```

As with anything else in Ruby, the `clients` variable is actually an instance of the `Array` object and therefore has several methods that you can call on. Here are some examples:

```
>> clients.size
=> 3
>> clients.class
=> Array
>> clients.empty?
=> false
>> clients.inspect
=> "[\"John Major\", \"Randy Bachman\", \"Louis Davies\"]"
```

If you want to add an element to an existing array, there's a method called `push` that adds your new object to the stack:

```
>> clients.push("Elmer Sotto")
=> ["John Major", "Randy Bachman", "Louis Davies", "Elmer Sotto"]
```

There are many other array methods. Earlier in this chapter, I discussed how you could find out how many methods are available for a given object. Later in this chapter, I also cover the Ruby documentation so you can find out how to use any method.

Hashes are the other common type of container class. The only difference between an array and a hash is how they're indexed; while an array is indexed with an ordered integer, a hash is indexed with a string value of your choice. This is what some people refer to as a *key-value pair*. Creating a hash is as easy as creating an array, except with a slightly different syntax:

```
>> myCar = {"Make"=>"Hyundai", "Model"=>"Tucson", "Year"=>"2008"}
=> {"Model"=>"Tucson", "Make"=>"Hyundai", "Year"=>"2008"}
```

Note the use of the curly braces instead of the square brackets. Just like the array, the hash has a set of methods available, and they should be quite familiar to you:

```
>> myCar.size
=> 3
>> myCar.class
=> Hash
>> myCar.empty?
=> false
>> myCar.inspect
=> "{\"Model\"=>\"Tucson\", \"Make\"=>\"Hyundai\",
   \"Year\"=>\"2008\"}"
```

You can also add new items to the hash by supplying a key to go with it:

```
>> myCar["Color"] = "Red"
=> "Red"
>> myCar.inspect
=> "{\"Model\"=>\"Tucson\", \"Color\"=>\"Red\",
   \"Make\"=>\"Hyundai\", \"Year\"=>\"2008\"}"
```

Now that you see how arrays and hashes work, let's see how they are often used together. In Ruby in general and Rails in particular, you'll find yourself creating arrays of hashes — that is, collections of individual objects that store multiple values. If you consider the example of `myCar`, you can imagine it might be more useful if I had a whole bunch of `car` hashes — one for each of the cars in my vintage collection of sports cars or maybe the cars on my lot if I'm a used car salesman. In Ruby, you might collect those objects this way:

```
>> cars = Array.new
=> []
```

```
>> carA = {"Make"=>"Honda", "Model"=>"Civic", "Year"=>"1998"}
=> {"Model"=>"Civic", "Make"=>"Honda", "Year"=>"1998"}
>> cars.push(carA)
=> [{"Model"=>"Civic", "Make"=>"Honda", "Year"=>"1998"}]
>> carB = {"Make"=>"Toyota", "Model"=>"Corolla", "Year"=>"2005"}
=> {"Model"=>"Corolla", "Make"=>"Toyota", "Year"=>"2005"}
>> cars.push(carB)
=> [{"Model"=>"Civic", "Make"=>"Honda", "Year"=>"1998"},
   {"Model"=>"Corolla", "Make"=>"Toyota", "Year"=>"2005"}]
>> carC = {"Make"=>"Hyundai", "Model"=>"Tucson", "Year"=>"2008"}
=> {"Model"=>"Tucson", "Make"=>"Hyundai", "Year"=>"2008"}
>> cars.push(carC)
=> [{"Model"=>"Civic", "Make"=>"Honda", "Year"=>"1998"},
   {"Model"=>"Corolla", "Make"=>"Toyota", "Year"=>"2005"},
   {"Model"=>"Tucson", "Make"=>"Hyundai", "Year"=>"2008"}]
```

Now you have just one variable, cars, that contains three hashes, each providing you with useful information about an individual car. So, how do you use that information? In Ruby, you use two constructs: blocks and iterators.

Blocks and iterators

You should already be familiar with the concept of an *iterator*; this is a means to step through every item in a collection. For example, in PHP, the most common iterator is the foreach() function. In Ruby, there are a number of iterators, which are methods that perform an action on each item in a collection. A common Ruby method for this is each. If you still have the cars array in your irb session, you can step through it with this code:

```
>> cars.each do |c|
?> print "I have a #{c["Year"]} #{c["Make"]} #{c["Model"]}.\n"
>> end
I have a 1998 Honda Civic.
I have a 2005 Toyota Corolla.
I have a 2008 Hyundai Tucson.
```

As you can see, the each method is available to the array instance cars. The do keyword follows along with a parameter within the pipe characters; think of that value as each individual item in the array going down into the block of code. So, in each run through the array, the value c holds a particular hash, from which you can pull the values.

Did I say "block"? Yes: The lines within the call to the each method belong to a *block*. This is a special language construct that yields to the value passed into it (in fact, there's a method named yield that explicitly uses whatever you pass into it). The line that does the printing accepts the value of the variable c — whatever it happens to be at the time — to perform an action. The block is defined by the do . . . end keywords. Another way to express a block is with curly braces:

```
>> cars.each {|c| print "I own a #{c["Make"]}.\n"}
I own a Honda.
I own a Toyota.
I own a Hyundai.
```

As you explore Ruby further, you'll find yourself using blocks all the time. They're a very elegant programming idiom.

If and unless

Like the other languages you've learned about in this book, Ruby has an if...else construction. But it looks a bit different from what you've seen; the Ruby version doesn't use brackets for the test expression or braces for the code block. Instead, you use the keyword end.

```
if name == "Hyundai"
     print "Found it!"
end
```

The missing brackets and braces make this code much easier to read than in the other languages I've discussed.

There's also an else mechanism as well as an elsif. Look carefully; there really is just one letter e in that one. Here's a complete example:

```
If name == "Hyundai"
     Print "Found it!"
elsif name == "Toyota"
     print "Sort of found it."
else
     print "Yeah, didn't find it."
end
```

These expressions can also be used in an abbreviated way. For times when you want to evaluate and act on an expression in one line, you can use either if or its opposite, unless. You can try this out in irb quite easily:

```
>> a = 1
=> 1
>> print "low number!" if a < 2
low number!=> nil
>> print "low number!" unless a >= 2
low number!=> nil
```

The Ruby interpreter sees when you're using if as part of an expression and doesn't require the end statement. This use really enhances the readability of your code, making it far more understandable. That's a big deal when you need to support it months or even years from now.

Finally, there's a ternary format in Ruby to give you a quick way to decide between actions in a single line:

```
>> a > 0 ? "A positive number!" : "A low number!"
=> "A positive number!"
```

Now that you have seen some of the basic Ruby syntax, you're going to put it to work building a framework for a real application.

The Invoicr Application

There's nothing like developing a real program to get an in-depth knowledge of a programming language. In the rest of this chapter, you'll work on a program that lets you create, track, and print invoices by using a command-line application built by using Ruby.

In the spirit of Web 2.0, I've decided to call this program Invoicr, omitting the extraneous vowel.

CROSS-REF
You can find the Invoicr project files on the website for this book: `www.wileydevreference.com`.

If you either intend to run your own business or you already do, then you'll understand the need for a way to create invoices; they are, after all, the lifeblood of your operation. With Invoicr, you can quickly create invoices, add individual line items, and then display their totals. You can include tax rates for your jurisdiction. And by using a PDF template that I provide, you can output your invoice in a clean-looking format for sending to the lucky client.

The first step in building any application is planning. Your Invoicr application is composed of two objects, which you create. These objects are:

- `Invoice`. This creates an invoice object, sets its values, and lets you save, recall, and print invoices
- `Lineitem`. This is used in an invoice, providing a way to add an item, with a description and cost per unit.

In the practice of good object-oriented design, you want the objects to do most of the hard work; they're responsible for managing themselves by using just simple directions from a main controller.

That controller is the main application, a file you'll write called (wait for it) `invoicr`. As a command-line program, this file is a shell script written in Ruby that accepts arguments on the command line, passing along commands to the objects as appropriate.

Let's begin by writing a framework for your application. In your text editor, create a new file and then type this text:

```
#!/usr/bin/ruby
arg = ARGV[0]
if arg == "list"
  print "listing...\n"
elsif arg == "create"
  print "creating...\n"
elsif arg == "additem"
  print "adding item...\n"
elsif arg == "print"
  print "printing...\n"
elsif arg == "help"
  print "Invoicer help! Command line arguments:\n"
  print "------------------------------------\n"
  print "list: show saved invoices\n"
  print "create: start a new invoice\n"
  print "additem: add a line item to an existing invoice\n"
  print "print: output an invoice to PDF\n"
  print "help: show this message\n"
  print "------------------------------------\n"
end
```

The script begins with the universal shebang prompt: the hash-plus-exclamation point (#!) that's the keyword for defining the shell script's designated interpreter. In Mac OS X, Ruby is located at /usr/bin/ruby, so that's what you put here.

The second line grabs the first of whatever argument will be passed in from the command line; this is done by pulling the first item from the ARGV array (remember, arrays are always zero-indexed, so the first value in an array has an index of 0). If you want to collect additional arguments from the command line, you can create another variable to capture ARGV[1], ARGV[2], and so on.

The rest of the program is just a wireframe. You use a series of if…elsif…else statements to direct whatever the user passes into the program. For all but the last command, you print only an acknowledgement of the argument passed in.

Let's give this a try. Save the program as invoicr. Then, open Terminal and change directories to where you saved the file. View a complete listing on that directory so you can see the file permissions on your new file:

```
achilles:invoicer aaron$ ls -l invoicr
-rw-r--r-- 1 aaron  staff  905  7 Oct 23:28 invoicr
```

As you recall from the discussion on file permissions back in Chapter 2, this new file is readable and writable by aaron and readable by both the staff group and the world. You need to change this so the file can be executed. Run this command and then view the results:

```
achilles:invoicer aaron$ chmod 744 invoicr
achilles:invoicer aaron$ ls -l invoicr
-rwxr--r--@ 1 aaron  staff  905  7 Oct 23:28 invoicr
```

The x bit on the user permissions means you can call the file directly, and it will run like a program. Let's do that now:

```
achilles:invoicer aaron$ ./invoicr help
Invoicer help! Command line arguments:
-----------------------------------
list: show saved invoices
create: start a new invoice
additem: add a line item to an existing invoice
print: output an invoice to PDF
help: show this message
-----------------------------------
```

Because you sent help as the command-line argument, the program parsed your intentions and displayed the carefully crafted documentation that you wrote. Good job! You can try sending the other suggested arguments, although you'll be less satisfied with these results:

```
achilles:invoicer aaron$ ./invoicr list
listing...
```

However, it's important to determine that your wireframe for the application is working. If you're still with me, give yourself a pat on the back — it's working!

Ruby objects

You've already seen a bit of Ruby's object-oriented structure at work. Now you're going to go into greater depth in order to understand it better. You start by creating the Invoice object, which is in charge of creating new invoices and setting their properties. Start by creating a new file and then type this text:

```
class Invoice
  attr :client, true
  attr :tax, true
  def initialize(client, tax)
    @client = client
    @tax = tax
  end
  def inspect
    print "Client: #{@client}, Tax: #{@tax}"
  end
end
```

There are a couple of interesting things going on in this code that you haven't seen yet. After you perform the standard practice of declaring your class (always remembering that a class name is capitalized), you have two statements that declare your attributes. The `attr` method is shorthand code that provides read and write methods for the given attribute. Remember the `Dice` example that I used earlier? In that code, I wrote a method called `sides`; the purpose of the method was to pull the value of that attribute. That kind of method is known as a *getter* method; its opposite is called a *setter* method, and it might look like this:

```
def sides=(num)
  @sides = num
end
```

This is pretty tedious stuff, especially if you have to write getters and setters for several attributes. Hence, the `attr` method. It takes two arguments: the name of the attributes you want to access and a Boolean value to determine if the attribute should be writable (that is, if there should be a setter as well as a getter). In this case, you do want both setters and getters for your two attributes.

NOTE
Why are there colons before the names of the attributes? The Ruby construct that places a colon before a non-quoted string is called a *symbol*. This symbol is a stand-in for the name of the variable. So, when you have a symbol called `:client`, it's referring to the name of the instance variable `@client`. And when you use `@client` in your code, you're getting the value of that variable. Therefore, when you want to refer to a variable getting its value, you express it as a symbol. Make sense?

The next piece of code is the `initialize` method that you've already seen; it's a standard feature of any class declaration. In this class, you're going to start it up with the name of a client and the tax rate charged on the invoice. If you think of all the items of information that are needed in an invoice, these are the two that I consider necessary at this global level; each individual invoice will require these two attributes.

Now, I advocate taking small steps in my development. As soon as I write code, I want to know whether it's working as I expected. So, I'm going to want a way to display the attributes of my `Invoice` object. You've already seen the `inspect` method in an earlier example; this is the Ruby method that provides a string representation of the given object. In this case, I want to override the object's default implementation of `inspect` and provide my own (better-looking) version. Any method that you implement that has the same name as an existing method replaces that method's functionality.

Let's try it out. Save the file as `Invoice.rb` in the same directory as your `invoicr` script. Now, go to Terminal, activate `irb`, and then run this code to test your new object:

```
achilles:invoicer aaron$ irb
>> require 'Invoice.rb'
=> true
>> i = Invoice.new("AwesomeCo Inc.", "5")
Client: AwesomeCo Inc., Tax: 5=>
>> i.inspect
Client: AwesomeCo Inc., Tax: 5=> nil
```

In `irb`, the console returns a value for every statement that you execute, as you've already seen. In this case, you can see that `irb` automatically assumes your `inspect` statement in displaying the return value from the `Invoice.new` method. If you want to see how it would look without your implementation of `inspect`, simply cut it from your code and then run it again in `irb`:

```
>> i = Invoice.new("AwesomeCo Inc.", "5")
=> #<Invoice:0x101143438 @client="AwesomeCo Inc.", @tax="5">
```

The default action shows the rather human-unfriendly ID number for the new `Invoice` object and then the value of the properties.

Incidentally, you can also test your individual accessor methods:

```
>> i.client
=> "AwesomeCo Inc."
>> i.tax
=> "5"
```

So far, your `Invoice` object is working well. You have two accessor methods and one regular method.

Let's set up your other object. Because you're using object-oriented programming (OOP) to write your application, you have to model your program on the real-world purpose that you're simulating — in this case, the invoice. While an invoice is a single item, it contains any number of individual line items — those line-by-line details of the work you've toiled over on behalf of the client. So, it makes sense to have a separate object, called `Lineitem`, that represents each individual line on an invoice. Open a new text file and then type this code:

```
class Lineitem
  attr :item
  attr :description
  attr :quantity
  attr :unitprice

  def initialize(item, description, quantity, unitprice)
    @item = item
    @description = description
    @quantity = quantity
    @unitprice = unitprice
  end

end
```

There are no surprises here; when you create a `Lineitem`, it will have an item name, description, quantity, and unit price. Save this file as `Lineitem.rb`, again in the same directory as the other files you've created. You can also test this in the console:

```
achilles:invoicer aaron$ irb
>> require 'Lineitem.rb'
=> true
>> l = Lineitem.new("Web design", "AwesomeCo. site project",
   "15", "85")
=> #<Lineitem:0x101143410 @quantity="15", @item="Web design", @
   description="AwesomeCo. site project", @unitprice="85">
>> l.item
=> "Web design"
```

I didn't write an `inspect` method for this, but you can if you want; it's enough for now to test that you can access the attributes that you set for the new object.

You have now set up a basic framework for your application: a controller that will act as the main interface to the application and two objects that will do the hard work. Now it's time to put these objects to work.

Connecting objects together

Perhaps in the back of your mind, you're wondering this: If an `Invoice` consists of multiple `Lineitems`, how do you connect one to the other? Good question. Simply put, you're going to create another attribute for the `Invoice` object, which will contain the `Lineitems`. It's very easily done; in your `Invoice.rb` file, add this line (in bold):

```
attr :client, true
attr :tax, true
attr :lineitems, true
```

The symbol `:lineitems` will represent an instance variable. This variable contains an array of `Lineitem` objects. To test that this is the case, you're going to put the line items to work. In your `Invoice.rb` file, you're going to add a method that totals the value of all the line items. Add this method definition after your `initialize` method:

```
def items_subtotal
  if @lineitems
    subtotal = 0
    @lineitems.each do |li|
      extension = li.quantity.to_f * li.unitprice.to_f
      subtotal += extension
    end
    return subtotal
  else
    return false
  end
end
```

This code is fairly straightforward. It begins by checking for the presence of the `@lineitems` variable; if for some reason it hasn't been set, then you'll exit by returning `false`. Otherwise, you'll use Ruby's blocks syntax to step through each line item, adding its total price to a running tally represented by the variable `subtotal`.

The `extension` variable is a calculation of the line item's unit cost and quantity. You'll notice that a tiny method is appended to each value in the equation: `to_f`. This method converts the values to floats, which you'll use to ensure that you end up with an accurate value; a *float* is a number that contains a decimal.

Save the file and go back to your console to try out this code. First, get the object files included:

```
achilles:invoicer aaron$ irb
>> require 'Invoice.rb'
=> true
>> require 'Lineitem.rb'
=> true
```

Then, create the new invoice:

```
>> i = Invoice.new("AwesomeCo Inc.", "5")
=> #<Invoice:0x10113f518 @client="AwesomeCo Inc.", @tax="5">
```

Next, create three line items for the invoice:

```
>> i1 = Lineitem.new("Web development", "Site design project",
   "8", "85")
=> #<Lineitem:0x101132e30 @quantity="8", @item="Web development",
   @unitprice="85", @description="Site design project">
>> i2 = Lineitem.new("Design", "Brochure layout", "4", "85")
=> #<Lineitem:0x101128890 @quantity="4", @item="Design", @
   unitprice="85", @description="Brochure layout">
>> i3 = Lineitem.new("Hosting", "Site hosting for September
   2009", "1", "50")
=> #<Lineitem:0x10111ac40 @quantity="1", @item="Hosting", @
   unitprice="50", @description="Site hosting for September
   2009">
```

So far, so good. Here's the key part: Now add those three line items, as an array, to the invoice's `lineitems` attribute:

```
>> i.lineitems = [i1, i2, i3]
=> [#<Lineitem:0x101132e30 @quantity="8", @item="Web
   development", @unitprice="85", @description="Site design
   project">, #<Lineitem:0x101128890 @quantity="4", @
   item="Design", @unitprice="85", @description="Brochure
   layout">, #<Lineitem:0x10111ac40 @quantity="1", @
   item="Hosting", @unitprice="50", @description="Site hosting
   for September 2009">]
```

Finally, execute the method that adds their values together:

```
>> i.items_subtotal
=> 1070.0
```

Neat! Now, if you really want to show off, why don't you output an entire invoice to the console? In `Invoice.rb`, add this method definition:

```
def invoice_totals
  subtotal = self.items_subtotal
  tax = subtotal.to_f * (@tax.to_f / 100)
  total = subtotal.to_f + tax

  # print lines and totals
  print "Client: #{@client}\n\n"
  lineitems.each do |l|
    print "Item: #{l.item}\n"
    print "Description: #{l.description}\n"
    print "Quantity: #{l.quantity}\n"
    print "Per Unit: $#{sprintf("%.02f", l.unitprice)}\n"
    print "Item Total: $#{sprintf("%.02f", l.quantity.to_f * l.
    unitprice.to_f)}\n\n"
  end
  print "------------------\n"
  print "Taxes: $#{sprintf("%.02f", tax)}\n"
  print "Total: $#{sprintf("%.02f", total)}\n"
  print "------------------\n"

end
```

This method actually calls your `items_subtotal` method to do some of the work. It then adds in the tax to come up with a grand total for the invoice. The next part is easy: Output the values of the invoice. The one new thing in this code is the use of Ruby's `sprintf()` function, which you use to format the totals as currency. The `sprintf()` function is taken directly from the C language, even taking its arguments in brackets rather than using dot notation.

Here's what the output of this method looks like, using the same line item data that I used before:

```
>> i.invoice_totals
Client: AwesomeCo Inc.
Item: Web development
Description: Site design project
Quantity: 8
Per Unit: $85.00
Item Total: $680.00
Item: Design
Description: Brochure layout
Quantity: 4
```

```
Per Unit: $85.00
Item Total: $340.00
Item: Hosting
Description: Site hosting for September 2009
Quantity: 1
Per Unit: $50.00
Item Total: $50.00
-------------------
Taxes: $53.50
Total: $1123.50
-------------------
```

Not too shabby for a night's work. But this isn't the finish line; you need to add some bling to this application. Fortunately, that's exactly where Ruby's gem system comes in.

Adding features with Ruby gems

You've already seen the gem system at work in Chapter 13. You used `gem` to install the Ruby on Rails environment — and don't worry, you'll make good use of that in Chapter 17! But you won't have to wait to take advantage of gems because you're going to use two of them right now.

The first gem is a tool that will let you save your invoice data by using a plain-text format called *CSV* (comma-separated values). The `fastercsv` gem that you install makes it easy for you to read and write data to these files, and you'll use them to store your invoices and line items.

The second gem will give you the means to create PDF copies of your invoices. Using the `prawn` gem, you can open an existing PDF, write your data on top of it, and output a fresh compiled version, ready to send to your client.

While Ruby is great by itself, this system of easy-to-add functionality is a real strength of the language and will make your life easier in many ways. Let's look at some of these gems now.

To install these additions, run the following command in Terminal:

```
achilles:~ aaron$ sudo gem install fastercsv prawn
Successfully installed fastercsv-1.5.0
...
Successfully installed prawn-core-0.5.1
Successfully installed prawn-layout-0.2.1
Successfully installed prawn-format-0.2.1
Successfully installed prawn-0.5.1
5 gems installed
Installing ri documentation for fastercsv-1.5.0...
Installing ri documentation for prawn-core-0.5.1...
Installing ri documentation for prawn-layout-0.2.1...
Installing ri documentation for prawn-format-0.2.1...
Installing ri documentation for prawn-0.5.1...
Installing RDoc documentation for fastercsv-1.5.0...
Installing RDoc documentation for prawn-core-0.5.1...
```

```
Installing RDoc documentation for prawn-layout-0.2.1...
Installing RDoc documentation for prawn-format-0.2.1...
Installing RDoc documentation for prawn-0.5.1...
```

I have placed an ellipsis (. . .) into the output here. If you run this command yourself, you may see more text in this spot. As I run it today, part of that text includes this rather stern warning:

```
Welcome to Prawn, the best pure-Ruby PDF solution ever! ...
Prawn is meant for experienced Ruby hackers, so if you are new to
Ruby, you might want to wait until you've had some practice with
the language before expecting Prawn to work for you. Things may
change after 1.0, but for now if you're not ready to read source
code and patch bugs or missing features yourself (with our
help), Prawn might not be the right fit.
But if you know what you're getting yourself into, enjoy!
```

Now, if you've ever been exposed to the world of open-source software, you know that almost none of that software is at a 1.0 version; the nature of this software is that it's always under development. Sometimes, you'll find some quirky behavior, but there are almost always work-arounds. I'm not sure why the Prawn development team felt they needed to scare off less-experienced developers. I, for one, am glad that I ignored this warning because I found Prawn more useable than other PDF solutions for Ruby, and I think that once you see it in action, you'll dismiss the senseless fears these guys put in your head.

You'll deal with Prawn later. For now, you're going to practice by using FasterCSV.

The ability to save and retrieve invoice data is an important foundation for most of this program's functionality, so you're going to be making changes to much of this program now.

To begin, you need to add a couple of require statements to the files that will use your gems. At the top of Invoice.rb, add these lines (in bold):

```
class Invoice
  require 'rubygems'
  require 'fastercsv'
```

The rubygems statement provides you with access to the means to use the gems repository and lets you call FasterCSV in your code.

With that done, you need to make a small change to your Invoice object. If you think of a CSV file as a database, then one of the items you need is a *primary key*, an integer that uniquely identifies every line in the table. After writing a line using a primary key, you can readily recall that line by looking for that integer. Therefore, you need to add an attribute to your Invoice object to support it. In your attribute list in Invoice.rb, add this line (in bold):

```
attr :client, true
attr :tax, true
attr :lineitems, true
attr :id
```

Unlike the other attributes, id will not be set outside this class file, so you will make it read-only.

With that done, you can add support for saving to your Invoice object. Instead of simply instantiating an Invoice, you should also save it to the text file.

In your invoicr file, add the following code (new lines in bold) to your "create" argument block. These lines support the user entering data (note the string of methods that pull information from standard input — STDIN — using gets) as well as trimming white space with the chomp method. Then, you add the save feature:

```
elsif arg == "create"
  # collect the data
  print "Create new invoice\n"
  print "Enter client name: "
  clientname = STDIN.gets.chomp
  print "Enter tax rate: "
  taxrate = STDIN.gets.chomp
  i = Invoice.new(clientname, taxrate)
  # save it to file
  i.save

  print "You entered #{i.client} and #{i.tax}\n"
```

As you can see, after you create the Invoice object, you're going to call a new method on it: save. Open Invoice.rb and then add this method after the initialize method:

```
def save
  # get any existing data from the CSV
  current_data = FasterCSV.read("invoices.csv")

  # create a line in the "database"
  @id = self.newid
  FasterCSV.open("invoices.csv", "w") do |csv|
    current_data.each do |cd|
      csv << cd
    end
    # now add the new data
    csv << [@id, @client, @tax]
  end
end
```

It doesn't take much code to save data to a file by using FasterCSV. Let's step through it. A save operation with a file is actually a two-step process: First, you have to get all existing data from the file and then you write it back to the file and append the new data. The first line of your code starts the process, putting the contents of your invoices.csv file into the variable current_data.

The next line takes advantage of your newly created primary key support in the `Invoice` object. When you're writing lines into the text file, you need a way to ensure that you're using a unique `id` value. So, you have to write a method that will parse the existing file, find the highest `id` number, and add one. You'll write that in a moment.

The next block is the key to your method. To write to a file, you invoke the `FasterCSV` object's `open` method, specifying the file name and the mode — `w` means write. You then pass the result of that method call into a Ruby block as the variable name `csv`. As I mentioned earlier, you need to first write the existing data into the file and then append the new data; `FasterCSV` doesn't let you just add on a line.

So, the first of the two steps is to use `each` to iterate through the `current_data` array, adding each line to the file. Then, you can add the new line.

Simple enough? Writing files is the hard part; reading is simple. Let's write the `newid` method so your `save` method has an `id` number to insert. Type this code at the bottom of your `Invoice.rb` file:

```ruby
def newid
  # determine highest id number in CSV file and return increment
  id = 1
  FasterCSV.foreach("invoices.csv") do |row|
    if row[0].to_i >= id
      id = row[0].to_i
    end
  end
  return id+1
end
```

Starting with the lowest possible ID number, you'll first use `FasterCSV` to read through each line of your `invoices` file. Then, you'll compare the assigned `id` variable to the first field of each line — that's the line's ID number. If that number is higher than your variable, you'll match it to the variable. Therefore, at the end of the loop, the variable is the same as the highest number in the file. Add one and then return it.

There's just one more thing to do. Create a new, empty text file and then save it as `invoices.csv` in the same directory as the rest of your files for this project.

At this point, you can test your new code, so save the file and then go to Terminal to type the following:

```
achilles:invoicer aaron$ ./invoicr create
Create new invoice
Enter client name: Great Hoodoo Ltd.
Enter tax rate: 8.5
You entered Great Hoodoo Ltd. and 8.5
```

So far, this looks like what you already had. But now, let's have a look in your new CSV file:

```
1,Great Hoodoo Ltd.,8.5
```

It outputs actual data.

Now that you have a way to get invoices in and out of a file, let's put it to use. One of the features in `invoicr` is to list any invoices on file. That's handy for the user to get a quick look, but it's also going to be useful for other functions that you'll be writing. Back in the `invoicr` file, alter the `"list"` block (new code is in bold):

```
if arg == "list"
  # list all invoices
  Invoice.list
```

As you can see, you're still trying to get the objects to do the hard work; the code in your main program file should be kept to a minimum. So, let's head back to `Invoice.rb` to implement that method call:

```
def Invoice.list
  #class method for all invoices in the list
  FasterCSV.foreach("invoices.csv") do |row|
    puts "ID: #{row[0]} | Client: #{row[1]} | Tax Rate:
    #{row[2]}"
  end
end
```

Do you notice anything different about this method and how it's called? Look at the method name. Usually, it might be just `list`, but here, you prepend the class name. That makes this a *class method*, as opposed to the normal kind, called an *instance method*. Think about those names to discover the difference; instance methods are used on instances of your object (such as when you create a new invoice and assign it to the variable `i`), while class methods are universal, intended to do work on all instances of a class. In this case, you want a list of all invoices, so you invoke the entire class to do the work for you.

The work of this method is pretty simple; it iterates through the file and prints out the values for each line. Save the file and then try it out:

```
achilles:invoicer aaron$ ./invoicr list
ID: 1 | Client: Great Hoodoo Ltd. | Tax Rate: 8.5
```

This is handy code. As you work on adding individual line items to invoices, you'll see this feature come back.

Much of what you need to do with line items is similar to how you managed your invoices. Open your `Lineitem.rb` file and then first add the `require` statements at the top that will give you access to `FasterCSV`:

```
require 'rubygems'
require 'fastercsv'
```

You also need to add another attribute to the object — a way to connect a line item with an invoice. For that, use the invoice's `id` attribute, so add this line to the end of your list of attributes (the new line is in bold):

```
attr :item
attr :description
attr :quantity
attr :unitprice
attr :invoice_id
```

And to support your new connection with the invoice, you need to ensure that the `invoice_id` attribute is there when a new `Lineitem` object is created. Modify your `Lineitem`'s `initialize` method to include this attribute (new code is in bold):

```
def initialize(item, description, quantity, unitprice, invoice_id)
  @item = item
  @description = description
  @quantity = quantity
  @unitprice = unitprice
  @invoice_id = invoice_id
end
```

If you added an `inspect` method to `Lineitem` earlier as I recommended, you should also update that to include the invoice ID:

```
def inspect
  puts "Invoice ID: #{@invoice_id} | Item: #{@item} |
  Description: #{@description} | Quantity: #{@quantity} | Unit
  Price: #{@unitprice}"
end
```

So, how are you going to use your newfound ability to tie line items to invoices? You'll use the `additem` argument in `invoicr`. Let's write that part now (new code is in bold):

```
elsif arg == "additem"
  # first we need the invoice we're adding to
  print "Choose an invoice to add to:\n"
  print "--------------------------\n"
  Invoice.list
  print "--------------------------\n"
  print "Enter ID of invoice to add to: "
  inv_id = STDIN.gets.chomp
  print "Enter item type: "
  item = STDIN.gets.chomp
  print "Enter description: "
  description = STDIN.gets.chomp
  print "Enter quantity: "
  quantity = STDIN.gets.chomp
  print "Enter unit price: "
```

```
unitprice = STDIN.gets.chomp

l = Lineitem.new(item, description, quantity, unitprice, inv_
  id)
l.save
l.inspect
```

Just as you did with the `"create"` block, you're collecting the information you need to build a line item. But first, you need to know what invoice this line item will connect to; hence, the use of `Invoice.list`. When that method prints the list of invoices, the user can type the right ID number, to which you'll apply the line item.

Once the program gathers in the ID, item, description, quantity, and price, you first create a new `Lineitem` object and then `save` and `inspect` it.

You have the `initialize` and `inspect` methods written. But you still need to write that `save` method. Open up `Lineitem.rb` and add it now:

```
def save
  # get any existing data from the lineitems file
  current_items = FasterCSV.read("lineitems.csv")

  # create a new line in the 'database'
  FasterCSV.open("lineitems.csv", "w") do |csv|
    current_items.each do |ci|
      csv << ci
    end
    # now add the new data
    # Invoice id, item, description, quantity, unitprice
    csv << [@invoice_id, @item, @description, @quantity, @
    unitprice]
  end
end
```

This method is very similar to the one you wrote for your `Invoice` object; the only difference is in the fields you write to the file.

Speaking of the file, let's create that one too. Create a blank text file and then save it as `lineitems.csv` in your project directory.

Now you can test your work in Terminal:

```
achilles:invoicer aaron$ ./invoicr additem
Choose an invoice to add to:
--------------------------
ID: 1 | Client: Great Hoodoo Ltd. | Tax Rate: 8.5
--------------------------
Enter ID of invoice to add to: 1
Enter item type: Web design
Enter description: Site design for hoodoo.com
```

```
Enter quantity: 15
Enter unit price: 85
Invoice ID: 1 | Item: Web design | Description: Site design for
    hoodoo.com | Quantity: 15 | Unit Price: 85
```

You can then have a look at your CSV file; in `lineitems.csv`:

```
1,Web design,Site design for hoodoo.com,15,85
```

Exactly right! There's one more task to implement in order to demonstrate your mastery of file management: printing an invoice. You do this by using the console for now; I'll show you later how to create a PDF.

In `invoicr`, modify your `"print"` block (new code is in bold):

```
elsif arg == "print"
    # first we need the invoice we're adding to
    print "Choose an invoice to print:\n"
    print "----------------------------\n"
    Invoice.list
    print "----------------------------\n"
    print "Enter ID of invoice to print: "
    inv_id = STDIN.gets.chomp

    i = Invoice.fetch_invoice(inv_id)
    l = Lineitem.collect(inv_id)
    i.lineitems = l
    i.invoice_totals
```

You can see that you're using the `list` class method again to help the user identify an invoice to print. Once you've grabbed the invoice ID number, you execute another `Invoice` class method, `fetch_invoice`, so you'll have an `Invoice` object to work with. By the same token, you need all that invoice's line items, so you call another class method: `Lineitem.collect`. Once you assign the line items to the `Invoice` object, you can call the `invoice_totals` method that you wrote earlier. Easy enough, right? You're two methods away from finishing, so let's get it done.

In `Invoice.rb`, add the `fetch_invoice` class method:

```
def Invoice.fetch_invoice(inv_id)
    FasterCSV.foreach("invoices.csv") do |row|
        if row[0] == inv_id
            @client = row[1]
            @tax = row[2]
        end
    end
    if @client
        return Invoice.new(@client, @tax)
    end
end
```

This class method takes the desired invoice ID as its argument. The operation here simply scans through the `invoices.csv` file, and when it finds the right `id`, it places its values into the instance variables `@client` and `@tax`. Once out of the loop, you create a new `Invoice` object by using those values and then returning it:

In `Lineitem.rb`, add the `collect` class method:

```
def Lineitem.collect(inv_id)
  items = Array.new
  FasterCSV.foreach("lineitems.csv") do |row|
    if row[0] == inv_id
      i = Lineitem.new(row[1], row[2], row[3], row[4], row[0])
      items.push i
    end
  end
  return items
end
```

This method works similarly to the other `FasterCSV` blocks you've seen; starting by creating an array that will hold your line items, you cycle through each entry in the `lineitems.csv` file, adding each matching `invoice_id` as well as adding those records to your array of items. After the loop, you return the `items` array.

You're done. Save both these files and then let's try our program out in Terminal:

```
achilles:invoicer aaron$ ./invoicr print
Choose an invoice to print:
----------------------------
ID: 1 | Client: Great Hoodoo Ltd. | Tax Rate: 8.5
----------------------------
Enter ID of invoice to print: 1
Client: Great Hoodoo Ltd.
Item: Web design
Description: Site design for hoodoo.com
Quantity: 15
Per Unit: $85.00
Item Total: $1275.00
-------------------
Taxes: $108.38
Total: $1383.38
-------------------
```

I think you'll agree that you've created a handy, functional program. Let's put the finishing touches on it by adding the kind of output that you can send to a client. Because, let's face it, what's the point if you're not getting paid?

Printing PDFs

The Prawn library is a handy tool for creating PDFs. Adobe's Portable Document Format is an open standard for creating and sharing read-only documents. Using this library, you're going to generate a document that you can send to your client. It will include an image of your company logo, a few lines of text, and a couple tables of information (your invoice line items and the totals).

To begin, you need to add support for Prawn to your `Invoice` object file, just as you did for `FasterCSV` (new code is in bold):

```
require 'rubygems'
require 'fastercsv'
require 'prawn'
require 'prawn/layout'
```

You're including two files here: the standard Prawn library and the Prawn Layout library, which lets you build tables.

Before you write that code, you should make a quick adjustment to the `invoicr` file. The code you wrote to display the invoice in the console doesn't belong in the `"print"` block, but you would like to keep it. So, you change the command it uses to `"display"` instead. Now you can write the real `"print"` block:

```
elsif arg == "print"
  # first we need the invoice we're adding to
  print "Choose an invoice to print:\n"
  print "--------------------------\n"
  Invoice.list
  print "--------------------------\n"
  print "Enter ID of invoice to print: "
  inv_id = STDIN.gets.chomp

  Invoice.print(inv_id)
  print "File saved as 'Invoice #{inv_id}.pdf'\n"
```

The block performs its usual routine: getting the ID of the invoice from a listing. Then, you can call upon another class method, `Invoice.print`, passing in the ID of the selected invoice. Finally, when that method is done, it displays a confirmation that the invoice is saved with the file name.

So, here's the final step. In `Invoice.rb`, write the `print` method:

```
def Invoice.print(inv_id)
  i = Invoice.fetch_invoice(inv_id)
  l = Lineitem.collect(inv_id)
```

```ruby
  i.lineitems = 1

Prawn::Document.generate "Invoice #{inv_id}.pdf" do |pdf|
  company_logo = "innoveghtive.png"
  pdf.image company_logo, :at=>[0,720]

  pdf.text "Invoice ##{inv_id}", :at=>[350,700]
  pdf.text "Invoice for: #{i.client}", :at=>[350,685]
  pdf.text "Invoice Date: #{Time.now.strftime("%B %d, %Y")}",
  :at=>[350,670]

  data = Array.new
  i.lineitems.each do |li|
    data.push [li.item, li.description, li.quantity,
  "$"+sprintf("%.02f", li.unitprice)]
  end

  pdf.move_down 80

  pdf.table data,
    :position => :left,
    :headers => ["Item", "Description", "Quantity", "Unit
  Price"],
    :column_widths => { 0 => 120, 1 => 270, 2 => 60, 3 => 70},
    :border_style => :grid,
    :header_color => 'efefef',
    :header_text_color => "000000",
    :row_colors => ["999999","aaaaaa"]

  pdf.move_down 20

  subtotal = i.items_subtotal
  taxes = subtotal * (i.tax.to_f / 100)
  grand_total = subtotal + taxes

  totals = [ ["Subtotal", "$"+sprintf("%.02f", subtotal)],
             ["Taxes", "$"+sprintf("%.02f", taxes)],
             ["Total", "$"+sprintf("%.02f", grand_total)]]

  pdf.table totals,
    :position => 350,
    :column_widths => { 0 => 100, 1 => 70},
    :border_style => :grid,
    :header_color => 'efefef',
    :header_text_color => "000000",
    :row_colors => ["999999","aaaaaa"]
  end
end
```

Now you can see how this code works. The first step is to get the invoice data, and you do it exactly as you did with the (now newly named) `"display"` block.

With that done, it's time to start generating your PDF. As with so many great things in Ruby, it's done within a block: You invoke the `Prawn::Document` class to call the `generate` method, passing in the name of the file you want to create. Then, with the `Document` instance sent through the block as the variable `pdf`, you can set the parameters of that new PDF.

You'll lay out the PDF in the order that the content will appear on the page. So, it might help to show what your final result will look like. Check out Figure 16.1.

Figure 16.1

A PDF generated by your script

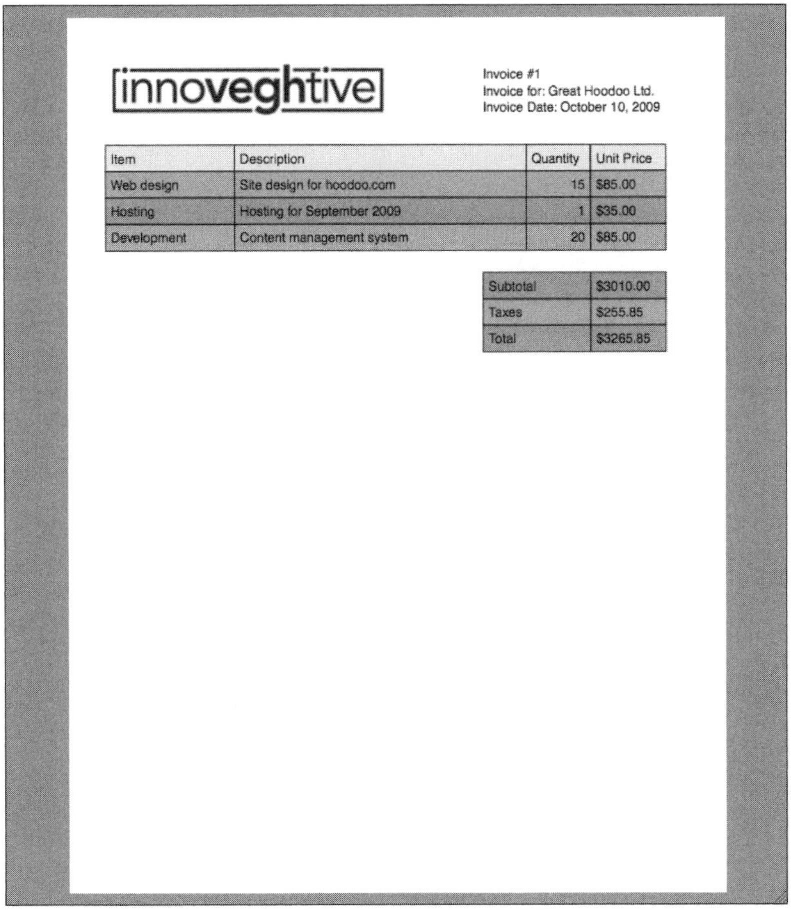

[innoveghtive]

Invoice #1
Invoice for: Great Hoodoo Ltd.
Invoice Date: October 10, 2009

Item	Description	Quantity	Unit Price
Web design	Site design for hoodoo.com	15	$85.00
Hosting	Hosting for September 2009	1	$35.00
Development	Content management system	20	$85.00

Subtotal	$3010.00
Taxes	$255.85
Total	$3265.85

It might not win any graphic design awards, but it's enough to demonstrate the full power of this fully operational PDF library.

So, take the elements as they come, starting with the logo image. I saved this as a PNG file (Prawn can also handle JPEGs) and then assigned it to the variable `company_logo`; feel free to insert your own logo here. Once you have the image assigned, you can place it by using the `image` method, which you can then position with the `:at` attribute.

NOTE

PDF coordinate math is hard. It works in *points*, which is a holdover from PDF's origins in print. Even worse, the *origin* — that is, where 0 and 0 meet — is at the bottom-left corner of the document. So, when you position an element, you have to figure out both how many points to put in your coordinate space and how long the document is. By default, Prawn produces a US letter-sized document (although you can specify otherwise), so once you figure it out, the elements will be better positioned next time. Nonetheless, there's a lot of trial-and-error in getting the position of elements right. Take heart: The numbers you see in this code were arrived at through scores of test runs.

The next step is to place a few lines of text beside the logo: the invoice number, client name, and date. The `text` method does this for you, and it also takes an `:at` attribute, allowing you to place it.

The remaining elements are the two tables: one to display the individual line items and the second to show the totals. Prawn's `table` library takes an array of arrays as its data; each array contains one row in the table, and it will generate rows until it runs out of arrays. So, for each line item, you need to place it in an array and then add it to a data array.

Then, to properly position the table you're about to create, you execute the `move_down` method, passing in a value of 30 points. This is enough distance to get the insertion point below the header elements you just created.

Now you can call the `table` method, passing it your data array. Tables in Prawn take a number of methods, and I've tried to show as many as possible here.

With that table generated, you use the `move_down` method again and then set about creating the `totals` table. You have to manually generate the data for this one, placing the values in the totals array.

That's about it! You can now save the file and then head back to Terminal.

```
achilles:invoicer aaron$ ./invoicr print
Choose an invoice to print:
---------------------------
ID: 1 | Client: Great Hoodoo Ltd. | Tax Rate: 8.5
---------------------------
Enter ID of invoice to print: 1
File saved as 'Invoice 1.pdf'
```

It doesn't look like much here, but you should find that file in your project directory, ready to send to your client.

Congratulations — you've just finished building a full-featured Ruby shell program. Feels good, doesn't it?

Using the Ruby documentation

Before you leave this chapter, it would be worthwhile to talk about the ways you can find out more about programming in Ruby. The language comes with built-in documentation, and there are some online resources that can also help you out.

For the quickest way to find the definition for a method, Ruby comes with a documentation system called `ri`. You simply invoke it on the command line, along with the name of the class you want to learn more about:

```
achilles:invoicer aaron$ ri Time
```

You get a listing that starts like this:

```
-------------------------------------------------Class: Time
Implements the extensions to the Time class that are described in
the documentation for the time.rb library.
-------------------------------------------------------------
Extensions to time to allow comparisons with an early time class.
-------------------------------------------------------------
Includes:
---------
Comparable(<, <=, ==, >, >=, between?)
Constants:
----------
CommonYearMonthDays: [31, 28, 31, 30, 31, 30, 31, 31, 30, 31, 30,
                    31]
LEX_FORMAT:          {      :year      => "%Y",       :month
                    => "%Y-%m",        :day       =>
                    "%Y-%m-%d",        :hour      => "%Y-%m-%d
                    %H",       :minute    => "%Y-%m-%d %H:%M",
```

You can press the spacebar to view more or press Q to quit the viewer and return to Terminal. You can also use `ri` to view documentation on a specific class method:

```
Achilles:invoicer aaron$ ri Time::now
-------------------------------------------------Time::now
Time.new -> time
-------------------------------------------------------------
Synonym for +Time.new+. Returns a +Time+ object initialized tothe
    current system time.
Returns a +Time+ object initialized to the current system time.
*Note:* The object created will be created using the resolution
available on your system clock, and so may include fractional
seconds.
```

```
a = Time.new        #=> Wed Apr 09 08:56:03 CDT 2003
b = Time.new        #=> Wed Apr 09 08:56:03 CDT 2003
a == b              #=> false
"%.6f" % a.to_f     #=> "1049896563.230740"
"%.6f" % b.to_f     #=> "1049896563.231466"
```

Ruby also provides a system called RDoc. This is how you'll most often view Ruby-related documentation. It's a system that scans Ruby source code and produces an HTML file that lets you navigate the given project's files and methods. Figure 16.2 shows the RDoc for the FasterCSV project.

Figure 16.2

The RDoc documentation for FasterCSV

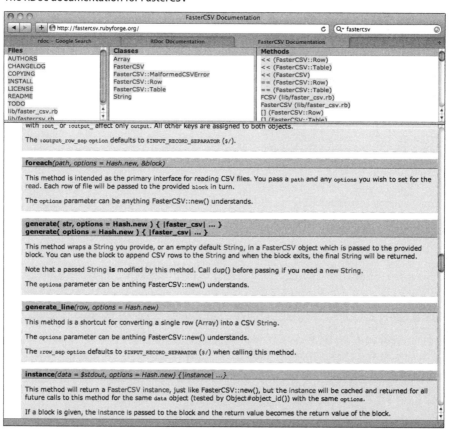

You can actually generate your own RDoc for the `invoicr` application. Of course, before you do, it might be a good idea to write some of that documentation. It's a simple thing to do: Before each method in your code, write a comment that describes it. For example, in `Lineitem.rb`, type the following comments (new code is in bold):

```
# creates a new Lineitem object.

def initialize(item, description, quantity, unitprice, invoice_
  id)
  @item = item
  @description = description
  @quantity = quantity
  @unitprice = unitprice
  @invoice_id = invoice_id
end

# Saves a Lineitem object to CSV format. To use, you must have a
  text file called "lineitems.csv".

def save
  # get any existing data from the lineitems file
    current_items = FasterCSV.read("lineitems.csv")
```

When you've finished adding comments to your methods, all you have to do is type the `rdoc` command in Terminal, inside your project directory.

```
achilles:invoicer aaron$ rdoc
Invoice.rb: c........
Lineitem.rb: c....
Generating HTML...
Files:   2
Classes: 2
Modules: 0
Methods: 12
Elapsed: 0.200s
```

Once that's done, you'll find a new directory called `doc` in your project. Open that up and then open `index.html` in your browser. You'll see the documentation for your `invoicr` application, as shown in Figure 16.3. Very cool.

You can always enhance your documentation, provide examples, and regenerate it all.

Finally, you can find resources online that will help you. Here are a couple of sites worth bookmarking:

- `www.ruby-doc.org`. This is one of the best-known sites that collates complete documentation for the Ruby language. Along with RDoc documentation for the entire Ruby language, there are articles and features to help you get started.

- `http://rubyforge.org`. This is the central repository for many of the gems that enhance Ruby. If you're looking for a way to do something more easily, start your search at RubyForge.

Figure 16.3

The RDoc documentation for your own application

Summary

I haven't been using Ruby for long, relative to the rest of my career. But since taking the time to learn this language, I've found myself delighted again and again by its elegance, expressiveness, and efficiency. Although its syntax might seem a little odd if you're accustomed to C and related languages, you should find that once you understand it, Ruby will make your life a lot easier. Of course, the other reason to learn Ruby is so you can learn Rails.

Ruby on Rails

Y ou have come a long way to get to this chapter — through seemingly impassable thickets, over bramble, and through the tumbled boulders of the dale. You have now climbed the last mountain, and the air is thin here. Few have come this far. Few indeed can say that they are familiar now with the great cluster of technologies that you've amassed in your vast tool belt.

Before you continue, I want to put one last tool in that belt. Perhaps the finest tool available to web developers, it's finely honed, beautiful to look upon, and devastatingly effective. But to use it correctly, you need to have learned and appreciated everything that's come before in this book. Every technology that has gone into Rails is a reflection of the different disciplines covered within these pages: system administration and network infrastructure; the core technology of HTML, CSS, and JavaScript; the principles of design and the tools to build beautiful and functional sites; and database applications. Even your time spent with PHP is instructive as you learn the elegance of the Ruby language as applied to web applications. In other words, this is where all your learning coalesces and where seemingly disparate technologies meld perfectly.

Ironically, Rails is intended to help people of differing skill sets to collaborate easily; systems administrators, designers, front-end developers, and back-end developers can readily (and independently) work on the same project. But you're all those people now. You're The One.

I could talk enthusiastically all day about this topic, but I should really get started.

What Is Rails?

I'll start by defining my terms. Ruby on Rails is a framework, written in the Ruby language, that brings together a number of technologies for developing web applications. It's the brainchild of a developer named David Heinemeier Hansson, who assembled the pieces of what is now Rails while building a product called Basecamp. Basecamp and its owner, 37Signals, are both standard-bearers for the entire Rails movement. The principles of the company, its products, and the Rails framework are the same: simplicity, elegance,

lower cost, and faster development time. And more than anything, the framework and its creator are extremely opinionated about how they work. In other words, if you play by the rules, you'll earn great dividends; try setting out on your own, and you'll find yourself in great difficulty.

Nowhere is this more evident than in Rails' essential structure. The framework is based on a design pattern known as *Model-View-Controller* (MVC). Among computer scientists, this design principle represents the three separate domains of any large program. When these components are properly separated, the developer will enjoy tremendous advantages, both in ease of development and, more importantly, in ease of maintenance.

When you use the MVC design pattern, you're coding in each of these three domains:

- **Models.** These provide the data for your application.
- **Views.** These describe the user interface.
- **Controllers.** These negotiate the movement of data between models and views.

Think of this in the context of a real application, such as the one you built in Chapter 16. In `invoicr`, you created two objects: an `Invoice` and a `Lineitem`. Both these objects are model objects; they act directly on the application data, both retrieving and saving your invoices. The `invoicr` file is both view and controller; it receives user commands and farms them out to the right model methods. It also presents the interface to the users, letting them type commands, and then displays the output.

For small applications, it's not uncommon to mix views and controllers. But as applications grow in size, it becomes advantageous to keep them separate. One of the chief advantages of the MVC pattern is that both models and views are highly reusable. Think about that: The way you interact with data is going to be similar, if not identical, among many applications that use the same data. The view can be thought of in the same way; the components that you'll use to present the interface are easily modularized by using HTML and CSS.

In fact, the only part of an MVC application that is truly not reusable is the controller code. It's the business logic for this particular application and should contain all the idiosyncrasies of your program's operating environment.

So, while in your Ruby program you do most of the work in the model objects, in a Rails application, it's the controller that does most of the work. But as you'll see, Rails provides features that make even controller code easy to write.

In Ruby on Rails, the MVC pattern is incorporated into the way the framework makes you write code. There's no better way to demonstrate this than to start looking at a project. In the first part of this chapter, I show you a very simple Rails application to demonstrate the basic concepts. Then, you'll spend the rest of this chapter building a real Rails application, where you'll get hands-on experience with Rails' major technologies.

If you installed Rails as instructed in Chapter 13, you should be ready to begin now; otherwise, go back to Chapter 13 to perform the installation before moving forward.

Your First Rails Application

You'll learn best if you follow along, creating this application step by step. If you're more of a reader, however, I've placed the completed project on the companion website. You'll probably want to get that code anyway so that you'll at least have the images that I'm using.

CROSS-REF
You can find the `todo` project on the website for this book: `www.wileydevreference.com`.

Open Terminal and create a new directory anywhere you like, calling it Rails. Then, move into that directory and execute the following command at the prompt:

```
achilles:Rails aaron$ rails todo
      create
      create   app/controllers
      create   app/helpers
      create   app/models
      ...
      create   log/server.log
      create   log/production.log
      create   log/development.log
      create   log/test.log
```

You see the long list of files being generated by the `rails` script, of which I'm only showing a brief excerpt here. This is the only time you use the `rails` script; it's only used to create a new application. Inside your `Rails` directory, you should find a new directory called `todo`. Open that in your text editor (you are using a text editor, such as TextMate, that can show you directories, right?), and have a look at the file structure, an example of which is shown in Figure 17.1.

There are a lot of files and folders here, but don't be overwhelmed! Most of them are safe to ignore — at least for now. Here are the important ones:

- `app`. This is where you write your program files. As you can see, this folder contains the three main pillars of an MVC application: `models`, `views`, and `controllers`. There's also a `helpers` directory, where you can compartmentalize code that can be used in multiple places.

- `config`. Rails keeps its basic configuration settings here. In the short term, you'll probably only care about the `routes.rb` file, which governs how Rails points URLs to the code in your `app` folder.

- `db`. Every Rails app uses the database to some extent, and this simple demonstration application is no exception. By default, Rails uses a database system called SQLite, which uses SQL syntax to manage data in plain-text files. Those database files are located here. If you instead want to use MySQL as your database, the configuration for that connection will be here. This directory also hosts the *migration files* that build those databases.

Figure 17.1

The Rails file system

Name ▲	Date Modified
▼ app	Today, 10:26 AM
▶ controllers	Today, 10:26 AM
▶ helpers	Today, 10:26 AM
▶ models	Today, 10:26 AM
▶ views	Today, 10:26 AM
▼ config	Today, 10:26 AM
boot.rb	Today, 10:26 AM
database.yml	Today, 10:26 AM
environment.rb	Today, 10:26 AM
▶ environments	Today, 10:26 AM
▶ initializers	Today, 10:26 AM
▶ locales	Today, 10:26 AM
routes.rb	Today, 10:26 AM
▶ db	Today, 10:26 AM
▶ doc	Today, 10:26 AM
▶ lib	Today, 10:26 AM
▶ log	Today, 10:26 AM
▼ public	Today, 10:26 AM
404.html	Today, 10:26 AM
422.html	Today, 10:26 AM
500.html	Today, 10:26 AM
favicon.ico	Today, 10:26 AM
▶ images	Today, 10:26 AM
index.html	Today, 10:26 AM
▶ javascripts	Today, 10:26 AM
robots.txt	Today, 10:26 AM

1 of 33 selected, 132.12 GB available
todo

NOTE

Dr. Richard Hipp, the creator of SQLite, spoke at the C4[2] conference in 2008. During his talk, Dr. Hipp said that SQLite doesn't compete with other relational databases; instead, it competes with C language's `fopen()`. In other words, this technology is ideal for smaller (that is, non-enterprise, massive data sets) applications, where developers might otherwise use something like FasterCSV. You can view this talk at `www.viddler.com/explore/rentzsch/videos/25`.

- `log`. This is where you find the logs that Rails generates for every transaction. Rails comes with three environments set up: development, test, and production. Each environment has its own log, and you'll find those logs critical to your development.

- `public`. You keep all your so-called public resources in this folder. Image, JavaScript, and CSS files all go here.

    ◉ `vendor`. When you want to use third-party add-on software — like how you used FasterCSV and Prawn in the last chapter — you install it here.

There are other directories that I won't go into now, but this gets you started.

Your `todo` application lets you manage lists of things: tasks, groceries, life goals, or whatever. You can create lists, and for each list, you can manage a group of items. You can add list items, mark them as complete, and delete them altogether.

As you go through the steps to develop this application, you'll take it from the perspective of those three major patterns that Rails uses: models, views, and controllers. You'll build each part in turn.

Rails models and migrations

Rails models are in charge of the objects that represent your data. In this application, you have two models: `List` and `Listitem`. Unlike your earlier experience with the Ruby program in Chapter 16, you don't have to laboriously manage the database directly. Rails takes advantage of a technology called ActiveRecord, which provides an opaque layer between the database and your Ruby code; whether your application uses SQLite or MySQL, your coding is the same.

Try this out. The first step to creating a model in Rails is to use the `generate` script. This is located in the `script` folder of your generated Rails application. From Terminal, inside your `todo` directory, you can execute this line, which generates several lines of output:

```
achilles:todo aaron$ script/generate model list
      exists   app/models/
      exists   test/unit/
      exists   test/fixtures/
      create   app/models/list.rb
      create   test/unit/list_test.rb
      create   test/fixtures/lists.yml
      create   db/migrate
      create   db/migrate/20091013175330_create_lists.rb
```

You'll use `generate` again soon, so keep this command in mind. When generating a model, Rails creates a number of files. You're interested in two of them: the `list.rb` file that defines the class and the `[date]_create_lists.rb` file that you're going to use to define the attributes of a list. The `[date]` will be the current date and time, formatted like this: yyyymm ddhhmmss.

Before you continue, generate the model for the `Listitem`:

```
achilles:todo aaron$ script/generate model listitem
```

This provides you with a `listitem.rb` class file and a `[date]_create_listitems.rb` migration file.

NOTE

Remember the Ruby convention of naming a class file in the singular? This practice is carried forward in Rails, where it's even more important. The functioning of the framework relies on your using the correct pluralization with your model objects. Hence, you have a `List` object and a `Listitem` object.

For example, if you open the `list.rb` file that defines your `List` object class, you don't see much:

```
class List < ActiveRecord::Base
end
```

Your class `List` is shown to *inherit* from a parent class called `ActiveRecord::Base`. This means that all the capabilities of the `ActiveRecord` object are available to your class without your writing a single line of code. I'll get to those capabilities in a moment. First, you need to set up a migration.

If you look in the `/db/migrate` directory, you find the two migration files that were created along with your model objects. There's already some code in there, so you need to add the code shown in bold here:

```
class CreateLists < ActiveRecord::Migration
  def self.up
    create_table :lists do |t|
      t.string :listname
      t.timestamps
    end
  end
  def self.down
    drop_table :lists
  end
end
```

This class is responsible for both creating and destroying table definitions in a database. The method `self.up` is run when the class is tasked with creating a table. The method `self.down` is run when the class is tasked with removing the migration. It's good practice to always provide the statements in the `down` method that undo your actions in the `up` method.

There are methods that work to create — and their opposites, which destroy. Table 17-1 shows those methods as well as their syntax.

Table 17-1 Rails Migration Methods

Create	Example	Destroy	Example
add_ column(table_ name, column_ name, type, options)	add_column :lists, :listname, :string	remove_ column(table_ name, column_ name)	remove_column :lists, :listname
create_ table(name, options)	create_table :lists do |t| t.string :listname t.timestamps end	drop_ table(name)	drop_table :lists

The purpose of migrations are to use Ruby code to build your database structure. As your project evolves, you often find yourself with the need to change your database tables and definitions. Migrations, with their date-encoded file names, act like items on a stack, working together as a navigable history of your database's schema. As you continue working with Rails projects, you'll come to appreciate the ability to manage your database without digging into SQL code.

For now, you'll create the migration for the `Listitem` object (new code is in bold):

```
class CreateListitems < ActiveRecord::Migration
  def self.up
    create_table :listitems do |t|
      t.integer :list_id
      t.string :item
      t.string :status_flag
      t.timestamps
    end
  end
  def self.down
    drop_table :listitems
  end
end
```

When you're defining your model's schema, you provide the data type (which corresponds roughly to the data types that SQL uses) and the name of the column as a Ruby symbol. Table 17-2 lists the data types that ActiveRecord makes available and their corresponding values in MySQL, which are used when creating a table.

Table 17-2 ActiveRecord Data Types

ActiveRecord Data Type	MySQL Data Type
:binary	blob
:Boolean	tinyint(1)
:date	date
:datetime	datetime
:decimal	decimal
:float	float
:integer	int(11)
:string	varchar(255)
:text	text
:time	time
:timestamp	datetime

The other line that's already found in any migration file is the `timestamp` command. This is a shorthand command that creates two columns in your table: `created_at` and `updated_at`, both of which are set to a `timestamp` type. These attributes are automatically handled by ActiveRecord as you put records into the database, and you can call on them as you can any other attribute.

Now you're going to activate your migration. In Terminal, ensure that you're still in the `todo` project directory and then run this command:

```
achilles:todo aaron$ rake db:migrate
(in /Users/aaron/Desktop/Rails/todo)
==  CreateLists: migrating ======================================
  ==============
-- create_table(:lists)
   -> 0.0014s
==  CreateLists: migrated (0.0016s) =============================
  ==============
==  CreateListitems: migrating =================================
  ==============
-- create_table(:listitems)
   -> 0.0009s
==  CreateListitems: migrated (0.0010s) ========================
  ==============
```

Rails' `rake` command is used to manage your database migrations, among other things. When run without any arguments, `rake db:migrate` runs all your migration files, ensuring your schema is up to date.

With your database set up, you can now interact with it. But instead of building a web application to do so, you can play with your tables by using a special version of the `irb` console, which is connected to your Rails environment. In Terminal, run this command:

```
achilles:todo aaron$ script/console
Loading development environment (Rails 2.3.4)
>>
```

You're now in a Ruby console that has access to your model objects. This is very powerful, and you'll find yourself relying on the Rails console to test your models. Here's how you create a new `List` record:

```
>> l = List.new
=> #<List id: nil, listname: nil, created_at: nil, updated_at:
   nil>
```

It's like creating an object in Ruby! You get back a reference to the object, with all values set to `nil`. Now you can populate those values:

```
>> l.listname = "Grocery List"
=> "Grocery List"
>> l.save
=> true
>> l.inspect
=> "#<List id: 1, listname: \"Grocery List\", created_at: \"2009-
   10-13 18:50:47\", updated_at: \"2009-10-13 18:50:47\">"
```

For this object, there's only one value. Once you save it and look at your object again, you find the `id` and `timestamp` values automatically filled in.

Just like the regular Ruby object initializer, you can create an object in one line of code:

```
>> l = List.new(:listname => "Dream Jobs")
=> #<List id: nil, listname: "Dream Jobs", created_at: nil,
   updated_at: nil>
>> l.save
=> true
```

You can get data out of the database by using the `find` method. There are many ways to use `find`, with perhaps the easiest way being to find all records:

```
>> List.find(:all)
=> [#<List id: 1, listname: "Grocery List", created_at: "2009-10-
   13 18:50:47", updated_at: "2009-10-13 18:50:47">, #<List id:
   2, listname: "Dream Jobs", created_at: "2009-10-13 18:52:46",
   updated_at: "2009-10-13 18:52:46">]
```

The `find` method returns an array of hashes if there are multiple records. If you're getting back a single record, it's just the hash. `Find` provides the keywords `:last` and `:first`, which can be useful:

```
>> l = List.find(:last)
=> #<List id: 2, listname: "Dream Jobs", created_at: "2009-10-13
   18:52:46", updated_at: "2009-10-13 18:52:46">
```

If you have a single record, you can immediately access its attributes:

```
>> l.listname = "Former Dream Jobs"
=> "Former Dream Jobs"
>> l.save
=> true
>> l.inspect
=> "#<List id: 2, listname: \"Former Dream Jobs\", created_at:
   \"2009-10-13 18:52:46\", updated_at: \"2009-10-13 18:58:05\">"
```

Of course, if you want to iterate through an array of hashes, you can use the `each` method and then run the array through a block, just as you learned in Chapter 16:

```
>> l = List.find(:all)
=> [#<List id: 1, listname: "Grocery List", created_at: "2009-10-
   13 18:50:47", updated_at: "2009-10-13 18:50:47">, #<List id:
   2, listname: "Former Dream Jobs", created_at: "2009-10-13
   18:52:46", updated_at: "2009-10-13 18:58:05">]
>> l.each do |item|
?> puts item.listname
>> end
Grocery List
Former Dream Jobs
```

The `find` method provides a number of other ways to get at your data. ActiveRecord provides dynamic method names for looking up attributes. So, you can look up a record by using its attribute name:

```
>> l = List.find_by_listname("Grocery List")
=> #<List id: 1, listname: "Grocery List", created_at: "2009-10-
   13 18:50:47", updated_at: "2009-10-13 18:50:47">
```

You can also provide conditional statements in the SQL format:

```
>> l = List.find(:all, :conditions=>"id > 1")
=> [#<List id: 2, listname: "Former Dream Jobs", created_at:
   "2009-10-13 18:52:46", updated_at: "2009-10-13 18:58:05">]
```

And if the Rails methods aren't robust enough for you (for example, you want to perform a join statement), then you can run it directly:

```
>> l = List.find_by_sql("select * from lists where id > 1")
=> [#<List id: 2, listname: "Former Dream Jobs", created_at:
    "2009-10-13 18:52:46", updated_at: "2009-10-13 18:58:05">]
```

Defining relationships

In Chapter 16, when you were building the `invoicr` application, you had to keep track of how `Lineitem` objects belonged to their `Invoice` objects. It required you to keep a reference to the `Invoice` object's `id` in the `Lineitems` table (known in database parlance as a *foreign key*) and manually ensure that you had the right `id` number before placing it in the database. Annoying, wouldn't you agree? It would be much better if you could simply define the relationship and then have the framework handle it.

Of course, that's exactly what ActiveRecord does for you. In the class files for the model objects, you can describe the kind of relationship these models have with each other. There are three kinds:

- **One-to-one.** This is where unique objects have a direct and exclusive relationship; for example, one baseball team has one logo.
- **Many-to-one.** This is where many objects belong to a single object; for example, a series of list items belong to a list.
- **Many-to-many.** This is where many objects can be related to many other objects; for example, many actors have roles in many movies, and movies have many actors.

A one-to-one relationship is so rare that I've never defined one in practice. Most relationships are many-to-one, with many-to-many a distant second. And in the latter case, you have to create a join table to connect the instances of each object together.

The terms you would use to define relationships are placed in your model files. They are:

- `belongs_to`
- `has_one`
- `has_many`
- `has_and_belongs_to_many`

Now put these to work in your models. In `list.rb`, change the code so it looks like this (new code is in bold):

```
class List < ActiveRecord::Base
  has_many :listitems
end
```

And in `listitem.rb`, add this code to define the other side of the relationship (new code is in bold):

```
class Listitem < ActiveRecord::Base
  belongs_to :list
end
```

Behind the scenes, ActiveRecord is using the foreign key that you included in the `Listitem` object's migration to tie those objects to a particular list. You can see how this works right away by using the console. At this point, if you're still running the console from your last example, it's usually a good idea to restart the `console` script to ensure that your new relationships are loaded in the application:

```
>> exit
achilles:todo aaron$ script/console
Loading development environment (Rails 2.3.4)
>>
```

You should be able to find your most recent `List` object still saved in the database. You can then assign it to a variable:

```
>> l = List.find(:last)
=> #<List id: 2, listname: "Former Dream Jobs", created_at:
   "2009-10-13 18:52:46", updated_at: "2009-10-13 18:58:05">
```

Now create an item that you can add to the list by using the relationship you just built:

```
>> i = Listitem.new(:item=>"Astronaut", :status_flag=>"open")
=> #<Listitem id: nil, list_id: nil, item: "Astronaut", status_
   flag: "open", created_at: nil, updated_at: nil>
>> i.save
=> true
```

Now for the real test. You're going to assign this `listitem` object to a list by using the assignment operator:

```
>> l.listitems << i
=> [#<Listitem id: 1, list_id: 2, item: "Astronaut", status_flag:
   "open", created_at: "2009-10-16 00:59:22", updated_at: "2009-
   10-16 01:00:15">]
```

The console responds with all the `listitems` that belong to the variable. With ActiveRecord's seemingly magical methods for handling relationships, your objects automatically gain a number of useful methods. For example, if you have a `List` object and you want to know its items, type this command at the prompt:

```
>> l.listitems
=> [#<Listitem id: 1, list_id: 2, item: "Some action", status_
   flag: "open", created_at: "2009-10-16 00:53:49", updated_at:
```

```
"2009-10-16 00:54:29">, #<Listitem id: 2, list_id: 2, item:
"Astronaut", status_flag: "open", created_at: "2009-10-16
00:59:22", updated_at: "2009-10-16 01:00:15">]
```

Or if you have a `Listitem` and you want to know what `List` it belongs to, type this command at the prompt:

```
>> i.list
=> #<List id: 2, listname: "Former Dream Jobs", created_at:
    "2009-10-13 18:52:46", updated_at: "2009-10-13 18:58:05">
```

These are the common methods that you'll use. Here's a list of some more methods that you might find useful:

- `List.listitems << Listitem` assigns a child element to the parent.
- `List.listitems` fetches all child elements.
- `List.listitems = (Listitem1, Listitem2...)` assigns specific child elements.
- `List.listitem_ids` fetches the id value of each child element.
- `List.listitems.size` fetches the number of child elements.
- `List.listitems.clear` disconnects the child elements from the parent.
- `List.listitems.find` allows you to search child elements by using the same format as you would for the regular `find` method.
- `List.listitems.destroy_all` deletes every child element.

This incredibly powerful relationship technology in Rails is a major reason for its rapid development and ease of use. Once you understand how this works, you'll write less code overall and spend more time developing your applications.

Writing the views and controllers

The next important component of a Rails application is the *view*: the HTML and CSS code that presents the interface your users will work with. In Rails, you're using a technology called ERb — embedded Ruby — to implement dynamic behavior in your web pages.

If you recall your work in PHP, then you'll quickly understand ERb. You'll use special tags to delineate your Ruby code, and this code is interpreted and acted upon by the server before being sent back to the client.

But views can't work without *controllers*. These are the files that handle the routing of requests from the client and which generate the data that views use.

Consider this example: You have a controller class called `list` and a method within it named `show`. The user navigates to `yourserver.com/list/show` to see a particular list. That method name maps to a view file called `show.html.erb`, which contains the HTML and ERb code for that request. Now give it a try.

In Terminal, inside your project directory, execute the following command:

```
achilles:todo aaron$ script/generate controller lists
      exists  app/controllers/
      exists  app/helpers/
      create  app/views/lists
      exists  test/functional/
      create  test/unit/helpers/
      create  app/controllers/lists_controller.rb
      create  test/functional/lists_controller_test.rb
      create  app/helpers/lists_helper.rb
      create  test/unit/helpers/lists_helper_test.rb
```

There are two notable items created here: first, a controller class called `lists_controller.rb` in the `app/controllers` folder; and second, a directory at `app/views/lists` for the views related to this controller.

Take a look at `lists_controller.rb`:

```
class ListsController < ApplicationController
end
```

You should be getting used to seeing basic class files by now. While the model classes come with most of their functionality already included, the controller classes require a fair amount of custom coding.

The methods that you add to the controller typically correspond to a page requested in the browser. So, when you think of what you want this application to do, you might come up with such methods as `show`, `create`, and `delete`. Add those method definitions now (new code is in bold):

```
class ListsController < ApplicationController

    layout 'layout'

    def show

    end

    def create

    end

    def delete

    end

end
```

You're also going to add one method call at the top of your controller class; the `layout` method indicates which template is used to render the views in this controller.

Leave this file for now and consider your views. If you recall your examination of PHP, you'll remember how you put a page together by using template functions. You'd call a function to produce the HTML for the `head` of the document, write your code for the `body`, and then call a function for the `footer`.

In Rails, you do the opposite. You write one template file that contains the header and footer, with a place in the middle where you *yield* — that is, hold this spot for — that page's code. This is better done than explained. In the `/app/views/layouts` directory, create a new file called `layout.html.erb`. In this file, place the following code:

```
<!DOCTYPE html PUBLIC "-//W3C//DTD XHTML 1.0 Transitional//EN"
    "http://www.w3.org/TR/xhtml1/DTD/xhtml1-transitional.dtd">
<html xmlns="http://www.w3.org/1999/xhtml" xml:lang="en"
    lang="en">
<head>
    <meta http-equiv="Content-Type" content="text/html;
    charset=utf-8"/>
    <title>ToDo</title>
    <%= stylesheet_link_tag "todo" %>
</head>
<body>
    <div id="wrapper">
        <div id="header"></div>
        <div id="contentarea">
            <%= image_tag("/images/todologo.jpg",
    :alt=>"ToDo", :style=>"margin-left:25px;") %>
            <br style="clear:both" />
            <%= yield -%>

        </div>
        <div id="footer"></div>
    </div>
</body>
</html>
```

This is pretty familiar HTML code, with some new code added. The tags delimited by the `<%` and `%>` are ERb. And just like in PHP, when a `<%` tag includes the equal sign, it's shorthand for `print`. Within this template file, you see some Rails methods that take the place of their HTML ancestors. The first is the `stylesheet_link_tag` method, which produces an HTML `link` tag. The difference here is that the Rails method takes a string as its argument, appends a `.css` to it, and then looks for that file in the `/public/stylesheets` directory of your project. So, create a new file in `/public/stylesheets` called `todo.css` and then type this text:

```
* {
  margin:0px;
```

```
      border:0px;
      padding:0px;
   }
   body {
      background-color: #e1ce48;
   }
   #wrapper {
      width: 900px;
      margin: 0px auto 0px auto;
   }
   #header {
      width: 900px;
      height: 32px;
      background-image: url("/images/page_top.jpg");
   }
   #contentarea {
      width: 900px;
      background-color: #FFF;
   }
   #footer {
      width: 900px;
      height: 32px;
      background-image: url("/images/page_bottom.jpg");
   }
```

Another method you see is the `image_tag` method. This one produces an `img` tag in HTML. All these methods that produce HTML tags are known as *HTML helper methods* and are intended to make it easier to include HTML tags within other Ruby methods.

One last Ruby method that you see here is `yield`. You've seen this already in Chapter 16; `yield` essentially gives way to the calling code. In this case, this is where the contents of the called page will go. You'll get to that now.

Thanks to the generate script you ran, you'll have a new directory: `app/views/lists`. Create a new file there, calling it `show.html.erb`. For now, you'll just place some basic HTML code in this file so you can see how it all works together:

```
<h1>These are the lists</h1>
```

Save this file. Before you start the server for the first time, you'll probably want to get the images for this project, which are included in the finished project that's posted on the companion website at `www.wileydevreference.com`. Add the files to `/public/images`, and you should be ready to start.

In Terminal, within the project directory, issue this command:

```
achilles:todo aaron$ script/server
=> Booting Mongrel
```

```
=> Rails 2.3.4 application starting on http://0.0.0.0:3000
=> Call with -d to detach
=> Ctrl-C to shutdown server
```

The server script launches a small web server called Mongrel. As you can see from the accompanying message, Mongrel launches on port 3000. While you can type the address `http://0.0.0.0:3000` to reach your project, I prefer using `http://localhost:3000`, as it's less awkward to type. In any event, visit either address now. You should see something similar to Figure 17.2.

Figure 17.2

The default Ruby on Rails home page

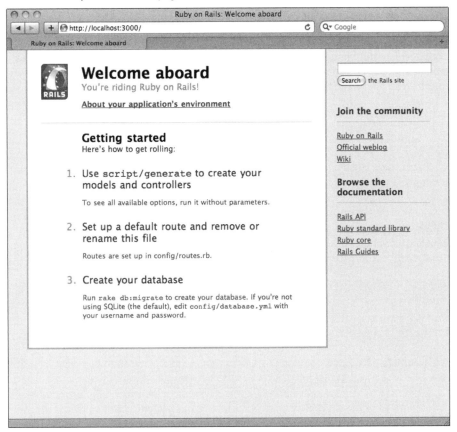

This is the default Ruby on Rails home page, served up from the file `index.html` located in the `/public` directory. If you want your default page to be something else, you need to delete this file, so go ahead and do that now.

Next, you have to set what your default file is going to be. This is done in the file `/config/routes.rb`. If you open it now, you see a lot of commented text, with two uncommented lines at the bottom:

```
map.connect ':controller/:action/:id'
map.connect ':controller/:action/:id.:format'
```

These instructions tell Rails to route requests through a named controller, then to its method, and finally to a method `id`. So, a URL that looks like `http://localhost:3000/lists/show/1` maps to the `lists` controller's `show` method, and it shows the list with an `id` of 1. The second line indicates that a URL can also specify a format; it can be an HTML page, a JavaScript page, plain text, XML, PDF, or another format.

The default setting in the `routes.rb` file is what you want, but you need to use this file to set a default page. Among the commented lines, you'll find what you're after: the `map.root` command. Type this line in the file (indicated by bold text) after the following commented line:

```
# You can have the root of your site routed with map.root -- just
    remember to delete public/index.html.
map.root :controller => "lists", :action => "show"
```

When you save the file, you can reload your browser. You should see your new page, including the template and text, as shown in Figure 17.3.

Figure 17.3

Your first look at the ToDo application

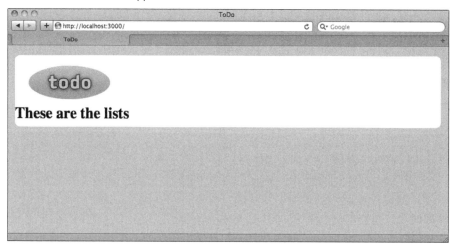

It doesn't look like much, but this should give you an idea of how your views work. You'll keep working on this application to make it more useful.

Go back to your controller at `/app/controllers/lists_controller.rb`. Make the following modification to the code (new code is in bold):

```ruby
def show
    @lists = List.find(:all)
end
```

Here, you're creating an instance variable and assigning to it the result of the `List.find(:all)` method call. This is exactly the same code you were writing earlier in this chapter in the console to learn how to query your models in ActiveRecord. When you create an instance variable in Rails, it becomes available to your views. So, save this file and then go back to the `show.html.erb` file. Delete the existing code and then type this code:

```erb
<div id="leftcolumn">
    <h1>Your lists</h1>
    <ul>
    <% @lists.each do |l| %>
        <li><%= link_to l.listname, :controller=>"lists",
    :action=>"show", :id=>l.id %></li>
    <% end %>
    </ul>
</div>
<div id="rightcolumn">
</div>
<br style="clear:both" />
```

I'll leave aside the discussion of the HTML code here; you should be an expert after having read Chapter 4. Instead, I'll pay attention to the ERb code. The first line simply puts the contents of the variable `@lists` through a block by using the `each` method that you learned about in Chapter 16. So, the code between this line and the `<% end %>` tags is run for every record in the array.

The only action you perform is to display each list by using an unordered list tag. For each item, you use a Rails HTML helper called `link_to`. For its arguments, it takes the displayed name of the link and the destination (or, in HTML lingo, the `href`). The `link_to` function is useful because it allows you to provide an explicit link to a controller and action; here, you're providing the same controller that you're inside of now as well as the same action. In effect, you're using this link to reload the page but with a particular list selected.

Before you check your work, you should add the CSS styles for this new page. In the `todo.css` file, add these styles:

```css
p, ul, ol, h1, h2, h3 {
    font-family: "Trebuchet MS", Helvetica, Arial, sans-serif;
}
h1 {
```

```
        font-size: 22px;
        border-bottom: 1px solid #999;
        width: 90%;
    }
    #leftcolumn {
        float: left;
        margin-left: 35px;
        width: 220px;
        padding: 0px 15px 0px 15px;
        border-right: 2px dotted #cfcfcf;
    }
    #contentarea ul {
        list-style-type: none;

    }
    #contentarea ul li {
        line-height: 170%;
        border-bottom: 1px solid #EEE;
        margin-top: 3px;
        width: 90%;
    }
    #rightcolumn {
        float: right;
        width: 550px;
    }
```

Try it out now: Save the file and then reload your browser page. You should see something similar to Figure 17.4.

Figure 17.4

Displaying your lists

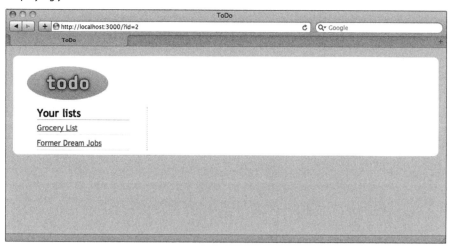

The lists you added should appear on the left side of the page. Now, go back to the controller to provide a means for the list items to be displayed. Modify the `show` method so it looks like this (new code is in bold):

```
def show
   @lists = List.find(:all)

   if params[:id]
      @list = List.find(params[:id])
   end
end
```

Just as in PHP, Rails receives its arguments through the `params` array. All you have to do is pull the desired value out of the array. In this case, you're first checking to see if the array value exists. If so, then you know that a link has been clicked on the main page, and you'll use that `id` parameter to find the list in question.

Save the file and then return to the `show.html.erb` file. Now add some content to the right column (new code is in bold):

```
<div id="rightcolumn">
   <% if @list %>
   <h1><%= @list.listname %></h1>
   <ul>
      <% @list.listitems.each do |li| %>
         <li><%= li.item %></li>
      <% end %>
   </ul>
   <% end %>
</div>
```

Again, in this code, you first check that the `@list` variable exists. If so, you do exactly the same thing that you did for the list of lists. Save and refresh your browser, and you should see something similar to Figure 17.5.

Figure 17.5

Displaying your lists, now with list items

Adding the remaining features

You've now demonstrated the ability to display list items within your web interface. Great! But it's still quite useless. You need to provide the ability to add and delete both list items and lists. Recode that left column to provide the ability to add and remove lists (new code is in bold):

```
<h1>Your lists</h1>
   <ul>
   <% @lists.each do |l| %>
      <li><%= link_to l.listname, :controller=>"lists",
   :action=>"show", :id=>l.id %>
         <%= link_to image_tag("/images/delete.jpg",
   :class=>"delete_box"), {:controller=>"lists", :action=>"list_
   delete", :id=>l.id}, :confirm=>"Are you sure you want to
   delete this?" %>
         </li>
   <% end %>
   </ul>
   <%= form_tag("/lists/list_create") %>
         <%= text_field_tag :listname, nil, :size=>"22" %> <%=
   submit_tag("New") %>
   </form>
```

The first thing you're doing is adding an image link to a controller action that deletes that list. To do that, you're combining two Rails methods in one line: `link_to` inserts an `image_tag` method as its link text argument. You can also add a special `confirm` attribute that ensures that the user needs to click a confirmation button before the action proceeds.

To create a new list, you use another Rails method called `form_tag`. It takes a file path to the method that will do the processing (in HTML parlance, the contents of the `action` attribute in a `form` tag). Inside the form, you have a single text field — again, using another helper method called `text_field_tag`. This one takes three arguments: the name of the field, its value (you pass `nil` so it has no value), and any HTML attributes you'd like to add. Add in a call to `submit_tag` with the value of the button, and you're done.

I added a couple more CSS declarations to support this HTML; go ahead and add these to your style sheet:

```css
.delete_box {
    float:right;
}
form {
    margin-top: 5px;
}
input {
    border: 1px solid #000;
    padding: 3px;
}
```

Now what happens when you choose to delete or create a list? You'll have to create two new methods in your lists controller to handle them. In `lists_controller.rb`, add this code:

```ruby
def list_create
  l = List.new(:listname=>params[:listname])
  l.save

  redirect_to :action=>"show", :id=>l.id
end

def list_delete
  l = List.find(params[:id])
  l.delete

  redirect_to :action=>"show"
end
```

There's nothing terribly complicated about these methods, but you should pay close attention to where the values that feed them come from. The `params` array passes in the values, and you can feed it directly to the call to `List.new`. This is exactly how you learned to create a new class instance in Chapter 16 and how you worked with ActiveRecord earlier in this chapter.

But then, having saved your new list, you do something new: a call to the method `redirect_to`. Normally, a Rails controller method automatically loads the view that corresponds to the method's name — the `show` method will load a view called `show.html.erb`. But in this case, you just want the method to do some work and then reload the `show` view. By supplying `redirect_to` with the proper action and list `id`, you can accomplish that.

There — your list management is complete. Reload the page to try it out; you should see something similar to Figure 17.6.

Figure 17.6

Add and delete lists

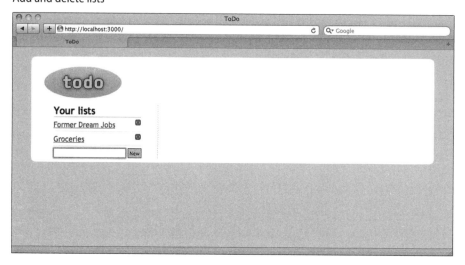

Now finish by giving the list items the same treatment. In the `show.html.erb` file, modify the content in the right column (new code is in bold):

```
<div id="rightcolumn">
<% if @list %>
   <h1><%= @list.listname %></h1>

   <% form_for :listitems, :url=>{:controller=>"lists",
   :action=>"create"} do |l| %>
        <%= hidden_field_tag :list, @list.id %>
        <%= l.text_field :item, :size=>"65", :id=>"listitem_
   input" %> <%= submit_tag("New") %>
   <% end %>
   <ul>
        <% @list.listitems.each do |li| %>
        <% if li.status_flag == "completed" %>
                <li><%= link_to image_tag("/images/checked.jpg"),
   :controller=>"lists", :action=>"edit", :id=>li.id %> <%= li.
   item %>
        <% else %>
                <li><%= link_to image_tag("/images/unchecked.
   jpg"), :controller=>"lists", :action=>"edit", :id=>li.id %>
   <%= li.item %>
```

```
        <% end %>
        <%= link_to image_tag("/images/delete.jpg",
  :class=>"delete_box"), {:controller=>"lists",
  :action=>"delete", :id=>li.id}, :confirm=>"Are you sure you
  want to delete this?" %></li>
      <% end %>
    </ul>
  <% end %>
  </div>
```

The new code accomplishes two tasks: It allows the user to enter a new list item, and it displays the current list's items along with the ability to both mark them as complete and delete them.

In the first example, you're using a `form_for` method to create a `form` tag. Why not the `form_tag` method that you used in the other example? Mainly to show you that there are two ways to create a form. In fact, Rails provides two groups of form helpers: one for forms that deal specifically with your instances of model classes and one for those that require a little more adjustment (or what I like to call manual intervention).

The `form_for` tag creates a form tied to the specified model class. So, this form is a `form_for` the `Listitem` object, and it contains a text field named `listitem` — the same name as the attribute in your object. When you submit this form to the controller method `create`, you can simply pass the object to the `Listitem.new` method, and Rails takes care of the rest.

Now I'll talk about the list items. You want to create a separate image for checked and unchecked states, so the first thing you do is create an `if` statement for each item in the list. If the state of the item is open, you'll show an unchecked box; otherwise, you'll show a checked box. In both cases, the image is a link to the `edit` controller method, which toggles the state of the item one way or the other.

Finally, you have one more image, which when clicked will delete the list item. This feature is implemented in the same way that you did the `delete` method for the main list objects.

Now go back to the `lists_controller.rb` file to add support for these new actions (new code is in bold):

```
def create
  li = Listitem.new(params[:listitems])
  li.list = List.find(params[:list])
  li.save

  redirect_to :action=>"show", :id=>params[:list]
end
def delete
  li = Listitem.find(params[:id])
  parent = li.list.id
  li.delete

  redirect_to :action=>"show", :id=>parent
```

```
  end
def edit
  li = Listitem.find(params[:id])
  parent = li.list.id
  if li.status_flag == "open"
    li.status_flag = "completed"
  else
    li.status_flag = "open"
  end
  li.save

    redirect_to :action=>"show", :id=>parent
end
```

In the `create` method, you can see how using the model-based form helpers makes life a bit easier; just pass in the `listitems` params array, and your `listitem` object is created automatically based on what's in that array. In this case, you're only supplying the `itemname`. Then, of course, you need to tie it to the list it belongs to. The list item's `list` attribute performs this task; you just supply the list `id`, which is provided by the hidden field in the form in your view.

The other methods are pretty straightforward. In each case, you want to return to the same list that you're editing, so you derive the `id` number of the list from the list item and then place it in a variable called `parent`.

Save your controller file and then reload your page, which should look similar to Figure 17.7. You should be able to add and remove lists, and individual list items should also be editable.

Figure 17.7

The completed application

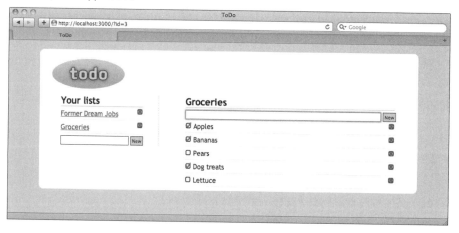

This is a complete, functional Rails application. Congratulations! Now that you've built a Rails application, you're going to do it again — this time with a more ambitious goal. I'm hoping that by seeing a couple of apps in development, you'll become more comfortable working with Rails.

Digging Deeper: Introducing the Pipeline Application

It's fair to say that the success of Ruby on Rails owes a lot to its ability to wow developers during demonstrations. In very short order, you can build a very functional application. There's a demonstration video on the Ruby on Rails website (`http://rubyonrails.org/`) that shows how to build a simple blog application in 15 minutes. And given your exposure to the previous list application, you can see that there's not a lot of code to write.

However, there's a big difference between putting together a quick demonstration app and building a long-term, maintainable web application. Fortunately, Rails also excels here — just not in as demonstrable a way.

For the rest of this chapter, you'll look at a larger application called Pipeline (see Figure 17.8). Pipeline is intended for single developers who are managing their own businesses. With Pipeline, you can determine the health of your business in a single view by showing the three pillars of your business — your accounts receivable (past work), your current jobs and tasks (current work), and your estimates for pending jobs (future work) — all in one place.

If you were thinking that there might have been some hints about Pipeline in earlier parts of this book, you'd be right. The invoicing application you wrote in Chapter 16 and the list manager you wrote earlier in this chapter will both contribute code to the Pipeline project. In fact, that's part of the point; if you do your job right, the Model-View-Controller design pattern will yield highly reusable code.

As with the list project that you just finished, you can find the completed Pipeline project on the companion website. While I highly encourage you to write this code yourself as I lay it out for you, I'm only going to cover the foundations: the models, data migrations, and initial home page view. After that, I'll only be touching on the major features of the rest of the application to demonstrate particular techniques.

CROSS-REF

You can find the `pipeline` project on the website for this book: `www.wileydevreference.com`.

If you do choose to start with an empty project, you'll want to take a couple of pieces from the completed application: the images and the CSS file. Feel free to simply copy those resources into your project.

Figure 17.8

The Pipeline main Dashboard

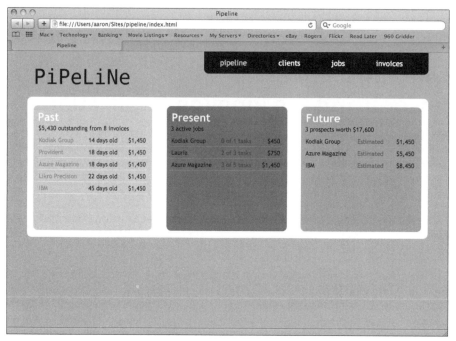

I'll start by enumerating the features of Pipeline:

- Using an `Invoice` model, you can manage invoices to your customers. The dashboard will show your invoices, ordered by date, along with the amount owed for each, the time since being sent, and the total amount owed (your accounts-receivable balance). You'll build on the previous invoicing application that you created in Chapter 16, with the addition of a separate `Tax` object, which will make your taxation situation more flexible.

- Using a `Job` model, you'll manage individual jobs, which will possess one or more `Task` model objects — think of the `List` and `Listitem` objects from earlier in this chapter. Your dashboard will show tasks completed and pending as well as the dollar value of each job.

- You can attach `Estimate` model objects to the `Job` model objects in order to both establish a dollar value for a future job and initialize a job in the system. In the `Job` model, you can set whether the job is pending (that is, it will appear in the Future column of the dashboard) or active (appearing in the Present column). I prefer to have all jobs go from Future to Present, but alas, that isn't always the case.

- Overarching all these models is the `Client` model, which takes its deserved place above the others. Every object depends on its attachment to a client. You'll also have the ability to manage separate contacts at a given client's company, so you'll also have a `Contact` model object.

The reason the application is called Pipeline should be clear now: You can see the entire life cycle of every job you do, and you have one place to keep track of it all.

Building the model objects

I always start a Rails application by building the model objects. The database is the spine of any application, so understanding the data that you need from the outset will make your life easier as you write.

Figure 17.9 shows a map of the relationship between your models. This map shows the fields that you'll be defining as well as the relationships between them. Take some time to study the map and become familiar with these objects.

NOTE

This map was generated with a Ruby utility called RailRoad (`http://railroad.rubyforge.org`); when the script is run in your Rails directory, it generates a diagram of your models, as you can see in Figure 17.9. The script isn't perfect, but the generated file is actually a text configuration that can be revised before using the open-source Graphviz utility (`www.graphviz.org`) to convert it to a PNG or PDF file.

One of the values of this project is in the variety of relationships between the models. In the last sample project, you only used the most-common relationship: the one-to-many. Here, you're taking advantage of the other two types: the one-to-one and the many-to-many. I'll explain them as you come across them.

First, you'll need to use Rails' `generate` script to create your models. I'll just include the commands in Terminal, omitting the output:

```
Achilles:pipeline aaron$ script/generate model Client
Achilles:pipeline aaron$ script/generate model Contact
Achilles:pipeline aaron$ script/generate model Job
Achilles:pipeline aaron$ script/generate model Estimate
Achilles:pipeline aaron$ script/generate model Task
Achilles:pipeline aaron$ script/generate model Invoice
Achilles:pipeline aaron$ script/generate model Invoiceitem
Achilles:pipeline aaron$ script/generate model Tax
```

Figure 17.9

Pipeline's model object map

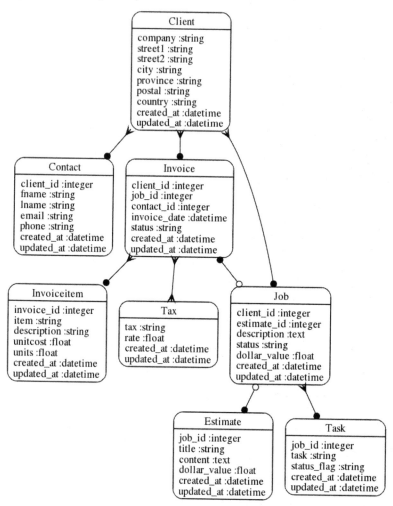

In your `/app/models` folder, you'll find these eight model files. You'll also find their migration files in the `/app/db/migrate` folder. You'll start by setting up your tables in the migration files. For each file, I'll show you the contents of the `self.up` method; simply complete each migration with the code here.

For the `Client` model:

```
create_table :clients do |t|
  t.string :company
  t.string :street1
  t.string :street2
  t.string :city
  t.string :province
  t.string :postal
  t.string :country
  t.timestamps
end
```

For the `Contact` model:

```
create_table :contacts do |t|
  t.references :client
  t.string :fname
  t.string :lname
  t.string :email
  t.string :phone
  t.timestamps
end
```

For the `Job` model:

```
create_table :jobs do |t|
  t.references :client
  t.references :estimate
  t.text :description
  t.string :status # "proposed" || "active" || "completed" ||
   "limbo"
  t.float :dollar_value
  t.timestamps
end
```

For the `Estimate` model:

```
create_table :estimates do |t|
  t.references :job
  t.string :title
  t.text :content
  t.float :dollar_value
  t.timestamps
end
```

For the `Task` model:

```
create_table :tasks do |t|
  t.references :job
  t.string :task
  t.string :status_flag # "open" || "completed"
  t.timestamps
end
```

For the `Invoice` model:

```
create_table :invoices do |t|
  t.references :client
  t.references :contact
  t.references :job
  t.datetime :invoice_date
  t.string :status # "pending" || "paid"
  t.timestamps
end
```

For the `Invoiceitem` model:

```
create_table :invoiceitems do |t|
  t.references :invoice
  t.string :item
  t.string :description
  t.float :unitcost
  t.float :units
  t.timestamps
end
```

And, finally, for the `Tax` model:

```
create_table :taxes do |t|
  t.string :tax
  t.float :rate
  t.timestamps
end
```

Much of what you see here should be familiar to you from the last exercise. However, there's one new method that's used here. The `references` method is used to help create an association between objects. Consider a one-to-many relationship, such as between a `Client` and a `Contact`. Because a `Client` might contain many `Contacts`, each individual `Contact` must have a way to tell what the `Client` record is. This is done, as explained earlier, by using a foreign key. In the last exercise, I created that association field manually by using a field name like `client_id` and an `integer` data type.

ActiveRecord provides a quick way to do that. By saying that `Contact` references `Client`, it automatically generates the proper foreign key field. So, if you're more comfortable seeing the foreign key spelled out, you now know that you can do it both ways.

Once you've saved these files, you can run the `rake` utility to migrate these files into your database (I'm omitting the output again for the sake of brevity):

```
achilles:pipeline aaron$ rake db:migrate
```

With the migrations complete, you can now visit your model object files and set up their relationships.

In `client.rb`:

```
class Client < ActiveRecord::Base
  has_many :invoices
  has_many :jobs
  has_many :contacts
end
```

In `contact.rb`:

```
class Contact < ActiveRecord::Base
  belongs_to :client
end
```

In `job.rb`:

```
class Job < ActiveRecord::Base
  belongs_to :client
  has_many :tasks
  has_one :estimate
end
```

In `estimate.rb`:

```
class Estimate < ActiveRecord::Base
  belongs_to :job
end
```

In `task.rb`:

```
class Task < ActiveRecord::Base
  belongs_to :job
end
```

In `invoice.rb`:

```
class Invoice < ActiveRecord::Base
  belongs_to :client
  belongs_to :contact
  belongs_to :job
  has_many :invoiceitems
  has_and_belongs_to_many :tax
end
```

In `invoiceitem.rb`:

```
class Invoiceitem < ActiveRecord::Base
  belongs_to :invoice
end
```

And in `tax.rb`:

```
class Tax < ActiveRecord::Base
  has_and_belongs_to_many :invoices
end
```

You'll notice two associations that you haven't seen before: the one-to-one and the many-to-many. For the relation between `Job` and `Estimate` objects, you know that a `Job` will only ever have one `Estimate`, so you use the method `has_one` for the `Job` model. On the other side, the `Estimate` model will use `belongs_to` to associate with the `Job`. Remember that both sides in every association must respond to the other; for example, every `belongs_to` is matched by `has_one` or `has_many`.

The other relationship is the most complex kind, so it's worth dwelling on. Your `Invoice` and `Tax` models are at issue here; for any given invoice, you'll allow the use of multiple taxes. On the other side, any given tax may be used in any number of invoices. This is a classic many-to-many situation.

In the many-to-one relationship, you create a foreign key to track the relationship. But in a many-to-many relationship, you actually need to create a separate database table to keep track of the joins. The table is named after the two models being tracked, in alphabetical order. In this case, your table is called `invoices_taxes`. This table contains just two fields: an `invoice_id` and a `tax_id`. You can create it by setting up a new migration by using the `generate` script:

```
achilles:pipeline aaron$ script/generate migration invoices_taxes
```

A migration simply creates a file in the `/db/migrate` folder. Go there now to supply the specifications on your new database table. Here's the complete file (new code is in bold):

```
class InvoicesTaxes < ActiveRecord::Migration
  def self.up
    create_table :invoices_taxes, :id=>false do |t|
      t.integer :invoice_id
      t.integer :tax_id
    end
  end
  def self.down
    drop_table :invoices_taxes
  end
end
```

You're passing an option to the `create_table` method; the `:id=>false` option ensures that this table won't have a primary key, which would otherwise be created automatically by Rails. Now you can return to the command line to rerun your `rake` migration:

```
achilles:pipeline aaron$ rake db:migrate
```

Your new database table is now created, providing you with a functional many-to-many model relationship.

Testing your work

At this point, it's usually an excellent idea to ensure that your models work as expected. What better place to do that than in the Rails console? You have a ready-made environment for working with your models. You'll now work on these objects in discrete units. First, you'll create a client and a contact and then tie them together. In the console, type the following:

```
>> c1 = Client.create(:company=>"Awesome Inc.", :street1=>"12
   Main St.", :city=>"Toronto", :province=>"ON", :postal=>"L0L
   0L0", :country=>"Canada")
>> con1 = Contact.create(:fname=>"Dean", :lname=>"Machine",
   :email=>"themachine@awesomeinc.com", :phone=>"939.333.3333")
>> c1.contacts << con1
```

Here, you create a client and a contact. With the assignment statement (<< to add one or more objects), they become connected. Now, if you have a client object, you can find out the available contacts by executing a simple method:

```
>> c1.contacts
=> [#<Contact id: 2, client_id: 2, fname: "Dean", lname:
   "Machine", email: "themachine@awesomeinc.com", phone:
   "939.333.3333", created_at: "2009-10-23 03:48:56", updated_at:
   "2009-10-23 03:51:14">]
```

Now you'll work with a `Job` object:

```
>> j1 = Job.create(:description=>"New website for Awesome Inc.",
   :status=>"proposed", :dollar_value=>"3500")
> est1 = Estimate.create(:title=>"Awesome Inc. Website",
   :content=>"Insert long-winded client proposal here...",
   :dollar_value=>"4300")
>> j1.estimate = est1
```

In this case, an `Estimate` object has a one-to-one relationship with a `Job` object, so you can simply assign the new estimate instance to the job. The `Job` object also has ties to the `Task` model, so you'll practice with that now:

```
>> t1 = Task.create(:task=>"Scope new site functionality",
   :status_flag=>"open")
```

```
>> t2 = Task.create(:task=>"Create graphical site mockup",
   :status_flag=>"open")
>> j1.tasks << t1
>> j1.tasks << t2
```

This should look pretty familiar. You can guess that a call to `j1.tasks` would reveal an array of all the tasks.

Finally, you'll work on the `Invoice` object:

```
>> i1 = Invoice.create(:invoice_date=>"2009-10-21",
   :status=>"pending")
>> i1.client = c1
>> i1.job = j1
>> i1.contact = con1
```

The `Invoice` object does very little on its own; instead, it relies on relationships with a client, a job, and a contact. So, you'll associate this invoice with the other model instances that you've already created. Then, you can add some information to the invoice:

```
>> item1 = Invoiceitem.create(:item=>"Web development",
   :description=>"Site development for Awesomeinc.com",
   :unitcost=>"85", :units=>"45")
>> i1.invoiceitems << item1
```

And you can finish by defining and including a tax:

```
>> gst = Tax.create(:tax=>"GST", :rate=>"5.0")
>> i1.tax << gst
```

If you've made it this far, then you've got some solid assurance that your data model is working just as you want it to. Well done!

But that was a lot of work, wasn't it? What happens if, down the road, you want to change the data model? You'll have to go through this whole exercise again, making sure that everything works together. As it does with most elements of web development, Rails foresees this issue and has a very elegant solution. *Unit testing* is a technique that isolates individual components of your application and automatically tests them against assertions that you set up in advance. So, whenever a change happens to your application, you can simply run a test, which gives you instant feedback on whether your code still works. Unit testing is outside the scope of this book, but there are plenty of great resources online; check Appendix B for details.

Setting up the views and controllers

Now that you have a working set of models, you can turn your attention to the views and controllers that provide access to your data. And thanks to your suite of tests on the data models, you now have some actual data to display!

This round of work on the application will give you a working home page (as shown in Figure 17.8). I won't go into much detail in areas I've already covered in the first example, but doing this exercise again will help solidify the knowledge that you've already been exposed to.

To begin, you're going to create a controller for the home page. You're going to call this the Home controller, and you're also going to make it the root controller; that is, when you type the domain name of the application, this is where you'll go.

You already know how to create a controller. Inside your project directory, execute the generate script:

```
achilles:pipeline aaron$ script/generate controller home
```

With that done, open the /config/routes.rb file to set the map.root path to this controller:

```
map.root :controller => "home"
```

Now turn your attention to the controller. Open /app/controllers/home_controller.rb and make the file look like this (new code is in bold):

```
class HomeController < ApplicationController
  layout 'layout'

  def index
    @current = "home"
    @invoices = Invoice.find_all_by_status("pending")
    @jobs = Job.find_all_by_status("active")

    prejobs = Job.find_all_by_status("proposed")
    @estimates = prejobs.collect { |j| j.estimate }
  end

end
```

The layout method should be familiar to you, and you'll create that template next. But take note of the creation of an instance variable called @current. You're going to use that variable in your template file to help you set up the navigation, so remember that you did this.

The rest of the index method gathers up data from your models, which you'll use on the home page. As you cover them in the view, you'll see how these values prove useful.

In the /app/views/layouts folder, create a new file called layout.html.erb. Here's your template file:

```
<!DOCTYPE html PUBLIC "-//W3C//DTD XHTML 1.0 Transitional//EN"
   "http://www.w3.org/TR/xhtml1/DTD/xhtml1-transitional.dtd">
<html xmlns="http://www.w3.org/1999/xhtml" xml:lang="en"
   lang="en">
```

```
<head>
  <meta http-equiv="Content-Type" content="text/html;
  charset=utf-8"/>
  <title>Pipeline</title>
  <%= stylesheet_link_tag "pipeline" %>
  <%= javascript_include_tag :defaults %>
</head>
<body onload="activate_current('<%=@current%>')">
  <div id="wrapper">
    <div id="header">
      <div id="navbar">
        <ul>
          <li><%= link_to "pipeline", {:controller=>"home",
  :action=>"index"}, :id=>"nav_home" %></li>
          <li><%= link_to "clients", {:controller=>"clients",
  :action=>"index"}, :id=>"nav_clients" %></li>
          <li><%= link_to "jobs", {:controller=>"jobs",
  :action=>"index"}, :id=>"nav_jobs" %></li>
          <li class="last"><%= link_to "invoices",
  {:controller=>"invoices", :action=>"index"}, :id=>"nav_
  invoices" %></li>
        </ul>
      </div>
    </div>
    <div id="contentarea">

      <%= yield -%>

    </div>
    <div id="footer">

    </div>
  </div>
</body>
</html>
```

Do you remember the @current instance variable? You saw it in use in the layout.html.
erb file. As you can see when you load the page, the navigation highlights the currently
selected section. This is an example of a commonly used technique in Rails: to apply some cus-
tomization to a template file that's used for every page on the site. By assigning the value of a
variable in the controller, you can influence behavior in the layout.

You do this by setting the argument of a JavaScript function to the @current page. That function, activate_current(), is called in the <body> tag's onload event. In Rails, there's

a JavaScript file automatically included in the page called `/public/javascripts/`
`application.js`, thanks to this tag in the `<head>` of your layout:

```
<%= javascript_include_tag :defaults %>
```

This tag also includes the Scriptaculous and Prototype libraries (both of which are discussed in
Chapter 6).

Let's edit the `application.js` file now, placing this code at the top. The function is pretty
simple:

```
function activate_current(current) {
    $("nav_"+current).className = "active";
}
```

As you can see, this simple script takes advantage of Prototype's `$()` function to grab the
required page element and change its class.

You also have a CSS file, but it's too long to print here. Instead, go to the companion website for
this book and grab the finished project. You'll find the file at `/public/stylesheets/`
`pipeline.css`; just copy that file over to your project.

CROSS-REF
You can find the `pipeline` project on the website for this book: `www.wileydevreference.com`.

You'll notice the images referenced in this CSS file; they're also included in the final website
project, so make sure you've copied them into the `/public/images` folder.

Next, you'll need to create the index file for the controller. In the `/app/views/home` folder,
create the file `index.html.erb`.

At this point, you can test the controller and your template. In Terminal, start the web server by
typing this command:

```
achilles:pipeline aaron$ script/server
=> Booting Mongrel
=> Rails 2.3.4 application starting on http://0.0.0.0:3000
=> Call with -d to detach
=> Ctrl-C to shutdown server
```

Then, go to your web browser to load the site. It should look similar to Figure 17.10.

Figure 17.10

The Pipeline template

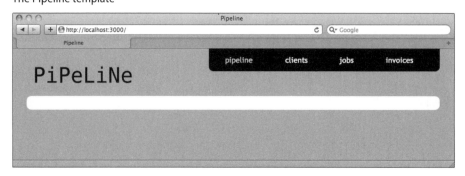

As a last step, you'll create the content that appears on the home page of the site. Open up /app/view/home/index.html.erb and then type this code:

```
<div class="home_box" id="past">
  <div class="title"></div>
    <div class="body">
      <p><%= number_to_currency(Invoice.all_owing)%> outstanding
  from <%= @invoices.size%> invoice<%= "s" if @invoices.size > 1
  %></p>
      <table>
        <% if @invoices %>
          <% @invoices.each do |i| %>
            <tr>
              <td><%= link_to i.client.company,
  :controller=>"invoices", :action=>"show", :id=>i.id %></a></td>
              <td><%= distance_of_time_in_words(Time.now - i.
  invoice_date)%></td>
              <td class="money"><%= number_to_currency(i.invoice_
  total)%></td>
            </tr>
            <% end %>
          <% end %>
      </table>
    </div>
    <div class="foot"></div>
  </div>

  <div class="home_box" id="present">
    <div class="title"></div>
      <div class="body">
        <p><%= number_to_currency(Job.active_total)%> pending
  on <%= @jobs.size %> active job<%= "s" if @jobs.size > 1 %></p>
```

```
      <table>
      <% if @jobs %>
        <% @jobs.each do |j| %>
          <% complete = j.tasks.find_all_by_status_
flag("completed") %>
          <% num_complete = complete.size.nil? ? 0 :
complete.size %>
          <% task_text =  num_complete.to_s + " of " + j.
tasks.size.to_s %>
        <tr>
          <td><%= link_to j.client.company,
:controller=>"jobs", :action=>"show", :id=>j.id %></td>
          <td><%= link_to task_text, :controller=>"jobs",
:action=>"tasks", :id=>j.id %></td>
          <td class="money"><%= number_to_currency(j.dollar_
value)%></td>
        </tr>
        <% end %>
      <% end %>
    </table>
  </div>
  <div class="foot"></div>
 </div>

 <div class="home_box" id="future">
   <div class="title"></div>
     <div class="body">
       <p><%= number_to_currency(Job.estimate_value)%>
potential from <%= Job.estimates.size unless Job.estimates.
size.nil? %> prospect<%= "s" if Job.estimates.size > 1 %></p>
       <table>
       <% if @estimates %>
         <% @estimates.each do |e| %>
         <tr>
           <td><%= e.job.client.company %></td>
           <td><%= link_to "Estimate", :controller=>"jobs",
:action=>"estimate", :id=>e.id %></a></td>
           <td class="money"><%= number_to_currency(e.dollar_
value)%></td>
         </tr>
         <% end %>
       <% end %>
     </table>
   </div>
   <div class="foot"></div>
 </div>
 <br style="clear:both" />
```

As you may recall, the page is divided into three separate areas: the Past, which displays invoices; the Present, which displays active jobs; and the Future, which displays estimates for pending jobs. For each box, you're going to provide a sentence that summarizes the content and then you'll list it.

There's a lot going on in this file, so you'll work on it one piece at a time, beginning with the Invoices section. The first step you want to take is to display a summary sentence: There are X number of dollars outstanding from Y number of invoices.

Determining the number of invoices is simple enough: In your controller, you simply use the `find` method to get all invoices that have a status of pending, and the `size` method returns the number. But getting the total value of the invoices requires a bit more work. For this, it makes sense to turn to a class method. You'll remember those from Chapter 16, where you learned that a class method acts on all instances of a class. What's true in Ruby can also be put to work in Rails, so creating that method means you'll go to the file `/app/models/invoice.rb`. Therein, add this method:

```
def Invoice.all_owing
  i = Invoice.find_all_by_status("pending")
  total = 0
  i.each do |inv|
    total += inv.invoice_total
  end
  return total
end
```

This method finds all pending invoices and iterates through them, adding their `invoice_total` values to the `total` variable.

Wait, did I say `invoice_total`? That's not an attribute of your Invoice model! How could it be? After all, invoices by themselves don't know what their items are. For that, you need to assemble their line items as well as taxes. So, `invoice_total` is, in fact, a method you'll write to do that for a given invoice. Below the `all_owing` class method, add this one:

```
def invoice_total
  i = Invoice.find(self)
  subtotal = 0
  taxes = 0
  # add up the total of all line items
  i.invoiceitems.collect { |ii| subtotal += ii.unitcost * ii.
    units }
  # add up the taxes
  i.tax.collect { |t| taxes += subtotal * (t.rate / 100) }
  total = taxes + subtotal
  return total
end
```

The call to `Invoice.find` passes in the current instance of `invoice`; hence, the use of the keyword `self`. This method first uses the iteration method `collect` to run through all the invoice's invoice items by using the relationship that you build between the models. For each item, you add to the `subtotal` the number of units multiplied by the unit price. Once out of the loop, your `subtotal` variable should have the sum of all the line items. Then, you do the same with the taxes; for each tax related to this invoice, you derive the total amount and add it to a `taxes` variable. Finally, you return the sum of the taxes and subtotal.

Now, back to your view. You're going to iterate through the `@estimates` hash, and for each item in the collection, you'll show the company name, the time since it was created, and the amount owed.

The first task is done thanks to ActiveRecord's relationships, pulling in the associated client to the estimate and then accessing its company name attribute. You're also making this text a link to the invoice detail page, which I cover later.

The time elapsed text is useful to have, and Rails provides a brilliant method to show how long it's been since you've sent that invoice. The method `distance_of_time_in_words` takes a `Time` object, which you supply as the difference between now and the invoice date.

For the last column, you'll use another useful method that converts a number into a dollar amount, called `number_to_currency`. You simply supply the `invoice_total` method, which you've already seen.

Now you'll move on to the list of current jobs. The summary line in this box has another need for a class method: You want the total value of all active jobs. So, you need to write that method in the `/app/models/job.rb` file:

```
def Job.active_total
  jobs = Job.find_all_by_status("active")
  total = 0
  jobs.collect { |j| total += j.dollar_value }
  return total
end
```

The structure of this method is very similar to the `Invoice.all_owing` method you wrote earlier.

For each active job, you want to show the company name, the status of the tasks, and the dollar value. Again, you can use the relationship methods to give you the company name of the job's client, and you'll make that a link to the job detail page, which you'll work on later.

The tasks present a more complicated challenge. You have to determine both the total number of tasks and those that are complete for each job. So, at the beginning of each loop through the `@jobs` hash, you do a few calculations. Here are those lines again for your reference:

```
<% complete = j.tasks.find_all_by_status_flag("completed") %>
<% num_complete = complete.size.nil? ? 0 : complete.size %>
<% task_text = num_complete.to_s + " of " + j.tasks.size.to_s %>
```

First, you use the job's relationship with its tasks to pull all completed items. Then, you want to get the number of completed jobs; but if none are completed, your call to the `size` method will return `nil` instead of zero. Therefore, you use a ternary statement to check the `size` of your result. If it's `nil`, you'll set the `num_complete` variable to zero; otherwise, you'll just use the `size`. Finally, you'll put together the complete text string for your tasks, which you'll use in the `link_to` method a couple of lines later.

The final block of code concerns the estimates that are pending. You will access your estimates by using the `Job` model; you can tell that a job belongs here if it is in a proposed status and has an estimate attached to it. Recall the controller, where you spent an extravagant two lines deriving this hash:

```
prejobs = Job.find_all_by_status("proposed")
@estimates = prejobs.collect { |j| j.estimate }
```

In other words, the `@estimates` hash will contain any estimate that's associated with a job in a proposed state. Once again, for your summary statement, you need a class method to provide a sum of the dollar value of your estimates. You'll put this in the `Job` model again, below the `Job.active_total` method you wrote earlier:

```
def Job.estimate_value
  ests = self.estimates
  total = 0
  ests.collect { |e| total += e.dollar_value }
  return total
end
```

Here, you pull the estimates from the current job and then accumulate a `total` by using the `dollar_value` attribute of each estimate.

For the other element in your summary statement — the number of estimates — you're going to use another class method. I've designed this so that the summary statement stands separate from the `@estimates` instance variable, which in this case contains the same information. But you might have noticed that `Job.estimate_value` also needed to know the estimates; it's useful to have a class method to call upon for all outstanding estimates. Here it is. Place this code after your `Job.estimate_value` method:

```
def Job.estimates
  prejobs = Job.find_all_by_status("proposed")
  estimates = prejobs.collect { |j| j.estimate }
  return estimates
end
```

Now you can move to the table of estimates. For each record, you're going to show the company associated with the estimate, a link to the estimate detail page (which I cover later), and the dollar value. The first line is really the only one worth talking about, as it takes a long route to get to the company name; the estimate accesses its `Job` object, which accesses its `Client` object, which accesses its `company` attribute.

So goes your dashboard page. Save and reload the page in your browser. You should now see something similar to Figure 17.8, albeit with fewer items in your lists.

The Finishing Touches: A Tour

There's quite a bit more work to be done on the Pipeline application, but with the foundation you've laid down so far, you've got a great head start. At this point, you're going to move from a line-by-line map of the application to a tour of the more general features. You've already seen most of the rest of the code: basic forms to manage the data in your models, navigation between your controllers, the use of a template, and changing state in your templates from the controller.

The remainder of this chapter covers the features you haven't seen yet. These include the following:

- Mixing models in a view so you can manage elements from multiple models in a single form
- Using AJAX technology to provide a more Web 2.0–like experience
- Using Rails partials to provide multiple-use blocks of view code

If you haven't already, download the completed project from the website and get it working on your system. You'll find that you're starting from scratch with your database, but you'll now have the ability to add and modify the data in your application. Take some time to explore Pipeline, and add some Clients, Jobs, Estimates, Tasks, and Invoices. When you've had a chance to familiarize yourself with Pipeline, come back to this section of this chapter, and you'll see how some of it was done.

CROSS-REF

You can find the `pipeline` project on the website for this book: `www.wileydevreference.com`.

Implementing AJAX in your application

If you've been paying attention to the Internet in the past few years, you've probably heard of Web 2.0. There are as many definitions as there are pundits, but a key feature of this new school of thought is greater interactivity in web applications. Rather than the old model of click-and-reload that characterizes most web pages, modern web applications tend to load new data without reloading the page.

The key to this capability is a set of technologies known as AJAX (Asynchronous JavaScript and XML). Thanks to a JavaScript addition to all web browsers, clients can send and receive information from the server without reloading the page.

Rails provides an easy-to-use technique for employing AJAX in your web application. Just as a controller passes the view on to an .erb file with the same name, it can also pass the view on to a file that ends in .rjs. RJS is Ruby JavaScript, a set of Ruby methods that generates JavaScript. So, instead of displaying a view, a controller can execute a set of JavaScript commands.

A typical RJS file contains a single line that specifies what page element is updated with new data and what data is passed to that element.

Here's how this works. In Pipeline, each main page features a table of records; when you click a row, details of that record appear in the right column, as shown in Figure 17.11. This is accomplished without a page reload, thanks to the power of AJAX.

Figure 17.11

Pipeline's Clients page; a detail view of the left-hand items appears in the right column.

In the file /app/views/clients/index.html.erb, you'll see that I've placed a JavaScript onclick event on each table row:

```
<tr id="client_<%=c.id%>" onclick="<%= remote_function(:url=>
  {:controller=>"clients", :action=>"contacts", :id=>c.id}) %>">
  <td><%= c.company %></td>
  <td><%= number_to_currency(c.billed_total) %></td>
  <td><%= number_to_currency(c.outstanding) %></td>
</tr>
```

The `onclick` event is a call to a Rails method: `remote_function`. It generates a chunk of JavaScript that will handle the event; all you have to do is pass in the URL parameters, just as you would with any other hyperlink method. The controller holds no surprises; in `/app/controllers/clients_controller.rb`, add the following:

```
def contacts
  @client = Client.find(params[:id])
  @contacts = @client.contacts
end
```

You simply take the parameter passed into the controller — the `id` of the selected client record — and derive from it the complete client record and its related list of contacts. With both values in instance variables, execution passes back to the view.

Under normal circumstances, Rails is looking for a file with the same name as this method, and with a file extension of `.erb`. But it will also accept an `.rjs` file if the `.erb` file is missing. So, you can create `contacts.rjs` in `/app/views/clients/` and add this code to the file:

```
page['box33'].replace_html :partial=>"contacts",
    :locals=>{:contacts=>@contacts, :client=>@client}
```

Say hello to Ruby JavaScript, a collection of Ruby methods that generates client-side code automatically. When you get into an RJS file, the system provides you with a variable called `page`; this is a reference to the currently active page (surprise!), allowing you to interact with it. By supplying the `id` of a page element in the DOM, you can execute methods directly on `page`. Here, I'm using the `replace_html` method, which places new content inside the specified `div` tag. This is but one of three methods that you might use:

- `insert_html`. This takes a named position (such as top or bottom) and puts the desired content within the specified `div` in that spot. You can see this in action with the invoice-creation and editing pages, which drop in new invoice line items dynamically.

- `replace`. This takes the `div` and the content and replaces the `div` — including its tags. This is known in JavaScript as the outer HTML of the element.

- `replace_html`. This is the same as `replace`, except it only affects the contents of the `div` — the inner HTML, in JavaScript parlance.

While you can supply any content to drop into the specified location, you'll most commonly use a *partial*, which is a reusable chunk of view code. I talk about this in the next section.

Reusing view elements with partials

There are a lot of places in a web application that call for code reuse. Your template files are just the beginning, specifying a header and footer. But inside your code, you'll often have places where single chunks of code could be used all over the place; think of a login form or a piece of navigation that appears on pages within a subsection. Rails has a philosophy: Don't repeat yourself. That applies in all elements of your code. But partials are a way to avoid repetition for your views.

In Pipeline, you use partials to represent a number of repeating objects: a block of information about a client, details on an invoice, and tasks for a job. When you click a specific row in each of these tables, a partial displays the related information.

In your view code, a partial is called by using the Rails `render` method. Here it is in the clients list, at `/app/views/clients/index.html.erb`:

```
<div id="box33">
  <% if @contacts %>
    <%= render :partial=>"contacts", :locals=>{:contacts=>@
  contacts, :client=>@client}%>
  <% end %>
</div>
```

The `render` method takes a partial as the argument. A partial is just another file, so you provide the name (here, `"contacts"`). That name is translated into a request for the file named `_contacts.html.erb`, located in the same directory.

You can also pass variables into the partial for execution. In this case, you pass in two variables from your current scope: `@contacts` and `@client`. When the variable goes into the partial, it becomes a simple local variable. Here's how that partial looks:

```
<ul class="object_options">
  <li><%= link_to "Edit Client", {:controller=>"clients",
  :action=>"edit", :id=>client.id}, :popup=>['Edit client', 'hei
  ght=500,width=600,resizable=yes,scrollbars=yes']%></li>
  <li><%= link_to "Delete Client", {:controller=>"clients",
  :action=>"delete", :id=>client.id}, :confirm=>"Are you sure
  you want to do this? You can't get it back." %></li>
  <li><%= link_to "Add Contact", {:controller=>"clients",
  :action=>"contact_add", :id=>client.id}, :popup=>['Create new
  contact', 'width=600,height=550,resizable=yes,scrollbars=yes']
  %></li>
<br style="clear:both" />
</ul>
<h2><%= client.company %> Contacts</h2>
<% if contacts %>
<table class="invoices">
  <% contacts.each do |c| %>
  <tr>
    <td class="invoiceitems"><%= c.fname %> <%= c.lname %></td>
    <td class="invoiceitems"><%= link_to "Edit",
    {:action=>"contact_edit", :id=>c.id}, :popup=>['Edit client',
    'width=600,height=550,resizable=yes,scrollbars=yes'] %>
  </tr>
  <% end %>
</table>
<% end %>
```

As you can see, this is just a harmless chunk of Ruby-enhanced HTML. Where you require access to the variables that are passed in, they're available.

Part of the brilliance of these partials is that you can pass in different variables. In the preceding example, you have the default setting for the partial; if the `@contacts` variable is present, then the partial is displayed.

But remember what happens when you use the partial with your RJS methods. That `@contacts` variable is set when a line in the clients table is clicked, the contacts method is fired in the controller, the `contacts.rjs` file is executed, and the `contacts.html.erb` partial is put into play. It may feel like a lot of steps, but this arrangement of files separates the vital aspects of your interaction between controller and view.

Managing multiple models at once

As you've seen with the List application, there are a couple of ways to link a form with your controller: the model-based `form_for` methods and the more manual `form_tag` methods. The latter methods all end in `tag`, allowing you to more easily tell them apart. While the `form_for` method is used for getting data into and out of a model, the `form_tag` method is used when you need to pass any arbitrary data to a controller.

The `form_for` method takes an instance of your model and passes it into a block that contains your form. The variable that passes into that block executes the methods of your form elements; you've already seen this at work. But what happens when you want to work with two models in one form?

The forms for creating and editing a job provide an example. While you have a separate `Estimate` model, your interface puts the editing interface for the estimate in the same form as the job. So, while the `form_for` tag points to the job, you have to have a way to also include the estimate. Because you're sending your form data using RJS, you can use a modified version of `form_for` called `remote_form_for`. The only difference between the methods is in how Rails handles the transaction between view and controller. In the traditional `form_for` method, the view is reloaded; in the `remote_form_for` method, the page is simply updated with the resulting data.

Now take a look at the code. This is `/app/views/jobs/edit.html.erb`:

```
<% remote_form_for @job, :url=>{:action=>"update"} do |c| %>
<h1><%= @job.description %></h1>
<div id="popup_container">
  <h3>Job Specs</h3>
  <p>Client</p>
  <p><%= c.collection_select(:client_id, Client.find(:all), :id,
   :company, {:prompt=>"Choose a client..."},
   {:style=>"float:none"}) %></p>

  <p>Status</p>
```

```
<p><%= c.select(:status, job_statuses) %>

<p>Description</p>
<p><%= c.text_field :description, :size=>55 %>

<p>Dollar Value</p>
<p><%= c.text_field :dollar_value, :size=>6 %></p>
<br style="clear:both" />
<% fields_for @estimate do |e| %>
  <h3>Estimate</h3>
  <p>Title</p>
  <p><%= e.text_field :title %></p>

  <p>Content</p>
  <p><%= e.text_area :content, {:rows=>5, :cols=>"55"} %></p>
  <%= e.hidden_field :id %>
<% end %>

<br style="clear:both" />
<%= c.hidden_field :id %>
<%= submit_tag("Save Job", {:onclick=>"refreshParent()"}) %>

</div>
<% end %>
```

I love the `form_for` methods. With very little effort on your part, the input methods (such as `text_field`, `text_area`, and others) automatically take on the values from the database. But when you want to include form elements for a different model, you clearly can't use them. In that case, you can use the method `fields_for`. Think of it as a way to create a new model instance within another form. You wrap this declaration around your estimate fields and pass a variable into the block. It's business as usual from that point.

Now, when you submit this form to the `update` controller method, you'll have two model arrays to work with. Here's the method in `/app/controllers/jobs_controller.rb`:

```
def update
  @job = Job.find(params[:job][:id])
  @job.update_attributes!(params[:job])
  if params[:estimate]
    @estimate = Estimate.find(params[:estimate][:id])
    @estimate.update_attributes!(params[:estimate])
  end
end
```

When the fields of the estimate subform are completed, you're passed an `estimate` array containing the fields from your form. You can easily test for the presence of that array, and if it's there, update the `Estimate` object.

Feature complete but never finished

Pipeline is a brand-new application, written for this chapter. The code included on the website for this book represents an initial effort to develop a feature-complete application. However, it lacks the polish that a truly useful application should have. So, if you're interested in experimenting with Pipeline further — either to hone your Rails skills or to actually use the application in your business — I have provided a way for you to do so.

GitHub (`http://www.github.com`) is a community of coders that shares its open-source projects. As Pipeline is being released as an open-source project, I've made the code available on that site. Using the Git version control system (you can learn more about Git at `http://git-scm.com` and install it by visiting `http://help.github.com/mac-git-installation`), you can download the latest version of Pipeline and see what's changed. If you want to add a feature or change the way a certain feature works, you can easily do so by *forking* — creating your own version of — the project on the GitHub site, thus creating your own branch. It's social coding at its finest, and I hope that you find it useful.

You can find the Pipeline project at `http://github.com/aaronvegh/pipeline`.

Pushing Rails to Production

Before I conclude this introduction to Ruby on Rails, it's worth going through the steps needed to go into production with a Rails project. Unfortunately, it's not as straightforward as with PHP, where you would create a new directory on your web server, drop the files into it, and then grab a beverage.

As you've noticed while running your sample Rails applications, your Mac's built-in Apache web server has not been involved. Instead, every instance of Rails comes with Mongrel, a web server written in Ruby and built for serving up Ruby on Rails applications. But Mongrel is no Apache; it lacks the raw performance that makes Apache so popular for large sites. Instead, production Rails sites have tended to use clusters of Mongrel servers, a group of server processes working in concert that could approach the speed of Apache. As you can imagine, there's some effort involved in getting such a system to work correctly.

But never mind that. You can use Apache now, thanks to the efforts of the kind, generous, good-looking folks at Phusion, a Dutch company that developed the Passenger module for Apache. It's also known as `mod_rails`.

You can install Passenger on Mac OS X, but I've never bothered to do so for development use. On the other hand, I consider this component vital on my dedicated Linux server, where I post my production sites.

Installing Passenger

Installation is easy. Assuming you have Rails set up on the server (the steps for which I covered back in Chapter 13), here's what you do:

1. **In the command shell, type** sudo gem install passenger.

2. **Once the Passenger library is installed, you can update Apache by typing** passenger-install-apache2-module.

You're asked to follow a few instructions and then everything is set up.

At this point, you'll be happy to know that your Apache server can run Rails apps. But to actually do so requires a few changes to your Apache configuration file.

As I suggested earlier, you can't just create a folder on your server and throw in a Rails project. While that's technically possible with the help of some configuration in Apache, I've never been able to get it working. Instead, I always ensure that a Rails application owns the entire domain. So, you'll create a virtual host on your server for each Rails project you want to run. If, like me, you need to run a Rails application in a development environment, it makes sense to create a subdomain on your main domain. For example, if I'm developing an application for Awesome Inc., I'll create the subdomain awesome.innoveghtive.com and host my Rails app there. In Apache's configuration file, it would look something like this:

```
<VirtualHost *:80>
    ServerName awesome.innoveghtive.com
    DocumentRoot /wwww/awesomeinc/public
</VirtualHost>
```

Clearly, you might have other configuration directives in this block, but this is the minimum amount of configuration necessary to get your server running.

Production pitfalls

By default, the Passenger plug-in operates in Rails' production mode. This can be quite different from the development mode that your application will run in while on your Mac. Take note of the differences:

- Rails provides separate databases for each of the development, test, and production environments. You can check the files used in each case (if your application is running a SQLite database) or the configuration for each (if your application is running a MySQL database) in the file /config/database.yml.

- There are places to set specific environment variables: in the /config/environment.rb file for global changes and in the /config/environments directory, where each environment has a separate file. Unless you have a code library that is set here, you likely won't use these files.

- The rake tasks that you ran in order to set up your database take place on your development environment by default. In order to specify the production environment, you need to include it by running this command in your Rails project directory:

```
achilles:pipeline aaron$ rake db:migrate RAILS_ENV=production
```

- The same is true for when you want to run the Rails console; the models that are loaded come from your development environment by default. To run your console in production mode, type this command in your Rails project directory:

```
achilles:pipeline aaron$ script/console production
```

The production environment makes use of caching mechanisms to dramatically improve the speed of your application. The downside of this is that you need to restart the server to see almost any change take effect. Passenger provides a shortcut that saves you from having to restart your whole Apache server. In the application's /tmp folder, create a file called restart.txt. Simply saving that file will reboot the Rails application and refresh the content in its cache. Suffice it to say, it would be ideal to have a mostly complete application before you move it to a production environment.

Summary

I clearly saved the biggest for last. After all the work you have done in this book, you have now learned the essential skills necessary to work with Ruby on Rails. It's tough to understand at first, and it requires you to place a lot of trust in the designers of the framework. But as I've learned — and as I hope you're coming to learn — this trust is well-placed. Once you learn the Rails way, you'll find yourself developing complex applications in a much shorter time frame. And that means more success for you and your business.

Running a Freelance Web Business

Now that you've read this book and mastered the technical side of running a freelance web company, it's time to talk about what really matters. While you may be skilled with the mouse and keyboard, what you may have trouble with is sustaining a long-term business. With this appendix, I hope to help you overcome that problem.

This appendix isn't exhaustive; in fact, it could be the subject of an entire book! Rather, look on this as a collection of advice or a sampling of the decisions you have to make. And above all, remember that the right attitude is the key to success.

Administration Basics

Getting your business off the ground is hard. You need to register your business, create business cards, build your own website, and set up a business banking account. But what are the decisions you have to make as a web developer? The following sections describe some of the important ones.

Getting an accountant

Unless you're already comfortable working with numbers, I can't say enough about getting someone to take care of your accounting. A full-service accountant can be a real asset to your business — not just in the preparation of your year-end statements and taxes but also in your month-to-month operations.

Consider the paperwork that goes along with a business: You have invoices, accounts payable and receivable, expenses, salary, and withholding of taxes, among other things. Keeping track of this paperwork can be a definite drain on your resources. I should know — I used to do it all myself. I probably spent five hours a month on accounting-related tasks (during normal times; tax season was even worse), and I resented every minute of it! I kicked myself for waiting so long to hire an accountant.

In This Appendix

Administration basics

Your service offering

Surviving in the long term

Now my accountant and I have a system set up: I send copies of all my paperwork — invoices, expenses, bank statements — and he takes care of the rest. He prepares monthly reports on the health of my business, and at year's end, he completes all the government paperwork and fills out the forms for my taxes. All I have to do is put a check in the envelope and mail it off.

Beyond the paperwork, a good accountant can give you advice on how to structure your business. For example, my accountant explained how splitting my income with my wife reduced the income taxes that we had to pay while putting more money in my pocket. He also explained how a computer lease is better than buying, thanks to the way the government taxes lease payments. This is advice specific to my jurisdiction; the point is, talk to your own accountant to take advantage of your local loopholes.

This suggestion to find an accountant perhaps falls under a broader category: outsourcing when you aren't an expert in something. I'll touch on that one again later in this appendix.

How do you find an accountant? The best way is to ask the people you know. Other businesses need accountants, and you'll often get a recommendation from them. If all else fails, find one in the yellow pages and then find out the answers to the following questions:

- How long have they been in business? See if you can talk to any of their other clients that have a similar profile to yours.
- What kinds of services do they offer to small business clients like you? Taxes? Year-end preparation? Day-to-day bookkeeping?
- Who in their firm will be looking after your business?
- Can they provide advice in the financial management of your business?
- What kind of turnaround do they have when you contact them? Are they readily available on the phone or in person?
- How do they charge for their services?
- What kind of software do they use, and do you also need to use it?

Of course, much of your decision will depend on the impression you get from your potential accountant. Heed that feeling because you're going to be relying on this person or company for the long-term health of your business.

Centralizing domain management with a registrar

There are some things that web developers do a lot of; buying and managing domains are two major functions. Every time you deal with a new client, you'll almost certainly handle the purchase of his or her domain name. Over time, you'll probably amass quite a collection of domains. I have over 50 under my management right now.

That's why it's important to choose a domain registrar that can be the home to all your domains. Early in my career, I used whatever registrar had the lowest price that day. Before long, I had to maintain a separate list just to keep track of what registrar belonged to a given domain, along with the credentials needed to log on to said registrar. It added a lot of overhead to a routine (and onerous) task.

Domain registrars grow like weeds on the Internet, so finding and choosing one isn't easy. Just like with an accountant, though, it's an important early step — and one not easily changed in the future. So, just like with an accountant, here are some questions you might ask as you peruse the websites of potential registrars:

- **What top-level domains can they handle?** It's not enough anymore to do `.com`, `.net`, and `.org`. A good registrar needs to let you register the whole gamut of up-and-coming domains as well as a good collection of country-specific domains, such as `.ca`. When your client wants something different, it's a real boon to know that your registrar can handle it.

- **How long have they been around?** Just as registrars grow like weeds, they also die like weeds. Make sure that this company will be around in the long term.

- **Are their prices reasonable?** You can do a quick comparison among sites, and you'll find that most registrars are within the same range. I would strongly caution you against making cost an important factor in your decision; this is a management problem, not a cost problem. Besides, you'll be billing your clients for the registration cost.

- **What additional services do they offer?** My registrar provides a complete management panel that gives me immediate access to all my domains. For each domain, I can manage its DNS, change WHOIS information, automatically renew it 90 days before expiry, and easily transfer domain ownership to another person.

And as with the accountant, do a gut check before committing. I've seen registrars with very sophisticated websites, but when you get beyond the surface, it's a guy sitting in his basement somewhere outside Orlando. True story.

Choosing a dedicated server for your business

Way back in Chapter 1, I talked about the different kinds of hosting services that are available, and I mentioned my own choice to use a dedicated server. It's been many months since I wrote those words, but my commitment remains the same. For a business that relies on the infrastructure of the Internet, you must have a solid hosting platform of your own. You'll need it if you want to host your own site, have a place to put projects for your clients that are in development, or host your clients' sites. Although you don't necessarily need a dedicated server, for my needs, it's the best option.

Dedicated servers are all about scale. With a price of at least $100 per month, a dedicated server represents a significant cost. On the other hand, if you host your clients' sites, you can charge for the service and offset — or profit over — the cost of the server.

To me, the performance of a good-quality dedicated server is worth the cost. They sit on a fat pipe (a very fast connection to the Internet), and they come with the complete resources of the entire computer. It's your machine to host as many sites as you can accommodate.

But . . . that cost. I wouldn't blame you if you wanted to make a prudent business decision and choose something a little more lightweight. The best (or second-best) option here is a virtual private server. Many companies offer servers that run as virtualized instances on powerful machines. It's not as fast as a dedicated server, but for a few sites, it can meet your needs — at half the cost.

When evaluating a hosting company, you'll examine a wide range of choices. When you narrow your vendors down to a handful based on features and price, use your favorite search engine to find out what others have to say.

Don't be put off by negative reviews either. Any hosting company will always have a disgruntled, vocal minority. Pay attention to all the reviews, and weigh them accordingly.

Providing clients with a selection of hosting options

When you start up your business is a good time to decide whether you will do any hosting. One thing I can guarantee is that you'll deal with clients who just want you to handle all aspects of their web presence. So, your decision really should be between hosting it yourself or selecting a third party to do it for you.

Clearly, hosting is not your core business; it's not something that you're likely to make any significant profit from. In fact, a savvy client can find decent hosting for a few dollars a month. You shouldn't bother trying to compete with that. Instead, I place the focus on the simplicity of having one person responsible for everything. And just as with your domain registrations, having many of your sites located on your server ultimately makes your life simpler. Not only will you need to remember just one set of credentials to access your sites, but you will also know exactly how the production environment is configured; that is, it's identical to your development environment. With a third-party hosting service, you often run into small surprises where the production server lacks some configuration or plug-in.

Technically speaking, you've already seen from Chapter 2 how easy it is to manage a web server. I've been running one myself for three years without any significant problems. Running a web server is not a specialized task that you need to outsource.

When I talk to clients about their sites and the question of hosting comes up, I'm fairly casual about my ability to host. All the same, I find that most of my clients are happy to pay $30 per month to host their site with me. It pays the hosting bill, and it makes life easier.

Your Service Offering

Once your business is set up, you'll start to deal with clients. The services that you offer and the conditions under which you offer them are important in determining your long-term survival. The following sections describe some areas you should pay attention to.

How to choose your rate

Like it or not, you need to have an hourly rate. Although I hate the very notion of it, an hourly figure can help your clients gauge your cost and level of expertise. But it is also a double-edged sword. To understand the details of what you charge, you should take a moment and consider the economics of your business.

I heard a quote once that I really liked: "I only eat what I kill." As a contractor, you're getting paid for the work you do. If you don't get work, then you don't get paid. Also, the work you do get is, by its very nature, rarely a neat, confined package with known start and end dates. You may structure your payments at certain project milestones, but those milestones are difficult to solidify.

Add to that the general reticence of clients to pay their bills, and you've got a potential cash flow problem. The only way to combat this is with a high enough rate so that when you do get paid, it's enough to carry you through the times when you don't.

When I bid for a job, I price at a fixed cost. This is so my clients can budget the expense, and it gives me a target to hit: if I work hard and things go smoothly, I might be done sooner and profit more from the job. But if I run into delays, then I lose. And I hate losing. Of course, the price I quote is based on the time I think the job should take, multiplied by my hourly rate of $85.

If I look at my annual sales and divide them by the number of working hours in a year, I actually appear to make $60 per hour. So, when you account for the fact that not every hour is billable, $85 appears to compensate for that difference.

Of course, your hourly rate is also a message to clients that this is what you're worth. Some people react with incredulity, believing the figure to be too high. But if you want to make a true living from this work, you need to calculate the numbers and understand what it takes to get the cash that you'll need to survive. You may not get rich being a web developer, but you should have every expectation that you can own a house and support your family doing it. Make sure your hourly rate reflects that need.

Subcontracting versus hiring

I've been fortunate in this business to have a fairly steady stream of work. While I've never been able to know whether I would still have work three months from now, it inevitably happens that another job comes up and life moves on.

Sometimes, work overwhelms me, and I'm filled with anxiety about the mountain of work in front of me. For a while recently, it was so constant that I began musing aloud about hiring someone to help me out. I spoke with a number of people that I trust, and I got a wide range of advice. Ultimately, I opted to hire temporary contractors instead.

Why? It's not an easy answer, and yours might be different. Let me list some of the reasons that affected my decision:

- **Cost.** A new employee is a serious commitment. You're responsible for the work environment, the equipment, the training, and, of course, the salary and benefits.

- **Mindshare.** An employee is someone you have to keep busy. When things are going well, that shouldn't be a problem, but what happens when things are quiet? I would be constantly worrying about whether I can afford this person.

- **Location.** I work from my home office. Where would this person go? The only option is to have someone local but remote, which is a tricky proposition. With the right person, it can work. But with the wrong person? It can go really badly. Which leads to the next factor.

- **Selection.** I actually interviewed a few local people to get a sense of the talent out there. My take? Good people are hard to find.

Conversely, finding a contractor is much easier. It's not a serious commitment; after all, if they don't work out, you simply don't use them again. They work from their own office and use their own facilities. Their cost is up-front and can be accounted for by the specific job. If you want, you can outsource the entire project to a contractor and add 15% to their bill.

Altogether, contracting out a job makes a lot of sense.

How to compete with the nephew in the basement

It seems that everyone knows someone who can build websites. Sometimes, after quoting a price for a job, I'll be told that they have a nephew who can do this job for, well, dramatically less. And I have no trouble imagining this nephew: a young man in a dingy basement, hacking away on his Windows XP desktop in between bouts of *Call of Duty 2*. Of course he can do it for dramatically less — he lives with his parents.

This response from a client is something of a pet peeve for me. Just getting the question probably suggests you won't be dealing with this client for long; they clearly don't understand the realities of business. Seriously, how often do people complain to their plumber that their crazy uncle Rusty can fix the toilet for less than a qualified professional?

So, if you don't intend to hang up on clients who pose this question — or, more likely, they pose it in a way that isn't insulting — there are a number of viable replies:

- **You get what you pay for.** A hobbyist (for want of a better term) will have limited experience to accomplish what most businesses are after. His or her attention to detail in meeting professional standards will obviously be less than stellar.

- **You get professional treatment with a professional.** I'll mention this in more detail shortly, but there's a relationship that matters when dealing with an agency. You can call at any time during business hours, and you can discuss change requests. Your hobbyist is probably at school during the day.

- **You get it done faster.** A professional will have the resources and experience to complete the job on time. Hobbyists will get it done when they feel like it. After all, there's not a powerful incentive on their part; they're doing this for fun and for beer money.

Sometimes, a client will say this as a way of opening up negotiations for lowering your price. I have no objections to dropping a few points off the price to get a job. In the long run, giving up 5 or 10% isn't going to affect your bottom line too much, especially if you don't have a lot of other work going on.

So, your job is to carefully listen to the client. Does he or she really believe that a hobbyist is a better option for the site or is he or she trying to lower the price? Figure out the difference, and you can end up with a happy client just by giving up a few dollars.

Don't worry: You'll get this money back when you add work to the initial contract as they change their minds and add new features.

Large versus small clients

Which is better: to make most of your money from a few clients or small amounts of money from a lot of clients? Having just a few clients is much easier to manage; you only need to keep track of a few people and remember the concerns of fewer websites in your head. If you have a lot of smaller clients, you'll need a scorecard to keep track of them, and you'll find yourself working away at dozens of sites in a given month.

I like to compare my client roster to a shopping mall. A good mall will have many stores, but it would be greatly diminished without its anchor stores — the large chains, such as Sears or JC Penney. Still, the experience is completed with the smaller-sized crowd of stores.

Just as with the mall, financially speaking, the larger clients are a great foundation, providing steady, high-margin business. But relying on just one or two large clients puts your business in danger. What would happen if you lost one of these clients? Your business would be seriously affected.

Having a group of smaller clients provides the kind of security that is good for the long-term health of your business. These kinds of clients are often shorter term; they develop a site with you and then you don't hear from them again for a year. For these clients, you'll do some minor updates for a few years, but then you'll be asked to do another large project.

If you have enough of these smaller clients, you won't suffer during these quiet times. And, of course, if you have a couple larger clients providing steady business, then your smaller clients can provide a nice bump in your revenues.

Ultimately, you'll probably take whatever business comes your way — I have a pretty firm policy to say yes to any job. But if you want to evaluate the health of your client roster, consider the mix of large versus small clients. You need both to succeed.

Getting new clients by keeping the old ones

I thought about doing a section on marketing, but, frankly, the field of advertising rarely works well for web developers. There are simply too many people who build websites, and most of them have marketing materials to promote themselves. Indeed, people are looking for skilled, reliable developers who will do the work they're being hired for. They keep on looking because such people are quite rare. I firmly believe that the people who succeed are the ones who actually show up and do what they promised to do.

That's why my favorite marketing technique is to run your business as if your new clients came exclusively from your existing clients. Because, well, that's exactly how it works. If you delight your current clients, they'll give your name to the next person they meet who's looking for a developer.

This is clearly easier said than done. Consistently delighting your clients means that you must set aside your ego, your dignity, and, sometimes, a slice of your profit margin. I don't always succeed at this, but it's a goal to aim for.

Let me give you an example. Many clients don't understand that changing their mind or adding features late in a project causes both delay and increased expense. It's a rare job that doesn't have a moment, late in development, where I have to stop the process as requests pour in. It's human nature; people don't know what they want until they see the almost-finished product. So, when I have to tell a client no, there's the potential for conflict.

One of my clients is a large company with hundreds of employees. My contact there had been under a lot of pressure from management to get the site done in record time. But as the site approached completion, a senior manager had taken his first look at it and declared it unviable without the addition of a major new feature that had never been discussed before. Also, there was no additional budget to pay for the new feature.

This is a difficult moment. Most developers I know would take a firm position at this point, either insisting on payment or postponing that major new feature to a second phase. I certainly exerted pressure on making either possibility happen. But they were firm: build the feature or the site won't be complete. My contact was in a really bad position, knowing the cost to me as well as not having a choice other than to finish it.

Ultimately, that's exactly what I did. I set aside my ego, my dignity, and a cringe-worthy slice of my profit margin to make the change. I saved my client's day, launched a brilliant new site that thrilled everyone at the company, and even got a letter from that senior manager thanking me for my sacrifice. Over time, I got more work from that company and recommendations to other clients thanks to the goodwill I built.

Of course, a story like this has to come with a warning. This was an unusual situation; if a client repeatedly demonstrates a last-minute change, then you've got a problem. But for those situations where you don't know, you may want to give them the benefit of the doubt. You'll earn dividends for it.

Up-selling your services for more revenue

In contrast to last-minute changes, there's the much more common case of features being appended as the job goes on. This has happened in nearly every project I've undertaken.

Every job seems to follow the same pattern: I begin by outlining the features that the client and I discussed, providing an estimate with a fixed cost, getting approval, and beginning work. During development, I'll post the website on my server so the client can review the progress.

Inevitably, there will be bugs and small misunderstandings about the way certain features are implemented. I consider this category of change requests a normal cost of doing business, and I do my best to accommodate my clients (especially by eliminating the bugs).

But some change requests turn out to be more substantive, and this can happen without the client realizing it. It's your job to be as clear as possible about the repercussions of their requests. When they suddenly want a search engine on the site, you have to explain how that's not a simple matter of adding a new text field and letting Google take care of the rest. This is when you can explain that there's a substantial amount of work involved and that you'll be happy to put together a quick estimate for the job.

This simple explanation either shuts the client down entirely or does something even more valuable: it up-sells your service. Having already signed up the client — an expensive and time-consuming operation — you've now just made them a more profitable one, with significantly less effort. And if you'd given up some profit margin on the front end, this is your chance to win it back.

Up-selling often happens from the client's perspective, but you can also initiate it. During development, I often suggest features that would improve the website. In fact, when figuring estimates, I try to include features that clients can consider in addition to the work we discussed, and I include the pricing so they can make a decision.

Surviving in the Long Term

Everything I've discussed so far has involved ways to successfully run your business. But doing this professionally is a long-term commitment. You're not in it to make a quick profit and get out; you're here to make a living. Here are some tips for keeping your career moving while also keeping your sanity.

Managing your time

As I discussed earlier when talking about bigger versus smaller clients, you can easily run into problems when you're working on several jobs at the same time. How do you choose what to work on at any given time?

The issue is complicated by the fact that many people have difficulty motivating themselves to work when they are the only ones looking over their shoulder! Fortunately, I have a wife, a young daughter, and a mortgage to keep me motivated; if I fail, then they'll suffer right along with me.

The best way to manage your day-to-day affairs is with the judicious use of lists. I rely heavily on iCal (which is included with every Mac) to keep track of my to-do items and appointments. It's not a perfect solution, but it does prevent jobs from being lost or forgotten.

When multiple jobs are in progress, I prioritize them according to the deadlines that I've been given and the needs of the clients. But just as important, I'm up-front to my low-priority clients when I have to stop working on their projects for a few days.

Ultimately, I always spend a few minutes at the end of each day organizing my actions and queuing up the list for the next day. Doing so will help you sleep better at night and make sure you get the job done.

Paying yourself

You should consider incorporating your business, as it's usually the most advantageous and it allows you to easily separate your personal financial affairs from that of the business. I have a business bank account and a business line of credit. When a check comes in from a client, it goes into my business account and adds to my annual revenues.

From those revenues, I pay expenses for everything that I own as a business: my computer lease (a new Mac every two years!), my car, even a portion of my house (because it's my office). But I also pay myself a salary. Every two weeks, I write out a check to myself, withholding income tax and other deductions (as required by the Ontario government — check your own jurisdiction for specific requirements). This is my income, and it's an amount that still leaves my business with enough cash to operate and pay for its expenses, with a modest amount left over to cover the taxes at the end of the year.

I've explained all this in order to warn you away from the alternative: Don't just write yourself a check whenever you need the cash. At some point, you'll need to report that income for your taxes, and you probably won't like the idea of sending the government $10,000 in April. If you do it right, you'll be just like any employee — except your boss is you and your office is at the end of the best commute anyone could wish for.

Staying relevant with new skills

As you can tell from this book, a professional web developer can't sit still — there are too many new technologies coming out. Once you've mastered the information in this book, you should have a good foundation for learning more. And once you've learned more about the next cool technology, there'll be something else that comes along.

It's easy to get carried away with the next interesting technology. But you have a business to run, and you have to focus on only adopting technologies that are going to make your life — and, by extension, your clients' lives — better.

For example, I learned JavaScript because clients were starting to see client-side interactivity and wanted that for themselves.

I learned CSS because I was wasting too much time building sites with HTML tables, and it was proving too unmanageable to maintain these sites.

I learned PHP because, back in 2001, it was the best way to provide database-driven applications, which were obviously the future.

More recently, I learned Ruby on Rails because it promised to help me build sites more quickly, leading to better profitability.

Choosing a technology is like getting into a relationship. It's very exciting at first, but then you come to understand its quirks, and you have to decide whether it's good for you. I've researched many technologies and rejected them — and I won't mention names because there are many people who love those solutions; they just weren't right for me.

But never make the mistake of settling in with your current skill set. The moment you do that, you'll stop caring about the real joys of web development. You don't want to lose that sense that all developers feel — of mastering something new, of developing the means to solve problems in novel and interesting ways, of discovering new paths to creativity. This career is a calling, and it's one that only the nerdiest and the most dedicated can successfully pursue.

You'll no doubt find more tips on how to run a freelance web business all over the Internet. In fact, Appendix B will point you to a few of those places. But when it comes to running a business, you need the right attitude more than anything else. If you have a passion for web development, you'll be rewarded.

Resources

Because this book covers a lot of subject matter, it's fair to say that it doesn't cover those subjects in a totally comprehensive fashion. As I suggested in the beginning, this book is about learning enough to make you dangerous; you know how to do the essential parts, but you'll surely find yourself looking for more specific information. Here, then, is a list of online resources that you can look to when you move beyond the book, arranged by each part of the book.

Internet Infrastructure

Internet infrastructure includes everything that you need to get your web development business up and running: knowledge of the way the Internet works, resources to help you pick the vendors you'll work with, and the applications you'll use to do your work.

- **Domain name system FAQs.** This page contains a complete explanation of the inner workings of the domain name system, explained in clear, plain language: `www.internic.net/faqs/authoritative-dns.html`.

- **List of domain registrars.** You can never be comprehensive enough when listing domain registrars, but Wikipedia tries anyway. They list the top 31 registrars, which should give you a starting point to choose one for yourself: `http://en.wikipedia.org/wiki/List_of_domain_name_registrars`.

- **Web-hosting forums.** This wide-ranging collection of forums provides very comprehensive and current knowledge about web hosting in general and can help you evaluate potential hosting companies. It's a great research assistant: `www.webhostingtalk.com`.

- **Macromates' TextMate.** To my mind, this is the finest general-purpose text editor available on any platform. It features intuitive and thoughtful code completion, syntax coloring, elegant file management, and a wide variety of plug-in features made available through an open-extension system. It's also super fast: `www.macromates.com`.

In This Appendix

Internet infrastructure

Client-side development

Design resources

Server-side development

- **Panic Software's Coda.** Coda is the one-window web development solution from Panic. I find it to be very powerful software, especially for sites in maintenance mode, where you have to edit locally and post remotely. Its text editor doesn't have the finesse of TextMate, but it's very close: `www.panic.com/coda`.

- **Linux distributions.** Take your pick! As described earlier, you can run any of hundreds of distributions, but I'll recommend two:
  - **Ubuntu.** This is available from `www.ubuntu.com`.
  - **Red Hat Enterprise.** This is available for free as CentOS from `http://centos.org`.

Running other operating systems

The Mac provides a number of excellent options for running other operating systems on your computer. For more information on each system, here are some sites:

- **Boot Camp from Apple.** This lets you partition your hard drive and reboot into Windows. However, it can be modified to boot into Linux: `http://wiki.onmac.net/index.php/Triple_Boot_via_BootCamp`.

- **Sun's VirtualBox.** This is the free, open-source virtualization package used in this book: `www.virtualbox.org`.

- **Parallels.** This company makes an eponymous virtualization product for the Mac, which provides better integration and graphics support: `www.parallels.com`.

- **VMware.** Longtime developers of virtualization products, VMware sells Fusion for the Mac. This is my current favorite: `www.vmware.com/products/fusion`.

Using Terminal

The Mac's Terminal application gives you access to the command line by using a program called Bash — the Bourne-again shell. Your expertise with the shell will give you extra power in your web development tasks. Here are some resources to help you learn more about Terminal:

- **Bash tips and tricks.** You can find this information at the *Linux Journal* site: `www.linuxjournal.com/article/7385`.

- **Gentoo Development Guide.** This is Gentoo Linux's Bash guide: `http://devmanual.gentoo.org/tools-reference/bash/index.html`.

- **Fifty Mac Terminal tricks.** It's not necessarily web-related, but you'll have fun while typing: `www.mactricksandtips.com/2008/02/top-50-terminal-commands.html`.

- **Running Mac OS X Tiger: The Terminal and Shell.** This free PDF describes how to use Terminal on the Mac. Most of the information is still current, despite its focus on OS X 10.4: `http://whitepapers.techrepublic.com.com/abstract.aspx?docid=323458`.

Client-Side Development

Here are some resources related to the front end of development: HTML, CSS, and JavaScript.

- **The W3C Validator.** The World Wide Web Consortium is the standard-setting body for the technologies that drive modern web development. Here, you can test your code against the specifications to determine if you have properly formatted your HTML and CSS: `http://validator.w3.org`.

- **HTML 4.x/xHTML 1.x Tag Reference.** This offers an alphabetical listing of all HTML tags, including examples of their use: `www.w3schools.com/tags/default.asp`.

- **CSS Reference.** This is a very good reference for CSS, including examples of each tag: `www.w3schools.com/css/css_reference.asp`.

- **Explorer Exposed.** This page outlines the major problems you'll encounter with Internet Explorer as well as solutions and workarounds: `www.positionis everything.net/explorer.html`.

- **JavaScript Reference.** This site provides a handy reference for the JavaScript language, including the Document Object Model (DOM): `www.javascriptkit.com/jsref/index.shtml`.

- **Prototype and Scriptaculous.** For information about the JavaScript framework and animation library, look no further than these sites: `www.prototypejs.org` and `http://script.aculo.us`.

Design Resources

Website design is about look and feel, functionality, and ease of use. These resources will help you get ahead with your own design process:

- **CommandShift3.** This is a great source for inspiration, with an ongoing contest of the best website designs. Browse the site and get some great ideas: `http://command shift3.com`.

- **Web 2.0 How-to Design Guide.** This is a rather long article on how to use the principles of design in the modern web context: `www.webdesignfromscratch.com/web-design/web-2.0-design-style-guide.php`.

- **Google Webmaster Tools.** This is Google's suite of tools for ensuring you're getting the most out of your site's visibility on the Google search engine: `www.google.com/webmasters/tools`.

- **Sitemaps.org.** This is the home of the Sitemap standard, demonstrating how to create an official sitemap file that Google can use to map your site: `www.sitemaps.org`.

- **960 Grid System.** This site provides examples and tools for creating grid layouts based on a 960-pixel width: `http://960.gs`.

Server-Side Development

These are the resources that you'll need when you develop web applications:

- **MySQL 5.0 Reference Manual.** This is the official guide to the MySQL database server. You'll use these commands to learn the syntax to manage your databases: `http://dev.mysql.com/doc/refman/5.0/en/index.html`.

- **PHP Documentation.** Just as PHP is easy to learn, its documentation is one of the best available. The PHP site is the best reference to the language, providing transparent access to the functions as well as examples and extensive user feedback: `www.php.net/docs.php`.

- **Ruby Core Reference.** The Ruby API provides complete documentation for every method in the language. It's a little difficult to navigate, but it should make sense in time: `www.ruby-doc.org/core`.

- **RailsGuides.** This site provides tutorials on the common workings of Ruby on Rails. If you need to know how even the most basic technology works, this is the place to start: `http://guides.rubyonrails.org/index.html`.

- **RailsBrain.** This site provides a JavaScript-enhanced reference guide for the Rails API. You can type in the method you want to learn about, and the list automatically displays what you're looking for. I find it much easier to use than the standard reference, which works like the Ruby documentation: `http://www.railsbrain.com`.

Glossary

AJAX (Asynchronous JavaScript and XML) A term coined to describe a process whereby JavaScript can request data from the server, receive a response, and update the current page, without reloading in the browser. AJAX technologies have created a series of more desktop-like applications on the web.

Apache The most-used web server software on the Internet.

array In programming, a collection of values indexed by sequential numeric keys.

Bash (Bourne-again shell) The default program that a user works with when running Terminal in Mac OS X; it also runs in most Linux distributions.

Boolean A variable type that defines `true` or `false` values.

breadcrumbs A type of navigation used on websites to show users where they are in relation to the home page.

BSD The Berkeley Standard Distribution of Unix. This is a completely free version of the popular operating system and is a direct parent of Mac OS X.

C A programming language developed alongside the Unix operating system. C provides developers with low-level access to system components, and other languages, such as JavaScript, PHP, and Ruby, borrow from its syntax.

CGI (Common Gateway Interface) A protocol for a server-side language to interact with a web server, such as Apache.

client side A reference to actions or code that runs on the user's web browser, as opposed to server side. This is also called the front end. See also *server side*.

colocation A form of web hosting that provides a network connection for a server that you own.

comment A syntax used by all languages to let you write code that won't be executed or to place notes to yourself when you return to the code later. Many developers use comments extensively.

compiler A program that takes computer code as input and then generates a machine-readable, binary executable file. Compiled languages such as C generate faster programs than interpreted languages.

cookie A piece of data from a web application that's stored on the user's computer when he or she visits a site; intended for later retrieval when the visitor returns to the site.

CSS (Cascading Style Sheets) A technology for separating the function of HTML from its form. CSS is a rule-based system for describing content in HTML documents.

database A mechanism for storing data in a structured format.

dedicated hosting A form of web hosting that gives you full control over the complete machine for maximum flexibility, although at an increased cost.

design elements The components that are used to create design, such as line, color, and shape.

design principles The theory that governs the discipline of design, incorporating concepts such as balance, harmony, and unity.

distribution A term used to describe a version of Linux. Because the components are open-source, developers can create their own distribution and give it a name. Popular distributions include Ubuntu and Red Hat.

DNS (Domain Name System) A system that's used to route requests made using names, which are translated into IP addresses.

DOM (Document Object Model) The mechanism that JavaScript uses to target elements within an HTML page.

domain A unique name for a network to identify it to others, such as `amazon.com`.

Dovecot A popular mail delivery agent; an IMAP and POP server for email.

DTD (Document Type Definition) A specification used by XML documents — including xHTML — to validate its format.

environment A term used to describe the scope of an application, either in development or in production.

event In JavaScript, a trigger for an action, such as clicking or moving a mouse over a specific element on the page.

float A numerical type that contains a decimal point.

framework A collection of code that adds functionality to a programming language or that targets a specific requirement. For example, Prototype adds capabilities to JavaScript, and Rails provides web application tools to Ruby.

FTP (File Transfer Protocol) One of the original Internet protocols. FTP is intended to allow the movement of data between remote systems. However, because FTP is unencrypted, it's being replaced by secure shell.

function In procedural programming languages (such as C, PHP, and JavaScript), a contained block of code that accomplishes a specific task.

GREP (Global Regular Expressions Print) A tool used on the command line to find text within text.

grid In layout, a system for determining how content appears on a page by using columns that evenly divide the page into sectors.

hex Short for hexadecimal, a notation for specifying colors in HTML. Hex values represent three sets of two-character values to describe the red, green, and blue (RGB) elements that make up a color.

HTML (Hypertext Markup Language) The most common language used on the World Wide Web. Its easy-to-learn set of tags allows web browsers to render documents as web pages.

HTTP (Hypertext Transfer Protocol) The communications foundation of the World Wide Web. HTTP allows web browsers to communicate with web servers.

IMAP (Internet Message Access Protocol) A relatively new protocol for delivering email, known for its ability to host messages on the server while clients sync to it.

integer A variable type, which can be a whole number, either positive or negative.

interface The part of a computer program or website with which users interact directly. An interface can be graphical or on the command line.

interpreter A program that converts scripting languages into actions on the fly. PHP and Ruby are both scripting languages that run through an interpreter.

IP address A unique numerical identifier for a computer on a network.

iptables A Linux-based firewall that uses a list (or, in `iptables` parlance, a chain) of rules to determine whether network packets pass through.

JavaScript A client-side (within the web browser) scripting language that has a C-like syntax.

Linux An operating system kernel developed by Linus Torvalds. Linux is the most pervasive example of the free software movement and provides much of the popular software in use today on Unix platforms, including Mac OS X. Unlike the Mac, however, Linux is available in a number of versions, known as distributions.

Mac OS X A modern operating system based on the work of BSD Unix and NeXTSTEP.

markup A simple code that takes the form of tags that surround human-readable content. HTML is the most popular form of markup.

method In object-oriented programming languages, such as Ruby, a contained block of code that performs a specific task.

MySQL An open-source relational database server and client system. MySQL commonly provides the data storage component of a web application.

package manager In Linux, a program that allows you to query, install, and remove software from online repositories. For example, Ubuntu includes `apt`, and Red Hat ships with `yum`.

PageRank An algorithm used by Google for determining the importance of a web page.

Perl A scripting language used to write web applications. Although still in use today, Perl has largely been supplanted by PHP. See also *PHP*.

permissions File attributes that determine who can read and write to the file. In Mac file systems, permissions are set for the owner, group, and world.

Photoshop Image manipulation software produced by Adobe Inc. Photoshop is a very popular choice for the development of graphical elements for the web.

PHP A server-side scripting language with a C-like syntax.

POP (Post Office Protocol) One of the original email delivery protocols. POP downloads mail directly to the client and then deletes it from the server.

port knocking A security technique that relies on a client knowing the correct sequence of server ports to ping in order to allow access.

Postfix A popular mail transfer agent, or email server.

process A running program on a computer.

Prototype A JavaScript framework that adds extended capabilities to the JavaScript language.

public-key cryptography A cryptographic technique that employs two keys: a private key that a user never discloses and a public key that is made available to others. Only by matching the two can communication occur. This is used in the secure shell system.

registrar A company that provides domain name registration services.

Ruby A dynamic, object-oriented, general-purpose scripting language.

Ruby on Rails A web-application development framework based on the Ruby language.

Scriptaculous A JavaScript framework that adds animation and events to JavaScript.

secure shell A client-server communications protocol that encrypts all traffic. This is used both to control remote systems through the command line and to move files (the commands `ssh` and `scp`, respectively).

selector In CSS, the means by which you specify the element you want to style.

SEO (Search Engine Optimization) A series of techniques used to improve a website's ranking in search engines.

server A program that responds to client requests. This may also refer to a computer that runs server programs.

server side A reference to code that runs on the web server, as opposed to code that runs on the client side. This is also called the back end. See also *client side*.

session The period during which a user browses a website. In a web application, sessions are used to contain variables that affect the operation of the site but are lost when the browser window is closed.

shared hosting The most common form of web hosting, which places a large number of client sites on the same physical machine. This is the cheapest but least flexible hosting option.

Shell script A file that contains shell commands that begins with a declaration of the scripting language that will execute it (such as Bash, Ruby, PHP, and others).

SQL (Structured Query Language) A language used to interact with relational database servers.

SQLite A file-based database system that implements a simple set of SQL commands. It's ideal for small-scale applications and is the default data storage option in Ruby on Rails projects.

string A variable type that contains text.

switch In the context of the command line, an argument passed to a shell script — usually a single letter preceded by a hyphen.

symbolic link Also known as a symlink, a pointer to the original file or directory. This is analogous to a Mac alias or a Windows shortcut.

Terminal The Mac OS X application for running the command line.

TextEdit The Mac OS X default word-processing application. This software is not the same as a real text editor.

type In programming languages, the kind of data that a variable will contain. Values include integers, floats, strings, and dates.

Unix An operating system developed in the late 1960s to allow multiple users on the same system. Unix is the foundation for many operating systems today and is the basis for Mac OS X.

usability The ease with which a computer program or website can be employed to satisfy the needs of its users. This is a discipline that considers the aesthetics as well as the purpose of a piece of software.

variable A programming construct that, as in algebra, represents a placeholder for a value.

VirtualBox The open-source virtualization product from Sun Microsystems. It is available for Mac, Windows, and Linux.

virtualization A technology that allows a program within a host operating system (such as Mac OS X) to run a different operating system (such as Windows or Linux). Virtualization provides the guest operating system full access to the hardware, thereby offering near-normal performance.

virtual private hosting A form of web hosting that virtualizes an operating system among others on the same physical machine. This provides great flexibility at lower cost but with reduced performance.

W3C (World Wide Web Consortium) The standards body for HTML and CSS. W3C is responsible for publishing the standards that drive these technologies.

web host A service that provides servers for running websites. Companies offer various types of hosting to accommodate a range of budgets.

web sharing The Mac OS X name for the service that starts and stops the built-in Apache web server.

wireframe A technique for quickly mocking up a site in a style that more or less reflects the final product, from a low (sketches on a napkin) to high (fully realized graphical mockups) level.

xHTML A new version of the HTML markup language that makes it a type of XML document, enforcing discipline in browser rendering.

XML (eXtensible Markup Language) A language used to standardize the transmission of data. XML is a strict format that either validates or is broken. It is the standard used with xHTML.

Index

Take the Book with You, Everywhere

How to purchase

Go to www.wileydevreference.com and follow the link to the iTunes store.

Wiley's Developer Reference app is free and includes Chapter 21, "Using the Game Kit API" from *Cocoa Touch for iPhone OS 3*. When you're ready for a full Developer Reference book, you can purchase any title from the series directly in the app for $19.99.

Want tips for developing and working on Apple platforms on your iPhone? Wiley's Developer Reference app puts you in touch with the new Developer Reference series. Through the free app you can purchase any title in the series and then read, highlight, search, and bookmark the text and code you need. To get you started, Wiley's Developer Reference app includes Chapter 21 from *Cocoa Touch for iPhone OS 3*, which offers fantastic tips for developing for the iPhone and iPod touch platforms. If you buy a Wiley Developer Reference book through the app, you'll get all the text of that book including a searchable index and live table of contents linked to each chapter and section of the book.

Here's what you can do

- Jump to the section or chapter you need by tapping a link in the Table of Contents
- Click on a keyword in the Index to go directly to a particular section in the book
- Highlight text as you read so that you can mark what's most important to you
- Copy and paste, or email code samples, out of the book so you can use them where and when needed
- Keep track of additional ideas or end results by selecting passages of text and then creating annotations for them
- Save your place effortlessly with automatic bookmarking, which holds your place if you exit or receive a phone call
- Zoom into paragraphs with a "pinch" gesture

Now you know.